Willkie

THE EVENTS
HE WAS PART OF—
THE IDEAS
HE FOUGHT FOR

BY

JOSEPH BARNES

Simon and Schuster · New York
1952

B
W736B

MANUFACTURED IN THE UNITED STATES OF AMERICA
BY H. WOLFF BOOK MFG. CO., NEW YORK

CONTENTS

Willkie

CHAPTER ONE

Germany and Indiana

O N March 12, 1941, the Nazi Ministry of Propaganda invited the American correspondents in Berlin on a special junket to Aschersleben, a small town in the Hartz Mountains in central Germany.* There, they were promised, the town archivist would show them records proving that a German coppersmith named Friedrich Willcke had died in 1859, that a family quarrel among his heirs had enabled a Jewish neighbor, Bernhard Gerson, to cheat them out of the coppersmithy, and that one of the sons, named Joseph, had packed up in disgust and sailed for America. According to Dr. Goebbels, this disposed of Wendell Willkie's statement that his grandfather had left Germany in 1848, as a protest against autocracy and as a demand for the right to live as a free man. The unsuccessful Republican candidate for President and the leader of the Republican opposition to President Roosevelt had made the statement a month earlier over a British Broadcasting Corporation transmitter in beleaguered London. British fliers were dropping copies of it in printed leaflets over Germany.

In New York, Willkie said he was amused and flattered that his statement had so worried Dr. Goebbels. "I do not pretend to have devoted any time to studying family history," he said. "If the talk I heard at home as a boy is correct, my grandfather came to the United States in 1848 as a result of the democratic revolution of that year, returned to Germany for a few years, married, and then returned with my father to the

* None of the reporters accepted the invitation.

United States in 1860, where he lived until he died. These things I know only generally by family tradition.

"I do know as a fact, however, that my grandfather taught my father a deep and abiding hatred of German autocracy and militarism, a passionate love and a warm and sympathetic understanding of the problems of the Jewish people and of all minority groups. I am proud that my father taught these same doctrines to his children, and I am firmly convinced, despite Dr. Goebbels, that millions of Germans enslaved by Hitler still cling to those beliefs."

This was nine months before Pearl Harbor. Patriotism had not yet glossed over the dilemma in which most Republican leaders found themselves on the problems of the war and President Roosevelt's foreign policy. Willkie's ancestry did nothing to make his position easier. Only once before in American history had a major party nominated an American for President whose father had not been born in the United States, and Alfred E. Smith in 1928 had had years of political activity in which to blend his Irish background, in the public imagination, with something as native as the sidewalks of New York. In the 1940 election, large pro-Willkie deviations from previous voting patterns were almost always associated with concentrations of German-Americans. In certain counties of Texas, traditionally Democratic, the German populations had voted overwhelmingly for Willkie and against Roosevelt's foreign policy. South Dakota, with 140,000 citizens of German extraction out of a total population of 650,000, had given Willkie a larger percentage majority than any other state, even Vermont or Maine.

During the campaign itself, the question of Willkie's German ancestry had been left by the Democrats, with a few scurrilous exceptions, to word-of-mouth discussion, but it had also played a real if unmeasurable part in lining up at least the more violent-minded interventionists against Willkie. One journalist, Louis Adamic, reported his "impression (which I can't document) was that between ten and fifteen million votes (most of them in such important states as New York, Pennsylvania, Illinois and Ohio) would go to Roosevelt either wholly or in part out of the 'old country' complex."

Germany and Indiana

If in 1940 many Americans, who had had too short a time in which to size him up, thought Willkie's German descent might lead him to oppose any involvement in the war, this was impossible to think in 1941. In the same month that Dr. Goebbels tried to rewrite the history of his family, a Republican Senator, John A. Danaher of Connecticut, charged on the floor of the Senate that Willkie had pledged all-out aid to Great Britain at a pre-election dinner at the New York home of Mr. and Mrs. Ogden Reid in order to secure the support of the *New York Times* and the *New York Herald Tribune*. Willkie denied this, too; it was only one incident in the great backwash of Republican second thoughts in 1941 about the candidate they had chosen in 1940. But Willkie's interventionist and internationalist convictions became a major reason for his repudiation by an important section of the Republican party,* and there were many in this camp who said openly that political worries about his German ancestry had led him to fall over backwards into the Roosevelt camp on foreign policy.

So his German ancestry was a problem for Willkie, but it was in political and not in personal terms. Willkie never spoke or read German, and never visited the country where all his ancestors had been born. Assimilation had moved with passionate speed in the Indiana of his father's generation. Even in World War I there had been in the Willkie family none of the problem of divided emotional loyalties which persisted for many Americans of German extraction who lived in more homogeneous communities than the farming land around Warsaw and Fort Wayne where his mother's and father's families, the Willkies and the Trisches, had settled.

There is no evidence, actually, to contradict the Willkie version of his grandfather's first emigration to this country after 1848 and subsequent return to Germany. This grandfather,

---

* Unimpeachable denials of the Danaher story were read into the *Congressional Record* by a Democrat, Senator Prentiss M. Brown of Michigan, who said: "Since no member of Mr. Willkie's party would rise to defend him from the charge that he bartered away his independence for support of the *New York Times* and the *New York Herald Tribune*, I thought, for old times' sake, that perhaps some old-line Democrat ought to rise up and say a word in his defense. And I do so."

Willkie

Friedrich Willcke,* lived long enough to leave his grandchildren memories of heavy German eating, an elaborate Catholic funeral in Fort Wayne when Wendell was four years old, and family tales of Germany in which early experiments with steam at the Aschersleben coppersmithy were described in terms of that vague but strong desire for a freer and more creative life which had driven so many Germans of Carl Schurz's generation to the United States. Even on Indiana farms at the turn of the century, German-Americans had a sense of common traditions stemming from their country of origin. In 1917, Wendell's father, Herman Francis Willkie, who was then sixty, went on a lecture tour around the country talking to groups of German-Americans. He was speaking in favor of the war, for the National Council of Defense, and all of his six children were in either the armed forces, the Red Cross, or civilian war work.

The search for freedom, a sense of self-reliance, and a hunger for an expanding material environment were Willkie's chief inheritance from his father's German ancestry. All three came to him equally strongly through his mother's family. She was a woman of considerable personal force, the first woman to be admitted to the bar in Indiana, her husband's law partner after she had given up teaching grammar school in Milford, where she had first met him. She raised a family of six children as if determined to refute by her personal example the entire German belief in *Kinder, Küche, Kirche* as the proper scope of a woman's life. Her family legends, even more than those of Willkie's father, belonged to the rapidly growing folk-myth of America as the dream and the haven of Europeans who had outgrown the narrow restrictions of the Old World.

Her maiden name was Henrietta Trisch and her paternal grandfather had been a wagon-maker of Erbach, in the Oldenwald, who had fled Germany after the revolutionary disturbances of 1830. His son, Lewis Trisch, met and married in War-

* The name acquired the new spelling, again according to family legend, through the mistake of a college registrar at Valparaiso College, then known as "the poor man's college," where Willkie's father studied for a year before transferring to the Methodist Episcopal College at Fort Wayne. The grandfather, Friedrich Willcke, died a Catholic but much under the spell of Carl Schurz and new American ideas.

6

saw, Indiana, a German girl named Julia Ann Dorothea Katherine von Hessen-Lois. Like Willkie's three other grandparents, she was a political exile from Germany but the details of her life must have sounded to the young Willkies as they grew up like notes for the standard novelist's treatment of the great nineteenth-century migration from Germany to the New World. Her father, Jacob von Hessen-Lois, had been a wealthy Hamburg merchant whose family acquired its name by marriage into the minor aristocracy and its liberal convictions by profitable enterprise with the growing middle-class traders of the new Europe which was struggling throughout the nineteenth century to throw off its feudal background. The family had been forced to a melodramatic flight from Germany, in 1848, via England to Indiana. There Julia met and married Lewis Trisch, and they moved farther west to Fort Dodge in Kansas, where they opened a store. Kansas was both a slave territory, after 1854, and a part of the new West. The young couple shared the growing bitterness over the compromise which had committed Kansas to slavery, and back they went to Indiana, again in flight.

Trisch became a blacksmith in Warsaw, where his family was still settled, edited the local paper, fathered two daughters, and died in 1873 at the age of forty. One of those daughters, Henrietta, became Willkie's mother; her sister, Jennie, studied medicine and became one of the first women doctors in America. Lewis Trisch's wife, Julia, Willkie's grandmother, was a Presbyterian lay preacher who rode horseback all over Indiana holding revival meetings. She was known as Mother Trisch throughout the region. The road was a long one which had taken her from a merchant's home in Hamburg through England to Indiana, to the pre-Civil War skirmishing and rioting in the Kansas which was John Brown's tortured land, then back to fighting the devil in the name of the Lord at Indiana prayer meetings. But it was a road traveled by a good many other Europeans in the middle years of the nineteenth century; the stubborn toughness and the restless passion which kept her going were as real in the making of America as the cornfields and the winding streams of Indiana where she settled.

Willkie

The notion that states like Indiana have always been peopled with native-born American stock, who were eating ice-cream cones in rocking chairs on the porches of their substantial homes when Columbus discovered America, is of recent origin and is more widely held in the East than it is in Indiana. It is true that the state, like all the Middle West, was to change during Willkie's lifetime; Booth Tarkington's characters rocked their chairs with a gravity which suggested that they had been there, solidly and respectably, for a very long time indeed. Yet Willkie grew up in a loquacious family where the stories of his footloose grandparents were told and retold into one version of the saga of the search for freedom which has become a great American folk-myth. He was always proud of his ancestors without knowing too many details about them, and the stories he remembered of them had nearly always to do with this hunger for freedom, for schools and libraries, for new jobs and new homes and new horizons, which had drawn them to Indiana in the first place.

Myth is the articulate vehicle of a people's wishful thinking. The German birth of all four of Willkie's grandparents was indisputably true, but it produced no wishful projection in terms of Germany—even on the Yorkville scale—among farm settlers in Indiana. It is also indisputably true that certain traits which are now called Middle Western—an anti-intellectualism, an undervaluing of cultural life, excessive respect for respectability, and idealization of the businessman—were also spreading when Willkie was born in 1892. These were to become important enough during his lifetime to help explain his eventual failure to win political support in just those groups where he most logically expected it. But this was a later process. By the outbreak of the First World War, Willkie was a grown man who had finished college, held itinerant summer jobs in a dozen states, gone off to Puerto Rico to work on a sugar plantation, opened his mind to all the winds that blew across this country just after the turn of the century. In this process his ancestry was enormously important, although what it gave him was not specifically German. Immigrants from other countries had settled in Indiana with comparable traditions. Only eight years

8

Germany and Indiana

before Willkie's grandfather, Lewis Trisch, came to the state as a baby, Robert Owen had broken through the ice in the Ohio River with his two sons and his "boatload of knowledge" to found New Harmony, in Posey County, Indiana. There they were to assemble more than one thousand persons in the first six months of their effort to launch an experiment in community of property and in business and social co-operation. This was not the Middle West that it later became for those who smiled at Harold L. Ickes's wisecrack about "the barefoot boy from Wall Street." * Willkie was never a farmer in his life, and seldom barefoot. The pull he felt towards Indiana throughout his life was strong with the vitality of the deeply cosmopolitan, eclectic, many-textured background which he acquired through his grandparents.

As Willkie's personality became a subject of wide popular interest after the 1940 election, it was easy to assign certain traits to his boyhood and his education in Indiana and to isolate these from the influences in New York, the nation, and the world which shaped him later in his life. It was much too easy. For Indiana, in the decade before Willkie was born, had experienced major technological and social changes which were at the very heart of a process which was, in fact, revolutionizing all of American life. These changes left in American minds a slightly bucolic dream-picture of the countryside on the banks of the Wabash; an ugly suspicion of more sinister forces at work in the cities; and a slowly developing awareness of the need for some new image of the state, both in itself and as a microcosm of the nation. The bucolic picture was universally recognized. The fears that industrialism and urbanization had changed it were acknowledged openly by very few Americans, and carefully fenced off as "problems" for experts to deal with or for fanatics to exploit. The hope that the older pioneer spirit could turn inward and work out a substitute for the frontier in the industrialized jungle which had grown up in America was fought for by an even smaller number. Yet all three reactions were close to the structure of Willkie's life, and

* The phrase was borrowed by Ickes from a newspaper column written by Jay Franklin.

9

they vitally affected both his personal growth and his political fortunes.

The bucolic picture was no invention; it was founded partly on fact and partly on the desperate hunger of an insecure urban middle-class and an equally insecure farming population to believe that all was for the best in the best of all possible worlds. One of Willkie's fellow-Indianans, Booth Tarkington, became the dean of American middle-class letters by giving Americans exactly this reassurance. In the notes which Vernon L. Parrington left for the uncompleted portion of his work on the American mind, he wrote that Tarkington "possesses the virtues of cleverness, optimism, humor, respectability. Honors all the Victorian taboos. Life is an agreeable experience—to the successful, hence it is well to rise. His chief theme, middle-class romance as exemplified in the 'valley of democracy': courtship of nice young people through the agency of parties and picnics. A skillful writer, with a light touch, but his art destroyed by love of popularity—a novel ends well that ends happily. A perennial sophomore, purveyor of comfortable literature to middle-class America."

This is the legend of an Indiana, and a world of values, which Willkie accepted at various times in his life, sometimes revolted against, more often simply slipped on and off like an old pair of comfortable carpet slippers. There is no denying that it was a central part of his background, affecting both his personality and his public reputation as long as he lived. It is personified in the class-book pictures of him as a young man which were dragged out of old files for the 1940 campaign, as it is in the feature stories which were ground out by the hundred in an effort, still strongly needed in 1940, to reassure Americans that there were no skeletons in the closet and no goblins under the bed, no unhappy endings in real life any more than in the movies. Willkie, who became a specialist in unhappy endings, was himself a part of this legend; yet much of the story of his life is the story of his efforts to rewrite it.

The myth of the great valley of the Mississippi as the Garden of the World continued to flourish like the tulip trees of Indiana. In May, 1940, before Willkie's nomination, Booth

Germany and Indiana

Tarkington got out of a semi-invalid's wheel-chair to meet the dark horse who was then being looked over critically by the Republican party. Here, he reported, was "a type familiar to us, a man wholly natural in manner, a man with no pose, no 'swellness,' no condescension, no clever plausibleness—in a word, a man as American as the courthouse yard in the square of an Indiana county seat. That is, we saw a good, sturdy, plain, able Hoosier—and as we ourselves were native Hoosiers, of course we instantly felt that we knew him."

It became a fact of political history that these Hoosiers were wrong in thinking that they knew Willkie. Yet it was an easy mistake to make. Willkie himself was so overawed by literary figures in 1940 that when Tarkington wanted to meet him, he considered this a more impressive sign of his rise in prestige than almost anything that could have happened to him. He said this to friends jokingly, but he was more than a little serious about it.

By 1940, this nostalgic picture of Indiana was as wide of the mark as Tarkington's estimate of Willkie. The idea of Willkie as a "good, sturdy, plain, able Hoosier" was a political boomerang which helped some of his worst enemies. "Willkie's own Indiana," Westbrook Pegler wrote in 1941 during the debate in the Republican party over isolationism, "has become an industrial state with an industrial population which is urban even in the country. The factories and works have spread out beyond the old city lines, which used to be the demarcation between soft comfort and hardy misery, sophistication and chew-tobacco innocence, 'way up into Michigan and over Ohio and Illinois. . . . I doubt that Willkie himself has really made that mistake, and suspect that his emphasis on open-faced, boyish political homeliness in the late campaign was something which the actors used to call hokum or hoke and now call corn. . . . His Indiana was dead and buried on the banks of the Wabash, and these people were frisking about in a very depressing burlesque."

The change in Indiana had begun a few years before Willkie's birth, when a gas boom started, in 1884, at Findlay, Ohio, failed there abruptly, and then started again around Muncie,

Indiana, which had been purely farming country until 1886. The boom was to peter out in less than a score of years, but it lasted long enough to transform Elwood, which became the center of a natural gas belt promising or threatening to transform the entire state. In an early Chamber of Commerce gesture, in 1890, the town gave fourteen acres on a farm near a well called "Vesuvius" to a tin-plate company. It became America's first big tin-plate plant. Governor William McKinley of Ohio dedicated it in 1892; it grew to contain twenty-eight mills and made huge profits for the families of William B. Leeds and Daniel G. Reed, who owned it. Before construction started on the plant, the company asked a lawyer who was also principal of Elwood's only school to report on the town's real estate offer. In the same year, 1892, on February 18, the lawyer's son, named Lewis Wendell Willkie, was born.

By 1893, some $300,000,000 had been invested in factories in Indiana established to use the cheap natural gas. Capital invested in all manufacturing plants in Indiana had doubled between 1880 and 1890 and was almost to double again by 1900. The statistical center of all manufacturing in the United States had moved by 1890 to a point eight and a half miles west of Canton, Ohio.

The natural gas boom was a local phenomenon, but what it represented in terms of American life was happening all over the country. Fortunes were being made in the new towns and cities which sprang up, but the drawing away of population from rural districts was so sudden and so drastic as to threaten many of them with complete paralysis. Professor Arthur M. Schlesinger, Sr., has reported that a map of the Middle West shading the counties which suffered the chief losses between 1880 and 1890 would have been blackest across central Missouri and in the eastern half of Iowa, northern and western Illinois, central and southeastern Indiana (which includes Elwood), southern Michigan, and central and southern Ohio. Most of the depletion, especially in Indiana, was due to the cityward flight, and not to the building up of agricultural country farther west, although this was also a pump drawing people away from the relatively stable farming world they had inherited from the pioneers.

"The men, women and children," Professor Schlesinger found, "who gathered in ten thousand schoolhouses to debate the farmers' grievances in the early 1890's had only vague notions about the intricacies of the free-silver question and its relation to prices and prosperity, but they were grimly aware that mysterious new forces in American life were robbing them of their traditional rural heritage of freedom and spiritual and material well-being."

On July 4, 1892, the year of Willkie's birth, thirteen hundred delegates met at Omaha to found the Populist party. They issued a "second Declaration of Independence" which described the nation in these terms: "The people are demoralized. The newspapers are largely subsidized or muzzled, public opinion silenced, business prostrated, our homes covered with mortgages, labor impoverished, and the land concentrated in the hands of the capitalists. . . . The toils of the millions are stolen to build up colossal fortunes. From the prolific womb of governmental injustice we breed the two great classes—tramps and millionaires."

These pressures set up strains and anxieties throughout the Middle West which were compounded in Elwood by the boom-and-bust cycle of the natural gas supply. In the spring of 1900, when Willkie was eight years old, the Amalgamated Association of Iron, Steel and Tin Workers, representing labor at the tin-plate plant, asked his father to represent it. This caused him some local disrepute, but not enough to keep him from accepting. He was still practicing law, in addition to his real estate speculation, which had by now made him the owner of one hundred renting houses on land he had bought close to the plant. The tin-plate mills then employed some four thousand workers, about two-thirds of the town's labor supply. It was in this same year that the gas supply began seriously to run out. With cheap fuel gone, the plant and the town slowly collapsed. A large number of Welsh workers who had been brought in to start the plant moved north to Gary; two of Wendell's brothers,

Bob and Fred, worked in Gary during summer vacations. The Pittsburgh Plate Glass Company, another industry which had been attracted to Elwood by the cheap fuel, closed its plant for good. Willkie's father got rid of his houses by jacking them up and selling them to farmers who used them for small barns or machinery sheds. The tin-plate mill staggered along for a decade, alternately closing down and reopening, while Gary was taking over the industry.

"The story of Elwood," Willkie wrote in 1940 before the election, "is the story of America and its problems. It's the perfect laboratory; I've always wanted to write the story myself." He blamed the town's collapse on two factors: "profligate waste of natural resources, and overindustrialization of an essentially agricultural community." He approved later efforts to rehabilitate the town, but he realized they could not succeed alone. "Elwood's experience," he said in 1940, "shows that individuals cannot carry through large-scale social readjustments—that society owes an obligation to its members when it leads them up a blind alley."

The mysterious new forces in American life which had been powerfully working in his native state for a decade before he was born remained close to the center of Willkie's interest as long as he lived. His awareness of them did not begin with his struggle against the TVA, his campaign for President, or his view of the world at war. To believe that it did was useful only to those who held the thesis that Willkie, like his greatest opponent, was "a traitor to his class," corrupted by ambition from the simple, clear, and honest view of the world which Booth Tarkington expressed for Indiana. The state was to produce, in Willkie's generation, a large number of citizens who clung to the simpler formula, and since most of these were Republicans both by background and by choice, they backed Willkie heavily when he seemed to give them reassurance that their world had not essentially changed. They abandoned him as it became clear, to him and to them, that such reassurance as he could give was useful only as a cushion to ease the bumps of still greater and more drastic changes.

Germany and Indiana

Indiana was typically American because it shared the wrenchings with which a basically rural society was becoming an urban, industrial economy. It was in 1893, the year after Willkie's birth, that Professor Frederick J. Turner published his essay, "The Significance of the Frontier in American History," in which he argued that this most decisive factor in the development of America had ceased to operate with the disappearance of the area of free land. Willkie was born just when "the bitterness of the frontier," as Parrington called it, was beginning to be recognized openly, in talk and in writing. "The Golden West of Mark Twain and the bucolic West of Whitcomb Riley," Parrington wrote, "had both slipped into the past and the day that was rising was to bring its discouragements that seared men's hopes as the hot winds seared the fields of rustling corn."

Meredith Nicholson's idea of Indiana as "The Valley of Democracy" disappeared in American literature while it was still a powerful political idea. This land of simple well-being, peopled by neighbors living like one big family in cozy "folksiness," wholesome, middle-class, dominated by the spirit of American democracy and equality, was to vanish from American writing after Sherwood Anderson, Theodore Dreiser, Henry L. Mencken, Sinclair Lewis, Zona Gale, Van Wyck Brooks, and a whole generation of writers and critics went cruelly to work on it. But in terms of political slogans it would be hard to argue—at least with an Indiana politician—that it is not as strong and as prosperous, even if as unreal, a land as ever. Willkie knew the change had taken place, and until 1940 he followed in his own life one of the main currents which were carrying men away from the world in which he grew up. When he was forced to find a political answer to the problem, in the campaign for the Presidency, he tried also to hold on to the older formula. His split answer—epitomized in the "barefoot boy from Wall Street" wisecrack—won him both friends and enemies. It never satisfied him, and until he died he was looking for political symbols which would combine some of the strength and quality of the Indiana he had known as a boy with

15

the bite and urgency of the new, ugly questions in people's minds which no amount of nostalgic reassurance from the past could quiet.

Willkie was by no means alone in this search. A list of the well-known sons of Indiana in his generation suggests that many of them were moved, as he was, by a hunger to understand the reasons for the shattering of the myths which had formed from the original frontier relations, as Henry Nash Smith has defined them, "between man and nature—or rather, even more narrowly, between American man and the American West." A surprising number of them left Indiana to find this understanding. The strains of industrialization and of increasing involvement with the markets of the world, which had destroyed what reality lay behind the older, simpler legends of Indiana, led many of them to one form or another of extreme deviation from inherited patterns. Eugene V. Debs and Theodore Dreiser came from Indiana; so did Roy Howard and Will Hays. Cole Porter and Hoagy Carmichael were born there. So was John Dillinger. All of them moved further away, in their personalities, than Willkie did.

One of the extremist answers some men found was a growth of native American Fascism probably as strong and deep-rooted as in any state of the United States. After the First World War, the Ku Klux Klan was stronger in Indiana than in the South. It was directed chiefly against the Catholics and the Jews; in practice, it worked out as an elaborate racket in which spoils were the lubricant of strong organization, and at one time it controlled the state government before its leader, or grand dragon, David C. Stephenson, was arrested and convicted after a girl he had raped committed suicide. John Gunther has told about one Indiana Klan official who understood the supremacy of practice over theory in politics so well that he remarked: "We're not against you Irish Catholics, but just against them *Roman* Catholics."

When Willkie was practicing law in Ohio, he fought the Klan, and won. But the spirit behind it has never been killed. Before and after World War II, Indiana was rife with silver-shirted or black legions of every kind, men who exploited the deep insecurities which had first grown up in the 1880's and 1890's and which had been aggravated by two wars, a great depression, and the slow but steady influx into the state of new settlers from the mountains and the mill towns of the South. One of these post-Klan bigots was Carl H. Mote, who published a magazine called *America Preferred* and tried to organize farmers into a "strike against strikes." Another was Court Asher, of Muncie, publisher of a Fascist paper called *X-Ray* and one of the seditionists indicted in Washington during World War II.

After reviewing the virulence of these movements in Indiana, Gunther wrote: "Considering some of these things, it seems remarkable that a man like Wendell Willkie could have risen out of the Indiana wastes. Willkie, as a matter of fact, only carried his home state by the narrowest of margins in 1940. I went to Rushville, to look at the house he lived in. It is comfortable, of red brick, ivy-bound, shaded by sturdy elms, and with a white-pillared stoop and an iron rail along the steps. A point that would astonish Europeans who know little of the normal topography of Middle Western towns is that, though in a good residential district, it is only twenty yards from the railroad tracks."

Earlier, Gunther came to the conclusion that earnest exploration of the reasons for this native Indiana Fascism revealed only that it "rose in the first instance out of simple antipathy to Roosevelt and the New Deal." The roots of both revolt and reaction in Indiana are much older than the New Deal, and part of their strength is a reflection of the strength of the older culture of Indiana which lost its meaning in men's lives, although not its power in political slogans, during the years in which Willkie was growing up. Neither Debs nor Dreiser, on the one hand, nor Mote and Asher and Stephenson, on the other, ever managed to answer the questions which sprouted in Indiana together with the factories, the cities, and the concrete highways lying among the cornfields under the same restless, continental wind.

For the wind went on blowing, the pioneer dream was never wholly lost except for those who fled from it, and Indiana was ripe for a man who could find and phrase an answer to the challenge of a new world which had burst upon it. Hugh McVey, in Sherwood Anderson's *Poor White*, lived for a time on a farm in Indiana, some forty miles east of Indianapolis, before he settled in Bidwell, Ohio. This was in 1892, the year of Willkie's birth; Elwood is forty miles northeast of Indianapolis. "In even the smallest of the towns, inhabited only by farm laborers, a quaint interesting civilization was being developed," Anderson wrote. "Men worked hard but were much in the open air and had time to think. Their minds reached out toward the solution of the mystery of existence. The schoolmaster and the country lawyer read Tom Paine's *Age of Reason* and Bellamy's *Looking Backward*. They discussed these books with their fellows. There was a feeling, ill-expressed, that America had something real and spiritual to offer to the rest of the world. Workmen talked to each other of the new tricks of their trades, and after hours of discussion of some new way to cultivate corn, shape a horseshoe or build a barn, spoke of God and His intent concerning man. Long-drawn-out discussions of religious beliefs and the political destiny of America were carried on."

This was a real part of Willkie's Indiana. The old frontier had lost its glamour as it disappeared from the map of a settled continent; the new machines and cities were wrenching life into new patterns; yet much of the older world survived in the texture of men's thinking. Crop reports were still published on the front pages of Indiana newspapers in the 1890's; local retail stores in the bigger towns were still overgrown country stores boasting names like "The Temple of Economy" and "The Beehive Bazaar." Elwood and Rushville, the two towns in Indiana which Willkie thought of as home, were both committed to the long and uncertain gamble of trying to marry their pioneer, agricultural past with a new, capitalist future. This had not been accomplished in Willkie's lifetime, but it was never clearly impossible. Rush County now raises 220,000 pigs a year and claims to be the best hog county in the world. After Willkie died, John Bartlow Martin, the most perceptive chronicler of Indiana, wrote about the landscape near Rushville: "This is Riley country. Cattle are browsing in the pasture beside a winding stream, and a man is selling watermelons at a roadside stand. Down a dusty side road walks a farm woman in bright flowered dress made from a flour sack, wearing a red straw hat and low black shoes, her shoulders stooped and her hair shingle-bobbed; she is going to catch the bus on the hard road and ride to Rushville with its stores and restaurants and massive red stone courthouse topped by a four-faced clock. Yet here where the rich plain flattens out are other things too: hybrid seed corn under scientific cultivation, enormous white farmhouses surrounded by hundreds of acres of corn. Wendell Willkie campaigned from the acreage of relatives here, but Hoosiers knew the acreage belonged to no poor farmer. This is one of the best corn and hog regions of the state, and here farming is a capitalist's enterprise, not a raggedy man's."

CHAPTER TWO

The Willkie Family

L EWIS WENDELL WILLKIE was the fourth of six children, and the third boy, born to his parents, Herman Francis and Henrietta Trisch Willkie. They lived in a nine-room frame house in Elwood on the corner of South A and 19th Streets. Both parents had been teachers and were partners in an active law firm. Herman Willkie used to wake the family in the mornings by shouting quotations up the stairs; one of his favorites was, "Oh, why should the spirit of mortal be proud?" Respect for literature and learning was a big part of the family atmosphere. In neither politics nor religion was the family frozen into any group affiliation. The children were all brought up in the deep turn-of-the-century belief that it is good for children to grow, in every way.

Lowell Mellett, who was to be a New Deal opponent of Willkie's, grew up in Elwood at the same time. He has recalled one vivid picture of him. "It is the picture of a tall, gaunt man, walking past our house with a small boy clinging to each of his hands. They were stubby little fellows and they had to reach high for the hand held down to them.

"For his part, the man not only accommodated his pace to theirs; he also kept a firm grip on their hands. If they stumbled —and they did, for the bricks of our sidewalk were uneven and their eyes were constantly roving in order not to miss anything—the man held on and a boy was sometimes left dangling in the air for a moment, never allowed to fall.

"One of those little boys was Wendell L. Willkie. The man was his father, known to those of my age as Hellfire Willkie, getting the nickname from his initials H.F.—while principal of the town's only school. He was a friend of my father, who considered him a very smart man."

His parents, Willkie once told a questioner, "were much interested in ideas, in books and in art. My father had a library of some six or seven thousand books. Eight of us, my father, mother and six children, lived in a constant atmosphere of reading and discussion in our home life, so when you ask me questions of what was my favorite book, it is difficult to answer as we read and reread everything in those days."

When Willkie was five years old, his mother was admitted to the Indiana bar and she practiced law as a career, hiring a housekeeper to run the house. She painted china, and won prizes for her quilting and her embroidery. She hated to cook, but she sang and played the piano, learned French and Spanish, and read omnivorously until her death.

She was a gifted public speaker. She helped to start the town library in Elwood, raising its initial thousand-dollar endowment. Her mother, Julia Trisch, had been the first head of the Woman's Christian Temperance Union in Indiana. Her parents had been Catholic and Presbyterian; she and her husband became pillars of the Methodist community in Elwood, and later joined the Presbyterians. The children were brought up on a reading diet which included both the Bible and the works of Robert G. Ingersoll. They all started life as Methodists, but there was no parental objection when Wendell, perhaps because he was then courting the daughter of one of the Welsh families in Elwood, became an Episcopalian.

From his mother, to whom he never felt as close as he did to his father, Wendell inherited some of the traits which were to help make him famous. She is remembered by those who knew her as a driving, restless, not very happy woman, of great ability and almost legendary strength, energy, and ambition. When she died in 1940, at the age of eighty-one, she still wore high French heels. She could still cut down to size her son's "big talk" about running for President, as if he had still been a schoolboy. After her death, when the Willkie sons wrote the epitaph for her tombstone in the Elwood cemetery, they called her "a woman driven by an indomitable will" and the words "to conquer" were omitted for reasons of affection rather than because they did not apply.

Herman Willkie had more to do with the conscious education of his most famous son. He seems to have been a man of restless character and steady habits, with a prodigious memory and a consuming curiosity. He had come to this country at the age of four, the brightest boy in a strongly Catholic family. They settled first at Yoder, near Fort Wayne. In his teens, he left the church after a bitter argument over indulgences. One younger brother left with him, but all the other members of the family remained staunch Catholics. When Herman Willkie went back to Fort Wayne for his father's funeral, his apostasy was mentioned in the service and this hurt and angered him.

A comparable influence on his life and on the atmosphere in which his sons were raised stemmed from his memories of German militarism and Prussian brutality. He used to tell the boys how, when troops were quartered on the civilian population in Germany, an officer had stumbled over him while he was playing on the floor, and had thrashed him hard in anger. During the 1914-18 war, his sons would bait him with tales of the British Navy or of the Belgian Congo, knowing that this was sure to provoke him to tell this favorite story all over again. Their father never spoke German at home, and when he visited Edward Willkie, Wendell's brother, in Belgium in the 1930's, he could hardly understand a word of the language.

Herman moved to Fort Wayne on his own while he was still a boy and worked his way, as a carpenter, through Valparaiso College and then the Methodist Episcopal College at Fort Wayne. He went to Milford as a teacher, married Henrietta Trisch there, and then settled in Elwood, where he was to live until his death. The town's population of one thousand in 1888, when he arrived, was to grow to eighteen thousand in the natural gas boom. He grew with it, switching from teaching to the law and then to real estate. After the panic of 1893, he found himself fifty thousand dollars in debt, but he managed somehow to send four sons and two daughters through college. The family was neither rich nor poor; it differed from many other families in Elwood chiefly because the house had so many books in it and the children were all sent away for advanced schooling.

There was a good deal of the crusader in Herman Willkie. His sons were never sure just how long he taught a non-sectarian Bible Class in the Methodist Church but an inscribed clock was presented to him on the thirtieth anniversary of his starting it. He invited distinguished men to speak to the class, and he was always proud that William Jennings Bryan and Vice-President Thomas R. Marshall had been among them. Elwood was a tough town, with thirty saloons and a red-light district when Wendell was a boy. Its population was two-thirds Protestant and one-third Catholic, and the Irish were the heavy drinkers. Herman Willkie found himself a friend and ally, in trying to clean up the town, in an exceptionally able Catholic priest named Father Bigel. He was so fond of him and so pleased to have help in the local-option elections on prohibition that he could even joke about the simultaneous campaign to persuade him to return to the church he had abandoned.

He made a good many local enemies in these crusading efforts. He was a six-footer, and he could lift his office safe without help. Four sons made a useful bodyguard when one was needed. There was nothing possessive in his attitude to his children, but they were quite simply what he lived for. A local politician named Pat Bradley called on him once, in his law office, on a Saturday afternoon, hoping to find him alone. Instead he found the four boys at their weekly chore of sweeping and mopping the floors. Bradley decided to broach his business anyway, and offered Herman Willkie ten thousand dollars to plead the saloonkeepers' side in a suit over a disputed local-option election. He could not understand why he was turned down, especially since the lawyer admitted he would get nothing for pleading the other side in the litigation. The fee offered was twice what Herman Willkie could make in a year. "If you really want to know why I won't take your case, Pat," Willkie finally told him, "there's the reason," and he pointed at the four boys.

The boom-and-bust cycle through which he lived in Elwood convinced Herman Willkie that neither the Garden of the World myth which Indiana had inherited from the pioneers nor the nineteenth-century dream of freedom brought with them by immigrants from Europe was the whole answer to the riddle of the American future. Nor were liquor and godlessness the only problems. He had long been an ardent Bryan Democrat, with labor sympathies, when the tin-plate mills reopened in 1908, after having been closed down in the panic of 1907. In June, 1909, the workers voted to strike and closed all but two of the twenty-eight mills. The company shipped in strikebreakers from Pittsburgh and by August fifteen mills were working. It was at this point that Wendell came home from a summer job, after college, to find his father trying to block a company injunction against the union.

Feelings were running high in the town. Two local bullies, hired by the company, tried to beat up Herman Willkie on the street and Wendell, who was with his father, got his first taste of political violence. The injunction plea was transferred to Indianapolis, and the union sent a delegation to try to interest Clarence Darrow in taking the case. Wendell went along with his father, and heard the famous lawyer agree to defend the union, for a twenty-thousand-dollar retainer and one-thousand dollars a day in court.

"Mr. Willkie," Darrow told Wendell's father, "it's a good thing for your son to learn now that there's nothing unethical in being adequately compensated for pleading a cause in which you deeply believe."

The union leaders turned it down. They went on hiring Herman Willkie for twenty-five dollars a day. He won the case, the injunction being denied by Edward M. Daniels, Master in Chancery of the Federal Court at Indianapolis. But the strike was already lost. It dragged out for a couple of years; by that time the union had been smashed and the company was on the brink of closing down its Elwood plant for good.

Wendell got from his father a first-class education and an insatiable hunger for more of it. This was what the father planned. He was himself absorbed in trying to understand the mysterious new forces which were transforming Indiana, and he wanted all his children to find out more about them than he could.

When four of them were at Indiana University together, there was a student riot in a Bloomington theater. Fred Willkie hit a policeman, Bob went to jail for a night, Wendell was stabbed in the free-for-all. The father was on a train the next day when an acquaintance told him the news. "If they were my sons, Judge," the man said, "I'd take them out of school fast."

"Was it a big riot?" Mr. Willkie asked.

"Big? The whole damn college was in it."

"Well, my friend," Mr. Willkie said, "if all the students were in it and my sons had not been in it, I *would* take them out of college."

He carried this belief in his sons' independence a long way. When any one of them came home from college, he made it a ritual to meet the train. He would greet his son, suggest that it would be nice if he spent a few days at home, and then give him a ticket to St. Louis or Chicago and a couple of ten-dollar bills, adding that he would be glad to see him again at the end of the summer. One of Wendell's brothers, after he had finished college, was visited by his father at a time when he was trying to support a family on a tiny income. Herman Willkie turned a deaf ear to a few discreet suggestions that a small loan might be helpful, until he stood on the station platform waiting for the train to take him home.

"My son," he then said formally, "there was once a King of England who dearly loved his son. He sent him off to fight the French, with an army. Soon the son sent a messenger home with a plea for reinforcements. There was no answer. A second messenger was sent. Again no answer. Finally, the

25

son sent a third messenger home to report that his army was in a bad way, that he risked a really serious defeat, and that he desperately needed help. The King replied: 'His Majesty is too good a soldier not to know when reinforcements are really needed, and too good a father not to send them when that moment comes.'" He then boarded the train and went back to Elwood.

Herman Willkie had no ambition to be anything more than what he was, to get anywhere, to pile up any fortune. He was glad to be called "Judge," or "Squire," or "Hellfire Willkie." When Wendell was practicing law in Ohio, a judge rebuked him once in court for some technical slip, and then asked him if he were Herman Willkie's son. "He would never make that mistake," the judge said. The story pleased Herman Willkie chiefly because it seemed good education for his son. He felt the same pleasure on another occasion when Wendell, deputizing for his brother Bob, assistant prosecuting attorney for Madison County, tried an arson case against his father, and the father won. When he died in 1934, the Willkie sons wrote the inscription for his tombstone: "He dedicated his life to his children."

Wendell's formal education was entirely in Indiana. He had a year at Culver Military Academy, about one hundred miles north of Elwood, but he was graduated from the Elwood High School, where he was elected class president in his senior year. He played a little football, but he was the shrimp in a family of big men, and he was never skilled in any competitive athletic sport. He learned to swim at Culver, and he could swim across Lake Barbee in Indiana, where his father owned a rustic lodge with a group of lawyers who shared it for summer vacations. But he was known as the weakling of the family through college. Not until he was in the army did he start to grow and to fill out.

In 1910 he matriculated at Indiana University, in Bloomington, where he lived in a house at 523 East 3rd Street, a few blocks from the campus. His older sister, Julia, ran the house while the other children went through college. Willkie is remembered by his classmates as a tall, thin, loquacious boy, often dressed in a turtle-neck sweater, known on the campus as a moderately good student, a debater, and a radically inclined gadfly. He was president of the Boosters' Club, and a director of the Jackson Club, an undergraduate Democratic society. Woodrow Wilson was his hero, and Wilson's New Freedom was the most exciting body of ideas he had yet found. He denounced fraternities until shortly before graduation when he joined Beta Theta Pi, the oldest and most exclusive fraternity at the university and always referred to at Indiana as Paul McNutt's fraternity. Both his opposition to the fraternity system and his final acceptance of it were part of his courtship of a girl named Gwyneth Harry, the daughter of a Welsh steelworker for whose sake he had joined the Episcopal Church.

He had been working at part-time jobs ever since he had a newspaper route when he was ten years old. In Elwood they were the odd jobs on which American boys grow up: tending cattle, sorting potatoes, collecting junk, driving a bakery wagon, distributing samples for an advertising agency. In the summer of 1908 he worked in the tin-plate plant in Elwood as assistant catcher in a rolling unit. Beginning in 1909, just before he went to college, jobs took him during summers through a large part of the West. He ran a tent hotel for itinerant farm workers in Aberdeen, South Dakota, harvested wheat in Wyoming, was a vegetable picker in California, did manual labor in a Texas oil field. He saw a good deal of the country, and learned to be independent. It was a restless way of growing up, in sharp contrast to the close-knit family of his boyhood.

After his graduation from Indiana in 1913, he went to the Coffeyville High School in Kansas to teach history and to coach the track, basketball, and debating teams. This job was no tryout of a profession; he took it to make some money so he could study law. The high school yearbook for 1914 shows that he threw himself into local and school activities with a good deal of energy. Other teachers who worked with him believe that he found a high school teaching job in a small Kansas town too cramping and that it was here he first decided that he must branch out. So he took a job the next summer as laboratory assistant in the Fajardo Sugar Company's plant in Puerto Rico, where his brother Fred was head chemist. Wendell was not a scientist by aptitude or inclination, but there was more money in it than in teaching, and a chance to see another country.

First he went to Oberlin for a refresher course in chemistry. His sister Julia had been planning to go to Heidelberg, and the family plan was to send his brother Ed with her to try a German school. Bryan, who was then Secretary of State and a good friend of Herman Willkie's, advised them not to go because of the chances of a European war. By this time, Oberlin was the only college which would still accept a late registration, so Ed matriculated there and Wendell went along partly to help out his younger brother. In this he failed; Ed was eased out of Oberlin into Annapolis, an All-American selection as football tackle, the Olympic wrestling team, and a highly successful business career. But Wendell brushed up his chemistry and went off to Puerto Rico.

A quarter of a century later, when he returned to the island on his trip around the world, he remembered little about it except its wretched poverty. Yet the experience formed an important part of the growing pattern of his mind. Gardner Cowles once asked Willkie what had kept him from thinking like a typical American millionaire. If it was any single incident, Willkie told him, it was a horseback ride in Puerto Rico with the manager of a big plantation. A native had stumbled out of the sugar cane, where he had been hiding for some days, a hungry fugitive in one of the revolts of the peonized *jibaros* of the island. The manager had hacked him with his cane knife, all but cutting off his shoulder, without stopping his horse or the conversation. Willkie and his host rode on, but Willkie never forgot it.

He went back to Indiana to study law and was graduated in 1916 with an LL.B. degree. His oration at his law school commencement was a free-swinging attack on the Indiana state constitution, which shocked some members of the faculty and is still remembered at Indiana for its boldness. It delayed for a few days the awarding of his degree. But he was much more serious as a graduate student than he had been as an undergraduate and he left the law school at the head of his class.

The Willkie Family

Wendell went back to Elwood and joined his father and mother in the law firm of Willkie and Willkie. He did not stay long, because he enlisted in the United States Army on the day America entered the war against Germany. He was twenty-five years old, a gangling but not a big man, with a restless, hungry mind. His education had equipped him with more than a profession. From his early boyhood on, he had absorbed the two rich inheritances of ideas which he shared with many Americans of his generation: the search, primarily for freedom, of nineteenth-century immigrants; and the fumbling of the American Middle West to bend its old frontier dream of the Garden of the World into the iron necessities of an industrial age. Both took him, as they took the United States, into a war in Europe and another step in the discovery of one world.

CHAPTER THREE

Akron, the Boom City

W ILLKIE saw no front-line action in the war, but he saw something of the world and a good deal of the United States Army. He was sent to officers' training school at Fort Benjamin Harrison in Indianapolis. Commissioned a second lieutenant, he was then sent to Harvard for further training under French infantry officers. Transferred to artillery, he was next moved to the School of Fire at Fort Sill in Oklahoma and assigned as a first lieutenant to Battery I, 325th Field Artillery, attached to the 84th Division. When he was finally sent overseas, his outfit landed in Glasgow and proceeded to a camp near Winchester for still further training. Six weeks after he landed in France, the war was over.

He stayed on for some months in France, appearing as defense counsel in court-martial cases, chiefly of soldiers who had overstayed their leave in Paris. He had been promoted to captain, and his appearance before courts-martial was voluntary, mainly in behalf of soldiers from his own regiment picked up AWOL. "This activity won for me no recommendation or promotion from my superior officer," he wrote later. "On the contrary, my immediate superior suggested that on account of it I was a nuisance and should be demoted."

Many years later, Willkie told how he had made a parachute jump during the war. He had been kidding another officer for griping about having to make a jump. The kidding led to a bet that Willkie would not jump from a plane just for fun; Willkie did and won the bet. He recalled the story in what was a real emergency, flying in a plane loaned by Cities Service Company on a Commonwealth and Southern field trip. The pilot was unable to find a field at Wheeling, West Virginia, and was running out of gas. By the time Willkie had finished telling his story of his wartime jump, the pilot found a break in the overcast. It was just in time, because the plane carried no parachutes. Willkie used to say that this emergency was the only time he had ever tried desperately to remember all of the small type on an insurance policy.

During a brief leave, Willkie had married Edith Wilk of Rushville, Indiana, on January 14, 1918. She had been the assistant librarian of the Rushville Library. (The librarian was Miss Mary Sleeth, who was later to manage Willkie's Indiana farms for him.) He had first met his wife when he was an usher and she a bridesmaid at the wedding of George De Hority, one of his Elwood friends who also married a Rushville girl. For three months Edith Wilk managed the library in Elwood which Willkie's mother had helped to found. "I think Edith married him for his brains, not his looks," Miss Sleeth once said. "Wendell wasn't any fashion-plate type, and some of the girls of the neighborhood commented on the fact he didn't know how to dance."

Willkie never had any sense of rhythm. Trying to keep step in the army was a big problem for him; later, he used to say with a grin, he had to give up being a pallbearer. He knew large chunks of poetry by heart, but when he groped for a temporarily forgotten word, he was likely to come up with one that spoiled the rhythm of the line. In reading a speech or a manuscript, it was almost impossible for him to put the emphasis where it belonged within a sentence, although he had no such difficulty when he spoke extemporaneously.

When he was discharged from the army, on February 28, 1919, Willkie's first impulse was to return to the law firm of Willkie and Willkie, in Elwood, but he was determined to use it as a steppingstone to a bigger field of work. He narrowly missed a political career at the very beginning. Dale J. Crittenberger, Anderson newspaper editor and a Democratic political leader in Indiana, offered him the Democratic nomination for Congress. He was deeply tempted, and he went to ask the advice of Frank C. Dailey, reform prosecutor of Indianapolis and a leading lawyer of that city for whom he always had great liking and respect.

Fourteen years later, in Washington, Willkie ran into Oswald Ryan, who had been practicing law in Indiana at the same time as Willkie and by 1933 was a member of the Federal Power Commission. "Well," Ryan told him, "you've got a couple of billions of other people's money now, Wen. How did you do it?"

"Luck, mainly luck," was Willkie's answer. "It's the breaks you get that matter. For me, it was a pair of swinging doors." And he went on to tell the story of his meeting with Dailey, while the nomination offer was burning a hole in his pocket. He had waited and waited for "Uncle Frank," as he called Dailey, and while waiting he made up his mind to take the offer. It would keep him in Madison County, where his roots were. He was sure he could beat the Republican incumbent. So he decided not to wait any longer. He got as far as the elevator, when he heard his name called. Dailey had glimpsed him through the swinging doors of his office. Willkie explained that he had figured out his own problem, and told him his decision.

"I think you're the God-damnedest, stupidest man in Indiana," Dailey told him. "Sure you'll win, with a war record. But it's a normally Republican district. You'll lose your practice. And you'll come back after a couple of years and be just another political lawyer in an Indiana county seat. Listen, Wendell, you've got to go places."

Dailey gave him a letter to Harvey S. Firestone and Willkie went to Akron to look into the new and highly speculative rubber business. The night he arrived he slept in a chair in a hallway of the Hotel Howe, which was jammed with convention delegates. Between 1910 and 1920, the population of Akron had more than tripled, going up from 69,067 to 208,435, and the city looked as if it were coming apart at the seams. The smells of rubber manufacture hung heavy over the sprawling boom town, especially on hot summer days. New workers were still streaming into the city to work 40 per cent of the world's supply of raw rubber into tires for the insatiable automobile industry. They came from the mountains of Tennessee and West Virginia, from the cotton fields of the South, and from all the Slav lands of eastern Europe. They jammed the town to overflowing, and still it grew.

On August 16, 1919, he took charge of an employees' legal department at the Firestone Tire and Rubber Company. His job was to set up a service furnishing free legal advice, drafting wills, deeds, and similar instruments, for Firestone employees. The job paid $175 a month, nearly double the $90 a month which he had earned when he taught at Coffeyville. He and his wife shared an apartment in the crowded city with another young couple. Their son, Philip, was born on December 7, 1919. In less than two years, Willkie was making $5,000 a year, and he rejected an offer to double this salary when he told Harvey Firestone in 1921 that he was resigning to join a private law firm.

"Young man, I like you," Firestone told him, "but I don't think you will ever amount to a great deal."

"Why not?" Willkie asked him.

"Because I understand you're a Democrat," Firestone answered. "No Democrat can ever amount to much."

Mather and Nesbitt, the law firm Willkie joined, had one of the most lucrative corporation practices in Ohio. Nation O. Mather, senior partner, had been a state Senator and a man who had done some pioneer exploration in the jungle of administrative law which was springing up around American industry. Roy Nesbitt, the other partner, was known as a brilliant trial lawyer, and it was under his tutelage that Willkie especially wanted to work. The firm's clients included the Erie Railroad, the Ohio State Bank and Trust Company, and several utilities including the Northern Ohio Traction and Light Company. This last was an operating concern which within a decade was to become, first the Northern Ohio Power and Light Company, then the Ohio Edison Company, then the Penn-Ohio Edison Company, which was a major unit in a new super-holding company called the Commonwealth and Southern Corporation.

Willkie's work in the firm, which became Mather, Nesbitt and Willkie within three years, fell into three main categories: courtroom practice, negotiating new franchises and rate schedules, and acquiring new business. He threw himself into all three with the passion of a man in a hurry. His whole generation was in a hurry. He found himself in a city with nearly a quarter-million population where there had been a small town of 42,728 in 1900. This decade of Willkie's life was given a fine-tooth-comb treatment by the New Deal in 1940, in a desire to pin personally on Willkie his share of blame for the evils of the boom which preceded the bust. As always in political partisanship, his enemies tried to prove too much: no single specific charge of labor baiting, or Wall Street speculation, or utility corruption has stood up against Willkie's Akron career. Yet if the indictment had been in terms of his complete acceptance of the business system and his almost breathless hurry to see it grow and work out the problems of his generation, it would have been unanswerable.

For many of these years Willkie was the firm's trial lawyer; in some of them he worked for two hundred days out of the year in courtrooms and night after night he worked in the office preparing cases for the next day. Nesbitt was an excellent teacher, and Willkie liked courtroom work. It was here that he learned the art of catch-as-catch-can debate as well as his life-long habit—not too common in modern politicians—of watching his audience. Many of his trial cases were damage suits against utilities, and there was strong public prejudice against utilities in Ohio. One of Willkie's enemies later counted 346 personal damage suits on the docket of the Common Pleas Court of Summit County, Ohio, between 1923 and 1929 against the Northern Ohio Traction and Light Company, and blamed Willkie personally for every verdict which gave a citizen struck by a trolley car less than he had sued for.

He became the most successful trial lawyer in Akron. In one of his early cases, he helped Nesbitt win a verdict for the streetcar company when he heard the judge, in chambers, say: "Nesbitt can go to hell." Willkie quoted the remark to the jury, which decided that the judge was prejudiced and brought in a verdict for Nesbitt's client. In another case, he threw doubt on the evidence of three girl witnesses who had all used the word "profile" in their testimony. He pointed out to the jury that the plaintiff's lawyer was a Harvard man, who used such words, and that the witnesses must have been coached. Again he won the case.

He was always out to win. One of his major clients was the local utility in a city swarming with recent immigrants and hillbillies from the South, and a good deal of litigation developed out of ignorance and confusion. So he inevitably made enemies. He took one case against Harvey Firestone, representing a claimant to a substantial disputed block of the rubber company's stock, and the zeal with which he pressed the case caused some bad feelings which were cleared up only much later when Willkie went to see his former employer just before the latter's death. But not even his worst enemy in Akron could charge him with sharp or unethical practice. On March 7, 1925, he was elected president of the Akron Bar Association.

"The representation of the local utility," Willkie later wrote of his life in Akron, "constituted only about a fourth of my business and income and had nothing whatsoever to do with legislative or Congressional matters." Most of his utility work was with the company's court cases, although he also appeared before the Ohio Public Utilities Commission to negotiate new franchises and rate schedules. That body was not famous as an independent champion of the people's rights against the power trust, and New Deal spokesmen later charged Willkie with having been a lobbyist who subverted public control to the needs of his utility clients. On the other hand, Willkie's Akron contemporaries recall that he did a good deal to help clean up graft and thus to improve the reputation of his clients in their relations with public bodies. Actually, he seems to have taken the system much as he found it, trying to improve it where he could but basically interested in making it work, in serving his clients, and in making money—the traditional functions of a lawyer in American business.

Willkie's firm signed one of the many legal briefs filed in Washington in the late 1920's in an effort to block Senate investigation of the public utility industry. He made a few trips to Washington in this connection but he was a very small operator compared to the others who were already involved in utility lobbying. His business was strictly in Ohio, and it was almost entirely there that he worked at it. In 1926, B. C. Cobb, who was later to take Willkie to New York and national prominence, wrote to an officer of the Northern Ohio Power and Light Company: "We should not let this young man get away from us. He is a comer and we should keep an eye on him."

The business of the firm trebled in eight years and other lawyers gave Willkie credit for much of this increase. He put his name in the telephone book three ways: Wendell Lewis Wilkie, a common misspelling; Lewis Wendell Willkie, his correct name; and Wendell Lewis Willkie, a transposition started by an army clerk which Willkie could not change and eventually adopted. He became a director of the Ohio State Bank and, at thirty-seven, of the Northern Ohio Power and Light Company. Although he did not play golf, he joined the Portage Country Club in order to meet more people.

A few of these, including the A. C. Blinns, of the power company, and the Frederic Attwoods—Attwood was a director of the Ohio Brass Company—remained close and permanent friends of the Willkies. Willkie once told General Hugh Johnson of his work in Akron: "I thought I was fixed for life. I wanted to stay right there." In a radio talk at the 1939 Goodyear Centennial, he said, "I spent some ten years—perhaps the happiest and most satisfying years of my life—in Akron." Later, in New York he became president for one term of the Ohio Society. His sentiment for Ohio was undoubtedly true and sincere, but Willkie himself was always a footloose American. He was wryly amused by the home-state loyalties of some of his friends, especially of those who could take life in New York only with a heavy coating of nostalgia for the states where they were born. Willkie liked to tell a story of going back to Akron after having been in New York for many years. He was walking along the street when one of his old friends saw him. He stopped, held Willkie at arm's length and looked him over appraisingly. Then he said: "Well, Wen, you haven't changed much. You still look like you came from Indiana."

At the very beginning of his stay in Akron, Willkie was interested in politics. He organized Summit Post No. 19 of the American Legion and was elected its commander in 1921. He spoke frequently, before local Rotary Clubs, the YWCA, the Boy Scouts, the Exchange Club, and similar organizations. First, it was on his experiences as a soldier, later on the futility of war, on Abraham Lincoln, on the League of Nations, on the Ku Klux Klan, and finally on the electric power industry. In the Presidential campaign of 1920, he was already well enough known locally to be picked to introduce Governor James M. Cox at a public meeting in the Akron Armory. "He was a promising young lawyer," Cox has recalled, "but even then a very commanding personality. He told me once that he was confirmed as a liberal in his political thinking through the complete overhauling of our state government during my administration."

In 1924, he attended the Democratic National Convention as a delegate from Akron. "I went to that convention," he wrote later, "as a lieutenant of Newton D. Baker, mainly for two purposes: first, to put the Democratic party on record against the Ku Klux Klan; and, second, to secure a straight-out plank in the platform endorsing the League of Nations. The fight against intolerance we won; the fight for international co-operation we lost, and lost largely because the New York delegation, under the leadership of Franklin D. Roosevelt and others, voted two to one against it."

This was the convention in the old Madison Square Garden in New York at which McAdoo and Smith locked the delegates in an endless, bitter series of ballots over the Klan and prohibition issues. William Jennings Bryan was there, a spellbinder out of the past, and Franklin D. Roosevelt, a young and talented orator who nominated Smith. Willkie voted for Governor Cox and then for Smith through the first ballots, then for Baker, for James W. Gerard, former Ambassador to Germany, and finally for John W. Davis of West Virginia, who was finally nominated with Charles W. Bryan as his running mate.

"My opinion about the political situation," Willkie told the *Akron Beacon Journal* in an interview when he returned from New York, "is that with John W. Davis and Calvin Coolidge in leadership of the two great parties we will have an able and dignified presentation and analysis of the issues, which will be corruption in public office (the influence of the Klan), the

League of Nations and tax reduction." He went on to report that "the Klan fight was very bitter. The fact that the resolution [naming the Klan] was defeated by only one vote means that the Klan was absolutely exposed. They didn't gain anything by keeping the name of the Klan out of the plank. It got just as much publicity. I consider that there was an absolute repudiation of the Klan by this convention."

While he was in New York, Willkie received a telegram from the Klan in Akron asking him "when he had joined the payroll of the Pope." To this, according to one of his friends, "he sent a reply that suited the occasion, and it was very short because he was running out of funds."

A year later, the Klan fight became a bitter local issue in Akron. The president of the local school board and three of its members were disclosed to be members of the Ku Klux Klan. The three non-Klan members of the board at once resigned. Willkie played a leading part in organizing a Committee of One Hundred "to keep politics out of the schools." The committee put forward its own slate of candidates for the school board, pledged to keep the Klan out of the schools. The committee's candidates won handsomely in the municipal election held in the fall of 1925.

Willkie's speeches before Rotary, Knights of Columbus, Kiwanis and other clubs during these years make it clear that his success as a business lawyer did not change in any articulate way the political ideas he had acquired as a boy, chiefly from his father, and later in college. Bryan, La Follette and Wilson had been the architects of much of his thinking on contemporary affairs. He still talked their language.

In terms of foreign policy he was not a pacifist but he spoke a great deal against war. His support of the League of Nations was strong and consistent; it was also filled with the special emotional fervor to be found in the moral revolt against war which swept large sections of the American people in the 1920's.

On civil liberties he remained a champion of the underdog. There is no record of his having sought legal work for unpopular causes while he was in Akron, but his opposition to the Klan was deep and bitter. Friends remember him as a deviant in conversation who was always glad to oppose the orthodox view in any argument. A newspaper once dubbed him "the Bill Borah of Akron," and the phrase was close enough to be remembered by his friends and quoted at him for years.

It can hardly be said that he resisted the pressures for social and cultural conformity which were especially strong in the 1920's, in the Middle West, and among the ambitious young businessmen on his economic level. He never even knew they existed. Golf, bridge, automobiles, a country home, the correct political connections, the socially and professionally useful friends—no novel about his generation and his profession in Akron would be accepted as credible without these, but none of them plays any part in the record of Willkie's life in Akron or in the memories of his contemporaries. He worked hard, made his friends where he found them, argued a lot, lived, dressed, and talked as he wanted to, and apparently gave no time at all to thinking about his orthodoxy in the burgeoning middle-class prosperity with which he was surrounded.

In terms of other political ideas, and especially those touching economics, Willkie left few clews in Akron as to what was going on in his mind. It is clear that he accepted the American business system as something new, exciting, and important. From it he seems to have wanted money and power in more nearly equal proportions than many businessmen. Within this system, the utility industry had a special lure for him. It was already big and it was certain, he believed, to grow still bigger. It related to whole communities, and to the whole of the lives of their inhabitants. This last aspect fascinated Willkie far more than specialized and technical business operations, like making tires.

Willkie also liked the freedom he found in business at his level. It is impossible to document from his speeches during this decade exactly what he meant by freedom, although it was one of his favorite words. The issues which were to bulk large in the 1930's were not common currency in conversation in the 1920's. Freedom of enterprise was not being directly challenged by the government. Freedom of speech, freedom of religion, and freedom from fear and want were not even slogans at that time outside of small liberal groups.

To Willkie freedom may well have meant at this time chiefly *la carrière ouverte aux talents,* the absence of checks to his own ambition. Any city growing as Akron did on a new industry would appeal to a man of Willkie's age, ambition, and energy. The rubber industry was almost entirely self-financed, out of profits, with few ties to Eastern banking interests. Willkie's chief utility client was Ohio-owned until its merger into Commonwealth and Southern in 1929. The city had few old families. The waiting list for money, or power, or fame, was no longer than a man saw it in his own mind.

Willkie was already a big, somewhat shaggy man, often needing a haircut or with his suit looking unpressed, full of energy and physical magnetism and self-confidence. The days were never long enough for all that he wanted to do, and the discipline of choice and concentration came hard to him. The masculine ideal of the 1920's, according to F. Scott Fitzgerald, who was only four years younger than Willkie, was "the old dream of being an entire man in the Goethe-Byron-Shaw tradition, with an opulent American touch, a sort of combination of J. P. Morgan, Topham Beauclerk and St. Francis of Assisi." This was a dream that served Willkie until he died, and it drove him hard while he was climbing the ladder of American success in Akron.

Throughout most of the decade, it was a curiously unpolitical dream. There is no record of any political activity by Willkie connected with the 1928 election. The New Era was a phrase coined in Washington and New York and hardly heard outside those cities. Businessmen everywhere were busy expanding plant, opening markets, developing new products, and Willkie lived as they did, so engrossed in operating a new era that he gave relatively little time to figuring out what it meant or what it stood for in political terms.

He was living in a boom city in a boom time. Fortunes were being made with astonishing speed, and by no means exclusively in stock market speculation. Willkie himself made a small fortune, on paper and for a short time, on the sale of a railroad until the deal, in which he had acted as counsel, was called off. He used to say later that he had become a millionaire in this deal but had lost it all after moving to New York, in spite of days on the telephone trying to save it. His sporting pleasure over having made so much money was obviously more genuine than any regret over having lost it. There were money, and power, and excitement for restless minds in American business in the 1920's, and both Akron and the utility industry were full of all three.

The cities were no longer threatening the rural areas, as they had been in Willkie's boyhood; they were literally swallowing them. A predominantly English-Scottish culture was being transformed at great speed into a nation of many diverse national origins. Puritanism was under bitter attack; the Protestant churches in many towns were seeing newer and bigger Catholic churches erected on the same block. Akron was intimately tied to the fastest-growing industry in the land; pneumatic tires had become one of the staple necessities for the United States economy and for the American culture which it supported. Akron, like the nation, had its distressed areas, its slums and its wretchedly poor people, but until 1929 life was in too great a hurry even to notice them.

Willkie's ten years in Akron were decisive years in the development of all his later thinking. They forced no break with the ideas he had taken there with him from an immigrant family in Indiana. They reinforced many of them. When he announced on August 8, 1929, that B. C. Cobb had invited him to move to New York, to join Judge John C. Weadock in legal representation of a giant new holding company in the electric utility field, it was clear that the same deep forces in American life were still operative which had taken his father to Elwood in the natural gas boom, and had brought his grandfather to the United States from Germany.

He made the move in October, 1929, a few weeks before the stock market crash. It was a big change for him personally. A few days after his arrival he was riding in a taxi with another lawyer, looking at the crowds on the sidewalk. He commented that in Akron he couldn't take a walk without meeting a friend. Then he looked back at the hurrying crowds and said: "My God, Herbert, there isn't a soul here I know!"

But in terms of ideas, he was still part of the older American business tradition which was based on expansion and freedom. He had been guaranteed a starting salary of $36,000 a year, a big figure in both Akron and New York. Yet he had no bridges to burn behind him either in becoming a big-business tycoon or in remaining a liberal Democrat who could and did vote for Roosevelt in 1932.

He had accepted in Akron, at least for working purposes, a set of values which was still the orthodox view of life held by articulate men in American business at the end of the 1920's. Like his own life, it stemmed from the frontier, from the great influx of European immigrants, and from the challenge to bend and blend these into an urban, industrial age. Progress through unlimited expansion was at the very basis of this view of life. Businessmen like Willkie postulated minimum outside controls over the struggle for survival in a free market. In the summer of 1929, they grumbled against control by Wall Street more than against Washington controls, and they were blissfully unaware of the degree to which business itself had already asked for both, thus betraying its own stated belief in freedom. And for many practitioners of business like Willkie, who had not inherited wealth, there was none of the corroding sense of moral guilt which was to take some of American business within the next decade into truly reactionary opposition to its own history and its own future.

CHAPTER FOUR

The Angry River

P RESIDENT WOODROW WILSON, early in 1918, ordered the construction of what was then named Dam No. 2 on the Tennessee River at Muscle Shoals, a thirty-seven-mile-long stretch of
the river above Florence, Alabama. This was a treacherous link
of rapids and connecting pools which had been studied by the
Federal Government since George Washington's Administration. Work was begun by the War Department in April, 1918,
on the dam and a power house to help the war against the
Kaiser by making nitric acid to replace imports of nitrate from
Chile.

By the time the war was over, construction was less than
one-third completed. Debate began at once on whether to complete it. Congress formally abandoned the project and work
was suspended, but only for a short time. The engineering instinct of the American people triumphed over even the "sound
business" concepts of Presidents Harding and Coolidge; the
dam, renamed for President Wilson, was finished and its power
installations were placed in commission in September, 1925.
But already this river and the effort to develop it had become
political symbols in the American search for a new theory of
politics to fit a new technological world. It had become a honey-
pot for men with a shrewd sense of the new power of publicity.
It had become a prize for every kind of enterprising spirit from
Senator George W. Norris to one-acre land speculators. For two
angry decades of American history, America's angriest river
was to make headlines through the efforts of men to control its
floods, to exploit its potential power, to ignore it. Only the last

failed utterly; before Willkie and the New Deal came to terms finally on the TVA the river had cut itself a deep channel in modern American history.

The river played a curious and now forgotten role in Republican Presidential aspirations before Willkie had more than heard of it. In 1918, Henry Ford lost the election for Senator from Michigan to Commander Truman H. Newberry, a Detroit representative of inherited wealth and gentility. This was so galling to the self-made automobile millionaire that he proceeded to force his rival's indictment and conviction (later overruled by the Supreme Court) for political corruption, and his expulsion from the Senate. This last was not easy, until the Democrats and progressive Republicans gained control of the Senate in 1922. By this time the "steady golden stream," as the *New York Times* called it, which Ford's men had been pouring out had created a climate of opinion which forced Newberry to resign. But also by this time, Ford's acquired taste for politics had become a minor passion: "Ford for President Clubs" were being launched around the country; W. J. Cameron, editor of his *Dearborn Independent,* announced that the only forces which might cheat Ford out of the Presidency were the "fertilizer trust," the power companies, and "Jewish propaganda societies." Ford himself was announcing to his campaign biographer, Allen L. Benson, the names of men whom he would appoint to his Cabinet, together with such pithy comments as "I don't like to read books; they muss up my mind."

The biggest single move he made in his campaign for the Republican nomination (like Willkie later, he had to overcome the handicap of having been a Democrat) was a bid on July 8, 1921, for Muscle Shoals. Keith Sward, his biographer, says that for sheer effrontery nothing in Ford's career can compare with it. On the one hand, he knew that a Republican administration was about to auction it off at a bargain price. He was already manufacturing farm machinery, the nitrate equipment at Muscle Shoals could make fertilizer, and he was advocating for the entire country a new agriculture based on mechanized, pooled farms on the Soviet model. He told Benson that he wanted the property more than he wanted "another billion dollars." On the other hand, Ford was one of the first Americans to combine what Mark Twain called "soul butter" with the most streamlined form of modern self-advertising. This was a Heaven-sent opportunity to advance his fortune, his Presidential ambition and his personal fame; he could promise exciting miracles which fairly smelled of piety and social altruism, and be sure of losing nothing.

It worked like magic. Rumors covered the land that Ford would soon give away a ton of fertilizer with every Model T. The *New York Times* reported that he planned to teach every farmer in the South how to harness the brooks on his place so as to "run the United States" by water power and that he would give his super-power network back to the people free after fifty years. This would make the government of the country self-supporting, and the Ford organization, the account continued, was ready to swing into action on the Tennessee on a few hours' notice.

This touched off a land boom in this "future mecca of the electrical age," this "city of Ford's dreams," which was to color the entire subsequent history of the valley. Old family estates were auctioned off to land promoters, streets and home sites were laid out, new-style pioneers swarmed into the region. The House of Representatives, the Senate Committee on Military Affairs, the American Federation of Labor, and the Federation of Farm Bureaus all gave the scheme their formal blessing. A whole new city was founded, on paper, called Highland Park, Tennessee, with offices in Detroit.

The catch in the scheme was that Ford proposed to do all this practically without cash. The details of his offer were confusing, but Senator Norris estimated that for a round sum of $10,000,000, half of which was to be payable out of compound interest on the other half over the ensuing century, Ford was proposing to acquire public rights worth at that moment $236,-000,000, and—on the same compound interest basis which Ford applied to half of his cash offer—worth at the close of the century some $14,500,000,000. The Ford offer was amended later

to include the issue of a special "Muscle Shoals Currency"—
Thomas Edison gave this his blessing—with which to complete
the construction of the dam.

A man in the White House who was also interested in the
1924 Republican nomination moved quietly into this feverish
situation and Ford was summoned to a personal conference with
Calvin Coolidge in early December, 1923. Within a few days
there were two public announcements: President Coolidge, in
a message to Congress, recommended the sale of Muscle Shoals
to private interests (without mentioning Ford's name) and
Henry Ford announced that the country was "perfectly safe
with Coolidge" and that he would not dream of running against
him on any ticket whatever. Some commentators guessed that
a bargain had been struck. The Muscle Shoals boom collapsed
more slowly than the Ford for President boom. Senator Norris
kept hammering away at the Ford offer as well as at all plans
for selling Muscle Shoals to any private interests. Bills to dispose of the properties to Ford passed both the House and the
Senate, but with amendments, and finally died through lack
of action in 1925 on the committee report reconciling the two
versions. Already, in 1924, Ford himself had given up with a
statement that he had been licked by "Wall Street."

Actually, the failure of "Wall Street" and of private enterprise
to show even Henry Ford's curious interest in the project was
a major reason for the failure of Presidents Coolidge and Hoover
to do more than block the goblin of public power for a decade.
Private capital made offers as low as Ford's, with conditions of
purchase almost as complicated. Conservative Congressmen,
who wanted as much as Hoover to sell the Muscle Shoals property, could only wince at the offers which came to them, with
Teapot Dome still as fresh as paint in the voters' minds. The
Haber process for fixation of nitrogen, developed by Germany
during the war when the Allied blockade had cut off access to
Chilean nitrates, proved to be so much cheaper than the older
cyanamide process that both the power and the fertilizer industries were acutely interested. But the plant already finished
at Muscle Shoals had been built under contract by the American
Cyanamid Company, under War Department supervision, to

use steam before the Wilson Dam was finished and to use the cyanamide process which was still too expensive to guarantee cheap fertilizer in time of peace. For what had already been built, private interests wanted, not unnaturally, bargain basement prices.

A second factor in the failure to turn Muscle Shoals over to private enterprise in the 1920's was the increasing public apprehension over the "power trust." The Federal Trade Commission was publishing, after periodic hearings, details about the lobbying and propaganda activities of the public utilities. These proved to be prime propaganda ammunition for the handful of Congressmen—a large number of whom were Republicans—who had grown up with Theodore Roosevelt's ideas on conservation. Congressional speeches at this time, not all of them by Senator Norris, show that public opposition to the "power trust" did not by any means begin with the New Deal. It was shown in the 1920's that the electrical utility concerns, as Charles A. and Mary Beard put it, "had secretly subsidized newspapers and slipped their doctrines quietly into editorial columns. They had surreptitiously hired leaders in women's clubs, college professors and publicity experts to promote their cause. To the chests of political parties they had contributed huge sums for election purposes. The 'red badge' of communism they had deliberately pinned upon their opponents to discredit men and women who refused to accept their program wholesale. Some of their undercover activities were so gross that the more reputable utility magnates were themselves flustered; and metropolitan newspapers, normally inclined to belittle Congressional inquiries, felt compelled to deplore such behavior." This is important to remember if the fact is to be understood that Congress, before the New Deal, not once but twice passed legislation to develop the Tennessee River power resources through government operation of the Muscle Shoals power plants.

A third important reason for the failure to sell Muscle Shoals was Senator Norris himself. It was he who secured the passage of the first bill for government operation of the plants in 1928, which was given a pocket veto by President Coolidge, and of the second bill in 1931, which was directly vetoed by President Hoover. Although he still called himself a Republican, Norris was deeply committed to the conservation of national resources and to their development under public control and public ownership. He had been involved in the launching of Ford's political ambitions, since he had been a leader in the fight to disbar Newberry after the latter's victory over Ford in the Michigan election for Senator, and he never blamed Ford personally for the more larcenous aspects of the Ford bid for Muscle Shoals. "I am certain," he wrote later, "that had Mr. Ford known about this [the speculative aspect of the offer], he would have frowned upon it and rebuked it with all the power at his command." But Norris led the campaign against any private development of the properties with crusading fervor and great effectiveness. It was by no means easy. When the Ford boom was at its height, special trains were run from New York City to Muscle Shoals filled with prospective land purchasers; a school was opened in New York to train agents to sell lots; every purchaser—and they were scattered over the country—became a one-man lobby against Norris. He was burned in effigy in some communities, and his mail was filled with threats against his life. When he visited Muscle Shoals, the army representative who showed him around the valley took the precaution of assigning to him an armed bodyguard in civilian clothes. "I would be distressed beyond words," he told the Senator, "if while you were under my guidance some fool should take a shot at you in order to have what he feels to be his revenge."

Norris saw a nine-year fight reaching its climax when both houses of Congress passed his resolution for the second time in 1931. It provided for government operation of the power plants if they could not be leased to private concerns on legitimate terms within a year from the passage of the resolution. The public utilities had not been alone in lobbying against it. They had been joined by the fertilizer industry, which was worried about price competition, by the coal companies, already apprehensive of the competition of cheap power, by John L. Lewis and his Mine Workers Union, who were afraid that the generation of vast amounts of electric power would throw many miners out of work. President Hoover himself stepped into the battle while the resolution was still before Congress with a public statement in which he urged the legislators not to waste their time on a matter of such small importance. When it passed anyway, he vetoed it and Norris was unable to muster enough strength to override the veto.

The Hoover veto criticized the conditions under which the plants were to be leased as too onerous. Modernization would require, he said, unknown and enormous expenses. For the government to operate the plants itself, the veto went on, would be to "break down the initiative and enterprise of the American people," to "destroy the equality of opportunity of our people," and to "negate the ideals upon which our civilization has been based." The resolution had required that those appointed by the government to control the project must believe in its wisdom and its feasibility. This one requirement, according to Mr. Hoover, would make it impossible to find responsible and worthy men to sit on the board.

"I hesitate," he said, "to contemplate the future of our institutions, of our country, if the preoccupation of its officials is to be no longer the promotion of justice and equal opportunity, but is to be devoted to barter in the markets. That is not liberalism, it is degeneration."

So the matter stood. Willkie was practicing law at this time in New York City, as a partner with Judge John C. Weadock in Weadock and Willkie, general counsel for the Commonwealth and Southern Corporation. This was the holding company which controlled the electric power systems most interested in the future of the Tennessee River: the Tennessee Electric Power Company and the Alabama Power Company.

Commonwealth and Southern had been put together in May, 1929. A few months earlier, J. P. Morgan and Company had formed the United Corporation, its first big move in the utilities field and a signal to the banking world that consolidation of utilities was becoming not only a profitable but an orthodox operation. An associated banking house, Bonbright and Company, had put together another top holding company called the American Superpower Company. These two banking houses and their

[Willkie's corporation, Commonwealth & Southern, controlled ten operating companies that supplied electricity to a population of 6,100,000 in ten states from Michigan to Florida. Crosshatching marks the properties sold to TVA.]

respective utility holding companies then combined to launch, on May 23, 1929, a third giant company, the Commonwealth and Southern Corporation. They did this by acquiring or exchanging stock of three already existing holding companies:

50

the Commonwealth Power Company and the Penn-Ohio Edison Company in the North, and the Southeastern Power and Light Company, which owned the properties near the Tennessee River, in the South. By the end of 1932, the total assets of C. & S. and its subsidiaries amounted to $1,136,542,942, which ranked it near the top of the biggest holding companies in the country.

Holding companies are peculiarly American. They belong among the many ingenious and corruptible devices with which this country tried, on a national scale, to industrialize a thriving agricultural economy without breaking step. They first became legal in 1888, when New Jersey gave corporations organized in that state the power to hold the securities of other corporations—a practice which had until then been either banned or severely frowned upon. Other states followed, with Delaware high in the list, and the new device proved to be an invaluable aid in speeding up the concentration of industry, especially after the turn of the century, and in extracting the maximum advantages from the new technology of mass production. Through holding companies, operations could be decentralized while financing was centralized and control made tighter and tighter.

They also proved to be popular with businessmen who wanted to avoid various social controls, including government regulation, since they usually crossed state lines, and since they could accomplish miracles of confusion in accountancy. Their possibilities for capital inflation, since the holding company can issue new securities against those of the subsidiaries held in its treasury, were not unattractive to men like Samuel Insull. He had pyramided his public utility securities upward to a three-billion-dollar figure before he fled to Greece, in 1932, when the pyramid collapsed. Investors were left with a mass of handsomely engraved but worthless stock certificates.

The new device had been particularly popular in the public utility field: during the decade between 1919 and 1928, there were 3,744 public utility companies which disappeared through consolidation. As the depression deepened from 1929 on, neither legislators nor citizens were likely to remember that new scientific advances in the long-distance transmission of power and new requirements for integrated supply of power to an industrial nation had also been important forces behind the development of holding companies in the utilities field. They were more likely to think of Insull, and of the reports which had been piling up in Washington of a Federal Trade Commission investigation under Judge Robert E. Healy of Vermont.

This investigation had been begun in 1928, backed by Senator Thomas J. Walsh, Montana Democrat, after an earlier Congressional investigation of public utility corporations doing interstate business through holding companies, made from 1925 to 1927, had failed to cure the evils it had revealed. The Healy hearings and reports filled one hundred volumes, and they provided a gold mine for the fledgling New Dealers. Much of the passion with which the first Roosevelt Administration moved into the reform of corporate practices can be documented from this patient and careful study launched under President Calvin Coolidge in 1928 by a Federal Trade Commission which was commonly believed to be friendly to big business.

"Nothing that Lemuel Gulliver saw in Brobdingnag," the Beards wrote, "not even corn as tall as trees, was more fantastic in conception and appearance" than what the committee found out about holding companies. One corporation, through a maze of holding concerns, was in control of railways, terminals, trucking companies, coal mines, orange groves, real estate developments, office buildings, a hotel, a bridge, a ferry, a heat, light and power plant, a dock and a winter resort, in addition to some other enterprises harder to describe. It was by no means an exception. The intricacies of holding company control made possible two developments which were to make the New Deal campaign against them popular: manipulation by the few insiders who could understand the maze they had contrived, and fantastic propaganda compaigns to conceal the manipulation.

One giant holding company, the Associated Gas and Electric Company, at one time had three classes of common stock, six classes of preferred stock, four classes of preference stock, seven issues of bonds and notes, twenty-four classes of debenture bonds, four series of investment certificates, and various options to buy authorized but unissued shares. Owen D. Young, testifying before Congress in 1933 on the Insull achievement in pyramiding control of utilities, said: "Well, I confess to a feeling of helplessness as I begin to examine the complicated structure of that organization. Great numbers of operating utilities, with holding companies superimposed on holding companies, investment companies and affiliates, made it, as I thought then and think now, impossible for any man however able really to grasp the real situation. I would say it was so set up that it was impossible for anyone to comprehend its entire aspect; and it was so set up that you could not possibly get an accounting system which would not mislead even the officers themselves of that complicated structure."

By the end of the 1920's, the public relations activities of the "power trust," chiefly through the National Electric Light Association, had themselves become big business. Representatives on faculties, church councils, all kinds of community enterprises, saw to it that indoctrination was never forgotten, and little direct bribery was needed. Holding companies endowed university chairs, supplied football players, financed foundations, produced educational motion pictures, supported struggling young writers. Textbooks were written in accordance with business ideas or corrected to get those ideas across. Merlin Aylesworth, director of the N.E.L.A., was credited with the remark at one of its conventions: "Don't mind the expenses. The public pays." One of his predecessors was asked by the Federal Trade Commission in 1928 if he knew of any means of publicity that had been neglected by his organization. "Only one," was the answer, "and that is sky writing. I don't believe we have tried with airplanes."

As early as 1928, during the Smith-Hoover campaign, Will Rogers had summed up the public attitude to this new industry in which Willkie was just beginning to become an important figure: "In Omaha Al relieved the farmers, in Oklahoma (near Claremore) he bawled out the Baptists, but in Denver he reached his peak when he told the truth about the power trusts. When you hop on the power trusts, you are standing on the very arches of the Republican party. I had a joke about the power lobby in the papers and I got so many letters from power magnets saying 'there was no power lobby' that it almost made me

lose faith in rich men. So sic 'em, Al. Yours for everybody
owning their own river."

These were years in which Willkie was learning the power
business and the new field of corporation management. He
had been thinking for a long time about how to redefine capitalist democracy in twentieth-century terms. From the very beginning of this effort, it was on more sophisticated lines than,
for example, Herbert Hoover's. Willkie knew that strictly
laissez-faire capitalism was dead, and that the corporation had
replaced the individual as the basic unit of enterprise. He rejected socialist solutions at least as much out of conviction as
because of his business associations. What he was looking for
was a dynamic business philosophy with built-in controls, a set
of democratic checks and balances within and not outside the
producing machinery of the nation. The frontier had provided
this, for better or worse, during the opening of the continent.
Willkie was in a new industry at what might prove to be the
start of a new economic cycle. Both his own experience and
everything he had studied convinced him of the organic relationship between freedom and abundance, between liberty and
productivity. For him, they were inseparable parts of the
American dream.

The electric power aspect of the dream was something new.
The modern use of an electric motor to turn machinery dates
only from 1893—the year after Willkie's birth—when a motor
was installed in a Connecticut textile factory. Although younger
than Willkie, it had grown like Jack's beanstalk. By 1929, some
53 per cent of all the power used in manufacturing, 63 per cent
in mining, 1 per cent in agriculture, was electrical power generated in central stations. In the same year, one-half of the
world's total electric light and power capacity was in this
country. New and more economical methods of long-distance
transmission of power had been discovered in the 1920's, the
interconnection of generating stations had made possible wide-
spread distributing of loads, the cost of generating power had
been reduced through radical improvements in design. All
these factors had caused an enormous growth in the industry;
new plant and equipment were being added at a $750 million

annual rate at the end of the decade. In the single year 1928, new construction added almost 1.3 million horse-power to the nation's water-power energy resources; by 1930 they had reached a total of 14.8 million horse-power.

From Willkie's first connection with C. & S. as a lawyer, he was aware that this growth was more than a profitable and exciting development within American business. He knew that electric power promised to transform an entire industrial system in important and unpredictable ways. Power owned and generated by factories actually decreased slightly in the United States between 1919 and 1929 while the power they purchased from this new generating industry multiplied many times over. It needed no security salesman to point out that this marked the end of one kind of machine civilization and the beginning of another. Dr. Glenn Frank, president of the University of Wisconsin, told a Midwest Power Conference in Chicago, in February, 1928: "In a machine civilization created by steam power, the worker must go to the power, but in a machine civilization created by electric power, the power can be taken to the worker; and that is a revolutionary fact which means that when we say 'machine civilization' in terms of 1950, we may be dealing with a machine civilization that is as different as imagination can conceive from the machine civilization which began when James Watt first harnessed the expansive power of steam to the processes of production." The difference was that between the natural gas boom at Elwood, Indiana, which had drawn Willkie's father to that town, and the dams on the Tennessee River which were to engross national attention over the next few years; it was a difference which Willkie understood.

This new electric power industry had become part of American business, and it was big business. It acquired almost at once both the glamour and the bad repute which American businessmen had been accumulating over several generations. Within the industry, there was a subtle line drawn between the operators and the bankers, between those who had grown up with power lines and generating stations and those who had moved in during the palmy days of consolidation and holding company financing. Willkie belonged technically to the latter group but his sympathies, from the start, were with the former. To the New York State utility leaders, who had already had their baptism of political fire in the running fight with Governor Alfred E. Smith, and to what was called then "the Morgan crowd," Willkie was to become known as "the Jesus Christ of the industry." This was because he was known, from before he became president of C. & S., to favor elimination of banking control from public utility holding companies, restriction of membership on boards of directors to men involved in the management of operating companies, and self-regulation by the industry to correct the abuses of the holding company system. This was a division within the industry which was never publicized and on which it is still difficult to get utility leaders to talk; as the struggle with the New Deal grew more intense, strong pressures were developed which tended to blur this difference inside the utility camp. Yet it persisted, and it was to color Willkie's eventual position on many of the issues developed in the TVA controversy. And it reflected, in microcosm, a deeper split, and an older one, within what could be called the American business mind and the public reaction to business.

Thorstein Veblen saw this split as an antagonism between industry and business, between "engineers and the price system." Henry Ford saw it as a conflict between producers and Wall Street. Other Westerners have interpreted it in sectional terms as a division between the nation and New York City. Marxists have bent it into their own terminology by analyzing the conflicts between "industrial capitalism" and "finance capitalism." Although none of these formulas fits all the facts, there is little doubt that most Americans, in 1932, were living with two quite separate and contradictory pictures of the businessman. On the one hand, he was the successor to the pioneer, working on the technological and social frontiers of a new kind of society, building a new and richer world, a modern folk hero. This was a real picture in many American minds even in the fourth year of the depression; *Fortune* was first published in 1930 and dedicated to the propagation of the idea of the creative function of business; Herbert Hoover had been repudiated as President, but his concept of the businessman as a social engineer was still accepted by very large numbers of Americans.

On the other hand, the generation-old revolt against big business, climaxed by the depression, had produced another picture of the businessman: confused and predatory, driven by the profit motive, a George Babbitt in taste and culture, helpless in the grip of forces which he had unleashed in his blind drive for self-aggrandizement. This second picture had many variants; they were all alike in rejecting at least a portion of the businessmen of America as socially useless.

The first picture could be documented from the speeches at almost any national convention of the early 1930's, from the Commencement addresses at almost any university, from the success story which was the staple appeal on which popular magazines, Hollywood, and newspaper editorials flourished. If it was an invention, it was the work of many hands, over many years: neither Horatio Alger nor the National Association of Manufacturers dreamed it up. And if it was an invention, it worked. Millions of Americans believed it. This was recognized even by those who rejected it: Veblen himself wrote: "By settled habit, the American population are quite unable to see their way to entrust any appreciable responsibility to any other than business men; . . . this sentimental deference of the American people to the sagacity of its business men is massive, profound, and alert." This was convincing evidence of the reality of the businessman's position in popular favor, coming from one of his most lethal critics, a man who himself saw the spirit of American business as "a spirit of quietism, caution, compromise, collusion and chicane."

At the end of 1932, Willkie was a well-educated, widely read, and thoughtful businessman. New York City had been his home for nearly four years and he had already acquired a taste for urbane and cosmopolitan friendships. He was always a hard man to overlook in a crowd, and his rise to a top position in C. & S. made him a marked man in many circles where business, its ethics, and its ideals were a central subject of conversation in the 1930's. He knew at first hand many of the evils in American business which were being noisily debated as the New Deal acquired momentum. He was, above all, under no illusions about how the public utilities had been financed and operated. He was not ignorant of the split in the personality of the businessman-hero in American folklore. It was his conviction then, and he never lost it, that American business was the arena in which the struggle for a true democracy in this country would be waged. The TVA fight, which broke around his ears within a few weeks, was to test this conviction more strenuously than anything else in his life except his campaign to take over leadership of the Republican party. In both, tactical situations forced him to take, at different times, different positions which drew charges that he was either a die-hard and unreconstructed tycoon, or an adventurer, a radical upstart, and "a traitor to his class." He himself was convinced that he was following the American business tradition which had opened the continent and then industrialized it, and that—given time—this tradition would reassert its hold over the minds of both businessmen and the public by adjusting itself to the changed conditions of a new world, and later of one world.

In 1932, this was not a hard thesis to defend. There was a small but growing number of American corporations which were pioneers in the reintegration of a humane and socially constructive business spirit. In 1932, A. A. Berle, Jr., and Gardner C. Means, in *The Modern Corporation and Private Property,* had laid the basis for vast new speculation on the strange and powerful managerial role of the businessman. American life, like the structure of corporate enterprise, seemed to be fluid enough and tough enough to have bent itself around four years of depression without either complete collapse or revolution. It was true that John Chamberlain, saying good-bye to reform in the same year of 1932—a few months before the greatest reform era in American history—spoke for many who were cynical: "Faced with a loss, only the most Quixotic man of business can engage in positive humanitarian tactics. Consciences may be salved by the practice of hiring outside efficiency experts to do firing and wage cutting, but the results are the same. Work may be 'shared' and staggered, but sharing on the basis of stationary or diminished total wages per week does not increase purchasing power. The progressive businessman, individually humane, is caught in a complicated net of aggregate weave. He cannot cut clear by himself. In business, in time of trouble, the most unscrupulous inevitably set the pace for the whole machine, just as in good times the ones out for the immediate gain set the pace."

Yet this was a minority report. Even President Roosevelt turned to business, through the NRA's Blue Eagle, to pull the country out of depression, and the slow recovery which followed in the next eight years was proof that the doctrinaire socialists and the conservative Cassandras had both overplayed their bets. By the time another world war had buried the depression and lifted Willkie into politics, the question of the reintegration of the pioneer-businessman-folk-hero was still open. Willkie's belief that business was still the arena in which the future of American democracy was being decided was hardly open to doubt.

CHAPTER FIVE

The New Deal

O N January 24, 1933, a few weeks before President Roosevelt moved into the White House with a mandate from the people to clean up the excesses of American business, Wendell Willkie moved into the presidency of the Commonwealth and Southern Corporation. His predecessor, Bernard Capen Cobb, remained as chairman of the board, but underwent a serious operation in July and suffered a nervous breakdown in January, 1934. By June of that year, he had resigned as chairman and director. Willkie then assumed the title of chief executive officer of the company, which function he had actually fulfilled from January, 1933, when he resigned from Weadock and Willkie and took over the corporation.

Willkie, himself a Democrat, had voted for Roosevelt although he was disappointed that Newton D. Baker was not the Democratic candidate. Although their law offices had been across the street from each other, Willkie had had no contact with Roosevelt while the latter was serving as Governor in Albany. There Roosevelt had already tangled with New York State utility interests, an experience which Oswald Ryan, later a member of the Federal Power Commission, believed to have decisively colored, in very somber hues, all of Roosevelt's later views of the "power trust" and "public utility magnates." C. & S. held no properties in New York State; in fact, its New York City headquarters was 480 miles from its nearest operating subsidiary.

The Democrats had promised in their 1932 platform to regulate holding companies in addition to security and commodity exchanges, and to establish Federal regulation of utility rates

The New Deal

across state lines. During the campaign, Roosevelt had made a speech at Muscle Shoals in which he promised to do something about giving America more electric power at cheaper rates. Senator Norris deserted the Republicans to support Roosevelt chiefly on the basis of this promise. Most of the utility leaders were on the Republican side anyway. But none of them, including Willkie, had any clear idea of what the New Deal power program was to be.

Nobody knew, least of all Franklin D. Roosevelt. He was on the record as favoring lower rates, the "prudent investment" basis for rate valuation, squeezing the water out of the capitalization of private companies, some control over holding companies, and government operation of Muscle Shoals. These remained fairly consistent goals of the New Deal, and within two years they had taken shape in the TVA Act and the Wheeler-Rayburn Act (popularly known as the death-sentence act) to control public utility holding companies. Both bills were immediately and powerfully attacked by private industry. Six years were to go by before the Supreme Court gave even a partial verdict in 1939 on the TVA, even then refusing to pass on its constitutionality. The Wheeler-Rayburn Act was approved by the court a year earlier, but its enforcement was still being challenged by Willkie as late as 1940, a few weeks before his nomination for President.

Both bills raised deep political issues which have been violently debated for nearly two decades by the American people. Both acts were so close to the structural center of the New Deal program that what they said was less important, in the long run, than how they might be enforced and how they would be opposed and challenged. The turnover in the "brain trust" at the White House was convincing evidence of Roosevelt's political pliability; this was matched, on the utility side, by a less overt but no less shifting strategy of maneuver. The power business became, more than any other American industry, the battlefield on which the courts, the public, the New Deal, and private industry fought out the major problems raised by the Great Depression.

President Roosevelt's program for Muscle Shoals and the

Tennessee River Valley was part of his message to Congress on April 10, 1933. The bill which resulted was sponsored by Senator Norris and Representative John F. Rankin. It moved quickly through both houses of Congress, and the Tennessee Valley Development Act became law on May 18. The act set up a three-man board to administer a Tennessee Valley Authority which was to maintain and operate the properties already owned by the government at Muscle Shoals, Alabama, in the interests of national defense and the development of agriculture and industry in the Tennessee Valley, to improve navigation on the Tennessee River, and to control the floodwaters of that river and of the Mississippi. It was authorized, to these ends, to perform a multitude of functions enumerated in traditional legislative fashion, and among them were to produce, distribute, and sell electric power to private corporations, individuals, states, counties, and municipalities.

It was precisely this last function that Willkie opposed in the hearings before the House Military Affairs Committee which preceded the passage of the act. He approved the general development plan for the Tennessee Valley but opposed robbing the private power companies of their markets. After the law had been passed, he added that "we also offered no objection to the government developing such hydro-generating plants on the Tennessee River as might be thought necessary in connection with the government's flood control and navigation program. We did, however . . . protest against the Muscle Shoals Board being authorized to build transmission and distribution lines in competition with private enterprise in a territory already more than adequately served."

Here, in the last phrase, was heresy to the older expansionist tradition of the American businessman. Long before the TVA had proved that the area could absorb a hundred times more power than private enterprise was giving it, Willkie was to regret having taken this position, but he was stuck with it. Some of his colleagues went a good deal further. E. A. Yates, vice-president of C. & S., told the hearings that "any line built in this territory is simply a duplication of existing facilities." He added that from an economic point of view, the six companies he represented would not build a single additional dam on the Tennessee River. J. A. Longley, vice-president of the Tennessee Electric Power Company, testified that his concern already had a large surplus power capacity.

None of these arguments affected the language of the bill, not even Willkie's insistence that it would make worthless $400,000,-000 of securities of Southern utilities companies. The fertilizer interests chimed in, but they could agree with the public utilities only in predicting disastrous overproduction. The League of Women Voters endorsed the general purposes of the bill, objecting only to government manufacture of fertilizers on a large scale. A Kentucky representative was closer to the spirit of the times—some banks were still closed and relief was being organized on a national scale—when he told the committee: "During the last Administration, the Red Cross fed the hungry Republicans down in our state and our Highway Department fed the Democrats. A lot of our people lost money in Insull investments and we want a chance for cheap power to help our people."

Once the act had been passed, the TVA and C. & S. tried for almost a year and a half to find some working agreement. It was by no means a honeymoon but it was less violent than the dogfight which lay ahead of them. The New Deal was not yet being denounced as Communism; bankers were still busy reopening their banks. The winter of 1933-34 broke records for cold in the North, and the public mind was bemused and apprehensive over street fighting in Paris which might become civil war, the "night of the long knives" in Berlin, and the assassination of Chancellor Dollfuss of Austria. Memories of the economic collapse under Hoover and fears of a war which might be imminent made it hard to get excited over tales of the long-term plans of some visionaries in Washington.

There were seventeen million unemployed in 1933, there was no open geographical frontier to drain off their pressure on the cities, and since the end of 1929 the leaders of the business world had seemed to offer no solution except economic anarchy, the devil take the hindmost, and selling apples on street corners. Wall Street speculation, and the holding companies which made it possible, were prime factors in the indignation with which the

American public turned against business leadership. "Yesterday before breakfast," wrote Will Rogers, who was certainly no New Dealer, on August 1, 1933, "the U. S. Treasury offered $850 million worth of bonds, and before they reached the ham and eggs, they were all sold. That means sold and paid for, and salted away, not part paid for and the rest on margins, till you sold 'em over the ticker to somebody else. If industry could interest some permanent buyers like Roosevelt can in his business, then they could truly call themselves industrialists. As it is now they are just manufacturing dice for Wall Street to shoot craps with. Nobody is buying a pair to keep."

Willkie made almost no public speeches during this period. He was feeling his way, for a deal or a fight, with the three newly appointed directors of the TVA: Dr. Arthur E. Morgan, David E. Lilienthal, and Dr. Harcourt A. Morgan. They were equally eager to avoid or postpone a public fight. Their new dams were still on blueprints, and their only electric power, generated at Muscle Shoals, was being sold to the Alabama Power Company, a C. & S. subsidiary.

A geographical division of the area into spheres of influence, on a trial basis, was negotiated during 1933 and embodied in a contract signed by C. & S. and TVA on January 4, 1934. Willkie agreed to sell to the TVA a transmission line near the site of the Norris Dam on which construction had already started, as well as various distribution properties in Alabama, Mississippi, Georgia, and Tennessee. Willkie announced that the annual gross earnings of the properties sold amounted to approximately $1,-000,000 of the $50,000,000 gross earnings of all the Southern companies in the C. & S. group. Legal complications kept the sale from being consummated except for the Norris Dam line and the properties in Mississippi, which were turned over in June, 1934. The territorial arrangement, however, remained in force until the beginning of 1937. It kept C. & S. from selling power in counties where TVA had purchased the distribution facilities, and prevented TVA from selling to C. & S. customers outside those counties. The deal was to be effective for five years or until the completion of the Norris Dam power house, whichever date was earlier. The Alabama Power Company continued to buy the Muscle Shoals output on a month-to-month extension of its old contract, which had originally been signed with the War Department in 1925.

These arrangements were made after lengthy negotiations between Willkie and Lilienthal. Two other points figured heavily in these discussions. The first was the need for increased use of electrical appliances, and Willkie could and did offer help on standardized design of less expensive models in return for the government assistance in financing their sale which Lilienthal could offer. According to Lilienthal, this was Willkie's own idea, for which credit has never been given him. He was glad to use Federal financing to increase his company's power sales through wider use of electric appliances. It was he who worked out the system of collecting appliance costs through the company's bills for electric power. As soon as banks and private finance companies moved into the field, seeing that it was both legitimate and safe, the government financing arrangements worked out by Willkie and Lilienthal were suspended for good.

On the second point there was no agreement between the two men. This was the "yardstick" which Lilienthal felt TVA power sales should supply for the measurement of privately generated power prices. Willkie was against this from the very beginning, as an unrealistic proposal, and he said so loudly.

It was not until the end of 1934 that the issue was joined between C. & S. and TVA along the entire front. During the late spring and midsummer of 1934 drought and hot weather had scorched the agricultural sections of the country; it was estimated that 300,000,000 tons of the nation's topsoil had blown away. Bad news from abroad had been crowded off the front pages by the birth of the Dionne quintuplets. Bruno Richard Hauptmann was arrested for the kidnaping and murder of Colonel Lindbergh's son. The first emergency phase of the New Deal was over, and there was a faint smell of normalcy in the air even if it promised depression-as-usual. Dr. William A. Wirt had begun to talk about a Georgetown dinner where he had heard some fledgling New Dealers make jokes about Franklin D. Roosevelt and Alexander Kerensky. Conservatives were beginning to wonder what we were coming to.

Willkie

From the very beginning, there had been interesting signs of an important line of cleavage inside the New Deal camp on the problem of electric power. The Federal Power Commission, then made up of Frank R. McNinch, Basil Manly, and Oswald Ryan, stood for a moderate approach to the problems of regulation and government ownership. They knew that the government had more than one *quid pro quo* to offer for co-operation by the industry: curbing of potential government competition; a fair return on actual capital investment; new and attractive fields for making profits through government subsidy of rural electrification and of cheap appliance sales. All three men—and there were others like them—were experienced administrators and negotiators, and they had friends in the industry.* There were plenty of precedents in American history for a peaceful and intelligent bargaining-out of the differences between Washington and New York on the problem of electrical power. Although few denied that there were many abuses to be curbed or eliminated, it is significant that the initial New Deal legislation introduced to do the job was neither radical nor novel in tone or language.

Anyone who expected a simple solution along this line would have reckoned without other forces which had been strengthened in the depression and given power by the 1932 election. There was, for example, Senator Norris, at last in sight of the victory for which he had fought during an entire generation. He had vision and obduracy; no one could call this elder statesman from Nebraska either a Bolshevik or a compromiser. His vision was part of the lure which brought to Washington a new generation and a new kind of public servant; they ranged from academic men like the two Drs. Morgan, respectively president of Antioch College and of the University of Tennessee, through state officials, looking for bigger horizons, like Lilienthal, to young lawyers like Benjamin Cohen and Thomas Corcoran. All these men were to play major and continuing roles in the TVA and holding company fights, but at different phases of the struggle they found themselves in shifting coalitions with

* Ryan had been a judge in Indiana when Willkie was practicing law there; they were old and good friends.

many of the curious elements which made up the New Deal in its palmy days.

The spokesmen for the Edison Electric Institute (successor to the National Electric Light Association), with other lobbyists and public relations experts for the public utilities, called nearly all these new elements "Reds" at one time or another; none of them was Communist or Communist-inspired.* It is curious, however, to note that even the extremists on the power issue inside the early New Deal owed much more to Theodore Roosevelt and Robert M. La Follette than they did to Marx or Lenin. Gifford Pinchot was an old-time Republican. Morris L. Cooke was a consulting engineer who had been a trustee of the New York State Power Authority. Rankin, co-author of the TVA bill, was a Democrat from Mississippi whose name was later to become anathema to liberals because of his position on civil liberties and human rights. Senator Norris, Senator Burton K. Wheeler, Representative Sam Rayburn, Rexford Tugwell, A. A. Berle, Jr., Raymond Moley, Harold Ickes, Henry Morgenthau, Robert H. Jackson, Homer Cummings, and Donald Richberg were in and out of the major White House discussions which determined the fluctuations of New Deal policy on electric power. Some of them wanted to go much further and faster than Roosevelt himself, some of them slower. The idea that the TVA was or might become a laboratory for some nebulous kind of native American socialism was born partly in this group of men, and partly in the imaginations expensively hired by the Edison Electric Institute, but not at all in the *Daily Worker*.

On the public utility side of the fight, the line of cleavage was far less visible but it was probably of equal importance. The extremists here were the utility bankers and promoters of the boom days. They opposed not so much the details of each successive New Deal program for regulating the power industry as the whole notion of government intervention and control. Their

* The trial in New York in 1951 of William Remington, Department of Commerce official convicted of perjury in connection with his Communist party connections, revealed that the Communists gave high priority to recruiting work around Knoxville when the TVA was being built, but the evidence also showed that they apparently had almost no success at all.

complicated holding company empires, their freedom to fix and agree on rates, their monopoly of decision on the rate of expansion of industry, and, above all, the common stock with which they had rewarded themselves for their empire building were all clearly at stake, and they operated on the sound notion that the best defense is a strong offense. As it became clearer and clearer that public utilities were to be both whipping-boy and guinea-pig for the New Deal, other die-hards in the private enterprise camp who had no direct stake in the electric power industry moved in behind the Edison Electric Institute.

The differences within the utility camp were much less widely reported, as the fight developed, than those within the New Deal. By May, 1937, *Fortune* admitted the bitterness of the die-hards: "There has indeed been an oversupply not of conservatives but of arch-Tories in this business, men of so simple and realistic a sense of power that they preferred to indoctrinate the people against public ownership by influencing the schools and universities rather than by the roundabout method of low rates and progressive selling."

Willkie's difficulties with this unreconstructed right wing of American industry and the public utility industry went largely undocumented although he talked about them, a decade later, with a mixture of amusement and profanity. He wasted a forty-minute speech in Washington in 1933, trying to dissuade his utility colleagues from a too-cunning plan to take over their own regulation at the very start by writing it into their NRA code under the supposedly unwatchful eye of the Blue Eagle. The plan never got to first base with President Roosevelt or General Hugh Johnson, NRA Administrator, but it helped to sour relations between the New Deal and the industry, and it helped to confirm the reputation as "the Jesus Christ of the industry" which Willkie had been earning on his own.

The existence of another faction within the electric power industry was never widely publicized, since it could hope to be effective only in measure as it was quiet. Corcoran, testifying before the Senate Committee on Interstate Commerce in 1935, explained this clearly. "As a matter of fact," he told the Senators about the government's plans for regulating holding companies, "none of these ideas originate with so-called 'radicals' and Bolsheviks. They are all ideas that have been put forward by the utility people at one time or another, although, of course, when the utility people come down here, they have to stand together. More than one of them has said to us privately, 'we have to say things and hang together with the gang in the front room, but we will tell you different things in the back room.' That is easily understood. If I were in that position I would hang together with my gang, too."

Willkie himself was never one of these men, and Lilienthal remembers him through years of negotiation as a tough, unyielding, sometimes irritable opponent. What compromises he could win from Willkie were within the latter's strategy, which was clear and logical but based on the assumption that the New Deal would prove to be a one-term aberration and that the country would soon return to normal. It was this belief which led Willkie to make his original deal with Lilienthal at the end of 1933, confident that it would serve only to bridge the time until the TVA went out of business. Later, the same assumption led him to underestimate the permanence of government grants and loans to finance municipal distributing systems; again he was sure that both Congress and the Supreme Court would block them. In both cases, the right wing of the utility industry saw the compromises he made without understanding or accepting the strategy on which they were based. It led to bitterness against him which was to continue, in some circles, until he died.

From the day he took over the presidency of C. & S. in January, 1933, Willkie showed that if the power business was the field of adventure which fascinated him, it was not the power business as Samuel Insull or the arch-Tories saw it. His first big job was to clean house inside C. & S.; this was a process which was to take nearly a year and a half before, at the annual meeting of stockholders on June 20, 1934, he achieved the resignation of four directors who were not engaged in operations, and the election to the board of five officers of the principal subsidiary companies in the C. & S. system. The four who left in-

BORN ELWOOD INDIANA
FEB 1892.-EDUCATED AS
LAWYER

ARTILLERY CAPTAIN DURING WAR

WAS OUTSTANDING
DEBATER IN COLLEGE

COMMONWEALTH AND SOUTHERN

ELECTED
COMMONWEALTH & SOUTHERN
PRESIDENT JAN. 1933.

FATHER A
CIRCUIT JUDGE
HAD HIM TRY
MOCK CASES
BEFORE HIM

NOW SUCCEEDS
B.C. COBB AS
CHIEF EXECUTIVE

Copyright New York *Journal*

[How a New York newspaper described Willkie, on June 23, 1934, when he was the youngest man in the United States to be chief executive of a major utility system.]

cluded Landon K. Thorne and A. L. Loomis of the banking firm of Bonbright and Company, C. E. Groesbeck, chief executive of the Electric Bond and Share group of utilities which held 1,605,-476 shares of the 33,673,328 C. & S. shares outstanding (another 5,000,000 were owned by the Bonbright-controlled American Superpower Corporation), and Ray P. Stevens of the engineering firm of Stevens and Wood—all men who had been active in the formation of C. & S. in 1929. The five who replaced them were Preston S. Arkwright, president of the Georgia Power Company, A. C. Blinn, general manager of the Ohio Edison Company, Jo Conn Guild, Jr., president of the Tennessee Electric Power Company, D. E. Karn, general manager of the Consumers

The New Deal

Power Company of Michigan, and R. S. Wallace, president of the Central Illinois Light Company. All these concerns were operating subsidiaries of C. & S.

At the same time, he proceeded to throw out all the local lawyers for the system, in seven states, who had owned C. & S. stock. It had been a common public utility practice to give both local law business and specially priced treasury stock to local lawyers who might otherwise be attracted to litigation against the absentee holding company; Willkie distrusted this as an insurance against trouble, and he disliked its business ethics. He simplified the system's complicated corporate structure, writing down its assets heavily, and set up an arrangement by which general management and other services were provided to the operating companies by the holding company at cost. His break with Bonbright and Company came after long arguments between Willkie and his friend Thomas W. Lamont, and after that firm ceased to be the company's bankers, Willkie was inevitably thrown into the financing side of the business. He later wrote, in answer to a savage criticism of him, that "after I was president of the company, I was, of course, in charge of its financial and general business. Also, as a matter of necessity, I made many arguments before committees of Congress and frequently testified before them on legislation affecting utilities—always in open and public hearings. [The] suggestion that as president of Commonwealth and Southern I did not manage the system would strike as exceedingly humorous those then connected with the company."

Willkie used to call himself "the world's best gadget salesman," and he learned to sell gadgets in the poorest parts of the country during the worst years of the depression. He would drive from town to town giving fight talks to local sales forces while he reviewed suits for damages, local franchises, and other legal business. These trips were sometimes made in automobile cavalcades, each car filled with New York City officers of the holding company; local expense accounts would list large items for new paint, he noted, just before each of these trips. When he hit a new town anywhere in the South, Willkie would desert his traveling companions and go first to the local newspaper editor,

71

then in turn to the town library, to the Chamber of Commerce, and to the Superintendent of Schools. He believed this procedure taught him about a town in the shortest possible time, and that only with this knowledge could he make intelligent decisions about what C. & S. policy should be in any locality.

These were bad years for the electric power business as they were for all business. The C. & S. system earned in 1931, after dividends on its preferred stock, 40 cents a share on its common stock. In 1932, it earned 12 cents a share on its common. In 1933, the system reported a loss of one cent a share and in 1934 a loss of 5 cents, with preferred dividends in arrears. The tide turned in 1935, with a profit of one cent a share, and by 1936 the company reported earnings of 13 cents a share. During these years, Willkie was engrossed in the political fights against the TVA and the holding company act, neither of which had any immediate relation to C. & S. current profits. But only a year after he had taken over the company, he had made public his plans for pulling it out of the red. These were chiefly four: the substitution of operating officers for representatives of banking interests on the board of directors; simplification of corporate structure through the elimination of many pyramided subholding units; aggressive leadership in perfecting promotional low-rate schedules regardless of the effects on rates of other companies; and a broad appliance sales campaign designed to educate customers to the benefits derived from wider use of electricity.

There was no great gap between this program and that of the moderates among President Roosevelt's advisers on the public utility problem in 1933 or 1934. Even Senator Wheeler told Willkie, when he was testifying in 1935 on the death-sentence act: "I am frank to say to you that probably if there had not been any more abuses in some companies than there have been in yours with reference to some of those matters, you probably would not have been faced with some of the provisions you are faced with." But all the pressures of the continuing depression were pulling the two camps apart, and it was the extremists on both sides who profited most. Sometimes, talking about this process later, Willkie used to say that he could have carried 65 per cent of the industry with him on a moderate reform program, sometimes it was "more than half." He never had a chance to prove either figure; the New Deal was proving to be a process rather than a program, and the process was setting up an equal but opposite reaction among the tycoons of the utility industry. The industry was still young, led by men who were bold and often reckless, who had no established traditions within the industry to fall back upon and a glittering gamble in front of them if they could only beat "that man" in Washington.

While the fight was at its height, Walter Lippmann watched it from what can be called a ringside seat on the private enterprise side, considering his general antagonism to the New Deal. He admitted that the utilities had grown with "many grave abuses of trust and much flagrant profiteering." But he castigated President Roosevelt for "the error of treating the industry as a unit instead of dividing it into its good and its bad elements. There are in the industry, as everyone must know, executives and financiers [he singled out Willkie as their leader] who are and have been dismayed and angry at the kind of thing represented by the Insulls, who fully recognize that the utilities are a public business and must be thoroughly regulated." This was half of the truth; there were irreconcilables on both sides, and it was they who set the pace in what was to become the most bitter continuing fight between the New Deal and business.

The general growth of discontent among businessmen throughout 1934 was neither slow nor vague among public utility executives. They were still clearly on the defensive in terms of public opinion. It was bad luck for them that John Dillinger was captured, in Tucson, only a few weeks before Samuel Insull was arrested on a Greek freighter in the Mediterranean on March 15; a pattern in public thinking was beginning to jell. The next month, the New York State Senate voted a special investigation of public utilities as a result of disclosures about the lobbying activities of the Associated Gas and Electric Company. The first announcement of TVA power rates had caused a slump in public utility stock prices. Nearly all TVA power was being resold under contract by a C. & S.

subsidiary, Alabama Power Company, at thirty times its cost, but Lilienthal lost no time in starting discussions with municipalities throughout the region for sale of power from the new generating stations under construction. The truce which had been worked out in January, 1934, would automatically end when the Norris Dam was finished, and this would be precisely the date when the TVA could start seriously to compete with private power companies. If this threat was to be met at all, there was no time to be lost.

Willkie had been no leader, in the first stages, in the hue and cry about the TVA as socialism. In April, 1934, he recognized publicly that Lilienthal and his associates had been "courteous, able, and ambitious" in the long negotiations leading up to the agreement of January 4. He was clearly hopeful about the increased profits which would result from government stimulation of appliance sales through the Electric Home and Farm Authority which Lilienthal had helped to set up. He was dubious about the need for more power generation; George B. Cortelyou, president of the Edison Electric Institute, was speaking for the industry when he said it had "an uncomfortably large percentage of excess capacity," and Willkie echoed this line until the middle of 1935, after which all mention of excess power capacity disappeared completely from his speeches. Finally, he was convinced that the "yardstick" would not work, and that government attempts to enforce it would lead quickly and irretrievably to heavy losses for investors in public utility securities.

This position changed during 1934 toward one of increasing denunciation of the whole experiment as socialism, and by the end of the year Willkie was clearly the public leader of the utility forces. The change can be seen in the quickened schedule of his speeches as well as in their tone. On September 26 he spoke to the American Statistical Association in New York, on October 30 to the Investment Bankers Association at White Sulphur Springs, West Virginia, on November 7 to the Rotary Club in Birmingham, Alabama. These were the first speeches he ever made in his life which were nationally reported in the press, and the accent of a spokesman for the industry was clear in all of them. In the first, he rebuked an earlier speaker for attacks on New Deal personalities; "to abuse men in public office will not save us." By the third, in Birmingham, he was full of sarcasm and raillery at Lilienthal and at Washington, appealing to Southern loyalties, and threatening a boycott of the region by New York capital if the TVA experiment continued.

"Mr. Lilienthal says he is riding the economic wave of our times," Willkie said in Birmingham, "and that it is as useless to buck this economic tide as it is to stop the tides of the sea. He, of course, may be mistaken about this. It may only be a political wave, or mayhap it is only a golden stream he is astride, which, when it becomes dry, as it surely will, may leave your territory washed and denuded of private capital."

More decisive than any speech was the beginning, in September, 1934, of litigation by holders of a small minority of the preferred stock of the Alabama Power Company to invalidate the sale of fourteen of its municipal distribution properties to the TVA. Willkie denied that he or C. & S. instigated the suit, which was to become known as the Ashwander case, and he was actually an indirect defendant, having negotiated at the beginning of 1934 the sale which was being challenged. But it destroyed a good part of whatever agreement had been reached in the January deal, and lower court decisions gave reason to believe that the suit might eventually result in the whole TVA being declared unconstitutional. The case was not finally decided until it reached the Supreme Court, in February, 1936, and it hung over the New Deal and the TVA like a sword of Damocles.

Whether this public utility campaign was a new offensive or a counteroffensive to earlier New Deal attacks on the industry, it was clear by the autumn that open war had been declared on both sides. President Roosevelt had two cards to play, and he played them both within a few weeks. The first was a threat to create still more TVA's; the second was a signal that he had only postponed, and not forgotten, his campaign promises of a drastic cleanup of the whole utility industry and its holding companies.

It was appropriately at Tupelo, Mississippi, the first city

with a municipally owned power system supplying TVA power, that Roosevelt made his first threat on November 18, 1934. He had been on a tour of the Tennessee Valley, and he waited to speak out until he reached the only town, except for the construction town at Norris, where his dream of lower rates had not been blocked by public utility litigation and opposition for a year and a half after the TVA had been set up. "What is being done here," he said, "is going to be copied in every state of the Union before we get through."

Willkie answered him immediately, saying that "the President is a fair-minded man with a pre-eminent sense of justice," but that he had been "obviously misinformed." He made five points: the TVA plants had been written down in value more heavily than privately owned plants; TVA paid less "in lieu of taxes" than the utilities' tax bill; government interest rates were lower than private industry could secure; certain overhead expenses had never been charged against TVA; finally, if C. & S. were given subsidies as large as these, it could compete with TVA on rates even in Tupelo. He scored one clear debating point: Roosevelt had paid a glowing tribute to the extraordinary sale of appliances under the TVA plan throughout the region, and Willkie thanked him for it—"we appreciate this statement very much because over 90 per cent of the appliances sold under that plan were sold by the operating units of the Commonwealth and Southern Corporation."

He did not mention the threat to duplicate the TVA in other states, but all utility executives were pondering it, and it became a major, if hidden, stake in the struggle which was to fill the air with so many claims and counterclaims for the next few years. Republican newspapers praised Willkie's answer to the President, and printed in full his detailed figures showing that the Tupelo rates were unfairly figured, but the citizens of Tupelo were happy and the American people showed the same reluctance to grasp the complicated statistics of kilowatt-hours and base rates which was to work against Willkie throughout the entire struggle. Will Rogers summed up the public reaction: "The President made one of his best speeches in Tupelo, Mississippi, Sunday. He told that the people could make their own electric energy cheaper than they were getting it. And say, by Monday morning he had all the companies talking 'new rates.' They all say the government can't do anything toward running any business, but they break their necks to see that it don't try."

The industry had already turned to the lawyers in its hope of both defeating the TVA and blocking action against holding companies, but it was not content with a minor action in an Alabama court. On November 8, ten days before his Tupelo speech, Roosevelt asked his old friend, Newton D. Baker, to come to see him because of a rumor that he had been hired by the Edison Electric Institute to fight the TVA. "One of my principal tasks," the President wrote to Baker, "is to prevent bankers and businessmen from committing suicide! . . . I am writing you thus frankly because it seems to me that in the public interest you and I should discourage suicide. If it is true that you have been retained, I should love to have a talk with you about the whole subject of public utilities. . . ."

Baker wrote back that he would come, and he had luncheon with Roosevelt at the White House on December 12. But it was too late. Roosevelt's power program had already been denounced openly and loudly by the public utility industry. Its official spokesman, the Edison Electric Institute, had released to newspapers a month earlier a legal opinion that the TVA was "palpably unconstitutional," and the opinion was attributed to Baker and James M. Beck, a former Republican Solicitor General. There was a parade of public utility executives through the White House. In a single fortnight in December, Roosevelt saw, besides Baker, Thomas N. McCarter, president of the Edison Electric Institute, Floyd L. Carlisle, chairman of the Niagara Hudson Power Corporation, Clarence E. Groesbeck, chairman of the Electric Bond and Share Corporation, Preston L. Arkwright, president of the Georgia Power Company, a C. & S. subsidiary, and Willkie himself.* The results were small

---

* It was after this meeting, the first between the two men, that Willkie telegraphed his wife, who was strongly anti-New Deal: "CHARM EXAGGERATED STOP I DIDN'T TELL HIM WHAT YOU THINK OF HIM."

indeed. McCarter presented a memorial to the President urging an early legal test of the TVA, saying that he had not come in "any spirit of antagonism," but it was turned over to Frank R. McNinch, head of the Federal Power Commission, whose reply was described in circles sympathetic to the utilities as "an ill-tempered tirade general against the power industry."

President Roosevelt told a press conference that all the conversations had been "entirely amicable." Washington correspondents were given hopeful reports about co-operation with the industry on appliance sales, and rural electrification was beginning to be talked about as still another field in which mutual advantage could be found by the New Deal and private industry. Of 6,000,000 farms in the United States, only 800,000 were electrified, and of these only 650,000 had "high line" service instead of their own plants. This was attractive bait, but the industry did not bite. For it was already common knowledge that two young lawyers, Tom Corcoran and Ben Cohen, who lived together in a little red house on R Street, were drafting for the President an act to control public utility holding companies. To the utilities, the TVA was already a nuisance and an exceedingly dangerous precedent, but this new threat was a frontal attack on the very citadel of their power.

CHAPTER SIX

The Death-Sentence Act

P RESIDENT ROOSEVELT'S conferences with Willkie and other
public utility executives in December, 1934, and January,
1935, were blandly and shortly reported in the press. Even
shorter and vaguer reports were published about another series
of conferences on the same subject which brought together
the oddly assorted groups and individuals loosely comprising
the New Deal. Some of these conferences were in the White
House, others at Warm Springs, Georgia. Their purpose was
to work out a strategy on the whole power problem, and the
key to this, in Roosevelt's mind, was the holding company.

In the electric power industry, concentration of control had
reached a point in 1932, when the Insull system was still intact,
where thirteen holding companies controlled 75 per cent of the
total privately owned operating utility business in the United
States. Three companies—Insull, United Corporation, and Electric Bond and Share—controlled 40 per cent. During the 1935
Congressional hearings it was shown that the Associated Gas
and Electric Company, by pyramiding holding companies ten
corporations deep, had given holders of $300,000 of securities
at the top control over nearly $1 billion in assets. The holding
company device was most developed in the power industry
but not confined to it. A 1936 study of the 475 largest corporations in the United States, in all industries, showed that 70
per cent of them were holding companies.

Federal regulation of interstate transmission and sale of electric power was also on the agenda of the Roosevelt conferences,
but there was little dispute about this. The Federal Power

Commission was instructed to cover the problem in Title 2 of the proposed act, which was eventually introduced by Senator Wheeler and Representative Rayburn. Title 1 of the act, aimed at the holding companies, was assigned to Corcoran and Cohen and James M. Landis, former dean of the Harvard Law School. This was the trio who had already written the legislation regulating the Stock Exchange. Their names were becoming synonymous in conservative minds with socialism and revolution. Willkie knew them all, and his personal friendship with Cohen survived the battle over the act. It did not keep the public debate over the bill Cohen helped to draft from becoming the loudest, one of the most prolonged, and the most bitter in the entire history of New Deal legislation.

Roosevelt himself wanted to wipe out all holding companies. He saw them as a device by which public utility stock had been watered, raising capitalization figures to such a height that any rates based on reasonable return to that capital would be prohibitively high. American business leaders had been sensitive to this criticism; a year before, during the Senate Banking Committee's investigation of J. P. Morgan and Company, representatives of that firm had opposed the pyramiding of holding companies and said that there should be only one layer of holding companies above operating companies in the power industry. But once the issue had been joined, the utility industry decided to take the offensive, and in the torrents of public relations material which soon covered the country from utilities sources, the possibility of self-regulation was forgotten as a theme in favor of the outright socialism of the New Deal.

The men around Roosevelt ranged from radical to conservative on this problem, but it would be too simple to divide them into two camps. Morris L. Cooke, then of the Rural Electrification Administration, stood for an extreme solution—that of wiping out all holding companies—and the President himself, on two separate occasions, defended this course. He later claimed that no one but himself deserved the credit or blame for thinking up and sticking to the death-sentence clause as it was finally formulated. Close to the opposite extreme were men like McNinch, then chairman of the Federal Power Commission. An old-time

The Death-Sentence Act

Bryan Democrat, he had been appointed to the Commission by Hoover in 1930. He was violent in speeches against "financial groups squatting on power sites" and the public utilities regarded him as a ringleader among their enemies; yet most of the men present at these strategy conferences agree that his weight was thrown in favor of regulation and against the death-sentence clause.

Somewhere between them were men whose positions covered the entire political spectrum of the early New Deal. Corcoran and Cohen, the chief drafters of the bill, were radicals only in the sense to which public utility propaganda stretched that word. Their final draft was actually milder than others submitted to the President. The three most interested members of the Cabinet were Henry Morgenthau, Jr., Homer Cummings, and Harold L. Ickes; of these, Ickes took the most extreme stand against the holding companies, and he was still being described in the newspapers as a former Republican. McNinch's colleagues on the Federal Power Commission were Basil Manly, an authority on national power resources, and Oswald Ryan, an Indiana lawyer. Others who played important parts in setting the strategy of the Wheeler-Rayburn Act were Herman Oliphant of the Treasury, Robert H. Jackson of the Department of Justice, Donald Richberg, and the shifting personnel of the "brain trust" in the White House.

Before the bill was decided on, two alternative solutions of the problem had come to nothing. The first was a plan, backed by Morgenthau, to use taxation as a means of killing the holding companies. By lifting exemptions, utility income could have been made twice taxable, a powerful deterrent to pyramiding holding companies. Supreme Court Justice Louis D. Brandeis is said to have quietly approved of this plan, stating that it was the only sure way he saw of avoiding the constitutional issue. But he never said this in public, and the plan never got anywhere.

The other suggestion came from Willkie. In October, 1934, before the White House power conferences had started, he was having dinner with Oswald Ryan in Washington. "I have an idea," he told him. "You ought to sell it to this man in the White

House. It will make him the most popular man in the country. Sure, there are abuses in the holding company system, but he can't get away with killing them all. Instead, let's set up what we'll call an 'objective rate'—a rate we can all work towards as an objective. Roosevelt is the best salesman in the country. He's already sold more appliances for C. & S. than any man we hire. With him behind it, this rate would roll across the country from coast to coast. The President should announce it, and dramatize it as meaning lower electricity costs for everyone in every region. I can bring him the backing of 65 per cent of the industry. All I'd need would be his guaranty that there will be no TVA in any region where the utilities accept his 'objective rate.'"

Ryan talked this over with McNinch and they agreed they would need Roosevelt's approval. "Well," the President commented, "maybe there's something in it. Why don't you work it out, Frank?" But this was in October, before the problem had become a major political issue inside the New Deal and in the newspapers. For a few months, both the FPC and the industry worked on the plan, but events were moving much too quickly for it.

The three most common abuses of the holding company device were generally agreed to be the writing up of values, also called loading the rate base because it made possible higher rates for electricity; upstream loans, which made many operating companies finance their holding companies, instead of the reverse; and gouging of the operating companies on fees charged by their parent concerns. The C. & S. record was clean on all three of these counts and Willkie's own proposals included legislation covering them. The real fight came over the so-called death-sentence clause in the bill, designed to force the dissolution, after a stipulated interval, of all holding companies except those which controlled single, integrated systems of operating companies in single regions of the country.

Willkie later claimed with pride that he invented the "death-sentence" phrase at one of the hearings; he believed the phrase had helped rally opposition to the bill. There is no doubt that Corcoran and Cohen wrote the clause. Raymond Moley, who conferred with them at the drafting stage, has recorded that the clause was originally included only for trading purposes and that the President and his advisers were sold on it only in the course of the legislative battle. Corcoran and Cohen, he wrote, "were in and out of the White House, day after day, night after night, reporting the progress of their campaign to 'put the heat on' reluctant Senators. Between them they generated enough indignation over the opposition to the bill to become the victims of their own strategy. The fight became a fight for all or nothing."

1935 was a year of violent talk. In May, just after the Senate had held its hearings on the holding company bill, the Rev. Charles E. Coughlin, a Roman Catholic priest who was head of a dubious organization called the National Union for Social Justice, came from Detroit to tell a packed Madison Square Garden that if capitalism stood in the way of social justice it should be voted out of existence. In the same month, the Supreme Court had declared unconstitutional both the National Industrial Recovery Act and the Farm Mortgage Moratorium law. In August, the month the holding company bill passed, a New Jersey advertising man admitted to a Senate committee investigating lobbying that he had suggested a whispering campaign that the President was insane. The Associated Gas and Electric Company ordered its subsidiaries in twenty-six states to burn all written records of what they had done to oppose the bill, but Howard C. Hopson, an important stockholder who was later sent to jail, told the Senate that his company's total expenditure against the bill might run close to $1,000,000.

The conservative revolt against all that the New Deal stood for was steadily gaining resonance, if not momentum. The farms were still blowing away in the Dust Bowl, and prosperity was nowhere to be found around the corner. But the Supreme Court was considering the constitutionality of a whole series of New Deal measures. The business community had been recovering its nerve ever since the winter of 1933, and this attack on electric power holding companies seemed to it a declaration of war against the whole system of private enterprise.

The crucial meeting inside the Administration was held at Warm Springs in January. It was followed by another at the

White House on January 21, 1935, when the final decision to press for a death-sentence clause was communicated to enough persons so that it leaked to the press. Two days later, Willkie, Groesbeck, and Harvey C. Couch, president of power and light companies in Arkansas, Mississippi, and Louisiana, were being told the bad news at a White House meeting presided over by the President. McNinch, Manly, and Lilienthal were also present. Couch was a former director of the Reconstruction Finance Corporation who was deeply interested in rural electrification. It was a clear bid by the White House to split the utility front by winning over three of its key members who had not yet been violently hostile to the whole New Deal. It failed. The fight had been gaining steadily in bitterness since the autumn, and the first few months of 1935 were to see it take definite form, with line-ups and plans which were to last for a long time.

On the same day as the White House conference which broke the news about the death-sentence clause, January 21, Willkie had appeared in his first full-dress public debate on the issue. It was before the Economic Club of New York at the Hotel Astor, with Lilienthal as his opponent. James P. Warburg, president of the club, was in the chair. Lilienthal was running a fever, and had to leave before the discussion. Willkie's stinging attack on the government won him more prominent coverage in the national press than he had ever had before. The grand ballroom and its galleries were packed with businessmen, looking desperately for a Moses to lead them out of Egypt. Here, many of them thought, might be their man.

Willkie's speech was an outline of the case he was to argue over and over again for the next few years. He attacked all government business enterprise as inefficient, vulnerable to political manipulation, and unfair to private investors. In spite of "the presence of my very charming and learned friend, Mr. Lilienthal," he explained the TVA as the result of agitation backed by men who "have become enamored with European economic and social concepts and seek their application to American life." He denied the charge that utility securities had been watered, he repeated the industry's claim that generating capacity was already excessive, and he turned the charge of propaganda back against the government. "I want to say that as propaganda artists we have come to learn that we were the most immature and bungling amateurs. The volume of publicity issued by Federal bureaus having to do with power and kindred subjects has literally flooded the newspapers of the country in the last year."

Finally, he defended holding companies with pride in being the head of one of the biggest of them. In a dramatic touch, he produced a letter written on November 5, 1926, by Franklin D. Roosevelt from Warm Springs to a C. & S. subsidiary, the Georgia Power Company, complaining about bad service from a local plant which was later taken over and improved by the holding company to which Roosevelt had appealed for help. He recognized the government's right to regulate public utilities, although he preferred state to Federal regulation, but not its right to compete with private enterprise or to legislate holding companies out of existence.

There was nothing socialist or even radical about Lilienthal's speech. He spoke shrewdly to the holders of the senior securities, especially bonds, of the public utility companies, warning them that their investments were being endangered not by the government but by the financial malpractice of holding companies and management companies. There was, he said, "serious doubt of the existence of any substantial equity for common stock in a very large part of the operating utilities of the country." The New Deal was trying to divide its opposition; one of the strategic errors of the Willkie attack, in its first major exposition as in its subsequent development, was that it tended to reduce rather than to strengthen the basic differences within the New Deal camp.

Less than a month later, the bill was being heatedly debated in Congress and the fight had become clear and inescapable. On February 26, Willkie reported to the directors of C. & S. that ruin was staring them in the face. "It is, of course, being said by those who seek under the guise of this bill to 'nationalize' the power business of this country that its passage will not work any hardship upon security holders, that the distribution of the securities of operating companies, owned by holding companies, among the several holders of holding company securities will eventually prove advantageous to such holders of holding company securities. This contention is obviously without merit.

"The debenture debt of your company must be paid in full upon dissolution prior to any distribution to preferred and common stockholders. Cash for this purpose could only be realized by forced sale of securities in a market which will be bereft of buyers by reason of the destruction of other holding company units and the prohibition in the bill against any aggregation of capital acquiring such securities."

Willkie was the lead-off man for the utilities in the hearings before the House Interstate and Foreign Commerce Committee and he played the major role in the later hearings before the Senate Committee on Interstate Commerce. Whatever differences had earlier separated his position from that of others in the utilities industry were no longer to be found in his testimony. C. & S. was relatively innocent of many of the charges brought before the committees; the only specific charges introduced against it were that it had carried $553,000,000 in allegedly watered capital values on its books for two years before writing it off in 1932, and that its Northern and Southern systems were not integrated. Willkie had moved to Washington to carry on this fight, and his tactics were those of the entire industry—an all-out campaign against the bill as an attack on the American system of private enterprise.

Theodore C. Wallen, covering the hearings for the *New York Herald Tribune*, wrote one of the earliest dispatches to recognize Willkie's new role as leader of the industry, even if it got the color of his hair wrong. "The forty-three-year-old corporation president and former lawyer," he reported, "whose tousled red hair and old-fashioned spectacles gave him the appearance of a youthful college professor rather than a Wall Street magnate, neither gave nor asked any quarter in his appearance before the committee." He did not sit at a table reading a prepared statement, "but strode up and down before the committee seated on a dais before him. At times his voice was angry as he turned to answer some allegation against holding companies. Again, it was soft and trembling as he told of the years of work, vision and dreams on the part of men who had brought

The Death-Sentence Act

holding companies into existence to make the power industry more efficient. 'A fine American romance that has made this country great' was what he called it."

It was clearly recognized at the time that the utilities were putting their least vulnerable representative up to speak for them, although some of the backers of the bill claimed that C. & S. had "got religion and cleaned up" only to head off the government's attack. Willkie told the Representatives about an investigator for the Federal Trade Commission who had congratulated him on C. & S. business methods after spending some weeks in the company's offices. When Willkie suggested that the commendation be included in the report, the investigator answered: "Oh, Mr. Willkie, I would be severely criticized if I put anything in my report favorable to a holding company."

Willkie's basic claim was that the bill threatened to wipe out $3,500,000,000 in holding company security values, thus placing "the ghost of fear and distress in the homes of 5,000,000 American citizens who have invested in these securities." He proposed an alternative program of his own designed to reduce the number of intermediate holding companies through tax concessions to top companies, and to control, through regulation, such evils as exorbitant profits for management companies, use of expense accounts to disguise use of company funds for propaganda, upstream loans from operating to holding companies, and write-up of capital values.

He lashed out at what he called "the myth of banking control," denying that C. & S. took direction from any financial interests and listing with pride the operating records and duties of the directors of the company. "As a matter of fact," he said, "I wouldn't know a member of the New York Morgan banking house if he walked unannounced into this room, unless I recognized him from pictures I have seen in the public press. All we use bankers for is to get their money. That banking control is one of those Orphan Annie 'goblins will get you if you don't watch out' bedtime stories. It is one of the great American myths."

Myth it may have been, but it was unquestionably a great one. Senator Wheeler, at a later stage of the hearings, pressed

Willkie hard on how the founders of C. & S. had succeeded in getting New York financing without losing their shirts. "I do not know," Wheeler said, "of any company of any kind or character that has gone into New York from the West but what had the experience that the New York bankers left them very little when they got through with them."

The hearings dragged on for weeks, with the public furore building steadily outside Congress. Utilities representatives made few concessions. When Samuel Ferguson, chairman of the board of directors of the Connecticut Power Company, admitted that holding companies should not make a profit from management services rendered to wholly owned subsidiaries, Senator Sherman Minton of Indiana commented: "The devil has hit the sawdust trail." The White House was equally reluctant to work out any compromise, and it whipped its straggling supporters together through a long, hot summer before the bill came to a final vote.

At one point, Willkie was interrupted in testifying before the Senate Committee by Senator Homer T. Bone of Washington. "I do not want to make a speech," the Senator said, "but I am just wondering what the effect on the public mind is going to be right now when millions of people are demanding, not this bill, but something infinitely more drastic with respect not only to your business, but all other forms of business. You gentlemen will have to pay the price along with the rest of us. I only suggest that you view this thing calmly, dispassionately, and realistically. We are dealing with forces over which we have no control."

The Senator was closer to the mood of the American people in 1935 than all the complicated memoranda on rates and security values which were being submitted to the Congressional committees or the quotations from Walt Whitman, *Hamlet*, and the Bible with which the hearings were studded. Serious propaganda warfare was being carried on outside the committee rooms with loud noise, high feelings, and relatively little consideration of the legal or constitutional issues involved in the dispute. Both the public utilities industry and the government

The Death-Sentence Act

were aware that the issue cut deep enough to require eventual decision in the court of public opinion, and neither side was neglecting this aspect of the conflict.

Even Will Rogers' sure hand could fumble with an issue as hot as this. On March 13, he used a wisecrack in his syndicated column: "Say, did you read about what Mr. Roosevelt said about those 'holding companies'? A Holding Company is a thing where you hand an accomplice the goods while the policeman searches you." By March 22, he had apparently been talked to, for his next reference ran: "I was shooting off the other day about holding companies. Mr. Roosevelt and lots of folks may think they are uncalled for, but the folks working for em think mighty well of em, it's the old fault of not calling your shots, by naming the bad ones, and not shooting into the whole covey." Even this failed to get him out of hot water, and he returned to the subject again on March 31:

"Seeing the Presidents headline about em, why I said, a holding company is like a fellow handing the other fellow the swag while they search you. Well I dident figure that little half witted remark would upset the whole holding company business. But I forgot that a remark generally hurts in proportion to its truth. If its so untrue as to be rediculous why nobody pays any attention to it. And on the other hand I dont want to get any remark that will be so true that it hurts, I mean really hurts. So I was in wrong both ways. Now I dont know what it is, but right or wrong, there must be some little teeny weeny bit of underground connivance connected with the idea of holding companies, or is there?

"Now be honest. In a straight forward legitimate business, a farm, a store, a little manufacturing concern, or any business, what makes the holding company necessary? Dont it have something to do with shifting the responsibility over to another company that are liable only for so much?

"You see here is something that any of us that write have found out, if we write or say something that agrees with you, why then we become quite a smart guy in your estimation. But if we should write or say something that dont agree witn

89

your idea of the same subject, then we become a 'menace' and should be eliminated from the public prints. So we are good only as long as we agree with you."

Will Rogers was not the only commentator who found the holding company problem hard to handle. Walter Lippmann had already been committed to the outlawry of all practices which restricted the free working of a market economy, including monopolies and holding companies, and at first he supported the measure. It was, he wrote on March 14, 1935, "a revival of old-fashioned, hundred per cent American trust busting applied to the complicated and gigantic trusts of the new era that preceded the New Deal." As the public fight grew more bitter, his columns illustrated the same dilemma Will Rogers had described. By July 4, he was arguing against the White House insistence on the Senate version of the bill, which unlike the House version at that stage placed the burden of proof upon each holding company trying to avoid dissolution. By the end of the year, on December 21, he was writing against the death-sentence clause, arguing that public utilities were relatively new industries, whose financial practices should be attributed to their reckless and pioneering spirit.

Willkie's testimony before Congress gave him his first real national prominence, and both the public utilities industry and the embattled leaders of other business groups rallied around him in launching the most serious wave of protest the New Deal had yet encountered. Willkie began to write and publish articles for the first time on a serious scale. His market in 1935 included *Forbes Magazine, Current History,* the *Wharton Review,* the *Public Utilities Fortnightly,* the *Journal of Land and Public Utility Economics,* and the *Magazine of Wall Street;* they were a workout and a build-up for the national-circulation, slick-paper market which lay ahead of him. He was also in heavy demand as a speaker. In May he addressed the United States Chamber of Commerce, in June the Harvard Business School Alumni Association, and the New York Town Hall Club, the Bond Club of New York, and similar organizations followed. He was strongly urged to take the presidency of the Edison Electric Institute at its annual convention in June at Atlantic City, but he decided against the propagandist reputation that body had inherited from its predecessor, the National Electric Light Association, and formed instead a Committee of Utility Executives to combat New Deal power policies.*

One of Willkie's devices for rallying support was a series of letters to C. & S. stockholders. On May 26, 1935, he wrote them that the market value of their stock "has declined with each successive Federal government attack, and is now 60 per cent less than the market value in May, 1933, when the campaign against private utilities was commenced by the passage of the TVA act. Similar declines have occurred in the securities of other utility companies. Many leading industrial stocks rose almost 100 per cent during the same period." A month later he mailed two hundred thousand copies of a similar letter, and each time he asked the stockholders to write again to their Senators and Representatives against the still-pending bill. In July, he mailed to ten thousand business executives a twenty-six-page legal opinion by the firm of Winthrop, Stimson, Putnam and Roberts on the unconstitutionality of the death-sentence act.

The continuing Congressional debate reflected the bitterness which was being developed in the public controversy. Much of the basic pattern of the anti-New Deal campaign was set in this debate, especially its antagonism to intellectuals and professors. Representative George Huddleston, Alabama Democrat, said: "This bill was written by Benjamin Cohen and Thomas Corcoran, two bright young men brought down from New York to teach Congress how to shoot. Some of us were here when both were yet in short pants. But these are days when experience and fidelity in public service or in business life are exceedingly disqualifying." He added that every syllable of the bill was "loaded with arsenic." It was, he said, "designed to baffle, to harass, to ensnare, to enmesh, to confuse, to produce a situation beyond the wit of anybody to get through with it." Representative John G. Cooper, Republican from Ohio, blamed

---

* This organization continued until July, 1941, when it quietly disbanded as defense needs boomed the national demand for power. Willkie resigned from it when he resigned from C. & S. in 1940.

the bill on ten to twenty-five of "these young brain trusters on the government payroll" who "occupied one long row [in the committee room] which was classified as intelligentsia row."

At the height of the debate, Senator Hugo L. Black, Democrat of Alabama, and later an Associate Justice of the Supreme Court, made a radio speech in which he charged that the power industry's fight against the bill "will be known as the $5,000,000 lobby." Willkie fired back the next day, challenging Black to summon witnesses before his Senate committee which was threatening to expose the industry's lobbying activities. He did not deny the figure, but he accused the government of financing a $4,880,000,000 lobby of its own. This figure was the total of the huge relief fund then being spent by President Roosevelt. The investigation petered out, but not until it had collected, through the Federal Communications Commission, a good many private and irrelevant messages along with the evidence of massive lobbying by some of the utilities. Few Americans were left in any doubt that an enormous lobbying and propaganda campaign had been fought by both sides.

The bill was before Congress for seven months before it was finally passed in August. It had caused a terrific uproar, with telegrams, letters, and lobbyists pouring in on Washington in unprecedented volume. It caused serious party splits, a temporary deadlock between the two houses of Congress, and a mobilization of special interest groups which threatened to demolish completely the entire pattern of party responsibility. The death-sentence clause passed the Senate by a margin of only one vote and was turned down, at first, by the House, where the Democratic majority split, 166 to 130, on this issue. In the Senate, 29 Democrats had joined the opposition, with the Republicans voting 15 to 8 against the clause. The final vote, when the bill became law with the death-sentence clause included, showed the South and West most united for utility regulation with the utilities strongest, in both major parties, in the industrial East and in the Middle West.

President Roosevelt signed the bill on August 26, four days after the final compromise version had been passed by the

House. This version met Roosevelt's original formula. The Federal Power Commission was given authority to regulate rates, facilities, and security issues of concerns engaged in interstate transmission of electric power. It was also stipulated that after three years all super-holding companies must be dissolved, and only those continued which were limited to single integrated systems and the business directly connected with the supply of power to consumers. On September 25, Willkie and Landis, then chairman of the Securities and Exchange Commission, drew up a statement after a conference in Washington in which eleven top public utility executives agreed to help the SEC draft its new holding company regulations without waiving their legal rights to challenge the legislation. This was hardly more than an armistice in the struggle. On November 7, Federal Judge William C. Coleman in Baltimore ruled that the act was invalid "in its entirety." At the same time the Ohio Edison Company, one of Willkie's subsidiaries in the C. & S. system, began a legal action, challenging the act as unconstitutional, which was to last for almost as long as the New Deal itself.

The lines had been drawn in a major and long-lasting fight. Both sides had been pushed in the controversy to extremist positions which would not have been defended a year before. President Roosevelt had now challenged the American business community as it had not been challenged by earlier New Deal measures, and it had responded with an all-out attack which froze into the vituperation of a long decade. Willkie had still called himself a Democrat before the Senate Committee in the spring of the year but he was now a determined and angry opponent of the Administration and all its works. In September, a rumor started in Washington that he might be named a member of the SEC and a Republican paper like the *New York Herald Tribune* could still describe him, in reporting the rumor, as "one of the outstanding liberal and progressive leaders in the industry." Willkie himself was inclined to discount the advantages of this reputation, considering what had happened in the year 1935. At its end, he summed up his position: "I have only one possible regret. If by spending more money legitimately the C. & S. could have prevented this destructive act from being passed, then I am sorry I did not authorize such additional expenditures."

In the course of 1935, he had become a public figure. He was now deeply involved in a struggle in which his own convictions, his business interests, and his sense of trusteeship for C. & S. stockholders all reinforced each other. His almost overpowering desire to win any fight he was ever caught in played its part. There was a final factor—the pressure of the steadily growing business revolt against the New Deal and all its works. Willkie had not originally been a part of this revolt, but the 1935 struggle over the death-sentence act pushed him, whether he liked it or not, steadily towards that leadership of it which was to reach its culmination in 1940. For it was growing as remorselessly as the New Deal it opposed, and pushing men into as strange alliances.

Once the bill had been passed, Roosevelt wrote to Roy Howard on September 6 that he saw "substantial completion" of the experimental phases of the Administration's program as far as business was concerned, and promised a breathing spell. Violence and death competed for the big headlines for a few weeks: Will Rogers and Wiley Post were killed in an Alaskan air crash on August 15; Huey P. Long was assassinated in Baton Rouge on September 8; the Italian Army invaded Ethiopia on October 4; Arthur (Dutch Schultz) Flegenheimer and three of his companions were shot to death in a Newark tavern on October 23.

It was a short breathing spell. On December 4, Clinton L. Bardo, president of the National Association of Manufacturers, told its annual convention: "Whether we like it or not, industry, much against its will, has been forced, in sheer self-defense, to enter the political arena or be destroyed as private enterprise." On January 6, the Supreme Court threw out the Agricultural Adjustment Act. The turn of the year had heightened, as it nearly always does, the public expectation of big change. On January 20, King George V died. On January 25, Alfred E. Smith told the first annual dinner of a new organization called the American Liberty League that the Roosevelt Administration

The Death-Sentence Act

was "socialistic on the Soviet type." American business leadership was moving down one road as recklessly as the New Deal
in Washington was moving down another; the fork where the
roads had split was somewhere too far behind for either to
recall it; for the next five years Willkie was traveling with men
in a hurry.

CHAPTER SEVEN

TVA and the Supreme Court

THE hard core of Willkie's original opposition to the New
Deal was his desire to salvage from the TVA threat the
Tennessee properties of his C. & S. stockholders. During 1935,
this issue had become part of a bigger fight—the struggle of
all the utilities to block the New Deal's nation-wide power program and especially its plans to control their most distinctive
device, the holding company. Facing the prospect of defeat in
this struggle also, Willkie and the public utility industry gradually moved the struggle into a third arena—an all-out campaign
against the entire New Deal.

The next four years saw the United States move closer to class
war than it had been since Andrew Jackson's time. Businessmen
stormed into politics with money, co-ordination, and far more
gusto than had been expected of them. They found no vacuum
there; the labor movement, organized farmers, college professors, old-style conservationists, and trust-busters were all
being equally drawn into politics by the momentum of the
continuing depression. From 1936 until the outbreak of the war
in Europe at the end of 1939, Willkie became steadily more and
more involved in the biggest drama of his time by forces which
were deep-rooted in him as they were in American life.

He was forty-four years old in 1936, a man of no accumulated
fortune but with a large income by any standard. In 1938, his
income as president of C. & S. was listed as $75,815.* He had no
thought of a political career, nor was he even a titular leader

* The average wage in the electric power industry, a figure frequently
thrown at him by his opponents, was $33.47 a week in the same year.

of either the legal profession or the public utility industry. He
was not a die-hard in his political convictions. Still technically
a registered Democrat as late as 1938, he found himself increasingly living and working with men who were Republicans.
His disagreements with them were frequent, especially at first,
on both objectives and strategy. In these four years, the pressure
of the struggle against the New Deal was to narrow steadily
the area of disagreement between Willkie and the Republicans
until at the end he became their leader and their candidate for
President.

Any change in his personal life was subtle and gradual. He
spent much more time in Washington, staying in a suite at the
Mayflower Hotel, testifying before endless Congressional hearings, getting to know the Washington correspondents, learning
at first hand the political processes of democracy. It is probably
accurate to say that no other candidate for President has ever
known Washington so well without ever having held an elected
or appointed Federal job; he was a high-class lobbyist in these
days, and he picked up a good deal of that special lobbyists'
wisdom about Washington that Senators have been known
to envy.

He continued to run C. & S. from its Pine Street office in the
heart of New York's Wall Street district, but his swings through
the South and West grew longer and more frequent. In New
York he lived at 1010 Fifth Avenue, in an apartment which had
the right address for a leading corporation executive but few of
the signs that a man of strong personal taste and imagination
was concentrating on the making of a home. His son, Philip,
went to school in New York until 1939, when he matriculated
at Princeton. Willkie was far too restless in these years to build
the home in Westchester or Long Island which was almost an
essential part of the public picture of a successful utility tycoon.

In January, 1935, he had acquired instead the first of five
farms in Rush County, Indiana, which were to give him as much
of a home base as he had for the next nine years. He bought
them and ran them as an investment, with an old friend, Miss
Mary Sleeth, who had been librarian at Rushville in 1918, managing the property and his tenant farmers. He went there on

nearly every vacation he could take. Indiana attracted him, and long before he had any thought of a political career he found his farms a useful device for keeping himself informed about what people were thinking and saying.

What was perhaps Willkie's most revealing personal habit during these years ran directly counter to the established pattern of the businessman moving into national prominence. Instead of taking up golf, he found an outlet for restless energy in insatiable reading. Eighteenth-century English history fascinated him; in August, 1939, before he had become a political candidate for any office, he reviewed for Irita Van Doren's *New York Herald Tribune Books* Lord David Cecil's *The Young Melbourne and the Story of His Marriage with Caroline Lamb.* A little later, he also reviewed in the same paper *Mr. Pitt and America's Birthright,* by J. C. Long. Another field in which he read extensively was the history of great American fortunes; still another was the history of the South. He held original and unacademic theories in many of these fields; he used to say that he would like to rewrite Gustavus Myers on American family dynasties with special emphasis on their real estate, and he would talk for hours on his belief that the southern and westward movement of the original settlers in the Southern states, driven by the soil depletion of the plantation system, constituted a unique case of a rich men's migration.

The pre-Civil War economics of the South was only one of the subjects on which he read omnivorously. William Pitt, William Loundes, Judge William Brooks, Yancey, and other early Alabama figures, the original settlement of Indiana, the rise of trade unions, the causes of decay in civilizations—these all fascinated him. Many businessmen looked on him, even at this time, as a Bohemian, a man who read too many books, an intellectual. Others remember him as having the distinction of being a literate person fallen among utility men. Neither kind of comment bothered him; he went on reading and talking. Newspapers were a vice with him like cigarettes; he bought them all in every city he was in and he acquired an expert knowledge of individual papers all over the country. Janet Flanner once called his memory "something like a boy's pocket," and she claimed that once, in answer to a reporter's challenge, he wrote down from memory all the Prime Ministers of England since the time of George I, with their dates.

Willkie read few novels. In 1936 the advertising manager of one of the C. & S. subsidiaries, the Georgia Power Company, asked Willkie to lunch with him and his wife. She had just finished writing a book, and they had their fingers crossed hoping it might earn enough for the down payment on a new house. Willkie, in an expansive and bighearted mood, sent a letter through the C. & S. system. "I am not suggesting that any of you necessarily buy the book," ran his letter, "but I thought that each of you might wish to do a little vicarious boasting. The novel has been very highly commended by the critics. I am commencing my reading of it tonight." The novel he was trying to boost was Margaret Mitchell's *Gone With the Wind*, total English-language sales of which were to reach four million copies. Later he arranged a raise in salary and position for her husband on the theory that it was bad for a man's morale for his wife to be so much more successful than he was.

These interests drew Willkie into highly cosmopolitan and urbane circles in New York where anti-New Deal businessmen were not often seen. Physically he was a hard man to overlook in any room: his size, his usually tousled hair, his uninhibited voice and laugh and gestures all made him an attractive guest even at parties where business and politics were unlikely subjects of conversation. Willkie was a good laugher and a good listener and he liked interesting conversation wherever he found it. There could be no important business advantage to him in social conformity, now even less than before, and he did not conform.

The reason for both his reading and his conversation was his tremendous curiosity. He asked questions about everything and drank in the answers. He would literally milk a new acquaintance, working in a field with which he was unfamiliar, of every bit of information he possessed. After spending an evening with Willkie, you found him almost as well versed in your business as you were, and sometimes he ended up by pointing out things to you that you had never noticed yourself. When he became interested in an historical person or a place, he would make side excursions on his trips in order to learn more about the subject. He would question everyone he could corner in a town to gather bits of information he had not found in his reading. Sometimes he did this just to confirm some point in which he had been interested, and when he was proved right he was boyishly pleased.

In 1937, he was elected to the Century Association in New York, a club which had been founded in 1847 by "gentlemen engaged or interested in Letters and the Fine Arts." The Century was a far cry from the yacht and country club gregariousness in which most American business leaders then engaged. There was nothing reserved about Willkie's pride in his election to it.

The Willkies were first listed in the New York Social Register in 1936, but social position did not change his habits or his associates. The Fifth Avenue apartment always had an indefinable but noticeable Indiana air about it. Willkie said in 1940 that he had never spent much more than $20,000 a year of his $75,000 salary, including insurance payments, and that he had saved and accumulated $500,000 before he went into politics. He gave away a good deal; once he tried to count the number of boys and girls he had helped to go to college, and he could remember the names or the parents of forty-nine.

Willkie sometimes smoked up to six packages of cigarettes a day, lighting, puffing, and stamping out far more than he finished. He drank moderately, preferring Scotch and never learning to like wine. He was careless of his health, seldom seeing doctors except for insurance examinations. He never carried a watch. Although he loved to ride in automobiles, especially on long trips through the country, he never drove himself. His father had once tried a case for a baker in Elwood who could not pay his fee and gave him instead an automobile. It was a side-crank affair, and Wendell's brother Ed became his father's driver. He tried to teach Wendell. The car had reached the breathless speed of twenty-five miles an hour on an Indiana dirt road when it hit a rut while Wendell was indulging in his passion for talking with expansive gestures. The car turned over on both of them, pinning them on a carpet of poison ivy. Willkie never drove a car again; he had been cured of wanting to.

TVA and the Supreme Court

Tennis, fishing, and betting on horses were in the same category as golf for Willkie; his body was too restless and his mind too hungry for any of them. One summer he tried his hand at a clock golf course which friends had set up around a house in Connecticut. If they could do it, he said, so could he, by God. He started for the first hole, which lay on the other side of a stone wall, as if he were driving a nail. He lifted the ball neatly over the wall and went around the course with almost a record score and never played again.

He always played a little poker, and he became very fond of all the variants of rummy. Albert Leventhal and Tom Bevans, two friends of his in the publishing business, taught him to play gin rummy on a train coming into Grand Central. He played badly at first and then became interested. The porter warned him to get ready just before the 125th Street Station, but Willkie brushed him away. The three of them sat in the empty train underneath 42nd Street until Willkie could finish the game, with the train crew kibitzing while cleaners swept the aisles. He carried the same tenacity and absorption into everything he did, including conversation. Friends remember him swinging a leg over the arm of a chair, or sitting on one leg, fidgeting, his coat riding up his back, but always with passionate interest in the talk that went on endlessly around him wherever he was.

Of the three major struggles in which Willkie was engaged in 1936—against the TVA, the death-sentence act, and the whole New Deal—the first was not only the oldest but also the one in which he felt most sure of himself and therefore most capable of political maneuver. The first major legal test of the TVA was the Ashwander case, which had been begun in September, 1934, by the group of holders of preferred stock in the Alabama Power Company who were challenging the right of their parent corporation, C. & S., to enter into a contract with TVA. In February, 1935, the district court returned a verdict against the TVA. Although this was to be reversed a year later by the Supreme Court, it led many to predict that the whole enterprise would be declared unconstitutional, and the year's delay before the final verdict gave Willkie and the public utility industry time to plan the general strategy of their respective campaigns.

The district court verdict against the TVA in the Ashwander case carried with it an injunction preventing seventeen municipalities in Alabama from accepting PWA funds for the construction of city plants. Together with the city of Athens, Alabama, they were also enjoined from purchasing power from the TVA. The Circuit Court of Appeals, later in the same year, upset the judgment. The use of PWA funds, in loans and grants to municipalities, was becoming a major political weapon in Lilienthal's hands against C. & S. Litigation kept the weapon from being fully used, even after the Supreme Court decision at the beginning of 1936, but the Norris Dam was still being built and the only power TVA had to sell was the surplus at the Wilson Dam. In the public debate throughout 1935, Willkie's case against the yardstick principle was steadily strengthened by this prospect of government subsidy to users of TVA power. But the number of towns and communities which were prepared to take the cheaper power and let the yardstick go grew mucn faster than the ranks of those who agreed with Willkie on the principle involved.

So there was jubilation throughout the Tennessee Valley when the Supreme Court decision in the Ashwander case was announced on February 17, 1936. Public celebrations were held all over the region, factory whistles blew, TVA officials felt for a short moment that they had won a final victory. The conservative press needed two days to analyze the verdict, and then it was seen that the TVA was still far from victory.

The Supreme Court actually handed down two decisions. By a five-to-four vote, Chief Justice Hughes, with Justices Butler, Sutherland, Van Devanter, and McReynolds, held that the stockholders who had brought the original suit did have a right to a hearing and adjudication. Justices Brandeis, Stone, Cardozo, and Roberts dissented on the grounds that the plaintiffs had no standing in court at all. By an eight-to-one vote, the Court then held that the Wilson Dam had been legally constructed and that the TVA had the right to sell surplus power from it to the Alabama Power Company. But no ruling was given on the major questions involved. The Court gave no opinion on the TVA itself, on the new dams it was building up and down the river, on the right of the government to acquire or operate or subsidize local distribution systems, or on the legality of TVA steam plants. "Though hailed in the White House and recorded in the press as a victory," the Beards summed it up, "the decision in itself was at best a dubious victory. In fact, it could be considered as a defeat for the Administration in that it flung wide the gates for endless litigation and left ample room for invalidating the essentials of the Tennessee Valley program whenever a broader question was raised for adjudication."

The line of battle had not yet been drawn sharply in political terms. A Republican, John Lord O'Brian, Assistant to the Attorney General under President Hoover, argued the Ashwander case for the TVA before both the Circuit Court of Appeals and the Supreme Court. The TVA legal strategy had been mapped out by James L. Fly, then its general solicitor, and Paul A. Freund, who was described in the press at the time as "a protégé of Professor Felix Frankfurter and a former secretary to Justice Brandeis," together with other lawyers in the Department of Justice. Willkie himself played no role in arguing the other side. He had been afraid from the beginning of the case that the Supreme Court might duck the constitutional issue, restricting itself to the narrow problem of Wilson Dam power, and Willkie had been willing from the start to buy this power from the TVA. His press statement after the decision made it clear that he was as disappointed as Lilienthal and President Roosevelt that their major difference, over the right of TVA to build new dams and sell their power in competition with privately owned utilities, had not been ruled on.

American business was far less reserved in its reaction. Dr. Hugh S. Magill, president of the American Federation of Investors, warned that the TVA, "which has the blessing of Socialists, Communists and radicals," would be a major issue in the coming election. "This ambitious Marxian scheme affects, first, the utility industry," he said when the verdict was announced, "but if it should ultimately win, it will affect every free industry in our country, for those who advocate it have as their goal government ownership and political management of all industry."

Willkie himself followed two courses after the Ashwander decision. On the one hand, he tried to work out with Lilienthal a territorial division under which C. & S. would sell to TVA its properties inside an area roughly following the watershed line of the Tennessee River, with TVA agreeing to sell power outside this "ceded area" only to C. & S. On the other hand, he began new litigation designed to test the constitutionality of the TVA Act itself; in May, 1936, nineteen public utilities operating in the region and headed by C. & S. brought a broad suit against the TVA, seeking an injunction against its entire power program "except to the extent the production and sale of power at Wilson Dam had been held legal." The Ashwander decision had been the only Supreme Court decision yet in favor of the New Deal, and there was excellent reason to hope that a new test of the TVA would kill the entire experiment.

The territorial proposal grew out of long talks Willkie had during 1936 with Lilienthal, who was then TVA director in charge of power. "American stockholders in TVA and consumers of Commonwealth and Southern power," Lilienthal's biographer, Wilson Whitman, later wrote, "would have been interested in and perhaps edified by some of the conversations between David Lilienthal and Wendell Willkie which took place in Knoxville or New York or when the 'two farm boys from Indiana' in Willkie's friendly but inaccurate phrase, took a walk around the Lincoln Memorial in Washington. Not that their political talk was important; during the Landon campaign, Willkie argued that Landon would win in a photo finish, with Ohio casting the deciding vote."

The TVA then had eight power dams under construction or proposed, to cost about $235,800,000. The 1934 contract between C. & S. and TVA was to expire ninety days after the completion of the power house at the first of these, the Norris Dam, and this was scheduled for August, 1936. From that point on, TVA competition with C. & S. would change from a threat to an actuality. In May, Lilienthal proposed tentatively to Willkie a power pool for the whole Southeast, with what he called a "pool gateway rate." Willkie opposed this, according to Lilienthal, because it left the TVA free to sell power directly to municipalities. Willkie's counterproposal of a "ceded area" was objected to by

Lilienthal since he felt, and President Roosevelt agreed with him, that the act setting up the TVA made it necessary for that agency to give lower rates to public bodies and this would have been impossible under the Willkie proposal to distribute TVA power outside the "ceded area" only through C. & S. The discussions produced only one important result other than a resolution of the TVA board on August 4, 1936, that "in future contracts the Authority will not agree to territorial restrictions on the sale of Tennessee Valley Authority power to public agencies." The resolution itself was less important than the dissent, when it was voted, of Chairman Arthur E. Morgan. This was the first sign of dissension inside the TVA camp, and Willkie was not the man to miss it.

The new litigation to test the constitutionality of the TVA was started in an atmosphere as unfriendly as Willkie's talks with Lilienthal had been friendly. On March 5, in an N.B.C. network broadcast, Willkie had stepped up his public language on the TVA, calling it "the most useless and unnecessary of all the alphabetical joy-rides." The huge lake made by the Norris Dam was already beginning to fill; generating equipment had been ordered and was ready for delivery. The Wilson, Norris, and Wheeler Dams alone would generate some 500,000 horse-power, one and one-half times the entire generating capacity then used in all Tennessee, and public utility officials stated coldly that "a market for the electricity now is wanting and may never develop."

Willkie was now operating C. & S. at a profit. Net earnings had risen from one cent a share in 1935 to 13 cents a share in 1936 and they were to climb to 18 cents a share in 1937. During 1935 and 1936, six of his subsidiary companies were among the top ten in the nation in sales of electric appliances. But he could still point out that the preferred stocks of his Southern companies were selling at 30 to 40 points below par, and that he was unable to refund their bond issues, to take advantage of lower interest rates, because of the uncertainty about TVA competition. By November, this uncertainty would become an ugly fact.

So the suit was filed, in Birmingham, Alabama, on May 29, by nineteen operating companies affected by the TVA, and it was soon followed by appeals for temporary injunctions in most of the cities of the region. Underneath the legal language there was real bitterness. On July 24, the Alabama Power Company began to stake out a line from Vinemont to West Point, Alabama. "In less than an hour," Willkie complained, "after this work had commenced, the TVA began work in the same location with a crew of more than 100 TVA employees who proceeded to dig holes and set poles within a few feet of the poles being erected by the Alabama Power Company. On the same afternoon, [TVA] crews began stringing wires which in some instances touched the tops of the Alabama Power Company's poles. [They] continued and completed the work on this line on Saturday, July 25." "This fight," the *Nation* reported, "has taken on many of the colorful aspects of the old railway right-of-way battles. One Georgia woman took a shotgun and warded off the utility pole setters until the TVA could get in. At other places private-company poles have been burned down. The people are on the TVA's side."

This was a situation which called for at least one more attempt at compromise, and President Roosevelt made it on September 17 when he invited Willkie, the TVA, other government agencies, and private interests to a conference to explore the possibilities of "a power pool or grid system" in the Tennessee Valley. The conference was held on September 30. Thomas W. Lamont of J. P. Morgan and Company, Owen D. Young, Alexander Sachs of the Lehman Corporation, and all the top officials of the government concerned with power were invited, yet Willkie and the President dominated public interest in it. It was clearly an olive branch, and there was some reason for thinking it might be accepted on both sides. The President wanted the litigation called off; the Supreme Court was much on his mind at that moment and he had small hopes of anything he considered good coming from it. The utilities industry wanted the government to stop subsidizing towns and cities to build their own distribution plants. Here was the basis for a possible agreement.

The joker was the imminence of the November election. No one could be sure how much the President was thinking simply of a gesture which would look good to the voters. The 1934 contract between C. & S. and TVA would expire on November 3, Election Day itself, leaving TVA free to sell its power where it wished. Willkie and McNinch issued a joint statement after the conference, agreeing on another effort to extend the contract. TVA transmission lines had already been built in Tennessee, northern Mississippi, Alabama, and Georgia, and arrangements were pending with Memphis, Chattanooga, and Knoxville for new city-owned distribution systems. Was the Administration offering some sort of lasting truce in this struggle, Willkie must have wondered, or only playing for time until the votes had been counted?

On October 10, a three-month truce was announced in order to allow the pool discussions to continue. These were under the chairmanship of Louis B. Wehle, nephew of Supreme Court Justice Louis Brandeis, acting as Roosevelt's personal representative. Both the TVA and C. & S. agreed to freeze competition for another ninety days, and detailed stipulations were included in the truce agreement to make sure that neither side secured a competitive advantage over the other while the pool talks went on.

This was the last occasion in the long fight when Willkie took a position independent of the other public utility leaders. He discounted the political motives in Roosevelt's intervention, seeing it as "an act of political statesmanship calling for an equal degree of business statesmanship on his part." In this interview, published in the *New York Times* on October 11, 1936, he explained that there was now a tremendous investment of public funds in the Tennessee Valley, that a large volume of power would now be available there for all time, whether he liked it or not, "and that the statesmanlike thing to do is to negotiate a permanent settlement." Other utility leaders disagreed with him. They had not been represented at the conference. The newspaper story concluded that "on the larger issue, most utility men continue to express considerable doubt, in marked contrast to Mr. Willkie's views and position. As they are not currently parties at interest, however, they are obliged to remain intensely interested observers of the developments in Washington."

They had good reason to doubt, and in the end they proved to be more nearly correct than Willkie about the results of Roosevelt's intervention, whatever his motives were. On the very day the three-month truce was announced, October 10, 1936, Ickes approved a grant of $3,092,000 to Memphis to build a municipal distribution system, and Judge J. Lon Forest in the Tennessee Chancery Court denied a request for an injunction to prevent Chattanooga from issuing bonds for the same purpose.

On November 13, just after the election, Corcoran went to see Moley and they found themselves talking about utilities. When Corcoran said they were "licked," Moley asked if this meant that TVA was going to try to take over Commonwealth and Southern.

"You're damned right it will—and all the rest of them too," Corcoran said, according to Moley's account of the conversation.

"You realize what that means?"

"Well, we're going to squeeze them for a couple of years at any rate."

Moley told him that this kind of squeezing was hard to stop, it had a way of staying done. "Yes, I suppose so," was Corcoran's answer. "It won't come fast, but twenty years from now the government will own and operate all the electrical utilities in the country."

Willkie was not the only one confused about the President's plans. Senator Norris wrote Roosevelt from Nebraska on November 13, after the landslide against Landon had been counted, that he was very much disturbed over negotiations going on between the TVA and Wendell Willkie. He was against making any concessions to C. & S.—"an outfit who would destroy you in a minute if they had the power." He concluded: "I hope, Mr. President, that you would not give up the advantage this national victory has given us in this power fight . . . for God's sake, do not give our laurels of victory to those whom we have defeated." The President answered him on November 16. "Dear George," he wrote. "Yours of the thirteenth has come just before I leave. Nothing will be done while I am away, nor can any commitments be made. I agree with you. Don't worry."

Nothing was done. The pool discussions dragged on for a few weeks. Another and more drastic injunction was granted against the TVA on December 22 by Federal District Judge John Gore at Nashville, preventing it for six months from making any new contracts. Legal paralysis was replacing the temporary truce. Senator Norris charged C. & S. with bad faith, alleging that the injunction violated the White House truce, and Willkie answered angrily that the injunction had been pending at the time of the White House conference, and that the agreement had not covered litigation. Wehle backed him up. But on January 26, 1937, President Roosevelt announced that he was discontinuing the power pool conferences. He did not directly allege bad faith, but he claimed that the sweeping injunction against the TVA which had been won by the nineteen companies precluded any working agreement. "The implication of the President's announcement today," Ernest K. Lindley reported to the *New York Herald Tribune*, "is that the penalty of the utility companies that seek refuge in the courts will be war—at least until the companies mend their ways and show a more co-operative attitude."

On February 3, exactly ninety days after the first expiration date of the contract, TVA and C. & S. began to disentangle their complicated systems. This meant the loss to the TVA of its principal customer, C. & S., which had bought $800,000 worth of electricity from it in 1936, almost two-thirds of its total revenue from the sale of power. The injunction prevented it from signing up new customers. C. & S. lost a prime source of cheap power, and Willkie announced that his companies would have to spend $10,000,000 at once on the construction of steam plants to make up the difference. But Willkie still had his lawsuit, and in two days' time, on February 5, Roosevelt was to give Congress his plea for reorganizing the Supreme Court. This contained the explicit statement: "I defy anyone to read the opinions in the TVA case or the Duke power case and tell us exactly what we can do . . . to control flood and drought and generate cheap power . . . that will not be nullified as unconstitutional." Finally, the break between Lilienthal and Dr. Arthur E. Morgan had broken into violent headlines. Willkie could afford to wait, not for another patched-up and dubious truce but for a showdown.

CHAPTER EIGHT

The 1937 Recession

Some time in the spring of 1937, stock market prices and industrial production began a decline which was called a recession by Administration and business leaders and uglier words by those who were losing jobs. After a three-year upswing in economic activity, there were still between 7,000,000 and 8,000,000 unemployed in the country, and now the number threatened to grow again. This was the year of sit-in strikes. The C.I.O., with 3,718,000 members by 1937, moved into automobiles and then into steel with new techniques and new militancy, and many employers countered with violence and extremism of their own. The Administration rode out the storm, opening the year with Roosevelt's battle against Congress over reform of the Supreme Court and closing it with an attempt to meet the bleak economic situation by making peace with business and directing the nation's attention to the threat of war abroad.

A few business leaders went along with it. But this was the year in which both camps in the struggle over the New Deal split wide open. Roosevelt's left wing had found, largely in the C.I.O. organizing drive, new procedures and new machines more attractive than anything the Democratic party could offer. At the opposite extreme, the right wing of organized business had begun to revise, after the 1936 Landon defeat, its estimate of how quickly it could expect the political pendulum to swing back in its direction. The American Liberty League was riding high. Mussolini was beginning to prove that in addition to running trains on time he could operate a civil war in Spain. The long depression, which had undermined many people's faith in business, had also undermined many businessmen's faith in people. Even when they stopped short of this, a good many solid citizens noted how the New Deal had moved from recovery to reform and wondered—especially after Roosevelt's statement on his second inauguration: "I see one-third of a nation ill-housed, ill-clad, ill-nourished"—how much further the process was to go.

Willkie was clearly one of these. He was no Liberty Leaguer, and his faith in the democratic process grew stronger as he became more embroiled in political fighting. But the record of his speeches and his writings shows a steadily growing opposition to the New Deal and all its works from 1937 on. He was obviously aware of splits within the New Deal and he began for the first time to develop a position which could take advantage of them. But there is no evidence that he saw any convincing signs of retreat in Roosevelt's policies or any move to consolidate ground already gained by the New Deal. Even if he had, he could hardly have admitted it in public, for the TVA fight was to keep him in the role of a spokesman for business until its final settlement in February, 1939. Nor could he easily disavow those businessmen who were taking a more and more defiant pride in being called "economic royalists." He shared with Roosevelt, naturally in lesser degree, the dilemma of the Frenchman in the revolution who said as the mob passed his window: "There go my followers. I must follow them, for I am their leader."

"Prolonged controversy on any subject is apt to engender such bitterness that fair and dispassionate consideration becomes extremely difficult," Willkie wrote in 1937. There was little that was either fair or dispassionate, on either side, in the final stages of the C. & S.-TVA fight. In the same year, according to James A. Farley, Roosevelt felt about the utilities as they felt about him. "Every time you do anything for them," he told Farley, "they want something else. I am ready to sit down and work it out, but you can never pin them down. I had Wendell Willkie of the Commonwealth and Southern in here for a talk, but I couldn't get anywhere with him: you can't get anywhere with any of them."

Willkie

The value of Willkie's by-line and picture was on a steadily rising market. By 1937 he was being asked to write not only for financial and utility periodicals but also for the *Saturday Evening Post*, the *Atlantic Monthly*, the *New York Times*, and *Life*. This market, like his business associations, forced him to broaden his position. By July, 1937, he was attacking the flood control provisions of proposed authorities under the title "The Back Door to Government Ownership" in the *Saturday Evening Post*, and warning that the power industry was only the entering wedge for socialism. He attacked the Post Office Department the next month in the *Atlantic Monthly*, claiming that the American Telephone and Telegraph Company could deliver the mail more cheaply. Another theme he used more and more frequently was his defense of American business. He had formulated this first in a radio address over C.B.S. on April 15, 1936:

"I want to say a word about businessmen because it has been my good fortune to know a great many of them. Don't let a politician ever tell you that a businessman is a fat, white-vested individual with a top hat, sitting in a mahogany office inherited from his father and exercising a mysterious power over his fellow-men. That myth is old and silly. The real truth is that by and large businessmen are men who started to work at wages that were less than relief payments are today. They became business leaders because they worked hard enough and intelligently enough to rise to positions of responsibility and trust. They are as a class simple, sincere and ardently patriotic men. They constitute the most potentially constructive force in America."

Willkie knew what it was to be a businessman. He was, he used to say, a super-peddler. During these years, he gave more than one hundred days a year to traveling his territory, talking to salesmen, pushing the merchandising end of the electric power business. Carl Saunders, editor of the *Jackson* (Michigan) *Citizen Patriot*, wrote about Willkie's contacts with the buying public long before he became interested in the voting public: "Willkie himself is as approachable as a Pullman porter and as democratic as a candidate for sheriff."

The 1937 Recession

He tried to make every C. & S. employee a salesman. In one city an elevator operator, not recognizing the president of the company, rode him to the roof and back several times while he tried to talk him into buying an electric refrigerator. The results showed in the company's operating figures. Profits were 18 cents a share in 1937, 14 cents in 1938, 13 cents in 1939. Net sales had risen from $5,199,475 in 1933, the year Willkie took over, to $17,396,262 in 1937. In 1939, including Tennessee Electric Power Company figures only for the eight months before its sale to TVA, they amounted to $8,712,683. As he was constantly promising to do in public speeches, Willkie saw to it that this increased volume produced lower rates for consumers. Average residential rates per kilowatt and annual average residential consumption in the regions served by C. & S. showed his success in this:

	RATE	CONSUMPTION
1933	$0.0498	663 kilowatt-hours
1934	.0437	722
1935	.0396	821
1936	.0353	955
1937	.0328	1,092
1938	.0315	1,173
1939	.0309	1,196

TVA supporters could claim, and did, that this was a result of TVA competition. Willkie could answer, and did, that rates had been lowered faster and further in the Northern areas of the system than in the Southern areas directly affected by TVA competitive rates.

While he was running his company, he concentrated in his public speeches on the TVA fight. His defense was a recital of the good record of C. & S., which was serving over a million customers in eleven states without any outstanding litigation over its utility rates, and repetition of his 1935 offer of peace with TVA, which had never been accepted. His offense was a series of elaborations on the general theme—it became one of his slogans—that "the Tennessee River waters four states and drains the nation." TVA's failure to pay taxes was a favorite debating point; he never admitted in public that the TVA did pay out large sums "in lieu of taxes" just as the TVA spokesman never admitted in public that these sums were smaller than the taxes paid by competing utility concerns. "Every time a citizen in Tupelo, Mississippi, turns on his light," ran Willkie's line, "all of you and your fellow-citizens contribute to the payment of his bill."

Willkie knew that the odds were against him in the fight for public opinion. Sometimes he admitted it. "The American people have been stirred," he wrote in the *Atlantic Monthly* in 1937, "by stories of what is happening to the soil in the great agricultural areas in the Middle West. Many thousands have seen the huge TVA dams with the water banked impressively behind them, and have seen green life returning to soil that was previously bleak and pitted. They have been told about plans to make the river navigable, about the plans to prevent floods. They have naturally been as enthusiastic about these objectives as about the general idea of 'cheap power.' The TVA has therefore appeared to be on the side of the angels in the controversy between it and the utilities. But the conservation program of the TVA is only a masquerade."

Here he quoted Lilienthal, Norris, and Roosevelt himself to prove that power was the real reason for the new dams. "There seems to be some inclination to forget that these dams are not being built for scenic effect," Lilienthal had said on March 1, 1935, in a speech at Knoxville. "These millions of dollars are not being spent merely to increase business activity in this area. These dams are power dams. They are being built because they will produce electric power. That power must be marketed in order to pay for the dams." Willkie quoted this up and down the country to prove the dishonesty of the "multi-purpose" aspect of the TVA. He coupled it with an estimate that the TVA expenditure for flood control was 250 times the average annual loss from floods. This was not true, even as a debating point, and in the spring of 1937, when the Ohio River went on one of its periodic rampages, the Tennessee River was under control, so Willkie's argument won few converts in that region.

But it reinforced his general warning that the TVA was a first step towards socialism. Another quotation he used extensively was from Norman Thomas, who had called the TVA "the only genuinely socialist product of the New Deal. It is a beautiful flower in a garden of weeds." It was socialism, Willkie argued, both because it put the government in business and because it endangered the property of private investors in competing utility concerns. His growing interest in politics, together with the pressures working on him as the fight grew rougher, led him to denounce the government in business, but as president of C. & S. he was still chiefly interested in what was going to happen to its properties in the TVA area. It is probable that Willkie knew as early as the end of 1935 that in the long run he would have to sell these properties to TVA. Once the Norris Dam was going up, Willkie was not the man to believe that anyone would pull it down again. But it could only help him in the sale to continue his attack against the TVA, lock, stock, and barrel.

It was true, of course, that he had no way of knowing what the terms of sale might be. In November, 1937, Willkie ridiculed publicly the government's claim that it had no intention of damaging private investors. He pointed out that Tennessee Electric Power 6 per cent preferred stock was selling at $50 a share. "It is earning its dividends by a very substantial margin," he said, "and it is paying them, and it has earned them right through the depression and it has paid them. You can go right out and get a 12 per cent yield, and if you believe the government, that stock is worth $100. This is the hottest market tip you ever had, provided you believe the government. Now understand, if you buy and lose, don't blame it on me!" Just fifteen months later, that same stock was redeemed for $100 a share, and anyone who bought it on Willkie's tip would have had his 12 per cent yield and doubled his investment, too.

Besides his speeches and his articles, Willkie used paid newspaper advertising as a weapon in his fight. His New Year's Day statement as president of C. & S. was published in this way and it summed up his entire case under the caption: "The Cost of an Unsolved Problem." After citing various figures to show that the Northern companies in the C. & S. system were doing better than the Southern companies, it pointed out that refunding of bonds and preferred stock at lower interest rates—impossible because of the "impending threat of competition and duplication by the Tennessee Valley Authority"—would save more than $6,000,000 a year, or one-half of the entire revenue received annually from the 400,000 domestic electric customers of the Southern companies. If the problem could be solved, Willkie promised, there would be rate reductions, more men would be put to work, security holders would be protected, and taxpayers would be relieved of heavy burdens.

When Roosevelt called off his pool conferences and the TVA—C. & S. contract finally expired, the dispute between Lilienthal and Dr. Arthur E. Morgan had become public, and it gave Willkie new ammunition. Since the very beginning of TVA the two directors had differed on a wide range of problems, from labor relations to the "multi-purpose" formula which was being slowly worked out in the Tennessee Valley. As early as January, 1937, this difference was becoming acute over the question of attracting industry to the valley from other parts of the country and over the subsidizing of municipal transmission and distribution systems. Both of these were Lilienthal schemes, approved by Harcourt Morgan, the third member of the board. Dr. Arthur Morgan believed that such policies were recriminatory, backed by the left wing of the New Deal in revenge for the past excesses of the utility industry, and he did not hesitate to say so publicly. "A sovereign government should not act in a spirit of retaliation," he wrote in the *New Republic* in December, 1936, "of getting even for past abuses. Wrongdoing should be stopped, abuses corrected . . . but in so far as honorable and necessary investments in power utilities are honestly administered . . . private power utilities should be looked upon as honorable undertakings, and investments in them should be given the same consideration as any other properly made investment."

Willkie was wise enough not to identify himself publicly with Dr. Morgan when this dispute first started, but the press was quick to pounce on it. "For a concededly honest man," Jay

The 1937 Recession

Franklin wrote, "Dr. Morgan could have done little more for the private utilities had he been on the payroll of the Commonwealth and Southern." Dorothy Thompson answered at once: "For Mr. Franklin, and for Senator Norris and Mr. Lilienthal, this is plainly not a question of finding the best method for giving the people cheap power and protecting their interests, but is a fight between the forces of good and the forces of evil. Such a fight, being completely subjective, is never compromisable."

Congress moved in, too, realizing that the President's cancellation of the pool discussions had been in effect an important victory for Lilienthal over his older and more conservative colleague. Senator Kenneth McKellar, of Tennessee, who had at first opposed the TVA and who was later to fight bitterly against Lilienthal, was temporarily on the TVA side, together with E. H. (Boss) Crump of Memphis, and he demanded angrily that Dr. Arthur Morgan resign "if he has cold feet." But the dispute simmered for months, while the TVA itself grew day by day more enormously visible in the Tennessee hills and the chief actors in the struggle over its future continued to denounce each other in public while they jockeyed for position in a final settlement.

Roosevelt, like the nation's press, was occupied for the first half of 1937 with the Supreme Court battle, and the legal fate of TVA clearly hung on its outcome. The Republicans, with less than one-fourth of the House and only fourteen Senators, were powerless to block the President, but the debate over the court issue split the Democratic party wide open. Roosevelt never got the legislation he asked for, which was defeated by the narrow margin of one vote in the Senate committee, but the Supreme Court began to hand down less conservative decisions, sustaining minimum wage legislation, the Wagner Labor Act, and the Social Security Act. Then Justice Van Devanter's retirement opened the way for Roosevelt's first appointment to the court. This was to help the TVA, by the time the suits challenging it reached the court, but the defeat of Roosevelt's legislative proposals on the court had already widened measurably the split inside the New Deal. If Willkie had known for some time that he would eventually have to accept a compromise settlement, there were now clear signs for Lilienthal and the public power group that they faced the same prospect.

The clearest sign of all was the fate of the President's request, which he sent to Congress on June 3, 1937, for "legislation for national planning and development of natural resources through seven regional authorities." The bill, which was introduced by Senator Norris, was dubbed "the seven TVA's bill," and Roosevelt's message in support of it was strong. It proposed an Atlantic Seaboard Authority, with jurisdiction from Maine to Florida; a Great Lakes-Ohio Valley Authority; a Missouri River Authority; an Arkansas Valley Authority; a Southwestern Authority, including the Colorado River basin; and a Columbia Valley Authority to cover the Pacific Northwest. This was a return to Roosevelt's threat made at Tupelo, Mississippi, more than two years before, when he had promised to repeat what was happening there "in every state of the union before we get through." *

The utilities were no less alarmed this time than they had been before. Willkie claimed that the scheme would cost $35,-000,000,000, approximately double the national debt. The press poured ridicule on the plan, and the utilities lobby moved in on Congress with all its force. But this was the last major bid of the public power group within the New Deal. Congress shelved the bill, and by October 6, 1937, Roosevelt himself repudiated its nickname, saying at a press conference that all he had had in mind was planning agencies while the TVA was also an administrative agency. The court fight had taken some of the starch out of the New Deal. By November, Roosevelt was engaged in another effort to make peace with Willkie and the public utilities, and although the bill was one of four items of legislation for which he had summoned a special session of Congress, it was allowed to die on its shelf without protest from the White House.

The day before the press conference at which Roosevelt abandoned his "seven TVA's bill," two separate events had taken place which were vitally to affect the development of the New

* See page 76.

Deal and thus of the Willkie-TVA fight. In Chicago, the President made a speech in which he called for a quarantine of aggressor nations in Europe; this was the beginning of the shift from domestic to foreign policy which eventually ended the New Deal. In Washington, Senator Black took Justice Van Devanter's seat on the Supreme Court, considerably advancing the breakup of the log jam which had held so many New Deal measures for so long. At the time, neither event could be seen in its true importance. The fight continued between business and the Administration. The District Court trial, designed to upset the whole TVA, began in Chattanooga in November with Raymond T. Jackson of Cleveland heading a battery of lawyers for the eighteen utility companies, and James Lawrence Fly, general counsel for the TVA, leading an equally impressive list of government lawyers. There was more than a year to go before any final settlement of the old dispute. But with the Supreme Court issue won, even if not in his own way, President Roosevelt was beginning to slow up the pace of reform, and once again events were to move more quickly than the minds of politicians, businessmen, or the public.

Conversations between Willkie and Lilienthal continued throughout 1937, but with no concrete results. On November 12, the President announced that he was calling still another series of conferences with utility heads, this time offering to make peace if the utilities would revise their methods of rate valuation. Willkie went to Washington from Chattanooga to see the President, but an infected tooth kept Roosevelt in bed, and the conference between the two men did not take place until November 23, when they talked for an hour and a half.

The core of Roosevelt's new proposals was an effort to persuade the utilities to accept the "prudent investment" basis of rate valuation, arguing that any other system would fail to write down the heavy overcapitalization which he charged was general in the industry. But he was conciliatory on other issues, pointing out that the TVA had not yet hurt operations of the private utilities in Tennessee, that government power projects could not at best serve more than 10 or 20 per cent of the country's needs, and that it was desirable to have the utilities expand their plants as much as possible. The scrapping of the Administration's "seven T.V.A.'s" bill was a tangible peace offering even if its effect was considerably diminished by the President's sending to various Congressional committees and Federal agencies, at the same time, a report by the New York State Power Authority showing the utilities' expenditures for propaganda against public power and presenting figures to show that the government could produce hydroelectric power at much lower cost than private utilities could produce power by steam plants.

After his conference with the President, Willkie left a memorandum at the White House. He accepted the "prudent investment" theory of rate valuation for future determination of values and he agreed that any other system, to be used for determining present values, should not be allowed to recognize watered capitalization of the kind the President had charged. The President, in reporting the talk at a press conference, withheld the text of Willkie's memorandum and summed up Willkie's position by quoting him on "a general feeling" around the country of government competition and interference which was preventing the utilities from contributing their full share to national recovery.

Floyd L. Carlisle, chairman of the Consolidated Edison Company of New York and of the Niagara Hudson Power Company, and other utility executives followed Willkie to the White House. The olive branch continued to look like a sword to the conservative press and to many businessmen. In the phrase "the general feeling," it was reported by Arthur Krock, Willkie "said a mouthful. He put his finger on one of the major reasons for that uneasiness in the business and financial community which is making a big recession out of a little one. Casual inquiry reveals that Mr. Roosevelt would get about the same reply from hundreds of other businessmen whom he has as much reason to respect as Mr. Willkie." The *New York Herald Tribune* rejoiced that "there are at least some feeble signs that the President is at last opening his mind, so far as his outlook on the future of the power industry of the country is concerned," but it concluded that something much more tangible would have to come from the White House before the deep breach could be closed.

The feeble signs were enough to arouse the advocates of public power. Representative Rankin called on the President to spurn any compromise with "purring" power leaders and Senator Norris repeated his old faith that the President would make no vital concessions. The full text of the Willkie memorandum eventually leaked to the press, and showed that Willkie had made a series of concrete demands, in order to abate "the general feeling." These included modification of the death-sentence clause in the 1935 holding company act, so as to eliminate all intermediate holding companies within three years but to leave parent companies in their present ownership of property; a requirement that TVA rates be set on the same cost-accounting basis required of public utilities by the Federal Power Commission; action to prevent towns and cities from building new distribution facilities without purchasing the existing private plants; a ban on Federal gifts or grants for this purpose; and a negotiated division of rural areas between the utilities and the Federal Government.

The fact that Roosevelt had not released these concrete demands might well have shown that the whole economic program of the New Deal was in course of revision. But at the time it showed Willkie's friends and supporters only the President's bad faith. His version of the conversation, the *New York Herald Tribune* commented, had been another weapon in the war. "One was asked to picture," the paper wrote in an editorial, "the usually informed and articulate Mr. Willkie stammering and stuttering as he attempted a hopeless defense of the position of the utilities—falling back constantly on a single refrain: 'It is the general feeling.'"

Yet the Administration's economic mind was deeply divided by the beginning of 1938. More and more olive branches sprouted in Washington, but they wilted quickly. At a January press conference, Roosevelt asked: "Why have any holding companies?" He explained later that this had not been a declaration of war, but business was too jittery to take this kind of comment in its stride. "One day, business was severely criticized," the Beards recorded; "the next day, it was appeased. Such oscillations continued until near the middle of February when at a regular press conference the President lapsed into almost complete silence on the battle over business interests. That, at least, was a novel feature of the political scene."

Inside the business community there was as little agreement as inside the New Deal over what were the next steps to be taken in the long struggle. Utility leaders continued their full offensive on the public front. Letters to stockholders, paid advertising in the press, and a steadily increasing propaganda campaign backed up the litigation which by now was well on its way towards final rulings. Willkie was one of the forty lawyers who appeared for the public utilities in the trial at Chattanooga which had started in November, 1937. They presented evidence for four solid weeks, with Willkie himself as their final witness. When cross-examination was invited, Fly picked up a bunch of papers, started toward the witness stand, but halted briefly for a conference with his staff. He then announced there would be no cross-examination. "I am sorry," Willkie commented.

Much of this direct testimony was devoted to an incident which showed how far business was from an effective united front. Edgar M. Queeny, then president of the Monsanto Chemical Company of St. Louis, was building a new plant at Columbia, Tennessee, and he had agreed on all contract terms for the purchase of electric power from C. & S. At the last moment, the contract fell through, Queeny charging, in a telegram which Willkie read to the court, that TVA operations in the region cast serious doubt on the financial responsibility of the Tennessee Electric Power Company, the C. & S. subsidiary involved. Willkie cited the incident to prove damage to his company by TVA. It was subsequently disclosed in court that Monsanto closed the contract with TVA instead. Six years later, Queeny was to be a prime mover in Missouri business circles which attacked Willkie for being too liberal in his alleged "me too" attitude towards the economic philosophy of the New Deal.

On January 6, 1938, three years after his first full-dress debate with Lilienthal on the TVA issue, Willkie debated Assistant

The 1937 Recession

United States Attorney General (later Justice of the Supreme Court) Jackson on America's Town Meeting of the Air. N.B.C. carried the debate on a nation-wide hookup; more than two million persons heard it. By this time, the arguments were familiar on both sides, and only their tone could serve to show what strategy each side was following. Both men were polite. Jackson carefully distinguished between Willkie and "that small but loud section of the business world which has been ganging up on democracy." He called Willkie "one of the pioneers—stimulated no doubt by a little competition from TVA—in the adoption of a low-price, high-volume basis for his industry. He ventured and it paid." Willkie noted the friendlier tone of Roosevelt's latest speeches and added: "I hope that at last we can have done with the epithets, the calling of names, the catchwords—catchwords which have been so glibly used, such as economic royalists, bourbons, moneyed aristocrats, banker-control, holding companies and the nonsense about sixty ruling families." His list of catchwords did not include socialist, Soviet, Bolshevik, foreign-inspired, or revolutionary—all of which were still being heavily overworked in utilities' propaganda—but neither did he use these words himself. Without them, he did to his opponent what General Hugh Johnson called "a nice job of cooperage on a particularly tough barrel."

A few weeks later, on February 28, he spoke before the Economic Club of Detroit, and it was clear that there was no peace, not even a truce. "If it is my baby that's hurt now," he said, "it may be your baby later. With all the earnestness of which I am capable I want to state that those who wish to prevent government invasion of their business had better begin to preach the doctrine now. At the same time I might as well warn you what will happen to you if you do. From personal experience I know very well what happens to those individuals who defend their causes against government attack. You may, for example, have your income tax examined several times with a magnifying glass. You may be called an economic royalist. You may be chastised in official speeches. You may be called down to Washington to be questioned as to your personal affairs. You may have your name dragged into political investigations by legislative committees of this or that state. You may suffer and your families may suffer by having your reputation smeared with the mud of false insinuation. All of that may happen to you, and I can assure you that it is not pleasant.

"But isn't the risk worth it when you consider what is at stake? Isn't the personal discomfort and annoyance a far less important thing than the preservation of the free enterprise which has been responsible for the extraordinarily high level of the American civilization?"

The language was full-blown, sounding unhappily like what the New Deal wanted the public to believe economic royalists sounded like. Willkie was doubling his bets, win or lose, and this was a lifelong habit which always put him in danger of caricaturing himself. Once caught in a bitter fight, it never occurred to him to ask how he had got there, or how he could get out of it except by winning. *Power,* a play produced in New York in 1937 by the WPA-financed Federal Theater, had a character in it called Wendell Willkie, heavily built, wearing unrimmed glasses like those Willkie used to wear, making speeches about the American Way of Life. Some of Willkie's speeches in 1937 read now as if he had been cribbing from this satire of himself, just as some of President Roosevelt's letters read as if he had used drafts prepared by his worst Union League Club enemies. This was the democratic process, which shapes leaders in the image of their followers. In times big with change, it gives the opponents of any man who sticks his neck out a chance to rearrange the features on his face without his even knowing it.

CHAPTER NINE

The Final Sale

THE first months of 1938 were full of bad legal news for the utilities. On January 3, the Supreme Court refused to allow power companies to use injunctions to stop Federal loans and grants to municipalities for the purpose of building competing plants. Another decision in a California rate case showed that the Supreme Court was at least well on the way to accepting Roosevelt's "prudent investment" theory of valuation for rate-making purposes. On January 21, Judge Florence Allen read the seventy-five-hundred-word decision of a United States District Court in Chattanooga rejecting Willkie's suit to hold the TVA unconstitutional. Finally, on March 28, the Supreme Court by a 6 to 1 verdict instructed utility companies to register with the Securities and Exchange Commission and to disclose their financial operations as required by the holding company act.

This was a series of major defeats for Willkie's side in the long conflict with the New Deal, and it marked a startling reversal of judicial policy. When the Supreme Court fight had been at its most bitter stage, in the spring of 1937, the court had thrown out the NRA, the AAA, the Farm Mortgage Moratorium, the Guffey Coal Act, and a long list of other New Deal measures. The court's sanction in 1936 of TVA power sales at the Wilson Dam and its verdict on the gold clause had been, in fact, the only New Deal measures upheld by the highest judicial body in the nation. By the end of 1938, the tide had completely turned and the TVA was the only extant New Deal creation which was still without some judicial sanction by the Supreme Court.

Yet the process of fission within both the New Deal and the

business community had gone too far to make possible any major compromise on the issues which had been sharpened in the years of public controversy. Negotiating the sale of C. & S. properties within the TVA area was at best a long, slow job and it was complicated by the multiplying splits within the TVA and the whole New Deal. Similarly, the working out of a formula under which the utilities could finally comply with the holding company act was slowed up by serious differences of opinion and strategy inside the public utility camp. President Roosevelt, from his "quarantine" speech on October 5, 1937, through the grim year of Munich, was turning more and more to foreign policy to hold together the disparate elements in his political support. Willkie, not yet in politics but already the most frequently headlined businessman in the country, could find a comparable rallying cry only in a constantly growing attack on the entire New Deal.

Most of his time was devoted to driving an exceptionally hard and successful bargain with TVA for his C. & S. stockholders. Yet his growing sense of political timing forced deliberate delays to secure the maximum profit from final court actions, from the Morgan-Lilienthal feud, and from the widening schism between Roosevelt and his more radical followers. He used these delays to denounce the TVA, and increasingly the whole New Deal. During 1938 and 1939, the pattern was set in the public mind which made possible Willkie's sudden emergence into political leadership in 1940. The same pattern made inescapable the polarization of political philosophy which gave Willkie, for a short time, the titular leadership of the most conservative elements in American business. A few years earlier, the same kind of forces in the party system under democracy had pushed Willkie's rival, Roosevelt, into titular leadership of far more radical elements than would have been indicated by his background or his convictions. Now the same process was pushing Willkie in the opposite direction. As he grew more prominent and more powerful, he grew steadily less able to stick to his own definition of the function of business in a democracy, or to pick his own path towards the industrialization of an agricultural nation which had engrossed him ever since he left Indiana. All that was suggested in the American mind by the phrase "big business" was thrust upon him in these years, and he had to work with it.

The Supreme Court decision validating PWA grants and loans to municipalities to build new municipal power plants gave TVA unrestricted use of a weapon against which Willkie and C. & S. could not hope to fight. The decision rejected a suit by the Alabama Power Company for injunctions against Federal aid to four municipalities in Alabama, and was unanimous, with Justice Black recorded as "concurring" presumably because he had been in the Senate when the act creating PWA was passed. The mere fact that the power companies might suffer loss from lawful competition, Justice George Sutherland held, did not establish the claim of the power companies that they had suffered a legal wrong. Willkie, who had planned the case for his subsidiary, the Alabama Power Company, was quick to point out that the decision contradicted President Roosevelt's recent assurances that the utilities had nothing to fear from government competition.

"It means," he said, "that the Federal Administration can continue its present policy of making outright gifts to municipalities with which to duplicate the distribution systems of existing utilities. Of course, no utility company can successfully compete with a municipal plant built with free money and upon which the municipality does not have to make a return. This is particularly true in areas such as the Tennessee Valley Authority where the municipality can buy its wholesale supply of power at below cost from the TVA.

"The decision is unfortunate from the standpoint of the utility, but the Supreme Court has spoken and it is the last word. No one can now change the policy except the Federal Administration itself."

Secretary of the Interior Ickes made it quickly clear that the decision was not academic. As PWA Administrator he announced plans to proceed in twenty-three states with sixty-one municipal power undertakings involving a total cost of $146,412,408. Of this sum, he was allocating $61,225,544 as loans and $38,412,408 as outright gifts.

The rate decision, which was announced on the same day, did not directly involve Willkie. The ruling was read by Chief Justice Hughes against the Pacific Gas and Electric Company, with five Justices joining him, Justices Pierce Butler and James C. McReynolds dissenting, and Justice Sutherland not participating. It held that original cost was valid as a measure of valuation for rate-making, and this was, if not a complete reversal of the Supreme Court's earlier position, at least a bad blow to the utilities' argument that reproduction cost less depreciation was the only fair method. Roosevelt had argued that this latter method opened the door for watered capital values and forced up the rates charged to electric power consumers.

If Roosevelt was thinking of peace with the utilities, there remained plenty of others in the Administration who were still full of fight. John M. Carmody, Rural Electrification Administrator, fired a blast at Willkie on January 10, charging that C. & S. was sabotaging the REA by refusing to sell power to a farmers' co-operative in Michigan, building spite lines to hamper the co-operative, and forcing power on farmers who did not want it. Willkie replied the same day—a habit of promptness he had learned in fighting the TVA and which he never forgot in later political campaigns—that no application for power had been made by the co-operative until ten days before. But the spite was there on both sides, whether or not it produced spite lines. The same week, commenting on Willkie's memorandum left with him on November 23, Roosevelt tossed off his comment which the press interpreted as a desire to eliminate all holding companies, of all types. At the same time, he hailed the Supreme Court decision on government grants to publicly owned power projects.

Again Willkie answered quickly, this time with a "suggestion as a last resort in a desperate situation." He proposed to sell out to TVA. Two-thirds of the total utility investment in the nation would be wiped out, he warned, if the President's suggestion should be followed by cities taking over private distribution systems. So he saw no alternative, he said, to selling out, and he proposed that the companies in the Tennessee Valley be purchased intact by the government at a price to be fixed by negotia-

The Final Sale

tion or to be determined by three arbitrators—one to be named by the President, one by the Supreme Court of the United States, and one by the utilities. This was not the first offer Willkie had made to sell out to TVA; it had been made in writing to Roosevelt on January 6, 1937, during the White House conferences on a proposed power pool. But its timing plunged Willkie into the middle of a stormy national debate over the still-continuing recession.

Senator Norris and Representative Rankin moved into the debate at once with approval of a new campaign against all holding companies and a blessing on the idea that TVA should buy the C. & S. properties, at "a fair price to the government," as Rankin quickly added. Robert H. Jackson, speaking at Rochester, told business that Roosevelt's assault on holding companies had been no emotional outburst but a deliberate statement of policy. Representative Andrew J. May of Kentucky, chairman of the House Military Affairs Committee, which was in charge of matters connected with TVA, opposed the entire plan of buying private utilities, although he said that he sympathized with Willkie's motives in making the offer because the latter was "right up against the wall." The public power group in Congress backed the offer warily, suspicious of its maker, and the reaction of business was summed up by a *New York Herald Tribune* editorial on January 17, 1938, which gave the plan an equally tentative blessing as having "much to commend it in equity." There was nothing tentative in its admiration for "the bulldog-like Wendell L. Willkie, head of the Commonwealth and Southern Corporation and 'unofficial spokesman' for the public utilities." The editorial called him "easily one of the most articulate of Administration critics. And he is one who ignores generalizations and talks facts; one who insists that the cards in the controversy be laid on the table at all times for the public to see, and one whom it is therefore difficult if not impossible to put off or satisfy with vague and shadowy reassurances."

C. & S. preferred stock dropped from $40 to $36.25 on the news of Willkie's offer to sell, the common stock dropping $.25 to $1.60. The *New York Herald Tribune's* financial editor reported that there was no doubt that business in general was in accord with Willkie's expression of despair. But he added, and this was illustrative of the divisions within the business world, that "statements to this effect were surprisingly lacking yesterday. There is an understandable desire, in these days of government regulation, to keep in the background."

Lilienthal went to see Roosevelt on January 18 with Harcourt Morgan, McNinch, and SEC Chairman (later Justice of the Supreme Court) William O. Douglas. He then issued a public statement rejecting the Willkie offer as "radical" and proposing instead the sale of C. & S. distribution systems to those cities wishing to buy, and of such transmission lines, dams, and power plants to TVA as the latter wanted to buy. "I need hardly say," he explained, "that TVA cannot and will not buy anything but useful physical assets. It has no authority nor has it any intention to pay for water or write-ups in these companies. Nor would TVA be a party to recommending that any municipality pay inflated prices." Willkie replied immediately that any piece-by-piece dismemberment of his operating companies would result in "tremendous" loss to the utility investors. "If the investment in this business is to be saved," he said, "these utility systems must be bought as systems."

The District Court decision upholding the constitutionality of TVA did not come until January 21, but Willkie had made his offer on a safe prediction that the verdict would go against him. Fly, general counsel for TVA, had been so sure of the verdict that when Judge Allen finished reading it—the decision required forty minutes to read—he had a prepared statement ready for the press terming it "a milestone in the conservation movement." Willkie announced at once that the decision would be appealed to the Supreme Court. A more immediate result was that the TVA, its legality affirmed, authorized Lilienthal to negotiate the possible purchase of utility properties. Governor Gordon Browning of Tennessee urged the President to accept the Willkie offer. This set off a political row with Senator McKellar, who was feuding with Browning and Senator George L. Berry, head of the A. F. of L. Printing Pressmen's Union and claimant against the TVA for some marble quarries which had been flooded by the Gilbertsville Dam. McKellar called Browning "the voice of

Fitzpatrick in the St. Louis *Post-Dispatch*

the private power trust," but a Tennessee primary fight was
going on and epithets carried little real meaning.

The fight was still more than a year from its final settlement,
and a major factor in the long delay was the public airing, at
long last, of the conflict between Lilienthal and Dr. Arthur E.
Morgan inside the directorate of TVA. Rumors of serious disagreement between the two men had been heard since the fall
of 1933. In 1936, the *Nation* had predicted that the "internal
policy war . . . will probably not be ended short of the retire-

131

ment of one or the other." Dr. Arthur Morgan had protested to Roosevelt, unsuccessfully, against Lilienthal's reappointment in May, 1936, and the dispute had simmered on fitfully, giving Willkie one of his chief reasons for holding out to the end. On March 4, 1938, Roosevelt released a bitter, nine-page attack on Dr. Arthur Morgan which Lilienthal and Harcourt A. Morgan had handed him during their January 18 meeting, and the feud flared into headlines which were to continue for many months.

One issue in what was essentially a personal conflict was closely linked to Willkie, since Dr. Arthur Morgan had argued almost from the start of TVA that it should purchase the C. & S. properties in the Tennessee Valley and set up a true yardstick to test the relative merits of public and private power ownership. Underneath this issue was a deeper difference between the two men which was also part of the central problem with which Willkie had been wrestling in his effort to define in his own mind the function of business in a new, postdepression America. To Dr. Arthur Morgan, as one Lilienthal supporter, J. Charles Poe in the *Nation,* put it, "nothing is sure except the experimental attitude and the belief that the people cannot always be trusted to make the right choices." He was interested in creating a new way of life in the valley, and many of his plans took little account of electricity. He was frankly skeptical of much in modern industry and of nearly all businessmen. "Business ability," he once wrote, "is a power which has no necessary relation to a high type of intelligence and character." He talked of reviving old folkways, and he encouraged the dancing, basket weaving, wood carving, and other handicrafts which were so much ammunition for the propagandists on Willkie's side when they tried ridicule against the TVA. He believed deeply in the scientific method of free inquiry and what he called "the engineering approach." And he saw no conflict with the privately owned utilities which could not be solved by reason and fairness.

Lilienthal reacted against something in this approach which seemed to him authoritarian. He was happy to have Dr. Arthur Morgan in charge of building dams, but they clashed whenever power or the planning of the valley came into question. As early as 1936, Lilienthal was stating his position in these terms: "There

The Final Sale

is, as I see it, no turning back from the machine. Perplexing as the problem is, we cannot admit defeat. We cannot return to a simpler standard of living, for that is to begin a retreat—a retreat which will only stop when we reach the level of the fourth century. I am against beginning that retreat. I am against 'basket weaving' and all that that implies, except perhaps as a temporary expedient. . . . We cannot confess our failure, we cannot prepare for 'the second coming of Daniel Boone' in a simple handicraft economy."

Lilienthal was also, unlike Dr. Arthur Morgan, in that faction of the New Deal which believed the fight with the utilities to be unavoidable. In 1934 he had gone to England to see at first hand the British "grid" plan for pooling power, a much-publicized example of co-operation between public and private enterprise. He had made a speech from London over a B.B.C. network in which he said: "To understand what is going on throughout America in these stirring times, there are two facts which you must have clearly in mind. First, you should know that President Roosevelt continues to hold the influence and the devotion of an overwhelming majority of American men and women from all classes and groups. And you should also realize that a powerful and reactionary opposition has begun a violent attack on his policy and on him. The outcome of this bitter controversy will determine the future course of American life."

During the January, 1937, crisis in the C. & S.-TVA conflict, this difference of opinion between the two TVA directors had already been public knowledge. When Willkie's article on "Political Power" was published in the *Atlantic Monthly* in August, 1937, the editors asked Dr. Arthur Morgan for a rebuttal, entitled "Public Ownership of Power," which they published in the September issue. W. L. Sturdevant, Director of Information for TVA and therefore a subordinate of Dr. Arthur Morgan's, wrote a reproachful letter to the magazine, complaining that both sides of the issue had not been presented. Willkie labeled this an "amazing statement" and insisted that both sides of the question had been given by the two articles. Other utility sources drew the more frank conclusion that Dr. Arthur Morgan was "getting kicked from under," as one of them phrased it.

On the same day as the President's release of the attack on Dr. Arthur Morgan by his two fellow-directors, Lilienthal and Dr. Harcourt Morgan wrote a letter to Willkie proposing negotiations for the purchase of all the C. & S. properties in the Tennessee Valley for a price to be determined on a cost-minus-depreciation formula. The offer to buy the systems intact was a real concession, partly to the views of Dr. Arthur Morgan, but the price formula was almost certain to be turned down by Willkie. Willkie accepted the negotiations, proposing a sixty- or ninety-day standstill period during which no PWA grants or loans would be made to municipalities and also suggesting that the negotiations be turned over to a disinterested committee. He suggested such men as Dr. Clarence A. Dykstra, president of the University of Wisconsin; Dr. Karl Compton, president of the Massachusetts Institute of Technology; and Professor Felix Frankfurter, later on the Supreme Court but then of the Harvard Law School. The bulk of his answer was a defense of a valuation formula worked out by J. D. Ross, Federal Administrator of the Bonneville power project, and this formula had been warmly defended by Dr. Arthur Morgan in a letter he had written to thirty-five Congressmen on February 16.

This was the key to the timing of all these moves. In the Lilienthal-Harcourt Morgan attack on their fellow-director, they accused him of unwillingness to be reasonable in "give-and-take" discussion, violation of "good sportsmanship" in refusing to abide by majority decisions, "obstructing" and "subverting" adopted policies, collaborating with "the former chief engineer of the Insull utility system" in a recommendation of power-pooling policy, "impugning the integrity" of his associates, and co-operation with a utility executive on a memorandum against a decision of the board. The last charge was the only one that was new. There seemed no doubt then that it referred to Willkie and to the Ross proposal—a question of vital importance in the settlement of a price for the C. & S. properties. Willkie said in New York: "It can't be I, because I never collaborated with Dr. Morgan on the preparation of any memorandum." It later developed that the charge actually referred to a memorandum on power pools which Dr. Arthur Morgan had prepared the preceding winter for Roosevelt. But there was no doubt in March, 1938, that Willkie and Dr. Arthur Morgan were both backing, openly, the same Ross formula on compensation for private systems taken over by the government.

Within a few days, the personal feud between the TVA directors had taken on the proportions of a public brawl, completely eclipsing in the newspapers the actual beginning of negotiations between Willkie and Lilienthal on the price to be paid for the C. & S. properties. All the Republican and anti-Administration forces of the country were hoping to find a Teapot Dome scandal buried somewhere in the New Deal record, and Roosevelt's hope to avoid a major investigation was doomed from the outset. "In the heart of America," Senator S. Styles Bridges of New Hampshire sounded off, "a new star has arisen in the constellation of authoritarian states—the state of Tennessee. And David Lilienthal is its Fuehrer." Representative Robert Low Bacon, Republican from New York, charged the TVA with not accounting for ten million dollars of expenditures and claimed that stock and bond markets had been rigged by persons receiving advance tips on Lilienthal's yardstick power rates. Newspapers were full of speculation about little black bags and big bribes and stolen money.

Faced with this developing scandal, Roosevelt summoned all three TVA directors to the White House. Senator Norris stated that the "green-eyed monster of jealousy" had so invaded Dr. Arthur Morgan's heart that it had warped his judgment, and he pressed for an investigation by the Federal Trade Commission, but the President was described as grim and emphatic in insisting that he himself would first hear the bitter charges and countercharges. It took three telegrams to get Dr. Morgan to appear; his answer to the first was a tip-off to his curiously egocentric attitude towards the whole dispute: "On considering the matter, in view of my experience with the other two members of the Board, I am convinced that the type of conference proposed with them and the President cannot now serve any useful purpose. Therefore, the President should not plan on my presence."

On March 11, the three men met with the President for six barren hours. "The drama was like *Hamlet*," one reporter wrote, "with Hamlet missing, or rather, sitting mute as a stone in the middle of the stage." Dr. Arthur Morgan stood on his charges, refused to amplify them, and demanded that the case be heard by a committee of Congress. The hearing was adjourned for a week, to give Dr. Arthur Morgan a chance to change his mind, but on its resumption, he proved to be no less adamant. Roosevelt gave him three more days in which to abate his "contumacy," concluded that he was "temperamentally unfitted to exercise a divided authority," and on the next day removed him as both chairman and member of the Board of TVA, effective March 23, 1938.

Dr. Arthur Morgan was successful in getting the Congressional hearing he wanted. A joint committee of both houses was set up and six Democrats and four Republicans were appointed to it. Francis Biddle was selected as committee counsel. The first meeting was in Washington on May 25, and hearings were held in the Tennessee Valley throughout the summer. Dr. Arthur Morgan's allegations against his fellow-directors filled 6,199 pages of testimony before the hearings were over, but they failed to support, or even to back up, his original charges of dishonesty. Before the hearings closed, 101 witnesses had been heard and 611 exhibits introduced as evidence. A total of 15,470 pages of testimony was taken, costing taxpayers $75,000. The committee made a 301-page report in which the majority concluded: "Dr. A. E. Morgan's charges of dishonesty, resulting in the investigation of the Authority, are without foundation, not supported by the evidence, and made without due consideration of the available facts." One Independent Republican Senator, Lynn J. Frazier of North Dakota, signed the majority report.

Willkie figured in these hearings chiefly because of Dr. Arthur Morgan's charge that his fellow-directors had sabotaged a friendly arrangement with C. & S. and their countercharge that Dr. Arthur Morgan had consistently furnished ammunition for Willkie's long campaign against the TVA. Dr. Arthur Morgan charged Lilienthal in particular with "a persistent attempt to build up in the public mind a false understanding of the attitude of C. & S." through his reports to the board of his conversations

with Willkie. He claimed that Lilienthal had frequently misquoted Willkie as either unwilling to sell or willing only on the
promise of a monopoly outside the TVA area. Lilienthal had carried this misquotation, Dr. Arthur Morgan said, to the point of
changing the minutes of board meetings. Lilienthal answered
that the alterations in the minutes were merely the normal doc-
toring of English speech to be expected when three persons had
to approve each record. He denied having misquoted Willkie,
insisting that he had fairly represented the latter's position to the
board at all times, and it was significant that Willkie did not
make any public contradiction of him on this point.

The countercharges proved to be equally vague. Lilienthal
was able to quote a statement from Dr. Arthur Morgan admitting
that he had read to Willkie a memorandum in the controversy
over power pooling, but Dr. Arthur Morgan explained that he
had done so only to learn if it accurately stated his position. It
was also shown that Willkie had seen a copy of Dr. Arthur
Morgan's *Atlantic Monthly* article before publication, but this
had been admitted long before by the magazine's editors.
Finally, Dr. Arthur Morgan was proved to have consulted Owen
D. Young and Samuel Ferguson, friends of Willkie's, on power
pooling, but no evidence was ever introduced to show any collusion between Dr. Arthur Morgan and Willkie even though their
public positions were often close to each other.

Other witnesses brought up Willkie's name repeatedly
throughout the hearings, usually in connection with the fantastic hullabaloo which had been fostered inside the Tennessee
Valley for five long years by both sides in the controversy. The
treasurer of a Citizens and Taxpayers Association in Chattanooga revealed that Willkie had contributed $20,000 of a $23,-
900 fund spent in an unsuccessful effort to defeat a referendum
on a municipally owned power distribution system. Willkie's
answer was, as it always was whenever he was accused of propaganda: he only wished he had spent more and accomplished
more. This was his implicit answer, at least, to another charge,
made by former employees of the Tennessee Electric Power
Company, that they had given away large quantities of whiskey

before the Chattanooga referendum, and had purchased two vacant city lots in the names of one hundred nonresident employees of the company to permit them to vote.

A more serious charge, which was later to hurt Willkie politically, was that C. & S. had forced the suspension, on December 6, 1939, of the *Chattanooga News* by cutting down its advertising in the paper and by subsidizing a rival newspaper, the *Chattanooga Free Press*. The latter had indeed grown from an advertising throw-away into a newspaper during the C. & S.-TVA fight, and it had been full of C. & S. advertising. George Fort Milton, editor of the *Chattanooga News,* had been a strong supporter of the TVA. Willkie was never happy about this incident on his record, although there had been extenuating circumstances. Milton was engaged in a personal struggle for control of his paper; his quarrel was more with local officials of C. & S. than with the system; Francis Biddle, later Attorney General but then counsel for the Congressional committee investigating the TVA and himself an ardent New Dealer, was listed as a stockholder in Milton's paper. But Willkie was never happy about the withdrawal of advertising from the *Chattanooga News.* Although there was no ethical reason why a company should advertise in a newspaper that was trying to destroy it, Willkie felt that to fail to do so constituted bad public relations.

In the middle of the Dr. Arthur Morgan-Lilienthal quarrel and Willkie's concurrent negotiations with TVA came the final Supreme Court decision on the 1935 holding company act. By a margin of 6 to 1, the court upheld on March 28, 1938, the verdicts of two lower courts in holding the act constitutional. Chief Justice Hughes wrote and read the decision, with Justice James Clark McReynolds the sole dissenter and Justices Stanley Reed and Benjamin N. Cardozo taking no part. The Electric Bond and Share Company had brought the test case, but it was announced a few hours after the decision became known that C. & S. would at last register under the act, and the move was followed by other utilities—roughly the half of the public utility industry, controlling some $7,000,000,000 in assets, which had not registered.

The Final Sale

The Securities and Exchange Commission had been following a liberal policy in respect to the "death-sentence" provision of the act, holding that the public interest was more important than any strict interpretation of the letter of the law. Willkie was in the Middle West on the day the decision was handed down, but W. G. Bourne, Jr., assistant treasurer of C. & S., filed the company's preliminary registration on the same day, on his behalf. A few weeks later, Willkie took the leading part in setting up a committee of five utility executives representing fourteen holding companies to co-operate with SEC Chairman Douglas in working out problems raised by Section 11 of the act, the "death-sentence" clause.

Within another two months, Willkie was negotiating for the purchase of the Michigan and Ohio utility properties of the Cities Service Company, a corporation which was primarily in the oil business and therefore required to divest itself of its utility holdings. This move was to give Willkie a more clearly integrated electric system outside his Southern properties, and it strengthened the belief that any funds which might be secured from a sale to TVA would be used in an effort to integrate still more the Northern subsidiaries of the company.

This was by no means the end of Willkie's fight against the holding company act. C. & S. continued to argue over the exact interpretation of the law, holding that the Southern and Northern systems of companies, although not physically interconnected and integrated, could still be joined in one holding company under a clause allowing this in cases where subsidiary systems, although not in adjoining states, could not be operated independently without the loss of substantial economies. By the spring of 1940, when Willkie's political career had started, the SEC moved to force integration, and Willkie fought back with the same fire and indignation and many of the same arguments he had been using since 1935. On May 31, 1940, on the very eve of his nomination, Willkie filed a thirty-six-page brief with the SEC questioning again the constitutionality of the order compelling divestment of ten subsidiaries of C. & S. Final settlement did not come until 1942, when C. & S. at last agreed to simplify its capital structure. Common stockholders of the company got approximately $4.50 a share, a substantially higher price than the stock had sold for during the entire fight. The last chapter in the C. & S. story was a bill from eighteen law firms for a total of $1,576,409 for their work in the final stages of the cleanup.

The story was much the same for the whole industry Willkie had defended so passionately from the "death sentence." By the end of the fiscal year 1940, the SEC had registered 144 public utility holding companies with total consolidated assets of fourteen and a half billion dollars. It is clear that both investors and consumers have done well out of it. Whatever the holding company act did, in the summary of one historian, Professor H. U. Faulkner, "it apparently did not injure the electric utility business, for it was one of the first to push out of the depression and by 1937 enjoyed the greatest gross revenues of its history. No company died that seemed to have the slightest excuse for living."

Men quarreled over the issues with real passion while the bill was still under attack. In March, 1938, Professor Felix Frankfurter of the Harvard Law School was invited to address an audience of bankers, brokers, and lawyers at the Harvard Club in New York City. Grenville Clark and C. C. Burlingham alternated in the chair. Some of Willkie's friends took him along to tackle the man who was popularly, and wrongly, believed to be the arch-radical of the New Deal. The hall was jammed and the audience was packed with men eager to see "the little Professor," as he was called, brought to account. The meeting became a three-hour, hammer-and-tongs debate between Frankfurter and Willkie, and some fairly rough language was used over the charge that the latter's students were subverting the United States.

The audience, nearly all of whom started on Willkie's side, spread the word that a new champion of business had been discovered, and Alva Johnston reported that within a few days five publishing houses had asked Willkie to write books for them. For Willkie it was the beginning of a warm friendship for Frankfurter. The next day he wrote him to apologize if he had said anything offensive in the earnestness of the discussion. "I have great admiration," he wrote, "for the work that you have done in the training of young men, and I know of no one who has done so much to advocate the principle of a high-grade civil and public service." Frankfurter answered at once that "vigor and courtesy are not antithetic," so there was no need for any apology, and he added: "We met in the simple, direct way in which two Americans should meet who have a common concern about great public issues, even though they may view them on the basis of different experiences and are preoccupied with different interests."

Final negotiations for the sale of his Tennessee Valley properties to TVA filled most of Willkie's waking hours throughout 1938 and nearly all of 1939. These were the long, drab months that led up through Munich in Europe to Hitler's take-over of Czechoslovakia and the eve of World War II. The business slump continued at home almost without a break, and Roosevelt was increasingly eager to stimulate a new flow of private investment into industry. The appeal to the Supreme Court for a final test of the constitutionality of TVA, which was filed on April 13, 1938, dragged on until January, 1939, and the Dr. Arthur Morgan-Lilienthal hearings until a final report was voted by the committee in April, 1939. Willkie had small hopes of victory for his side in either of these long-drawn-out contests, but he sensed correctly that time was on his side as far as the terms of settlement were concerned.

The course of the actual negotiations betrayed the steadily increasing breakup of both sides in the conflict. The first passionate ardors of the New Deal had clearly cooled; 1938 was to see the President's ill-fated attempt to purge recalcitrant Democratic Congressmen and the equally ill-fated attempt of the La Follette brothers, who had been Lilienthal's original political mentors, to found a third party in Wisconsin. A severe attack of fever from drinking unpasteurized milk sent Lilienthal to the hospital for many weeks during this period. Former Senator James M. Pope of Idaho took Dr. Arthur Morgan's place on the TVA board and on January 26, 1939, promoted J. A. Krug, later Secretary of the Interior, to be chief power engineer and to take over the negotiations with Willkie. Ickes and Norris remained unreconstructed public power champions, and the former brandished a heavy club over Willkie's head throughout 1938 by repeated offers to lend the city of Chattanooga funds to duplicate the Tennessee Electric Power Company's plant, which accounted for one-third of the company's income. But the mood of the Administration had clearly changed, and the die-hards like Ickes were restrained from carrying out their threats. The 1938 elections were a defeat for the Administration, even if not a serious one, and individual New Dealers were beginning to think about their individual careers. By February, 1939, no less a New Dealer than Harry Hopkins told the public utilities in a speech at Des Moines that the government's war against them was over. The speech, broadcast nationally, was a persuasive document, his biographer, Robert E. Sherwood, has pointed out, "and generally reassuring to businessmen, but it was too carefully prepared, too meticulously conciliatory to all groups, to be a characteristic expression of Hopkins himself. . . . The political overtones and undertones of this Des Moines speech were so obvious to any trained observer that Farley referred to it as 'Hopkins' Acceptance Speech.'"

On the business side, defections were equally destroying the united front which had seemed to be so firm in 1937. The Supreme Court case was filed in April, 1938, by eighteen companies; by November of the same year, when it was being argued before the court, the appellants had shrunk to thirteen, nearly all of them C. & S. subsidiaries. Associated Gas and Electric Company and Electric Bond and Share Company, the two other major holding companies affected by TVA, were making separate deals with the government for the sale of their smaller properties, and so withdrew from the case. The incentive to make deals was strong: the threat of PWA-financed competing facilities. The government's tactics had left Willkie virtually isolated.

Until Krug replaced him, just before the final settlement, Lilienthal was the man with whom Willkie argued through this period as he had from the beginning of the fight. They met in New York, Washington, and Knoxville, and in spite of violent disagreement they had learned to meet on a personally friendly basis. Both men had been born in Indiana, both were first-generation Americans of German-speaking ancestry, both were inheritors of the old immigrant search for freedom and the richer life. A good deal has been made out of the fact that Lilienthal, who went to Harvard and came from a Republican family, was on the New Deal side, while Willkie, son of a maverick Bryan-Wilson Democrat and graduate of Indiana, was on the side of private enterprise. But this was a paradox which in reality carried little meaning.

Actually the two men got along well enough together but never became close friends. At the end of the first meal they ever ate together, according to Lilienthal, the check lay in the middle of the table until, without any grabbing by either man, each contributed half of the total. The practice continued whenever they ate together during the negotiations. When they were not talking about TVA, Lilienthal was conscious of a poignant effort by Willkie first to bulldoze and then to wheedle out of him the reasons why an extremely able man with his qualifications should be willing to work for a government salary. In the long run, Lilienthal now believes, Willkie had to learn the answer for himself, and he did it the hard way. In the reverse direction, Willkie used to say that he was never sure he had convinced Lilienthal why he felt so strongly that he had somehow to take his case to the people before he could be completely sure that he was right or wrong.

Lilienthal remembers Willkie as a rough fighter but a likable antagonist. He was never stuffy. Dr. Arthur Morgan had given Willkie, early in the conflict, a one-sided view of Administration policy in regard to the TVA. Lilienthal, as chief power negotiator, had had to correct this version but he never felt that Willkie was in collusion with Dr. Morgan or that he was anything but eager to learn the true TVA position. It was always Lilienthal's suspicion that Willkie would have been on his side in his fight to keep the TVA a kind of decentralized operation, dealing with people and things in the Tennessee Valley and free from Washington bureaucracy, had the fight over power not made them opponents from the start. It was Willkie's belief that Lilienthal would grow beyond the expert's attitude towards problems of government, and in the long run agree with him that only the people could really decide an issue as basic as the conflict between them. They were essentially very different men. It was a tribute to the democratic process that their relationship survived the C. & S.-TVA fight and became friendly when the war raised issues on which they could and did agree.

Willkie's public statements all stressed his desire for arbitration. He had first proposed the Supreme Court, then a panel of citizens including Dykstra, Compton, and Frankfurter. By the fall, he had switched to proposing the SEC, and this was the burden of his testimony before the Joint Congressional Committee to investigate the TVA when he was finally summoned to the witness stand in November, 1938. He repeated his basic belief that TVA should dispose of its power to the utilities at the switchboard, taking the government out of the power business, but he said he was not hopeful that this position would be shared by the committee. So he urged that the question of price be referred to the SEC for a quick and final settlement of the old dispute. "The quickest way to test the sincerity of this proposal," he said, "is to accept it." The next day he produced a legal opinion from a New York firm to counter the argument that TVA could not legally agree to arbitration, but it was to no avail. Krug turned the proposal down and it was clear that the principals would somehow have to agree on a price themselves.

Willkie's appearance before the committee had been preceded by a request by Francis Biddle, the committee's counsel, for permission to examine income tax returns between 1927 and 1935. Biddle insisted that he was interested only in corporation returns, in an effort to check depreciation figures, but Willkie and his friends were convinced that this was another attempt to smear him personally. As far as he was concerned, Willkie said, "they can have my personal income tax returns; all they ever gave me was a headache—I hope they give whoever looks at them the same."

On the stand, Willkie lashed back with some emotion at Biddle and at Representative Graham A. Barden, Democrat from North Carolina. It was a hearing with loud-speakers set among the marble columns, and both Biddle and Willkie were specialists in courtroom fireworks. One Senator questioned Willkie's argument that investors were frightened by the danger of gov-

ernment competition; "don't these investors take into consideration the past history of a company?" he asked.

"If they considered the history of the better utilities these
would be the most popular securities in the country," Willkie
retorted.

"You included the word 'better.'"

"That takes in 85 per cent."

"Fifteen per cent of bad apples in a barrel is a lot."

"Well," replied Willkie, "two of the Apostles went wrong—
maybe three—out of twelve."

The hearings were exhaustively reported and Willkie had
never before in his life enjoyed such press acclaim. Arthur Krock
gave him a column headed "Portrait of a Business Man on the
Spot," which pointed out that he had not appeared frightened.
"Some of his industrial confreres in far easier circumstances have
shown marks of terror visible to all Washington. Others have
made the terms commanded, smoked peace-pipes, issued fra-
ternal statements—and then gone home to explain that, while
they didn't want to do these things, there was no alternative. It
may be that Mr. Willkie, standing almost alone in court, threatened by PWA loans to Southern communities unless he takes
what the TVA offers for his properties, and faced by a searching
quiz into all his activities, will also yield his position. But his
manner and words at the inquiry today did not indicate that he
had been brought to that attitude."

The *New York Herald Tribune* singled out for sarcasm the
comment of Representative Barden, who had reprimanded Willkie during the hearing by telling him, "You would be more helpful if you were not quite so partisan." The paper commented on
November 28, 1938: "It is not surprising that a spokesman as
articulate as Mr. Willkie gives the palace politicians at Washington the jitters. For if it were not clear before the elections, then
it should be now, that the man in the street is as quick to resent
excesses on the part of government as he is abuses in private
enterprise."

Underneath the question of arbitration was the question of
price. The TVA wanted to pay as close as possible to historic
cost, what the properties had originally cost to build, less depre-

ciation, and Lilienthal kept pointing out that C. & S. had figured high depreciation in paying its corporation income tax. Willkie wanted a price based either on what it would cost to reproduce the properties or on a capitalization of its earning capacity. There were endless snarls over accounting procedures, but the basic disagreement hinged on this basic question. Willkie testified in 1940 that the initial price offer made to him was $55,000,000 less discounts for depreciation which were later estimated at between $10,000,000 and $15,000,000. His asking price started at $94,000,000, which was the valuation on which rates had been fixed by the state of Tennessee. In the difference between these two figures lay the questions of whether the bondholders and preferred stockholders would be paid in full and whether anything at all would be paid on the common stock.

On January 30, 1939, the Supreme Court ruled that Willkie's utility companies had no right to bring suit against the TVA on grounds of constitutionality. Raymond T. Jackson had pleaded the case for Willkie, Fly and O'Brian for TVA—the same line-up that had appeared before the District Court. Justice Stanley Reed excused himself from the case for having argued a similar case for the government before, and Justice Cardozo had died during the summer, no successor having been named. Justice McReynolds dissented, as he had done in the 1936 Supreme Court decision in the Ashwander case, and Justice Butler sided with him. But five Justices backed the majority decision read by Justice Roberts to a courtroom full of New Deal notables. This did not pass on the constitutionality of TVA, which has never yet been confirmed by the Supreme Court. But it eliminated the question by leaving open no legal channels for attacking the TVA power program. In effect, the court ruled that the utilities had no legal standing to bring the suit, and thus the old fight was ended by default.

Just two weeks before, Willkie had returned to his New York office from a trip through the Northern system of C. & S. It was then the third-largest public utility system in the United States and Willkie never gave up his active administration of the company even when he had to spend most of his time in politics and in Washington. On January 31, 1939, the SEC itself turned down Willkie's proposal that it arbitrate the sale, and on the next day, Willkie saw Krug and Joseph Swidler, a TVA attorney, at his 20 Pine Street office and reached a tentative agreement on price. Willkie was realist enough to know when a fight was over, and he announced at the same time that there would be no more utility suits against the TVA. Krug and Swidler returned to Washington the same night to get Administration acceptance of the deal and on February 4 the announcement was made in Knoxville and in New York that C. & S. was selling its Tennessee properties to TVA for $78,600,000 in cash.

The outstanding bonds and preferred stock of the Tennessee Electric Power Company amounted to approximately $72,000,-000. This meant that Willkie had won $6,600,000 for the common stock, in addition to the value of certain transportation and other properties of the company, estimated to be worth about $3,000,000. This was the first time that TVA had ever purchased private facilities at a price recognizing that there was anything but water behind the common stock. Wall Street saw the deal as a decisive victory for Willkie. The TVA top officials, assembled at the Norris, Tennessee, home of Lilienthal, were equally elated at the end of the long and bitter struggle.

It was still many months before the deal could be celebrated. Willkie pitched in to help persuade Congress to pass the necessary legislation, continuing meanwhile to needle the President with frequent demands to put in writing assurances that the new arrangement marked the end of government intervention in the power business. There was a mass of detail to be worked out in arranging the collective purchase, which involved thirty-three co-operating power districts and municipal agencies. The contract was officially signed by Willkie and Dr. Harcourt A. Morgan in Chattanooga on May 13, but Congress was slow in passing the appropriation required to carry it out. For this, Willkie himself was to blame. "His campaign was so successful," a *New York Herald Tribune* reporter said, "that he not only obtained an offer from the TVA to purchase his properties in Tennessee at a fair price, but he aroused such strong opposition in Congress to government ownership that there is now some question as to whether the necessary funds will be appropriated for the TVA to complete the deal."

Thirty bondholders of the Tennessee Electric Power Company also slowed up the deal by bringing suit in New York on the technical grounds that their bonds should have been redeemed at the call price of 105 instead of at 100. (They represented only $200,-000 of the roughly $40,000,000 in bonds outstanding, and they were finally turned down in the courts in June, 1940.) Senator Norris held up the bill in Congress until the House could be persuaded to delete a provision in the bill restricting TVA operations to the Tennessee River watershed. Finally, on August 15, on the sixth floor of one of New York's oldest and richest banking institutions, the First National Bank of the City of New York, Willkie took a part-payment check for $44,948,396.81 from Lilienthal under the glare of news photographers' flashlights and the heat of newsreel cameramen's flood lamps.

"Thanks, Dave," he said. "This is a lot of money for a couple of Indiana farmers to be kicking around. For this I give you the deeds of the Tennessee Electric Power Company."

CHAPTER TEN

The Political Build-up

"IT IS impossible to think of a career like that of Wendell Willkie in Europe," Harold J. Laski wrote, "save as the outcome of the breakdown in a social system." To this English authority on the American Presidency, Willkie's sudden rise to political leadership was proof that "the American system reveals a capacity for the discovery of new men, an anxiety to test new things, an interest in absorbing new experience, which remain notable even when all allowance is made for a visible loss, here and there, of important fluidities."

What happened to Willkie in 1940 was unique even in American political history. It was surprising enough to cause many men to wonder if there had not been, in fact, at least a partial breakdown in a social system. A registered Democrat in 1938, he became a year and a half later the Republican candidate for President. A public utility tycoon—traditionally believed to be tops in what was politically undesirable—he became a figure of very considerable glamour to American voters and some politicians. Finally, in the same year, he exchanged the public reputation of a conservative lawyer and businessman, spokesman for Wall Street and holding companies, for that of a crusader for the common welfare with a few dangerously liberal ideas.

This last change, least noticed at the time, suggests the massive scale on which the accumulated pressures of a decade of depression were changing both him and American public opinion. For he unquestionably became a symbol of hope to large numbers of Americans to whom the New Deal had failed to offer, or to deliver, its own brand of hope, and the most impassioned early statements of belief in Willkie as a liberal leader proved to be, as events developed, more accurate than the cynical wisecracks which explained this political miracle in terms solely of manipulation.

Manipulation played its part, and it was a steadily increasing part up to November, 1940. So did the American capacity for the discovery of new men, and Willkie's capacity to recognize and stimulate the restless, ill-defined forces in American life which had already shaped his life so strongly. The measurement of the respective roles played in his career in 1939 and 1940 by expert politicians and by the relatively inarticulate American public is a fascinating and rewarding study of the function of leadership in a democracy. Yet in the end both forces combined to cause the loss of important fluidities, in Laski's phrase. Willkie had already seen this process at work during the ten-year struggle over utility regulation and the New Deal: it had forced him into positions, and a spokesmanship for these positions, which he had not deliberately chosen. He was now to see the same pattern repeat itself in political terms.

He now understood the process better, so that his own efforts to resist it produced, by the end of 1940, a double image of himself in the public mind. The utility fight had given him public recognition by 1939 almost exclusively as a successful, anti-New Deal practitioner of what was called free enterprise. By the end of 1940, many saw him as the defeated Wall Street candidate, and many others as a successor to William Jennings Bryan. Yet the two were the same man. Both of the large public issues in which Willkie figured during the decade of the 1930's produced a visible loss of important fluidities, and in both cases the loss was inseparably linked with the scale and the speed of social change in the United States.

During the ten years leading up to his nomination, Willkie's involvement with the electoral processes of politics had been confined exclusively to the Democratic party. His father had been a hard-bitten Bryan Democrat, and Willkie's own boyhood, with his early jobs in Indiana and Akron, had grooved his interest in Democratic politics steadily deeper. He had gone to two national conventions, in 1924 at Madison Square Garden in New

The Political Build-up

York and in 1932 in Chicago. Just before he died in 1944, Willkie wrote for the *Birmingham Age-Herald* his memories of the gallant but futile effort of Newton D. Baker to commit the 1924 convention to the League of Nations.

"I shall never forget those early morning hours," Willkie wrote, "when Baker, physically a slight man, would return exhausted to his room to tell us—ardent, young and uninitiated in the obduracy of mentally-set politicians—of his battles in the committee and to get fresh stimulation from our naïve and infectious belief that so just a cause, so ably advocated, could not lose."

Willkie was especially fond of one quotation from the minority report Baker made to the 1924 convention when the cause had indeed lost. "I sat in that room across the street," Baker had said, "for five days and nights and heard talk about 'expediency' and 'votes' until I am sick. I am talking about life and death and love and duty. We have no logic for luck. There is no calculus for expediency. But we do know how to do that which is right, and that is the only rule we need follow if we want to win and deserve to win in politics."

Baker lost again in 1932, this time the nomination itself. Willkie's disappointment—he had gone to Chicago with the "Baker boys" hoping to cash in for Baker on a deadlock between Roosevelt and Smith—was deep, but it had not soured him on politics. Instead, it had turned his interest from the electoral machinery of politics to the manipulation of government institutions. The years of struggle over the TVA and the holding company act in Washington gave Willkie an unorthodox but extremely realistic view of politics in the United States, and a burgeoning sense of his power to use political means to serve his ends. He never earned his living from politics and he never proved that he could master the techniques of election—this was the basis for the charge that he was an amateur in politics. But politics goes on in a democracy between elections, and at this phase of it Willkie was no amateur.

From the very beginning of the electric power struggle, his work in Washington had forced on Willkie associations, loyalties, and ideas which stood in growing contradiction to those he had brought with him to New York in 1929. It required an entire decade for him to shift his formal political affiliation from the Democrats to the Republicans. The same pressures which produced this shift in Willkie were moving other Republicans— and notably many of the businessmen with whom he was most directly associated—into the Liberty League, the America First Committee, and other extremely conservative movements. He was to become the titular leader of all Republicans in 1940, but the record of his ideas during the 1930's makes clear that this is better explained by the amorphous character of the party system in the United States than by any sudden conversion of Willkie himself.

The conversion was, in fact, tentative and partial, and it was very slow. As early as 1935, when Willkie at forty-two was the youngest man in the country to be chief executive of a major utility system and was already in bitter dispute with the New Deal, he was elected to the New York County Democratic Committee, together with Mrs. Willkie, James A. Farley, Bernard M. Baruch, and Frank C. Walker, in a Tammany-controlled district. He had joined the district club in June, 1934, and he paid dues for two years before dropping out. In the same year it was widely rumored that he would succeed Joseph B. Kennedy on the Securities and Exchange Commission, which was then one of the chief targets of the anti-New Deal camp. Yet at the 1935 annual meeting of the United States Chamber of Commerce—the first such meeting to be completely boycotted by President Roosevelt—Willkie made what the papers called "the most militant attack on the New Deal." He admitted in this speech that the country had made some progress, "but it is clear that the progress has halted, and we have not yet achieved that economic recovery which is our earnest desire."

At the end of 1935, Willkie was quoted in the press as having said that he wished he had back the $150 contribution he had made to President Roosevelt's campaign fund in 1932. Three of his old friends in Akron, Murray S. Parker, Frank M. Enright, and George S. Carson, wired him that they would be glad to reimburse: "Before you became a plutocrat you were a good Democrat, and we now are astounded to know that you contributed only $150. Not being owners of any holding company stock, we still like the New Deal." Willkie wired back acceptance of the offer, advising all "disgruntled Democrats" to take similar action. It was all in good fun, without any bitterness.

The bitterness came from his allies and supporters in the utilities fight sooner than it came from Willkie. These were years when there was already a marked vacuum in the leadership of the anti-New Deal coalition of businessmen, Republicans and disgruntled Democrats, and newspaper columnists were professionally eager to fill this vacuum. One of these newspapermen, in the *Sun* in New York City, which was bitterly against the New Deal, gave Willkie one of his earliest political build-ups in a profile published on November 2, 1937. It pointed out that Willkie "gets no mention in connection with the new offensive by the utilities against New Deal 'strangulation,' but certain informed persons tell this writer he is planning the attack and calling the signals. The long, lean Hoosier, landing here via Akron, is a career standout of the depression years and in recent months has appeared to be the white hope of the utilities." Willkie used to laugh off such talk, but the counterpoint between what he said himself and what was said about him by "certain informed persons" was a major factor in his emergence into political prominence.

The bitterness also came from the steadily worsening climate in which political discussion took place in the 1930's. John Chamberlain pointed this out in the *New Republic* on November 8, 1939, in one of the first public comments to link Willkie's name with political ideologies. "To argue," he wrote, "for government ownership or control of the TVA dynamos is, for example, not at all the same thing as arguing for government registration of white leghorn chickens. Philosophies of centralization or decentralization must be put forward in this year of Stalin, Hitler and Wendell Willkie with precise demarcations; else the 'either-or' boys will twist you beyond recognition, making you into a Fascist, a Communist or a Rugged Individualist as suits their demagogic convenience." The warning was universally disregarded.

It was not until August, 1939, that money changed hands in the TVA deal, and until that date most of Willkie's increasing prominence in the public eye was keyed directly to the electric power issue. But he was becoming steadily more articulate. He had been widening his attack to include more and more Roosevelt policies. The newspaper press, the radio, and the big magazines were beginning to make him a minor national figure. In 1938, he became president of the Economic Club of New York, a position which gave him frequent newspaper publicity as moderator or presiding officer at meetings featuring speakers as newsworthy as Homer Martin, head of the United Automobile Workers, Philip F. La Follette, former Governor of Wisconsin, Thurman Arnold, who was redefining the slogans of American business, and Senator Millard E. Tydings, who successfully defeated Roosevelt's 1938 attempt to purge him. Willkie was a member of the board of trustees of the Town Hall Club in New York, the only board he served on outside his business. He was forced to ration himself on public speeches; his portrait was painted for the first time in 1938; by the end of 1939 newspapers were just beginning to pay him the ultimate flattery of a democracy by using his name without an immediate explanation, between commas, of who he was.

Until only a few months before his nomination, Willkie still had to explain just who he was. He went back to the University of Indiana in May, 1938, to speak at that institution's Foundation Day. He had been out of college for twenty-five years, and his summary of what he had learned during this time was given as an attempt to redefine liberalism. He gave his undergraduate audience an unorthodox warning that he saw no great moral crisis at hand, no crossroads for the world to choose: "New Deals and New Freedoms, Red Perils and the iron hand of militarism have confronted us day in and day out, and we have managed to carry on." He told them he believed Big Government had succeeded Big Business as the chief threat to the liberal tradition, but he was clear that it was still only a threat. He was defining his own position when he challenged the students "to strike a true balance between the rights of the individual and the needs of society, like a man rowing a boat who, when the boat swings to the right, pulls on the left, and when it swings to the left, pulls on the right."

The Political Build-up

That Willkie himself had no concrete political goal in mind at this time is also clear from the record of what he said. At a *New York Herald Tribune* Forum on October 26, 1938, summing up a panel discussion of management, labor, and government problems, he referred directly to "the Democratic party, of which incidentally I am a member." No man aiming at the Republican nomination would have gone on to say, as he did: "Personally, I think that the Administration has been right in many of the social and economic proposals which it has put into effect. For one thing, our industrial activities and our social needs have outgrown regulation by states alone. . . . The New Deal has realized that conditions of poverty and insecurity beyond the powers of the state to handle have created the need for social legislation in Washington."

A few weeks later, on December 1, James A. Farley had luncheon with Willkie. "In a general discussion of the political situation," Farley recorded later, "Willkie professed great admiration for the President and his program. He said he disagreed with him only on the power question, where Willkie felt Roosevelt was being led astray by Thomas G. Corcoran and Frank McNinch of the National Power Policy Committee. Willkie told me he was a firm Democrat and had cast his vote for Governor Lehman and the rest of the Democratic ticket."

There is no evidence that Willkie formally changed his party during the following year, or that any thought of an imminent political career led him even to think of it. He was still on the make in terms of political reputation, and still deeply engrossed during 1939 in the final Supreme Court fight and the haggling over price with TVA lawyers. He sounded off in public against Big Government and against government investigations, notably against the Dies Committee's methods in looking for radicals. In a speech for the annual American Design Award, he kidded "the artistic fellows" for giving us Victorian furniture and bustles, and his close friendships with artists, actors, and writers multiplied as he became more and more a minor celebrity around New York. A small private dinner was given in his honor at the Century on March 21, 1939, by his friend Gano Dunn, electrical engineer and president of Cooper Union. Austin

Strong, the playwright, presented him with a goose-feather quill to mark his new status as a writer. "Our wish," he said, "is that you will conquer and master this stubborn thing and squeeze through its point all the elements we admire in your character: your wit, your clarity of thought, your devastating hold on truth, your born leadership, your mule-like insistence on facts, and your ornery, common or garden cussedness!"

The big change in Willkie had relatively little to do with party affiliation; men like John G. Winant, Harold L. Ickes, Fiorello LaGuardia and a host of disgruntled Democrats were stepping over party lines without much difficulty as the 1930's drew to their end. The change was rather that he had grown up as a man, and had become a mature and self-confident personality. When he had first come to New York from Akron in 1929, Cobb, who was then head of C. & S., had persuaded him to replace a gold inlay in a front tooth with a white porcelain one, and had checked up regularly on his having his hair cut. A decade later, it was another friend, Irita Van Doren of the *New York Herald Tribune,* who helped to speed an incomparably more important change—his acceptance of himself as a potential leader with original and important ideas. Besides helping him on the drafting of speeches and magazine articles, she filled the more important aspect of an editor's role by stimulating him to work out his own position on major problems and to accept himself without self-consciousness both as a writer and as a thoroughly educated thinker in political science.

Willkie kept his name in the newspapers; it was becoming fairly widely known for the first time, but not in connection with any party or with any White House prospects. As late as March, 1940, an American Institute of Public Opinion poll showed that Willkie's name was given, in answer to the question "Whom would you like to see elected President this year?" by fewer than 1 per cent of those answering the question. What was true of the general public was not true of the manipulators, who went seriously to work some time towards the end of 1939. First, in point of time, came the reporters and commentators, then the editors, then the public relations experts, and finally the politicians.

The Political Build-up

The newspapermen had continued to be Willkie's friends throughout the TVA fight. He called most of them in Washington by their first names, drank with them, and talked to them all with disarming frankness. A political career was seldom mentioned, even in kidding. "What are you going to Washington for, Mr. Willkie?" was the standard query. "Oh, to see that my contempt for the New Deal remains founded on familiarity," was the standard answer.

In 1939 the friendly interviews continued, but with a different note. One columnist, Jennings Perry, says that as early as 1938 Willkie pooh-poohed to him the idea that he might be interested in the Presidency—"but showed me a large sheaf of letters, carefully preserved, suggesting that he run." The first such letter to appear in print was in the *New York Herald Tribune* of March 3, 1939, from G. Vernor Rogers, a vice-president of the McClure Syndicate, signed only by his initials. An earlier mention in print had been on February 23, when Arthur Krock published a column of political gossip in the *New York Times* in which he suggested Willkie as "the darkest horse in the stable: 1940 will be a little early to bring out a utilities man." But he pointed out that Willkie owned two farms and worked them, a fact full of meaning to political reporters, and that "he still has his haircuts country style."

On May 22, 1939, David Lawrence discussed him as a Republican possibility: "his name is one that fits the demand the Republicans are making for confidence and fair dealing in the government's relations with business." In Wendell Willkie, Lawrence wrote, "the Republicans would have an independent Democrat with a business ability and a leadership capacity which would fit the pattern that nine out of ten Republicans really want but do not venture to ask for."

Willkie wrote him a longhand letter. "My dear Dave," he wrote, "I have refrained from writing you heretofore in appreciation of that article you wrote about me for fear that I would seem a bit too sentimental in my thanks. I am utterly devoid, I believe, of political ambition but no man could be honest and at the same time indifferent to the suggestion from one such as you that he was qualified to lead the country in

157

these times." He ended by wishing Lawrence "all the luck in the world and for myself that no one takes your suggestion seriously."

It is the business of editors in a democracy to go to work on such dark horses, and they went to work on Willkie in 1939. In February, Alva Johnston wrote a piece in the *Saturday Evening Post* called "The Man Who Talked Back." It included no hint of a possible political future, featuring Willkie as an articulate businessman with no allergy to good public relations for his company. In May, Willkie himself wrote "Brace Up, America" for the *Atlantic Monthly*. In June, the *Saturday Evening Post* featured his "Idle Money—Idle Men." Both pieces discussed national issues, but not in party terms. Other magazines and the newspapers followed suit. By July 31, 1939, he had achieved the distinction of his picture on the cover of *Time*, with a profile treatment marking the end of the TVA fight. It ended by calling him "the only businessman in the U.S. who is ever mentioned as a Presidential possibility for 1940" and then calling the suggestion "mildly fantastic."

It was still a strictly nonpolitical build-up, and the exact point at which it became "Presidential talk," either in Willkie's mind or in those of the public relations experts who moved in, is difficult to determine. On November 21, General Hugh S. Johnson, who was then a columnist, was answering questions about possible candidates after a prepared speech before the Bond Club in New York City. "How about Wendell Willkie?" someone called out. Johnson expressed his approval in strong language. Willkie was then in Atlanta on a business trip. When reporters asked him for comment, he replied: "In view of the speed with which the Federal Government is taking over my business, I'll probably have to be looking around for a new job. General Johnson's is the best offer I've had so far."

Later, in his column, Johnson claimed that he "not only first insisted on the availability of Mr. Willkie, but did it oftenest and most consistently—here, in magazines, in speeches and on the air. That was done while some of the other 'I saw him's' were silent or were referring to Wendell as a devoutly desirable but wholly unattainable dream." By this time, with the election only a year away, several columnists were considering Willkie as a dim possibility. General Johnson's claim to priority was less well-founded than his observation that even Willkie's backers thought his chances exceedingly slim.

In December, Willkie recognized the "Presidential talk" about himself in a personal letter to Krock: "I would not go through the pretense of saying that if a major party nominated me for President on a platform in which I believed I would decline the nomination. By the same token, I would not accept a nomination on a platform in which I did not believe.

"Now, please understand me—I have no illusions that any party is going to nominate me. I merely make the above statement, in view of the talk, in order to preserve my intellectual integrity."

After the conclusion of the TVA deal, in August, Willkie was for the first time in many years a man without a cause. A good many projects tempted him, and one was a return to practicing law. Former Governor Nathan L. Miller of New York was retiring from active practice in one of the city's largest firms, Miller, Owen, Otis and Bailly, which had always been headed by a prominent national figure. One of the partners, Harold J. Gallagher, proposed Willkie as a new senior partner for the firm. Willkie dined with several of the partners at Governor Miller's apartment in the Hotel Pierre, at the beginning of January, and over cigars and brandy Miller told him: "Wendell, you know and I know that the businessmen of America, if they had a free choice, would make you President. You know and I know that there just isn't a chance of this. But you are a public figure anyway and the place for you to be a good one is at the bar. We want you to come back to the practice of the law."

"You know, Governor," Willkie answered, "that I'm no shrinking violet. But I still don't know if I could practice law again. You men must be sure in your own minds."

He was deeply attracted by the offer. He wanted to discuss it with his wife and friends, especially Langdon Marvin, who had been instrumental in his first going to Commonwealth and Southern, and Frank C. Dailey of Indiana. The plan was delayed at first by the formal C. & S. reorganization, which had to be completed by July, but concrete details were discussed at later meetings between Willkie and Gallagher. After the Presidential boom started, Willkie was afraid people might think he was running away from the public utility business just before the convention. By August, Gallagher himself had abandoned law practice to help on the campaign, and the matter was not discussed again until the day after election.

Through the end of 1939, Willkie had handled direct talk about his Presidential possibilities with an amused and incredulous air. When people asked him if he were going to run, his stock answer was: "Wouldn't I be a sucker to say 'yes'?" There was no doubt that he found the idea amusing at first, and that he liked to laugh about it. He was always a wisecracker and a josher, rather than a wit. Klieg lights and cameras never fazed him or slowed up his comebacks. Clifton Fadiman told him, on an "Information Please" program, that he had quite a career behind him. Willkie answered: "I don't like that word 'behind.'" When a reporter asked him if he were a millionaire, as rumored, Willkie told him: "I put what money I had before the depression in good sound Ohio bank stocks. I wasn't going to get hooked on Wall Street. I got through paying my last double assessment on that bank stock last year." The wisecracks were never polished or epigrammatic, but they came fast and they never stopped coming.

It was early in 1940 that he began to accept wholesale the invitations to speak which were beginning to pour in on him. He spoke to business groups, colleges, churches, and Chambers of Commerce, on the radio, for newspaper interviews, everywhere he could get an audience. He wrote articles for almost anyone who asked him, for the *New Republic*, for *Fortune*, for the Hearst newspapers. It takes time to build a name into national prominence in the United States, and Willkie—once he had decided to make the gamble—was in a hurry.

He had some notable assets. One was the catch-as-catch-can technique he had learned in arguing with the New Deal. He was already a master at timing releases, issuing denials before edition time, adding punch to a prepared speech, or making one on the spur of the moment letter-perfect enough to have been memorized, treating publishers, editors, and reporters with the skill needed to suggest to each that they were the sole beneficiaries of his gratitude and his confidence. On the radio, he was still a beginner, but he wanted to learn.

His personality and his face served him excellently. Picture editors found it easy to play up news shots of him—a big man, an inch over six feet and weighing 220 pounds, his hair usually mussed up, his suit looking unpressed (actually he wore a freshly pressed suit every morning but inside an hour it usually looked as if he had slept in it), his arms raised in old-fashioned speaking gestures. And in the same way, what he said made good copy. Usually, it was unrehearsed, and human. Until January 30, when he first said publicly and flatly that he would accept the nomination if he could get it without strings, in a speech at Wooster College in Ohio, the routine was always the same. The presiding chairman at each meeting would make some remark about Presidential timber. There would be mixed laughter and cheering. Willkie would then deny he was a candidate or would have any chance if he were one, usually in a wisecrack or with an anecdote to make the point. Repetition of the denial served only to confirm the clear fact that he was running, and running hard.

In the two weeks after a Willkie article called "We the People" appeared in *Fortune,* accompanied by what was practically a nomination of him by the Luce editorial board, he received two thousand requests to speak. He accepted a staggering number of them, in Kansas, Nebraska, California, Minnesota, Boston, all over the country. There was nothing very subtle about his call on former Governor Frank M. Lowden of Illinois and on Alfred M. Landon, Republican candidate in 1936, in Topeka. "I'm the cockiest fellow you ever saw," he told the crowd at the Topeka railroad station. "If you want to vote for me, fine. If you don't, go jump in the lake and I'm still for you." This kind of good humor was something new in national campaigning, and it caught fire. On April 9, he broke one of the oldest rules of politics by appearing as a guest expert on the "Information Please" radio program with a panel of professional wits who would have been delighted to slaughter him. Instead, he ran away with the program, and a national audience, most of whom never heard of Commonwealth and Southern, now knew who Willkie was and liked him.

Another asset was the support of a small group of passionate political amateurs. At the public relations assignment which was given them, they included both professionals and amateurs, but there were no professional politicians among them, and they shared a crusading spirit which teetered close to something like religious faith. There were important publishers in this group, including John Cowles, Minneapolis newspaper publisher, and his brother, Gardner Cowles, Jr., of *Look* and the *Des Moines Register and Tribune*; the Reids of the *New York Herald Tribune*; Roy Howard; Henry Luce of *Time* and *Life* and *Fortune*. There were businessmen, prepared to put up money, although Willkie paid his own expenses right up to the convention.* These included John W. Hanes, Harold E. Talbott, Jr., Colonel Henry Breckinridge, who had been Assistant Secretary of War under Wilson, Robert C. Johnson, magazine publisher and former president of the Civil Service Reform League, and Samuel F. Pryor, Republican National Committeeman from Connecticut. There were editors, writers, a small number of big Broadway names. Finally, there was a hard core of men who were prepared to work as hard as Willkie himself.

One of these was Oren Root, Jr., a young lawyer and grand-nephew of Elihu Root, who opened a campaign for Willkie on April 10 among Yale, Harvard, and Princeton graduates. He had never met his candidate. One of his friends ran an advertisement in the Public Notices column of the *New York Herald Tribune*, appealing for help "to organize the people's demand for Willkie," and the Willkie clubs which followed mushroomed so quickly that Root had to take a leave of absence from his law firm to manage the volunteers who joined him, with an improvised headquarters at 660 Madison Avenue in New York. "Talk Willkie, breathe Willkie, live Willkie, and we'll nominate

* They amounted to about four thousand dollars, chiefly travel expenses of himself and his secretary, Fred Rahter.

him," Root told his cohorts. By June 8, petitions were coming in, each with fifteen signatures, at the rate of five hundred a week. "The movement is taking on the force of a decentralized snowball rolling downhill," Root told a *New Yorker* reporter. "We were baffled but impressed," the magazine commented.

Another of those volunteers was Russell Davenport, who resigned as managing editor of *Fortune* on May 2, against Willkie's advice, to work for the Willkie nomination as the nearest thing to a campaign manager Willkie had until the convention. An advertising executive, John Orr Young, started an advertising campaign on the chain letter principle which reached a total circulation of 93,000,000, all except the first ad bought and paid for by contributions from voters. Charlton MacVeigh, who helped to set up one of the earliest of the "Willkie Mailing Committees" in the Murray Hill Hotel to send out copies of "We the People," was one of the few members of this group who had had any political experience, and he was far from being a professional politician. These were all men with command over techniques which were relatively new in political campaigning, and they combined these skills with an almost fanatical belief in their candidate.

Meanwhile, Willkie was getting nowhere in the more conventional aspects of the race. In the Republican primaries, Governor Thomas E. Dewey was taking a commanding lead over all the other contestants. Willkie did not run in a single primary. Dewey's name also led all the public opinion polls right up to the convention. The engineering of the Willkie boom by journalists and high-powered advertising men has been severely criticized by some scholars studying the American party system who believe that it made a mockery of the Presidential preference primary machinery. It has certainly not been hidden or understated by those who took part in it. "Neither Willkie's personality, nor the weight of his ideas, could conceivably have produced even a fraction of the phenomenon that we lived through," Fred Smith, a public relations specialist in the prenomination campaign, has recorded. "It should never be forgotten that the 'Willkie boom' was one of the best engineered jobs in history."

Yet for all the skill and the ballyhoo, Willkie was still a long way from the nomination after five months of hard campaigning.

Public opinion polls showed a steady increase in Willkie's popularity through the spring, but the increase was slow and it never gave him the lead before the convention. The American Institute of Public Opinion figures showed the following percentages among rank-and-file Republican voters:

	MAY 8	MAY 17	MAY 31	JUNE 12	JUNE 21
Dewey	67	62	56	52	47
Vandenberg	14	13	12	12	8
Taft	12	14	16	13	8
Willkie	3	5	10	17	29
Hoover	2	2	2	2	6
Others	2	4	4	4	2

Where Willkie had been piling up support was neither in the party machine, which ran the primaries, nor in the general public, which can be measured by opinion polls. It was among rank-and-file Republican (and some Democrat) party workers who wanted something newer than the New Deal, and especially among independent citizens with no formal party affiliation but an active interest in politics. One major reason why Willkie could organize these people into the pre-convention boom was that he was more honestly himself in this period than he was to be again for a long time, once the political experts had moved in on him with their unanswerable arguments of compromise and expediency. He wrote his own speeches much of this time, and made many of them off the cuff. He was not frightened by unpopular causes. In March he wrote a piece for the *New Republic* called "Fair Trial" in which he attacked what he believed was the political prosecution of both Fritz Kuhn and Earl Browder. It took courage, while the Nazi-Soviet pact was still in force, to write: "Now, you may hate Communism even more than you hate Fascism (and I am surprised at the number of people who do) but if you truly believe in protection of civil liberties, you will wonder whether Browder was sentenced to

four years in jail and a $2,000 fine because he made a false state-
ment on a passport application or because he was a Communist
party member."

Before the convention, Willkie had a support in liberal groups
which was simply forgotten later by those who argued that he
had changed his position after 1940. On April 11, 1940, the
Nation published a profile of him by McAllister Coleman which
was ironical but friendly and which clearly recognized his native-
rooted radicalism. On June 17, the *New Republic* stated that
"his two heavy handicaps are: first, that he was a registered
Indiana Democrat until five years ago; and second, that on the
whole his outgivings since his backers began to groom him as a
dark horse, have been too candid and too decent."

From January until June, as the Willkieites became more fervent and more consecrated, Willkie himself seemed to grow
steadily more frank, more courageous, and more gay. There was
a deep streak of gambler in Willkie, and like all good gamblers,
his muscles loosened up when the stakes got high. He made no
bones about his past. "If any of you have any doubts about my
availability because I'm in business," he told a crowd at Lincoln,
Nebraska, "go ahead and vote against me. I'm in business, and
proud of it. Nobody can make me soft-pedal any fact in my business career. After all, business is our way of life, our achievement,
our glory." He treated his party irregularity in the same
way: "Some reference has been made to the fact that I was a
Democrat in 1932 [he was back-dating this by at least six years]
but I want to say that the New Deal wasn't on the ticket, and
the New Deal has no reference or relationship to democracy."
General Johnson quoted an unnamed industrialist who sat in on
a very private meeting with Willkie to discuss financial support
of the campaign if he should be nominated. Let's have no misunderstanding about this, Willkie told the group. The party
would need money. But he would make no pledge or obligation,
expressed or implied, to anyone. This included ambassadorships.
"Did they resent that?" the industrialist reported. "They ate it
up."

The time was ripe for unorthodoxy, and for a new voice which
sounded fresh and honest. In April, the Nazis moved into Nor-

way, in May into the Low Countries, in June into Paris. There was no agreement among Americans as to the course to be followed, but there was a general sense of expectancy, of living on tiptoe. No one knew exactly how Willkie felt about the war. In "We the People" he had come out resoundingly for "a foreign policy we can trust," whatever that might prove to be. On May 21, he said in New York: "In my judgment a man who thinks that the results in Europe will be of no consequence to him is a blind, foolish and silly man." He was beginning to look like a big, strong man to have around in case of trouble. Dorothy Thompson, an old friend of his, wrote a column from Paris, just before the city's fall, proposing the adjournment of party politics and the joint nomination by both parties of a Roosevelt-Willkie ticket. ("I shall be delighted to see Dorothy Thompson when she comes back," Roosevelt wrote on May 18 to Morris L. Ernst. "Do try to get this silly business of Wendell Willkie out of her head.")

The idea that he could be President was by now in many heads. It was still weeks before Willkie was to be afflicted with the full line-up of strange, ill-assorted allies who are the inevitable price of a major party nomination and whose disparity and confusion were eventually to cost him the election. But even before the convention, the Willkie camp was becoming a motley crowd. After the shouting was over, the public relations professionals were to claim that they had engineered the closest approach to a miracle in American history. Some deeply emotional enthusiasts spoke of a miracle as having been more reputably worked. New Dealers said that Wall Street had quietly picked its man. Isolationists charged that the King of England had given Willkie the nod. Some die-hard Republicans came to believe that the man had been foisted on them by a conspiracy between the White House and the Communists. Actually, there is no good reason to doubt that Willkie himself ran for and took the nomination, and that his strategy, his timing, and his self-confidence were all based on his belief in the strength of the independent vote even inside a party convention.

Events over the short run proved him right. Over the long run, they proved the opposite, because the old problem re-

mained of organizing for continued political action the vitality
and the imagination of the independents to whom Willkie was
talking between January and June, 1940. One of them, Heptisax,
who wrote a weekly column for the *New York Herald Tribune*,
came out for Willkie on June 7, three weeks before the nomination, in a personal statement which was an unconscious exposure
of both the strength and the weakness of the Willkie boom. He
was no joiner, he wrote. He had an aversion to movements and
meetings and a highly cultivated resistance to political spell-
binding. Yet he made a contribution, took the the Willkie button,
and called himself an "enlisted private" in the Willkie-for-President movement. Here he spoke for all the amateurs in politics
who were beginning to find that a little of it could be fun. Then
he cautioned his readers that as a self-declared liberal, Willkie
approved of certain modern trends that he did not. This was
what many Republicans were going to think a little later. Third,
he backed him "because I want Roosevelt out"—this was to be
the strongest cement of the entire Willkie campaign, and it was
excessively negative. Finally, he wanted Willkie for President
because he knew how to succeed, a "boy who can start from
scratch and work himself up into a $75,000 job." These four
themes—the amateur distrust of professional politics, misunderstanding of the sincerity of Willkie's liberal convictions, the
passionate desire to defeat Roosevelt with anyone, and the deep
confusion of success with money—were to run consistently
through the entire story of Willkie's ill-fated courtship of the
Republican party. What they contributed to initial success was
small change compared to what they did towards ultimate
failure.

After Willkie's nomination, he told a press conference that
May 11 had been the date on which he had first taken seriously
the idea that he might win it. He had debated against Ickes before the American Newspaper Publishers' Association in New
York at the end of April, and immediately after this the Cowles
brothers had dinner with him at the home of Russell Davenport.
It was the first real talk they ever had with him. Willkie outlined
what was then his plan: to make no specifically Republican
speeches, to play for a deadlock in the convention, and then to

gamble with the Connecticut delegation and eight New York delegates, which was all the strength he had.

Both John and Gardner Cowles told him this was nonsense. His background alone would kill him as a dark horse. What did he have to lose by trying out a straight Republican meeting in Iowa or Minnesota? There was still time to pick up delegates. With Willkie's reluctant agreement, they picked a dinner of Republicans which had already been scheduled in St. Paul for May 11. They had some difficulty persuading Governor Harold E. Stassen to introduce their man; Stassen was being reserved on all candidates. They put up the money for a limited broadcast of the speech. It started very badly. Willkie read a prepared and very mediocre speech, and the applause was so brief that the announcer could be heard saying: "Now we return you to the studio." Willkie, still standing, threw his unstapled speech into the air; it was a big ballroom and the pages fluttered down over the audience while Willkie began all over again: "Some damn fool told me I had to read a speech to you. Now let me tell you what I really think."

He caught fire and made a truly impressive speech. More than seven hundred Minnesota Republicans caught fire, too, and when he finished jumped to their feet yelling "More, more." This was by no means the normal reaction to a speech by a dark hopeful at a political rally in strange country, and it changed Willkie's whole strategy. He repeated the same performance in Des Moines, with much the same success, and from that point on determined he would meet every single delegate to the convention and take the nomination without a deadlock.

After May 11, it was serious business with Willkie, and he was on the go every minute of every day. On May 19, he returned to New York and issued a statement repeating that he still did not regard himself as an avowed candidate but that the movement had grown to such an extent that it needed some coordination. So he asked anyone working in his behalf to keep in touch with Davenport at his office at 17 East 49th Street, where the campaign was being planned. Root kept his separate office for the Willkie Clubs, and the Voluntary Mailing Committee continued to operate in the Murray Hill Hotel. All he could do himself was to go on talking, to pledged delegates about what they would do on the second ballot, to New Jersey Republicans who gave him a 19,865 write-in vote in a primary on May 22 which recorded 340,744 votes for Dewey, and most of all to the people of America.

"I doubt if there be any country," Lord Bryce had written about America in 1893, "where a really brilliant man, confident in his own strength, and adding the charm of a striking personality to the gift of popular eloquence, would find an easier path to fame and power, and would exert more influence over the minds and emotions of the multitude. Such a man, speaking to the people with the independence of conscious strength, would find himself appreciated and respected."

CHAPTER ELEVEN

Miracle in Philadelphia

WHEN the campaign managers and party big-shots began to check in to Philadelphia hotels on June 16, 1940, eleven days before balloting was to start, the Dunkerque evacuation had been completed, Italy had entered the war, and Nazi troops were taking over Paris. What great event might take the next day's headlines away from the convention was a brooding question in the minds of gathering delegates as well as reporters. There were quick answers to the question in bars, over after-dinner coffee in hospitable Republican homes in Philadelphia's Main Line suburbs, and in the newspaper copy of the trained seals and the more cosmic-minded columnists. But the answers were quick—as always at such times—with deep ignorance. The professional politicians, whose business it was, did not know who would be the candidate, nor what kind of world he might have to face the day after his nomination, nor what kind of program the Republican party would give him with which to meet the growing crisis.

The war in Europe was only one factor in this uncertainty. Far deeper was the ambivalence within the Republican party which matched, and had in fact grown out of, the deep split chiseled in American business by the Great Depression and the New Deal.

In 1940 there was no doubt in the minds of the Republicans assembling in Philadelphia that their party was pre-eminently the party of businessmen. Through eight years of public wrangling over the New Deal the party had consistently taken the side of business against government intervention and control,

Fitzpatrick in the St. Louis *Post-Dispatch*, March 6, 1938

"We must reinterpret to the nation the political and economic philosophy with which the Republican party faces the new circumstances of this new age."—Dr. Glenn Frank

but this had been nothing new. "The business of the United States is business," Calvin Coolidge had said, summing up what was the basic axiom of all the Republicans who held power in Washington for more than three-fourths of the period between the Civil War and the first Roosevelt election. Their policies had ranged from giving businessmen large chunks of the public domain to enlightened and socially useful support of free enterprise and a fantastic increase in the standard of living of a nation. The Republican party was still accepted as the champion of all those expansive, enriching, morally suspect, and seemingly all-conquering forces which had made the United States the greatest power in the world.

Since 1932, the party had faced a new challenge which seemed to be at the same time a challenge to the business world it represented. In Federal taxes, as Herbert Agar has pointed out, the New Deal found something to give away even more appealing than the public domain. President Roosevelt and the New Deal had given tax money away in large and growing amounts for eight years, in pensions, crop subsidies, slum clearance projects, unemployment relief, cheap power projects like the TVA. What they got in return was, in effect, a farmer-labor political base which had last been effective in the United States a century earlier, under Andrew Jackson. Farmers in the South and in the West were prepared for reasons of pure self-interest to vote with industrial workers in the cities, especially in the East, and to vote against the party which had traditionally stood for business and prosperity.

In continental Europe, the wrenching of the Great Depression, the New Deal handouts of public money, and this resultant change in voting behavior might have produced a revolution. They would certainly have produced a revolutionary party and a reactionary opposition. There were powerful and articulate forces in American life in 1940 which were moving in that direction. Yet the fact is that it did not happen. The American business mind proved to be as divided on politics as it had been on economics throughout the eight years of New Deal legislation. The Republican party proved to be as divided in terms of program and objectives as the businessmen it represented. The reasons for this are deep in American history, and they were not new: Theodore Roosevelt had split the Republican party wide open within the memory of living men, taking part of it with him into a liberal protest against many policies associated with American business. Yet Willkie was a very large and possibly decisive factor in the nation's refusal in 1940 to divide along class lines. By the time he died, events had not justified his belief that the Republican party could become again, as it was in some respects justified in calling itself, the historical party of true liberalism. Yet his deeper belief had been proved conclusively: that a large part of American business was still dreaming expansive, hopeful dreams, and that it was not ready to become entrenched and beleaguered in political re-action. His nomination in 1940, whether it was a triumph of manipulation or a grass-roots miracle, was a profoundly im-portant American refusal to adopt the right-left, reactionary-revolutionary line-up which was already taking shape all over Europe, and his campaign helped to groove American political development into a different line-up for a long time to come.

Willkie's own split reactions to New Deal reforms, over the preceding decade, made him the ideal man to play this role for both business and the Republican party. He did not so much create the role as fill it. Just like the public utility industry, Re-publicans were actually of two minds about what Roosevelt had done. In public, again like the public utility industry, they denounced the man, his family, and all his works, although many of them were prepared, in private conversation, to con-cede a good deal. As early as 1934, William Allen White, who was still recognized then as "the conscience of the Republican party," had stated that he was by and large for the New Deal: "It is neither communism nor fascism. Much of it is necessary. All of it is human. And most of it is long past due." Republicans like him could not easily forget that they were the party of Lin-coln, Theodore Roosevelt, and La Follette, of abolition and the Sherman Anti-Trust Act, and of conservation. Those who later denounced Willkie for "me-tooism" forgot that the liberal spirit was deep in the traditions of their party, and still alive in the business mind of America.

The professional politicians were the last to accept Willkie in 1940, lagging even after the public opinion polls. The sharp polarization of political debate was only partly responsible for this. The party bosses were inevitably closer to the spokesmen for business, especially in Congress, than they were to business itself, and these spokesmen had been euchred by the democratic process into a tactical position of all-out opposition to New Deal reforms which was not shared by all businessmen or by all

Republicans. There were, in addition, two complicating factors which had nothing to do with the great debate over the role of government in business. One of these was the concern with freedom, with the liberties of the individual, whether businessman or plain citizen, in a society growing steadily more collectivist. On this, Willkie's personal record and position both carried wide appeal. The other was the question of American destiny in the world, and especially our part in the frighteningly spreading war in Europe. On this, Willkie's personal position could have split the party wide open, as Roosevelt's could have split the Democrats. This actually happened, after the election. But Willkie's public record was innocent enough to conceal under an apparent ambivalence what was actually a deep split within the Republican party. Roosevelt's campaign double-talk performed exactly the same function for the Democrats.

It was this ambivalence within the Republican party which was chiefly responsible for what seemed to be a miracle in Philadelphia. A Willkie trend in public favor had been visible to political experts for a few weeks. On June 15, it had been reported by Washington correspondents, but they added quickly that only two delegates were known in the entire country who had said openly that they would vote for Willkie on the first ballot. He had no headquarters and no official manager; not a single state organization was on his side. Small wonder that Henry L. Mencken, experienced reporter of conventions, wrote that the event was "shot through with evidences of a miracle. At one time I actually saw an angel in the gallery reserved for Philadelphia street railway curve-greasers. To be sure, the angel had on a palm beach suit, but nevertheless it was clearly an angel."

During the days of private jockeying just before the convention opened, Dewey was the front runner, with the largest number of pledged delegates, backed by the smart professional money. Then District Attorney of New York County, he was considered by some to be not yet ready for the White House, and he was handicapped by a rancorous feud with Kenneth F. Simpson, national committee member from his own state. Simpson was an undiplomatic, redheaded Irishman who was too liberal for Dewey's right-wing supporters; the feud cost Dewey 32 of New York's 93 votes even on the first ballot. But Dewey was still the odds-on preconvention favorite, followed closely by Senator Robert A. Taft and Senator Arthur Vandenberg, both of whom had the disadvantage of being too openly isolationist even for those Republicans who wanted to conceal this conviction beneath a public straddle for the sake of votes. Willkie was mentioned only as a very dark horse right up to the opening of the convention, along with Frank Gannett, newspaper publisher, Governor Arthur James of Pennsylvania, and Herbert Hoover.

Senator Vandenberg described in his diary a breakfast with Willkie on the Tuesday preceding the convention at the Carlton Hotel in Washington at which Willkie asked him for his support. "I thanked him," Vandenberg wrote, "and told him that I thought the final decision would come between the two of us (in which I was wrong). We parted good friends—but nothing doing." On June 25, Dewey sent a message to Vandenberg offering him the Vice-Presidency for his support. The Senator answered with a sporting proposition to meet Dewey at eleven o'clock "and flip a coin to see which end of the ticket we each take." He never heard from Dewey again until the final voting on Thursday night, "when he phoned me with appeals to do something to 'stop Willkie.' But it was too late."

The first moves at the convention all went against Willkie. A Dewey supporter, Herbert K. Hyde, was elected head of the platform committee. Dr. Glenn Frank, former president of the University of Wisconsin, reported a two-year study of what the party should stand for, and it proved to be an extremely conservative document. Meanwhile the clans were gathering: lobbyists, Congressmen, delegates, reporters, national figures, spokesmen for pressure groups of every kind and variety. The war news grew more gloomy every day. These were times, it was clear to every professional politician, for his candidate to watch his step and hoard his delegates.

Instead, the times were a setup for a man like Willkie. He was not even in Philadelphia at first, having gone out to Bay City, Michigan, to dedicate a new power plant to his eighty-year-old

"On His Way"

former law partner, John C. Weadock. His spokesman was considered to be Representative Charles A. Halleck of Indiana, an Old Guard conservative and isolationist, who was already scheduled to nominate him. On June 20, Davenport opened a Willkie headquarters at the Benjamin Franklin Hotel. Within the next two days, the Philadelphia *Evening Public Ledger* and the Scripps-Howard newspapers came out for him; Root announced that 4,500,000 persons had signed his petitions; 500 young men showed up in Philadelphia from the Willkie Clubs to sell Willkie to the delegates in the hotel lobbies.

Miracle in Philadelphia

Willkie's original team at the convention included Halleck, Davenport, and Root, Representative Bruce Barton of New York City, who was to second his nomination, Representative Frank O. Horton of Wyoming, and the Willkie amateurs: MacVeigh, Emmons, then chairman of the Voluntary Mailing Committee in New York, Smith, then head of the Associated Willkie-for-President Clubs, Eugene Rose, publicity director, and William H. Harmon, former vice-president of the Baldwin Locomotive Works and head of Willkie's Pennsylvania followers. Not until June 22, five days before the first ballot, did his strategy committee include professionals like Governor Raymond E. Baldwin of Connecticut, Senator Styles Bridges of New Hampshire, Mayor Rolland B. Marvin of Syracuse, and national committeemen like Simpson of New York, Pryor of Connecticut, Walter S. Hallanan of West Virginia, and Sinclair Weeks of Massachusetts. Even these men were hardly thought of as speaking for the truly powerful city and state machines or in the important smoke-filled hotel rooms. When President Roosevelt appointed two independent-minded Republican leaders, Henry L. Stimson and Colonel Frank Knox, to his Cabinet on June 21, the reporters had reason to think that the professionals and the die-hards had the convention in the bag.

On June 22, Willkie came to town, two days before the convention was formally to open. It was a noisy arrival, undignified, tumultuous. On his way to his hotel, he got himself into a street debate over reciprocal tariffs and aid to the Allies. He wore a straw hat, tilted to one side, and the grin which was to be plastered all over the country in the next few months but which few crowds had yet seen. He set out to woo delegates, the galleries, and the American people. He saved himself a lot of time by going without sleep. From early morning until early morning, he talked to people in his suite, six small rooms on the top floor of the Benjamin Franklin Hotel, in hotel lobbies, and in the headquarters of state delegations. He lived on coffee and cigarettes. His hair and his clothes were always rumpled, whether he was appearing before a song-fest of three thousand slightly crazy Willkieites in the Academy of Music or being photographed with Republican elder statesmen of impeccable bankers' decorum. He kept both his good humor and his sense of humor, and he won nearly everyone he talked to.

Together with the candidate came the mail. Telegrams, letters, and postcards arrived literally in an avalanche. Simpson found 3,000, addressed to him personally, when he checked in at his hotel, and received a total of 100,000 in twelve days. By the day the convention opened, the letters and telegrams to delegates were estimated at over 1,000,000. The city buzzed with jokes about them. The mother of one candidate was reported to have wired him: SON STOP YOUR FOOLISHNESS AND GET BEHIND WILLKIE HES FASCINATING. A delegate was said to have had a telegram from the surgeon who had just operated on his daughter in St. Paul: OPERATION SUCCESSFUL DAUGHTER DOING WELL DROP TAFT AND VOTE FOR WILLKIE. Besides the mail and the telegrams, Philadelphia was seeing new faces, not those usually seen at political conventions. "The station wagon set had come down from New York for the big show," Marquis W. Childs later recorded. "The town was gay with the right hats. There were good parties all over the place."

There was nothing especially novel about this technique except its timing. Willkie and his amateurs had realized the grotesque absurdity of a carefully managed political convention in June, 1940, with the world on fire, and every move they made was aimed beyond the delegates at the galleries, and beyond the galleries at the anxious American people. The other candidates and their managers helped them nobly by growing more cautious and more mealymouthed as Willkie tore the convention wide open. "The Republican party is at present much too divided and confused," Walter Lippmann wrote on June 26, "to take a clear position on any great question." In the same Republican paper, the *New York Herald Tribune,* on the same day, Dorothy Thompson was writing: "There is not the slightest indication at this convention that the leaders of the Republican party know the facts of life as they are in the world at this moment."

It is hard to explain the Willkie miracle except in terms of this vacuum of leadership and the urgency of the times. William Allen White, who was reporting the convention for the North

Dowling in the Omaha *World-Herald*

American Newspaper Alliance, called on Willkie and later said his candidacy was making great strides. "Dewey has most of the delegates," he said, "Taft has most of the king-makers, and Willkie has most of the enthusiasm." Dewey told a press conference on June 22, answering a question about the still-fledgling Willkie boom: "I'm lost in admiration for the technical skill with which the job has been done." Three days later, Senator Gerald P. Nye of North Dakota said: "I have just sensed something

179

about this Willkie campaign that hasn't been apparent before. It looks to be a little too well organized. I sense a reaction against all the pressure." Willkie went right on grinning. "If there is any pressure at work," he told the reporters, "I'm not exerting it. I am having a great time. Things are wonderful."

Willkie was doing more than putting on a good show. He was talking to delegates with deadly seriousness. His first big break came on June 23, the day before the convention formally opened, when Governor Baldwin of Connecticut retired from the race, announced he would second Willkie's nomination, and thus gave him in effect Connecticut's 16 votes on the first ballot. The next day Governor Ralph L. Carr of Colorado followed suit, with his state's 12 votes. Betting commissioners in Wall Street began quoting Willkie at even money, ahead of all the other candidates, but these were gamblers' odds and the politicians in Philadelphia laughed at them. Representative Karl E. Mundt of South Dakota called a special meeting to deflate the growing Willkie boom, chiefly on grounds of Willkie's party irregularity, his support of reciprocal tariffs, and his suspected sympathy for an interventionist policy in Europe. It was attended by forty Representatives and five Senators, and some of them signed a strong warning against letting the boom develop any further. Senator Charles L. McNary of Oregon, Republican leader of the Senate, was at the meeting and was quoted by the newspapers as sympathizing with the statement although he did not actually sign it.

Willkie was answering all questions and hedging as little as he could. He told a group of Negro delegates about his fight against the Klan in 1924, and assured them that Commonwealth and Southern had Negro employees. "I don't know how many of them or in what categories, but it's a hell of a lot of them." He assured delegates from Tennessee that the TVA dams were solid concrete and that no one in his right mind would ever tear them down again. The avowed isolationists, led by Mundt and Representative Harold Knutsen of Minnesota, forced him to hedge on reciprocal tariffs by saying that Hitler had killed them as an issue. "I do not change my position," he said. "I merely state to you that all old positions are obsolete, as dead as last week's newspaper, and that any man who aspires to leadership must think wholly in the present and its future, and let the dead past bury its dead." For Willkie, who believed in reciprocal tariff agreements all his life, it was the first big compromise, but not the last.

Stassen formally opened the convention on June 24 in a keynote address which defined the straddle on foreign policy which both candidates and both parties were to adopt in the hope of being thought pro-peace but not pro-Hitler. All possible aid without war was the formula, wholehearted support of the Allies (which at that moment meant Great Britain) without American troops. The isolationists were as afraid to show their hand as the interventionists, and although Willkie knew better than most that this formula would simply leave the ultimate decision of peace or war in Hitler's hands, he was in good and numerous company in pretending that it made sense.

Dewey was the first candidate nominated on June 26, by John Lord O'Brian of Buffalo, in a speech which was liberally sprinkled with references to "lifelong Republicans." Halleck's nomination of Willkie was unorthodox in mentioning the candidate's name at the start, violating one of the oldest of convention rituals, and he went on to ask: "Is the Republican party a closed corporation? Do you have to be born in it?" Dewey's ovation lasted twenty-five minutes, Taft's—the loudest—nineteen, Willkie's twenty. The galleries were admitted by everyone to be two-thirds for Willkie. Underneath the excitement, the carnival spirit, and the growing tension, some observers felt a truculence in the "We want Willkie" chants from the galleries, and a sullen resistance from the delegates on the floor below.

It was also on this day that Stassen, who had been unwilling to invite the public utility executive into Minnesota a few weeks before, swung the Minnesota delegation into the Willkie camp. It had been divided between Vandenberg, who had most of its votes, Dewey, and Taft. Stassen, himself too young to run for President, had made the convention's keynote speech but he had carefully refused to commit himself to any candidate. John Cowles had worked on him, as had Raymond Clapper, the late columnist. (Clapper had been a Willkie backer for many months, but without his heart in it. If Willkie should be nominated, he had written in April, he would have to "stop talking blunt horse sense" and repeat instead "the drooling phrases of campaign ghost writers.")

Stassen had refused to talk candidates in Philadelphia until he had given his keynote speech, and his earlier meetings with Willkie, in St. Paul and in a private interview in New York, had left him impressed but uncommitted. The two Cowles brothers, Willkie, and Stassen finally got together at one o'clock in the morning of June 25. For an hour, they went over a state-by-state review of Willkie's chances, in great detail and with great frankness. Then Stassen announced that he would support Willkie, but only on condition that he could be his floor manager. He felt he had to be sure that no mistakes were made. There was no other deal, not even discussion of how it should be announced.

A relaxed mood followed; all four men had been tense until the decision had been made. "Well, Wendell," Stassen said, "the time may come when I'll ask you to return the favor." He would be glad to, Willkie answered, he had a feeling that for himself it was now or never. There was some more talk about what might happen in four years' time, Stassen repeating his warning that he might be around asking for help and Willkie assuring him that he would certainly be welcome. At least two of the men present agree that no bargain was struck and that there was no firm commitment which extended beyond the next day's session, but twisted memories of the conversation by both Willkie and Stassen helped to spoil their relationship by 1944.

At 10:55 on the morning of June 26, without any prior hint and five minutes before a scheduled meeting of his state delegation, Stassen told Roy Dunn, national committeeman from Minnesota, that he woud support Willkie. An hour later, it was announced officially that he would be Willkie's floor manager when the balloting started. This was not the kind of procedure which wins friends among politicians; it caused some hard feelings in Minnesota. But its short-term meaning was clear, and Willkie was no longer a dark horse. Willkie communicated to many delegates and newspapermen his own infectious optimism, while he kept to himself and a few close friends the cool appraisal

Miracle in Philadelphia

of his chances which he was constantly making and revising. "I'm in front of a trend," he kept on telling people. But late at night, in his hotel room, he would sit on the bed and spell out to a few people just what he had done during the day, whom he had seen, what he thought his prospects were. This score was candid in the extreme, and it was not always favorable.

Senator James Watson of Indiana has told his version of one of the incidents designed to chill Willkie's optimism. Willkie had known him for many years, and Willkie was, after all, Indiana's favorite son.

"Jim," Willkie asked the Senator, "couldn't you be for me?"

"No, Wendell, you're just not my kind of Republican."

"I admit I used to be a Democrat."

"Used to be?"

"You're a good Methodist," Willkie pleaded. "Don't you believe in conversion?"

"Yes, Wendell. If a fancy woman truly repented and wanted to join my church, I'd welcome her. I would greet her personally and lead her up the aisle to a front pew. But by the Eternal, I wouldn't ask her to lead the choir."

The next day, June 27, the miracle was wrought. The morning started well with a front-page editorial in the *New York Herald Tribune* asking the convention to nominate Willkie. "Such timing of the man and the hour does not come often in history. We doubt if it ever comes twice to a political party," the paper said in language which stood up for eleven years, anyway, before the paper used it again in another front-page editorial for General Eisenhower. Convention Hall was jammed with 22,000 men and women on the swelteringly hot afternoon when the balloting started. They had been reading for some days that they were the voice of the people, and they made it loud and raucous. The first ballot gave Dewey 360 votes, Taft 189, Willkie 105. These were not hopeful figures but the crowd was not discouraged. Willkie ate a steak and a bowl of raspberries in his hotel suite while the second ballot was being taken. Dewey slipped to 338, Taft climbed to 203, Willkie to 179. This set the trend of all the voting still to come.

Willkie had predicted, as early as June 8, that he would be

nominated on the sixth ballot, and had later unwisely revised his guess to the third. He first took the lead on the fourth ballot. On the fifth, Landon threw the 18 Kansas votes to Willkie. He had had a late private conference with Willkie the night before, and was reported to have received satisfactory answers to some questions about Willkie's Wall Street connections. Arkansas and Iowa, released by favorite sons, had moved into the Willkie column. If Pew had switched the Pennsylvania votes from Governor James to Taft on this ballot, the outcome might have been different. Martin refused a Bricker request for a recess, and the sixth ballot started with the crowd sensing that the Willkie trend was about to become an avalanche.

Shortly after midnight, it did. Michigan switched to the Willkie column, Senator Vandenberg releasing the delegates pledged to him. Oregon did the same, released by its favorite son, Senator McNary. A last-minute attempt to make a Taft-Dewey deal failed, and at 1:05 A.M. Pennsylvania threw all its 72 votes to Willkie. Governor John W. Bricker of Ohio moved to make the nomination unanimous. Seconding the motion, Governor James of Pennsylvania paid the new, still-unknown Republican candidate for President his most spontaneous tribute by calling him "Mr. Winkell."

Not everyone was prepared to credit the miracle to Mencken's angel in the palm beach suit. Old grudges die hard, and Willkie already had enemies. Senator Norris called him "Insull the Second" and charged that the power trust had bought the nomination for him. The legend that Wall Street bankers had bought it for him, in return for a promise to go to war on England's side, still rises and dies away with every turn in the fortunes of American Fascists. C. Nelson Sparks, former Mayor of Akron and campaign manager during the convention for Frank Gannett, later published a variation on this tale, charging that T. W. Lamont, the Morgan partner, had bought Stassen's support for Willkie through John Cowles. Cowles' flat denial also revealed that between the fourth and the fifth ballots Willkie had received and turned down two offers of Taft votes, one in return for a promise of a Cabinet post, the other for an agreement on an individual to run for Vice-President.

"After all she has said about glamour boys."

"After hanging up the telephone," Cowles reported, "Willkie turned to me and said, 'Apparently Taft is going to be nominated on the next ballot and we've lost. But it's been a good fight and I'd rather lose the nomination than win it by making any deal. Let's slip out of here and get away from the crowds before Taft is nominated.'"

The charge that it had been a rigged stampede died equally slowly. There was no question that there had been a vast campaign of pressure on the delegates. The Western Union Telegraph Company's superintendent in Convention Hall stated that his men had delivered more than 40,000 telegrams to delegates on Thursday and Thursday night alone, the night of the nomination. Former Justice William F. Bleakley, chairman of the New York State delegation at the convention and a Dewey supporter, said he had received 22,500 telegrams and letters urging him to vote for Willkie. There were men with long memories who compared this with the methods used by the power companies in their 1935 campaign against the holding company act. But the difference was that this time the telegrams were genuine, and in a check of its messages Western Union could find no person denying a message which bore his signature. Another check, made by Editorial Research Reports on a sampling of delegates from five states, showed that 30 per cent of them had been influenced by telegrams, 50 per cent by personal talks with Willkie, 20 per cent by other delegates. None admitted having been influenced by the galleries.

Willkie himself said quietly, when inquiries were threatened during the convention, that not one call or telegram had been sent or inspired from his headquarters. The tidal wave of public pressure was, in fact, partly a symptom of the troubled times, partly a logical result of the volunteer, grass-roots campaign which Willkie supporters had been conducting before the convention, and partly a spontaneous public reaction to Willkie himself. A few weeks later, the Senate Campaign Expenditures Committee, after reviewing several charges made to it of high-pressure tactics by Willkie followers, decided there was not enough evidence even to warrant an investigation.

The convention adjourned quickly, in something of a dazed mood as far as the politicians were concerned. They hoped this might be the beginning of a beautiful friendship between Willkie and the Republican party, but at best it was no more than a beginning. Taft hurried back to Washington, to conduct hearings on the confirmation of Stimson as Secretary of War, and to be kidded about Willkie. "To Taft this was no laughing matter," it is reported in Stimson's memoirs. "Neither was it to Stimson; he sought no conflict with the son of his old friend and chief, and the only regret he carried away from the hearing was that the questions put to him by Robert Taft should have been so pointedly unfriendly." Willkie was not the only man who was breaking party lines, and the Republican party was being forced by the pressure of events even more than by Willkie to take a new, hard look at its own past and at the future.

Senator McNary, whom Willkie had never even seen, was picked as his running mate before the convention broke up. The only other candidate for this honor in the voting was Representative Dewey Short of Missouri, who within a year was to make a speech in Congress about "Wee Windy War Willkie—a Bellowing, Blatant, Bellicose, Belligerent, Bombastic Blowhard." (He was the second ranking Republican on the House Military Affairs Committee.) Willkie announced that "I think it is a very good platform"—even the *New York Herald Tribune* could go no further than to admit that "of the platform the less said the better in most respects." The defeated aspirants weighed in with public pledges of support in the campaign to come, but the galleries had taken most of the enthusiasm away with them.

Willkie told the last session of the convention: "So, you Republicans, I call upon you to join me, help me." In his *Fortune* article, "We, the People," he had written a few months before about "You, the politicians of both parties," but Republicans had hoped he would now consider himself one of the boys. It was an honest use of the pronoun, but it was to prove steadily more galling to the party stalwarts as the campaign progressed. Within the week, on July 2, Willkie was to file his first application for membership in the National Republican Club. But first he combed the confetti out of his tousled hair, faced the newsreel cameras, said he was looking for one hundred hours of lost sleep, and disappeared on Roy Howard's seventy-three-ton yacht, the *Jamaroy*.

CHAPTER TWELVE

The Hoarse and Urgent Voice

IN THE simple, Horatio Alger story of an Indiana boy who had made a lot of money, taken on and defeated the long-haired New Dealers from Washington, and won himself a Presidential nomination on clear merit and the irresistible demand of the people, the next four months of Willkie's life were anticlimax. The high moment of this version of the Willkie legend was incontestably that early morning in Philadelphia, with a Scandinavian voice from North Dakota calling out a vote for "Mr. Vilkhie." Men and women all over the country listened to their radios with the exultant feeling that the dark horse had won, the underdog, the citizen in the melting pot, the amateur who is the ultimate sanction of democracy. People read the news in the papers with hope that this Hollywood happy ending was an augury of things to come, the party bosses beaten, the Nazis on the run, the prophets of change proved wrong, the world secure, old virtues rediscovered strong and unconquerable. For those who accepted this legend—and the mass media of the entire nation went to work to make sure that even those who could not accept it were still stirred by it—the campaign which followed was a tawdry business.

For Willkie himself, it was only a beginning, and in terms of the multiple and tangled forces which had actually produced his nomination, it was still far from a climax. He was only forty-eight years old, with a physical energy which matched his ambition, almost no hostages given to fortune, and a world to conquer. Politics was new to him, but not the reality of American life. What some of his more starry-eyed admirers were to call compromise—a slow blurring of the idealized pictures they formed of him, and these were many and contradictory—Willkie himself saw as the give-and-take at the heart of the democratic process. There seem to have been surprisingly few persons who knew him well as a human being in 1940, instead of as a public utility executive, or a lawyer, or a political critic of the Administration. But those who had some sense of his personality agree that he plunged into the campaign with a strong feeling of being in the driver's seat, and a confidence that he could go right on fusing the disparate elements in his support into a strong, durable, personal political movement.

After Willkie's major campaign trip was over, Marquis W. Childs wrote for the *St. Louis Post-Dispatch* a brilliant, unorthodox account of watching Willkie across the broad sweep of the American land through which he moved. From trains, airplanes, and automobiles, with sirens screaming, crowds cheering, eggs being thrown, and quiet-faced men and women sizing up this new man "with the raucous voice and the free gestures," Childs saw a puzzled and uncertain nation, hungry for leadership, a beautiful, strong, and lonely country. His reporting was later republished under the title "The Education of Wendell Willkie." It deserved the praise and fame it won, including the comment from Fitzpatrick, his paper's cartoonist, that Childs seemed "to be taking a last, lingering look at the corpse." Childs wrote: "I could see what he meant. I felt that the country was on the verge of a profound change. I think the people sensed it, too, that fall. Much in the America we had known was to go. A greater, richer, stronger America might come out of the ordeal ahead of us. Or we might forfeit our birthright, the wonderful heritage of spirit, of earth, of people. But nothing would be quite the same again. The high wind of change was in the air!"

Willkie himself sensed this as clearly as anyone, and it helped to give his campaign a high, emotional, and slightly shrill tone from the very beginning. This might have happened in any case, without the ominous war news from Europe and the mood of anxious expectancy in which Americans were living through the summer of 1940. Once he had been nominated, Willkie was forced to try to lead an orchestra of very different players, some

Hungerford in the Pittsburgh *Post-Gazette*

"How the old place has changed!"

of whom had never played in a political band before and few
of whom were in tune or even playing the same piece. The dis-
cord between the amateurs and the professionals around him
was loud enough to make news before the campaign ended. But
it was only one of the many contradictions which followed
inevitably on the nomination. On the problem of the war, on
that of race relations, on civil liberties, on agricultural relief
and crop control, on labor and collective bargaining, the Republicans were forced by their own internal split to seek support on the extremes instead of in the middle. So Willkie found

himself in one camp with Father Charles E. Coughlin and Colonel Theodore Roosevelt, with some German, Jewish, and Irish-Americans who hated Britain and most of the English-speaking Union, with Southern Bourbons and some of the most aggressive Negro leaders in the country, with isolationists like Hamilton Fish and internationalists like William Allen White. The third-term issue brought some important Democrats to his side to join Republican politicians with an eight-year-old thirst for Federal patronage. Before the campaign was over, he could look over his shoulder and see John L. Lewis side by side with those bankers who sincerely believed that Hitler was a lesser danger than Roosevelt. All Willkie really had to work with were his own personality, his legend, and the restless mood of the American people. He worked them hard.

From Philadelphia he returned to New York to resign from his $75,000-a-year job with Commonwealth and Southern, his directorships in the system's operating companies, and his place on the board of the First National Bank of New York. He was in high and cocky spirits, having made up some of his lost sleep, and he was not yet even thinking about problems like the possible public reaction to a candidate who traveled from Philadelphia to New York on a private yacht. On his first day in New York he held two press conferences, wound up all his business affairs, lunched with Stassen, spoke with Dewey three times by telephone, outlined a rough schedule of his campaign, and stopped the show at *Life With Father*, which he went to with his wife, his son, and Root. When Howard Lindsay, playing the part of Father, looked at the morning paper and exploded: "God! Why does God make so many fools and Democrats?" the audience, which had earlier broken out in the now-familiar "We want Willkie" chant, was his and he knew it.

He had a week of the heady taste of this new fame, in New York and Washington, before he went to Colorado Springs for the vacation which a Presidential candidate traditionally takes in order to do, without admitting he is doing it, the hard work of counting up his political assets and planning his campaign. He exercised his accepted right to reorganize the party's national committee, persuading Martin to become its chairman in place of John D. M. Hamilton, who continued as executive director. New and younger men were put in some key positions, Dewey and Taft backers were given prominent places in the hierarchy, Stassen became chairman of an advisory committee, and a picture of streamlined harmony was unveiled to the press. Actually, from the very beginning, no serious attempt was made at any organic fusion between the chief groups of advisers with whom the candidate had to deal. Hamilton remained titular chief of the professional politicians, in charge of what could be called the tactics of the campaign, with Pryor his chief lieutenant in the East. Martin replaced Stassen as chief planner, in charge of strategy. Davenport continued as Willkie's "personal representative," with Root in charge of the Willkie Clubs and other volunteers. In effect, Willkie was making a public show of party regularity; the subsequent history of the members of his executive and advisory committees showed how few of them were Willkieites in any true sense of the word.

White was one of the few dyed-in-the-wool Republicans to warn him against these concessions. He called on Willkie in New York right after the convention and urged him not to give a free hand to men like Hamilton, Pryor, and Pew, blaming Hamilton for the "foolishness" of reading Stimson and Knox out of the party. He approved of Martin as chief strategist, but disliked Pryor's appointment. Willkie's failure to force through a merger of his personal forces with the party machine was to cost him more and more as time went on.

Governor Carr had persuaded Willkie to go to Colorado for his vacation; this was another tip of the hat to sordid political reality. The Democrats, with traditionally strong farm support, have picked nineteen nominees from Eastern states compared to nine from the rest of the nation, while the Republicans, as the party of businessmen with strong backing in the East, have reversed the ratio with a seventeen to five count in favor of nominations from west of the Alleghenies. So it behooved Willkie to try to look like a Westerner. His earlier protests that he had never been a practicing farmer were gradually played down. Colorado seemed to be a politically smart location for a summer of political build-up as a true son of the frontier, of humble and rural origin, a man with his heart in the West.

He flew out on July 9 with his family, Fred Rahter, his secretary, twelve reporters and four photographers. He took five books with him to read on the plane: Carson McCullers' *The Heart Is a Lonely Hunter*, Morris L. Ernst's *Too Big, The Dissenting Opinions of Mr. Justice Holmes*, Mason Wade's *Margaret Fuller, Whetstone of Genius*, and Carl Snyder's *Capitalism, the Creator*. They were anything but bucolic, or hammock, reading; they gave a truer picture of the kind of man he was than the publicity handouts which were already being mimeographed at party headquarters.

He stayed at the Broadmoor Hotel in Colorado Springs, working on his acceptance speech and his campaign plans, and seeing an endless succession of notable visitors. Here was the true process of dilution with which a democracy, through its free press, cuts down to size the individuals who seek to lead it. Willkie had had between a few weeks and a few months in which to set an image of himself as a person in the public mind. Luckier than most politicians in this respect, he had been able to enter national politics at the top, with the initial image clear and individual. It was confusing in the degree it failed to fit accepted stereotypes, but it was still an image of himself. From this point until his death, there was nearly always someone else in the picture—an adviser, a local big-shot, a crowd, the Shah of Iran or Generalissimo Stalin or, at the very least, awareness in his eyes and his smile that he was not really alone. This was as true of studio portraits as it was of newspaper pictures, and truest of all of the images forming in the public mind. Here at Colorado Springs he dined with Colonel Robert R. McCormick, publisher of the *Chicago Tribune*, lunched with former President Herbert Hoover, was photographed with Landon, with Elliott Roosevelt, the President's son, and with literally hundreds of state officials, Congressmen, candidates, publishers and businessmen, disgruntled Democrats, hopeful world-savers, tourists and sightseers, all the curious people with whom an ambitious candidate must shake hands, smile for the camera, and establish some form of identification. The identification makes votes, directly or indirectly, but it also blurs the lines of a human personality in the public mind. It speeds the process by which every American sees in a public figure the multiple images of other men, types whom he can classify, according to his own loyalties and prejudices, more quickly and with less need to think for himself.

In the middle of August, Willkie flew from Colorado Springs in a chartered plane to Rushville in Indiana, where his farms were located, and on August 17, drove to Elwood to make his formal acceptance speech. This was the town, with a population of 10,798,* where he had been born and raised, gone to school, started work and the practice of law. His speech was given in an Indiana grove, with the thermometer reading 102 in the shade, to a shirt-sleeved crowd estimated by the reporters as 250,000 strong. Shipwreck Kelly was perched on top of a flagpole, advertising a brand of coffee. State police fought with an insoluble traffic problem. The candidate arrived wearing his flat straw hat, which was already going out of fashion, accompanied by Mrs. Willkie and her mother. The perspiring crowd bought pop, hot dogs, and Willkie souvenirs, and everyone commented—as had been planned—on how distinctively American the whole show was.

"I have an engagement to keep in this town," Willkie said. "It was made a long time ago with a young man I knew well. . . . As I look back upon him, I realize that he had plenty of faults. But he also had three steadfast convictions. He was devoted to the ideal of individual liberty. He hated all special privileges and forms of oppression. And he knew without any doubt that the greatest country on earth was the United States of America.

"That boy was myself thirty or thirty-five years ago. I still adhere to those convictions. To him, to his generation, to his elders, and to the youth of today I pledge my word that I shall never let them down."

The speech went on to outline in general terms the compromise between the Republican platform and his personal convictions on which Willkie was going to campaign. It had a good but

* This was nearly 8,000 less than at its peak in the 1890's when Willkie was a boy there.

not ecstatic press. Several prominent Democrats, including Alfred E. Smith, John W. Hanes, Alan Valentine, president of the University of Rochester, and Lewis W. Douglas, one-time budget director for Roosevelt, felt that he had staked out an unanswerable claim to the support of true liberals, while the Republicans read his speech as orthodox party doctrine. Norman Thomas, already nominated as Socialist candidate, struck the only jarring note. He called the speech "a synthesis of Guffey's First Reader, the Genealogy of Indiana, the collected speeches of Tom Girdler and the *New Republic*. He agreed with Mr. Roosevelt's entire program of social reform and said it was leading to disaster."

"Back Home in Indiana" was inevitably one of the Willkie campaign songs, and for the next few weeks he did his best to give it some kind of political meaning. This was the phase of the campaign which gave rise to the "barefoot boy from Wall Street" wisecrack. Rushville was his base, a town with a normal population of six thousand. Edith Willkie's Class of 1908 at the Rushville High School could still gather a substantial number of its members for a reunion when "Rush County's favorite son-in-law" came back, shortly after his acceptance speech. Willkie genuinely liked his farms there, his manager, Miss Mary Sleeth, his tenant farmers, and his neighbors. He understood their problems far better than most national political figures did. "I am forty-eight years of age," he said at Rushville, "and thirty-seven years of it I have lived in the Midwest. During the last eleven years all of my business interests have been in the Midwest and in the South. There comes to me an overwhelming sense of humility when I think that I am called to a position of leadership in one of the most critical moments in the world's history, to preserve the kind of life that you people live here. Of all the ways of life in all the country and in all the world, it is the most precious form of life."

The Willkies lived in a three-story red brick house lent to them by an old friend, Mrs. Charles Mauzy. It was surrounded by lawn on one of Rushville's maple-shaded streets, not far from the home of Mrs. Willkie's mother, Mrs. Cora Wilk. Willkie's press conferences were usually shirt-sleeved affairs with the reporters sitting on the grass. His campaign office was on the second floor of a two-story frame building on Main Street owned by Mrs. Wilk, sandwiched between a drugstore and a grocery. This Rushville month was dedicated in spirit to the memories of Booth Tarkington's Indiana and to the hopes of inspiring support all over the country among small-town and rural voters who had no love for the New Deal.

Yet the outer world kept on intruding. The town's Western Union facilities had to be increased seventeenfold. John Donaldson, a retired businessman and volunteer campaigner, directed a staff of eight secretaries on the job of opening, sorting, and answering a mail which fluctuated between one thousand and three thousand letters daily. Willkie's personal secretary, Fred Rahter, and his personal stenographer, Grace Grahn, handled a constant stream of visitors and incoming long-distance telephone calls. The latter numbered thirty-nine on one typical day. His press secretary, Lamoyne (Lem) Jones, a newspaperman who had formerly worked with Dewey, and his assistant, Jules Dulce, had the job of satisfying a press corps which seldom fell below fifty in number.

The contrast between the setting and the activity boiling around the candidate gave a synthetic and unconvincing flavor for many Americans to the whole Rushville performance. The world was burning up; great issues would not wait; yet here was the candidate going through an act which looked as if it had been dreamed up by the editor of a national picture magazine. "Forgetting politics for a time," read the caption on the inevitable barnyard picture released to newspapers, "Mr. Willkie looks over the cattle on one of his five Rush County farms, which have a total of 1,400 acres," and all the picture really showed was that politics was the one thing he was not forgetting.

"It's getting so," Miss Sleeth commented with the candor that made Willkie like her, "every time a cameraman shows up, the hogs run right over and strike a pose."

On September 13, six days after the Nazi Air Force had begun its all-out raids on Great Britain, this pastoral phase of the campaign ended. When Willkie's campaign train pulled out of Rushville, the candidate could begin to look and act more like himself. The campaign opened officially with his speech on September 16, at Coffeyville, Kansas, where he had taught school, but Willkie stumped the tough industrial districts of Chicago on the way, and gave unending rear-platform talks as the train crossed Illinois and Iowa. By the end of the first day, his voice had dwindled to a whisper, beginning the dependence on a microphone which was to last through the whole campaign. In the next seven weeks, his train was to cover 18,789 miles, through thirty-one states. In fifty days Willkie made 560 speeches, 520 of them extemporaneous. He shook the hands of uncounted thousands of Americans. He was betting everything on the sheer power of his personality. He was playing for another miracle, and this campaign train seemed to him the best way to give a miracle every possible break.

Nothing like the *Willkie Special* had ever been seen before in a Presidential campaign. A lounge car had been fitted out as a workroom for the press; there was a special darkroom near the head of the train for photographers; together with radio and newsreel men, there were seventy-five reporters in all assigned steadily to the train. At the rear was a private car for the Willkie family. Mrs. Willkie smiled and waved to the crowds but never made a speech. The bands played "Let Me Call You Sweetheart" and she invariably received a warm reception. In the middle of the train were the several staffs of experts, each with typewriters, filing cabinets, reference libraries, and mimeograph machines. The train started out with twelve cars, grew to sixteen, ended with fourteen. It was a migratory hotel, camp headquarters, traveling carnival, and smoke-filled politicians' hangout, all in one. Newspapermen called it "the Squirrel Cage." By the end of the seven weeks, when the train pulled into New York on November 2, there were a good many men on it who never wanted to see each other again as long as they lived.

Those on the train had very little in common except the desire to see Roosevelt defeated. Besides his immediate family and his personal staff of secretaries, the candidate had with him his younger brother, Edward E. Willkie, as a constant companion, a six-foot-six barrier against the crowds of well-wishers and curiosity-seekers. John Hollister, Senator Taft's law partner, Weeks, Pryor, and Horton were on the train for most of the trip, with

Willkie

Martin, Stassen, Senator Henry Cabot Lodge, and others joining it for longer or shorter times. Halleck was the train's tame professional, good-natured and smiling but largely window dressing as far as the reporters could judge. He sat in on the conferences, Childs recorded after the trip, "with the publishers and the high-powered publicists who were constantly advising Willkie, but he readily confessed that his voice in the councils was a small one. That, incidentally, is one minor conclusion which seems fairly obvious on the basis of Willkie's experience. Publishers make poor political advisers. They were always hopping on and off the campaign train, ready to pour out torrents of advice. They were working as hard as they could for Willkie and he was naturally inclined to take their advice."

The publishers and the publicists were in one sense Willkie's personal friends: he knew more of them and he knew them more intimately than most Presidential candidates. But they were all Republicans, too, indulging in the quadrennial frenzy of President-making which is apparently one of the reasons men want to be successful newspaper publishers. There were others on the train who belonged more exclusively in Willkie's personal entourage. They included Davenport, and his wife, the writer Marcia Davenport, Root, Paul Smith, of the *San Francisco Chronicle*, and Pierce Butler, Jr., son of the Supreme Court Justice. William J. Gallagher, New York lawyer and later to be Willkie's law partner, had the thankless task of managing the entire train; he was the only man on the train who knew how to say "no." A long list of friends and businessmen were constantly getting on and off, in addition to the local Republicans in each state who automatically joined the caravan. There were a few specialists. Raymond L. Buell, for example, was on the train as official campaign adviser in foreign relations until he was succeeded by Brooks Emeny. Elliott Bell, former newspaperman, was the specialist on finance, Bartley C. Crum, San Francisco lawyer, the specialist on labor problems.

Of the fifty-one nights between the train's departure from Rushville and its arrival in New York, Willkie passed forty-two in his private car, called Pioneer, five in hotels, and four in his New York apartment. Whenever he could, he would escape from his quarters and his advisers and join the newspapermen for a little relaxation, but he could never escape for long. At this pace, it was inevitable that the train should have become a nightmare for many of those on it and a legend for the reporters. Incidents happened so fast that they became anecdotes before anyone could discover what had actually happened. One girl reporter was discovered to have been planted on the train by the Democratic National Committee; she was found out only when President Roosevelt used some paragraphs in one of his speeches which Willkie had written and intended to use in one of his. An important state leader of Republican women fell off the back platform of the train when she started to make a speech just as the engineer decided to move on; when Willkie himself pulled the emergency brake signal, the train reversed and almost ran over the lady.

Willkie found the endless succession of new towns confusing, and he inevitably ran short of local color for his impromptu speeches. As a result, he sometimes found himself "glad to be near the town where Mark Twain was born" when he was two states away from Missouri. He invariably gave away his major speeches in advance talks with the reporters; it was impossible for him to keep a speech secret until he had delivered it. Irving Berlin had given him the right to use "God Bless America" as a campaign song; even though the Democrats crossed this up by using it too, those on the Willkie train heard it so often that its opening bars made the whole train wince. The two inflexible rules Willkie never broke were that he would not wear an Indian headdress or go fishing.

The pattern of campaigning produced under these circumstances ran surprisingly true to form. On issue after issue, and in situation after situation, Willkie began with a statement of his position which was relatively simple and honest. Within days, and sometimes within hours, it would become loaded with political hedges and reservations, on the one hand, and on the other with the peculiar quality of shrillness which his campaign acquired when "vibrant," "fervent," and "crusade" had become— as they did—its catchwords. This was no simple question of professionals versus amateurs, with Willkie in the middle. The times

Fitzpatrick in the St. Louis *Post-Dispatch*

were moving too fast for any actively campaigning candidate to stick to simple speech, and especially for one burdened with the inevitable problems and contradictions of the Republican nomination.

In addition, the old personal antagonism between Willkie and Roosevelt, bristling now with nearly a decade of real differences and misunderstandings, worked heavily against Willkie's effort to establish a firm, consistent program of his own. Roosevelt never once mentioned Willkie's name in public throughout the campaign, and for most of it, until October 23, he refused even to answer challenges and charges. This left Willkie galled and angry, with no one to debate what he sincerely believed were real issues except the Democratic spokesman whom he bitterly referred to as "that sterling statesman from the Bronx, Mr. Edward J. Flynn." Finally, this was a situation in which Willkie's own competitive, all-or-nothing spirit took charge. He had to win as only a man has to win who has never lost. He had to win big. And each time something went against him, he had to double his bets. This is the kind of man Willkie was, and it is small wonder that as the shouting grew louder, his voice disappeared, and as his campaign grew more strident, it was harder and harder to be quite sure what it was all about.

Two major questions of national policy broke through the campaign oratory during the late summer, and on both Willkie's position showed clearly this dilemma in which he found himself. Willkie approved of both the destroyers-for-bases deal with Britain and selective service legislation, but strongly disapproved of Roosevelt's methods in securing them. The crescendo of emotion in his public statements on each of them reflects his struggle with forces inside himself and inside his campaign train more than it shows any careful plan to win votes.

Winston Churchill had written to Roosevelt on July 31, outlining the swap of British bases for overage U. S. destroyers substantially as it was finally accomplished. But secret negotiations were required on the details, since the transaction involved new concepts of international law besides skirting dangerously close to a U. S. statute against the delivery of warships built for a belligerent. Willkie was sounded out early, through Archibald MacLeish, then Librarian of Congress and a White House intimate, and his friend and former fellow-editor of *Fortune*, Davenport, to make certain that the deal did not become a campaign issue. But most of the contact between Roosevelt and Willkie was through William Allen White.

White's Committee to Defend America by Aiding the Allies had six hundred local chapters and thousands of active volunteers behind it, and he was the logical man to act as intermediary.

He never allowed this role to conflict with his personal support and close friendship for Willkie, but even he was baffled by the human problem. "It's not as bad as it seems," he wired the President on August 11. "I have talked with both of you on this subject during the last ten days. I know that there is not two bits difference between you on the issue pending. But I can't guarantee either of you to the other, which is funny for I admire and respect you both. I realize you in your position don't want statements but Congressional votes. Which by all the rules of the game you should have. But I've not quit and as I said it's not as bad as it looks."

At first, Willkie ducked any open answer, since no legislation had yet been introduced to authorize the deal and he felt what White called "a natural diffidence about assuming Congressional leadership before his ears are dry." But the President knew from White that Willkie was in general for the plan, and he also knew, although he did not tell White, that he was not even going to try to get Congress to authorize the deal. A Gallup poll showed 62 per cent public support for it, and even the *Chicago Tribune* approved. But Roosevelt had a shrewder estimate of the strength of isolationism among Republicans in Congress than Willkie had. On August 20, Churchill told the House of Commons that the deal was under discussion and that it would involve Britain and the United States still more closely in each other's affairs. "I could not stop it if I wished; no one can stop it. Like the Mississippi it just keeps rolling along. Let it roll. Let it roll on—full flood, inexorable, irresistible, benignant, to broader lands and better days." With this on his side, Roosevelt did not need the Congressional approval White thought he did.

The final exchange of letters between Churchill and Roosevelt took place on September 2 and was made public the following day. Willkie announced at once that he backed the deal, but added his regret that the President had done it without either Congressional approval or public discussion. "We must be extremely careful in these times," he said, "when the struggle in the world is between democracy and totalitarianism, not to eliminate or destroy the democratic processes while seeking to preserve democracy."

Within a few days, the pressures had been at work and the language had been sharpened. Willkie was now calling the deal "the most dictatorial and arbitrary act of any President in the history of the United States." Roosevelt answered him in a press conference by claiming that what he had done as Commander-in-Chief was only what Jefferson had done in the Louisiana Purchase. Here the President was in complete error, for Jefferson did submit the Louisiana Purchase to the Senate, where it was given an almost unanimous vote of approval. But public sentiment was on the whole behind the destroyers-for-bases deal, and Willkie's original objection to the way it was concluded was soon forgotten in campaign oratory and public apathy.

Personal acrimony and the dead weight of Republican Toryism in the public mind embittered even more the problem of the Selective Service Act. Its first draft had been written by a Republican, Grenville Clark. It was introduced in Congress by Senator Edward R. Burke, Nebraska Democrat, who had broken with Roosevelt on the Supreme Court issue, and Representative James W. Wadsworth, New York Republican, both of whom were Willkie backers. Polls throughout the summer showed large and growing public support for the bill, even among the super-nationalists who wanted no part of the war in Europe. As with the destroyers-for-bases deal, Willkie was in favor of it. Yet once again the pattern of political and personal forces worked against his one-man assertion of leadership.

As early as August 12, Roosevelt wrote to Representative Edward T. Taylor, chairman of the House Appropriations Committee who had urged a conference with Willkie to work out an agreement on the issue: "I did not answer your telegram before this as I was feeling out the Willkie situation. The story in Saturday morning's paper makes it perfectly clear that he has no desire to co-operate and is merely playing politics. I am inclined to think that the best approach is an appeal to the patriotism of Joe Martin and Charlie McNary." Five days later,

Willkie came out in his acceptance speech in favor of the bill as "the only democratic way in which to secure the trained and competent manpower we need for national defense." Martin, interestingly, had begged him not to come out for selective service during the campaign, and Willkie had shown real courage in doing so.

Roosevelt had not been far wrong in suspecting that politics would be played with the bill, but it was not Willkie who played it. Before the bill was passed, Willkie denounced an amendment, backed by Senators John H. Overton, Louisiana Democrat, and Richard B. Russell, Georgia Democrat, which would have given the Secretaries of War and Navy blanket powers to take over factories and other property. Willkie called this an effort to "sovietize" the country and challenged the President to state where he stood on it.

"I put this up to the President now," he said, "and I hope that he does not answer with any quip about how Wendell Willkie loves property and he loves humanity. I say, without any personal criticism of the President, that it has been his good fortune at every stage in his life to possess and enjoy more wealth and more income than I have. This is as true today as it was in the past.

"The issue at stake cannot be intelligently set in such terms. The issue is the form of government under which we shall live, the way of life for which we shall stand. The issue is also our power to defend ourselves. In my view, the present amendment would weaken us further.

"The President in his own judgment has declined to debate such issues. That is his privilege, but in this instance so much is at stake that I put this question to him directly: Is he for or against the Overton-Russell amendment?"

Roosevelt had no burning desire to seem partial during the campaign to either exempting property from the draft or the sovietization of the nation. So he simply kept quiet, and never committed himself. The amendment was modified in the House, to prevent arbitrary seizures of property, and the bill was signed on September 16. Willkie never got his debate with the President on the question, but only a day of ridicule on the

The Hoarse and Urgent Voice

Senate floor. Senator Josh Lee, Oklahoma Democrat, suggested that "there should be a new popular song dedicated to Mr. Willkie entitled 'I Did Not Raise My Dollar to Be a Soldier.'" No single incident in the campaign served as much as this to remind the voters of Willkie's Wall Street background and his property-conscious backers.

Financial details of an election campaign make sordid reading, but nothing illustrates so clearly the strength of the party system against a candidate with pretensions to independence. On the day of his nomination, Willkie told a press conference in Philadelphia that his first request of the treasurer of the national committee would be observance of the recently passed Hatch Act which restricted individual contributions to a maximum of $5,000. "I hope," he said, "the contributions are in smaller amounts than that, and very widely diffused among the people who have been interested in this thing."

In the end the Republican National Committee reported to the Senate expenditures of $14,941,143, compared to a Democratic figure of $6,095,357, and Senator Guy M. Gillette, Iowa Democrat, estimated that unreported expenditures would bring the total cost of the election to between $50,000,000 and $60,-000,000. Since the Hatch Act did not bar individuals from making multiple gifts to different party committees, one family —the du Ponts of Delaware—gave the Republicans $186,760; another—the Pews of Pennsylvania—gave $108,525. These figures were very much smaller than the sums given by the same families in the 1936 campaign. But the names of other families who were big contributors to the Republican campaign fund included: the Pitcairn family of Philadelphia, $29,115; Ira C. Copley of Aurora, Illinois, $30,900; Mr. and Mrs. Alfred P. Sloan, Jr., New York City, $36,000; the Culver family of St. Louis, $25,600; the Widener family of Philadelphia, $23,750; Mr. and Mrs. Donaldson Brown of New York, $27,000; the Queeny family of St. Louis, $42,325; Mr. and Mrs. E. Parmalee Prentice, $17,000; the Rockefeller family, $59,000. All were names associated in the public mind with great wealth rather than with the "crusade for liberty and the democratic way of life" about which the candidate was talking.

Willkie

The 1940 campaign spawned more nonparty agencies than any other in United States history. Roosevelt could claim the National Committee for Agriculture, which spent $77,489 to re-elect him; the Businessmen's League for Roosevelt, which spent $59,973; the Hollywood for Roosevelt Committee, $12,983; the Non-Partisan League of Clothing Workers, $12,405; and a long list of others. Willkie's *ad hoc* committees raised more money than popular enthusiasm. Their names borrowed more slogans from the party's platform than from Willkie's speeches: the National Committee to Uphold Constitutional Government, $377,381; the People's Committee to Defend Life Insurance and Savings, $58,871; Pro-America, $37,950.

Willkie had some nonparty mass organizations on his side. Republican servicemen were organized as the Willkie War Veterans, and spent a campaign fund for him of $78,001. The Associated Willkie Clubs of America reported a total expenditure of $1,309,925 on the campaign, and after the election was over, Root sent letters to more than 11,000 individual contributors offering them their choice between a 7 per cent refund and contribution of the unexpended sum to a good-government movement. Even these figures showed that some of the contributions were large; the Committee to Defend America by Aiding the Allies, raising funds in the same manner and at the same time, reported by November, 1940, a total of only $230,000 contributed by almost exactly the same number of donors as the Willkie Clubs reported.

But these were still the small contributions Willkie had wanted, and they came from people who backed him personally rather than the party machine, and who were ready to contribute a very large amount of volunteer time and energy. No other candidate ever raised so much money in this way, but the total was still not enough to give him the independence he wanted.

The first tomato was thrown by a high school student in a Los Angeles suburb on September 19, the day after the campaign was formally launched. It was followed by a good many others, and eggs, cantaloupe, apples, potatoes, light bulbs, telephone books, rocks, a chair, even a wastebasket dropped from a hotel window, gave Willkie's campaign a touch of the violence which was loose in the world and in many men's minds in the autumn of 1940. A famous newspaper photograph showed Willkie just after a frozen egg had hit him in the eye, with Ed holding him back. In Chicago it was proved that children had been paid silver quarters to throw eggs and tomatoes. But no one was seriously hurt, and most of the culprits proved to be rowdy school children or hoodlums. Yet it happened in city after city and for the first time in a modern Presidential election. When a man was arrested loading a revolver in the aisle of Madison Square Garden, just before Willkie's wind-up speech, many memories were jogged into real alarm.

Violent ideas were in the air, and rough speech lay just beyond the sober edge of a lot of conversation during the campaign. A certain amount of whispering about the private lives of all the major candidates was inevitable in such a climate of anxiety. A few Republican publishers secured copies of letters allegedly written by Wallace which might have been used to smear the Democratic Vice-Presidential candidate. Charles Michelson, then publicity director for the Democratic National Committee, has described the perturbation this caused in New Deal circles, especially in Harry L. Hopkins, who "suggested expedients that would have made admirable chapters in an Oppenheim novel (for he regarded the matter as of tragic importance) but fitted into no conception of practical politics." Michelson believed until his death that these letters, which he described as "silly rather than evil" and of highly doubtful authenticity, were not made public because the Republicans could not find a publisher. The fact was that Willkie was under considerable pressure to authorize their use by several publishers and that he flatly refused to do so. "We're not running that kind of campaign," he said, and the letters were never used.

Much of this bitter partisanship was sopped up by the circus aspects of an American election. In Philadelphia, Willkie was greeted by a platoon of pretty girls carrying banners: "Hello, Mr. Willkie—We're for Roosevelt." In New Haven signs reading "Roosevelt for the Poor; Willkie for the Big Shots" were carried by little boys chiefly interested in the big parade. The World's

Fair was drawing to a close in New York, the Reds beat the Tigers in the World Series, and the election was, after all, the biggest show of all.

Willkie took the body-breaking schedule in his stride, and at the end of the campaign he still looked fresh and vigorous. Theodore Roosevelt and Bryan were certainly the only other candidates in history who possibly campaigned as hard. Willkie knew his own personality, his size, his grin, his informal manner, and his unruly hair were his assets. In his campaign biography, Stanley Walker wrote that Willkie, "in any gathering, is about as anonymous and inconspicuous as an old buffalo bull in a herd of range cattle," and millions of people found out for themselves what this meant. Campaign news pictures exploited his free, unpracticed gestures for those who never saw the candidate himself. Everyone who did see him got an impression of vast, unflagging energy, passionate conviction, and a hoarse and urgent voice.

The voice was the only personal asset which let him down. He had to apologize for it after the first day of heavy campaigning, but he was intolerant of friends—like Walter O'Keefe, radio star and advance man for the Willkie train—who urged him, first, to take lessons on how to save his voice and, later, to give it even elementary medical care. Willkie felt that he was challenging not only Roosevelt but all the skilled modulation of the fireside chats and of slick radio technique. He sometimes seemed to caricature his own "Indianer" accent, with "power" becoming "parr," and "America" sounding like "Amarrca." At least as many of these dropped syllables disappeared because he talked quickly as were the result of his Indiana boyhood. And there was a defiant sort of pride in the whispered croak his voice often became. A Hollywood voice specialist, Dr. Harold Gray Barnard, was added in Kansas City to the experts on the train, and he somehow kept Willkie's voice going although he never succeeded, day or night, in persuading the candidate to give it a rest. His bill, figured at $250 a day, was later protested and renegotiated by party leaders, but he had had no easy task. Willkie was a bad patient in every way. He kept on talking, and his raucous voice became an audible expression of the urgency and rough passion he was pouring into his crusade.

For a crusade it was, in steadily increasing measure. As the contradictions of his position multiplied, Willkie's passionate intensity grew. "Whether you or others like it or not," he had said at Rushville in September, "I never, during the course of the campaign, will state anything in which I do not believe. I will not talk in quibbling language. I will talk in simple, direct Indiana speech." But this resolution did not last long. The man tended to disappear beneath the candidate, for the professionals could not be denied. A release stating that the candidate "saw little opportunity to attend church today" was to be remembered by him with distaste as long as he lived, for he had never been a regular churchgoer and he disliked posing as one. But pose he did, and the pictures of him going to church were duly released to the nation's press. All this pressure drove him to a growing fervency. "This is not a campaign," he cried to a crowd at Long Beach, California, as early as September 19, "it's a crusade. I call upon each and all of you to join it. I ask each of you to be a soldier in the fight to keep our liberties." It was hard to raise the emotional voltage of this language, but Willkie did. Before the campaign was over, he broke into a prepared speech at the Empire City Racetrack in Yonkers to say: "After having seen millions of Americans and realizing more than I ever did before how precious a thing this American way is, I want to say to you that if we do not prevail this fall, this way of life will pass."

Willkie was not alone in believing this. On October 17, Herbert Hoover wrote to Chief Justice Charles Evans Hughes what he himself called a fantastic suggestion: that Hughes resign "with a declaration to the country of the complete necessity for a change in Administration." Hoover added: "I would not do [this] if I did not believe that the whole future of the American people hangs upon the decisions of this election." Hughes refused to take the suggestion seriously, but it showed the mood of many Republicans in the 1940 campaign.

When the great day came, on November 5, Willkie voted in

Willkie

a New York City public school and went to his Commodore Hotel headquarters to await the results. It was a long and bitter wait. He was so keyed up that, unlike McNary and the party leaders, he refused to concede defeat when he went to bed at 2 A.M. He had broken the unhappy night by a short fight-talk to a ballroom full of loyal but dejected followers. The first news of the Democratic victory was so stunning and complete that days were required before he and others realized that his 22,304,755 votes (against 27,243,466 for Roosevelt) were more than any Republican candidate for President had ever received. The electoral vote was 449 to 82, but Willkie had carried ten states, and a relatively small shift of votes from rural to urban areas would have made the electoral vote as close as the popular vote. Roosevelt had taken every city in the country with more than 400,000 population except Cincinnati; and his pluralities in New York City, Chicago, Los Angeles, and other big cities were big enough to carry the most important states. Yet Willkie had crowded him down to a majority of only 224,000 in New York, the smallest Roosevelt margin in New York since his original election as Governor in 1928. Besides adding nearly 6,000,000 to Landon's 1936 vote, Willkie had held his opponent to a smaller total than he had had in 1936, and to the smallest plurality any winning candidate had had since 1916.

"Don't be afraid and never quit" was what Willkie had told his dismal cohorts in the middle of the night. He was to follow his own advice, but the campaign fever had first to subside. This did not take long, and those who had been more interested in Willkie than in the Republican party machine dragged their heels in bitterness less than the professionals. "I am in no way excited about the election of Mr. Roosevelt," White wrote to another editor. "I voted for Mr. Willkie with enthusiasm. The dirty cracks on one side were as bad as the dirty cracks on the other, and twenty-two million against twenty-five [*sic*] million levels it up so we are in no danger of a dictator. I never thought we were. The old ship is going to keep right on sailing along."

CHAPTER THIRTEEN

Why Did Willkie Lose?

T HE most detailed study of the 1940 campaign, on an Erie County, Ohio, sampling by the Bureau of Applied Social Research of Columbia University, confirmed the conclusion of many of the reporters who covered it: that religion, economic level, and residence were the determining factors in the outcome. The survey found that a voter who was Catholic, poor, and lived in a poor urban neighborhood was likely to vote for the Democrats. A voter who was Protestant, well-off, and lived in a high-class neighborhood or in the country was likely to vote for the Republicans. It further indicated that the campaign itself was relatively unimportant, serving only to confirm already committed voters or to speed up changes in voting habits which had begun before the speeches started.

The basic truth of this explanation can hardly be challenged. The United States in 1940 was still living out the chapter in history which began with the Great Depression. Roosevelt was already changing his own view of his job from "Dr. New Deal" to "Dr. Win-the-War" but he had not yet coined the phrases and the change was not yet clear to the public. For most Americans, memories of the depression were even more vivid in 1940 than fears of war or of dictatorship, and the farmer-labor coalition which had ended twelve years of Republican rule in 1932 was still electorally invincible.

Yet Willkie's campaign may have had an importance beyond any simple formula of "haves" and "have-nots," of rural and urban groups, or of conservatives and liberals. In the first place, he carried enough agricultural states to prove that the Democratic farmer-labor alliance, made in depression, could be badly cracked. In the second place, he polled a total vote which was clearly far in excess of any estimate of the economically privileged in the country; this was an important demostration that the party system in the United States was not yet clearly established on class or even income lines. Finally, his own brand of liberalism, although it was defeated at the polls and later repudiated by the Republican party, won enough support across the nation and especially in business circles to keep the American political system, for at least another decade, from freezing into any clear conservative-radical alignment.

None of this would have happened had—say—Taft been the nominee. Willkie represented elements and ideas in the business world which had more vitality (and may still have) than they were credited with in the depression-born stereotypes of the American businessman. They were not new in politics: Theodore Roosevelt in 1912 and La Follette in 1924 had fought campaigns which sought to mobilize the older, expansive, liberal traditions of American free enterprise. In 1940, they were not strong enough to win the election or even to take over the Republican party. Yet they came close enough to give real importance to the study of why Willkie lost. These half-forgotten Republican traditions which Willkie sought to revive were opposed not only by the New Deal but also by many newer traditions within the Republican party.

The platform—bad as it was and was recognized to be—was no great handicap to him. Most Presidential candidates pay their respects to the platform in an acceptance speech and then proceed to ignore it. Willkie was no exception. But the same forces which had been at work in the committee at Philadelphia drafting the platform were also on the campaign train. They were unable to enforce strict party discipline on their maverick candidate, but they did help to shape his program and his speeches because they were representative, in the most direct way, of the different and contradictory elements within the party. The Republicans had no party mechanism in 1940 with which to compromise their differences. So on many of the important issues, the differences within the party and between the party and

Berryman in the Washington *Star*

"One way of looking at the country."

Willkie were evaded. Concealing them was a tougher job.

The record showed, for example, that McNary had voted in the Senate against a substantial number of the ideas Willkie was backing. (McNary, who had never made a single oration in twenty-five years in the Senate, gave this advice to Willkie when they met for the first time after the convention: "Don't forget, young fellow, in politics you'll never get in trouble by not saying too much.") Coming from the power-conscious Northwest, he had backed TVA from the beginning, the Bonneville and Grand Coulee Dams, and all other Federal power projects. He had voted for the Securities and Exchange Commission. He had opposed all reciprocal tariff agreements and

213

especially all measures tending to ease the supply of war materials to the Allies. His presence on the ticket with Willkie was a clear reminder that the Republican party, like American business at that stage of its development, was condemned to be for and against government subsidy of cheap electric power, for and against government control of Wall Street, for and against a policy of high tariff protection, for and against the risks involved in supporting the nations fighting Hitler. It could be argued, as Willkie himself believed, that such contradictions were by no means fatal in a party system, and that they were, in actual fact, a chief reason for the existence of the American party system, which serves, in theory, to work out coalitions between fractional group interests before elections, and not after them as, for example, in France. But the Republican party had neither the authority on top levels nor the clear channel for vigorous back talk from below which might have made these contradictions fruitful of good debate and effective political compromise.

In the 1940 campaign, both the strength and the weakness of the Willkie candidacy were to be seen in his program for economic recovery, his foreign policy, and his political independence. All three became inseparably tangled in the election. His position on each was hammered out in the course of the campaign, and against very heavy handicaps which were by no means accidental but grew out of the generation in which he lived.

Willkie was clearly hurt by the plain fact that his championship of free industry in a competitive society came from a man identified with a powerful monopoly. It is hard for any public utility executive to talk about the healthy social effects of competition. During the long struggle with TVA, Willkie himself had never budged from the position that one system or the other should have the customers, not both. A good many of his personal advisers kept prodding him to take up the cause of the small businessman; some of them believed this could be the core of the positive program the Republicans needed so badly, and that it might bring trust-busters and New Dealers like

Why Did Willkie Lose?

Thurman Arnold, whom Willkie admired greatly, into his camp. He made some halfhearted gestures in this direction; at New Haven, for example, in the center of New England's small manufacturing economy, he proposed a network of government-backed laboratories to do research work for small business. But the small businessman had already become such a stereotype in American politics that it was hard to rouse him into action with oratory. And Willkie was basically as divided in his mind on this question as the business community he represented. He was too deeply aware of the real meaning of modern technology to be able to put his heart into any crusade for small business. He had grown up in expansive phases of American business history, in the Indiana gas boom, in Akron rubber, in the electric power revolution, and the curse of bigness was never much more than a slogan to him.

The Democrats, naturally, made as much as they could of Willkie's dilemma on the public utility problem. The Commonwealth and Southern record was too clean to provide much political ammunition; during the campaign the SEC carried on an investigation of charges that a C. & S. subsidiary, the Georgia Power Company, had contributed to political campaign funds in Georgia, but this never made headlines. Instead, Wallace, Senator Norris, and Secretary of the Interior Ickes pounded away in the press and in speeches in regions where public power was a real issue, at Willkie's change of position on the problem. At Portland, Oregon, on September 23, Willkie said that the people, rather than the government, should decide whether private companies or public power districts should sell the new, cheap, government-generated power. "If you want to take over the private utilities," he said, "that is your business, but you should do it by a determination of fair values so that capital will not be driven out of this area."

This represented important concessions from Willkie's earlier public positions, even though it may have been close to what he had privately believed for a long time. The Democrats dug up one of his more fervent statements during the TVA fight, made before the Economic Club of New York on January 21, 1935. "I do not like to make personal references," he had said then, "but I want to say to you that no duty has ever come to me in my life, even that in the service of my country, which has so appealed to my sense of social obligation, patriotism and love of mankind as this, my obligation to say and do what I can for the preservation of public utilities privately owned." Not content to contrast the two statements, the Democrats charged that this was an admission of private loyalties transcending even loyalty to his country when he had been a soldier. Republicans fired back that this was a dastardly smear on a war veteran, asking what Roosevelt's war record had been, and the original issue was fairly quickly lost in campaign fireworks. But it stayed in some voters' minds, and Willkie did not carry a single state, even McNary's Oregon, in which the control of electric power was an important issue.

The core of Willkie's personal economic program was, in fact, expansion. His differences with the New Deal were far more real to him than they seemed to his conservative backers, who were already muttering "me-tooism," or to many voters who saw little to choose on this issue between the two candidates as far as their promises were concerned. Willkie stormed across the country denouncing the New Deal for (1) too many regulations on business; (2) too many and too sudden changes in these regulations; (3) ill-defined and shifting limits to the areas in which business might expect direct government competition; (4) a tax structure which did not provide incentives for new enterprise; (5) a generally defeatist attempt to recover prosperity by limiting production instead of by increasing it. These points added up in his own mind to an economic program, and one in which he deeply believed. But he failed to make it stand out as a positive program in its own right, because he never succeeded in translating his own belief in an expanding economy into a credible program of action.

It was during the campaign that he first used the phrase, "Only the productive can be strong, and only the strong can be free." He said it over and over again; no single sentence came so close to summing up the man and what he stood for. "American liberalism," he had said in his acceptance speech, "does not merely consist in reforming things. It consists also in making things. The ability to grow, the ability to make things, is the measure of man's welfare on earth. To be free, man must be creative. I am a liberal because I believe that in our industrial age there is no limit to the productive capacity of any man. And as I believe that, I likewise believe that there is no limit to the horizon of America."

His central difficulty lay in translating this into a positive program rather than simply into criticism of the New Deal. The latter was not hard: one-third of the nation was still living in some degree of need; the unemployed numbered between 8,000,000 and 10,000,000; the national debt was climbing higher and higher; most important of all, the New Deal had not worked out any long-term solution of the depression. He tried hard to criticize the New Deal for what it had failed to do rather than for what it had done, but the daily reaching for the crowd and for the headline forced him into an essentially negative statement of his own central position: the need for a release of constructive energy on a tremendous scale, for an enormous increase in production.

With twelve years' hindsight and a threefold increase in the U. S. national production, it is easy to see that Willkie's expansionist program for America was more solidly based on the facts of national capacity than the defeatism of tired New Dealers who laughed at him as a salesman and a blowhard. Even during the campaign the signs were there: official figures showed 400,000 jobless men going to work in August, 500,000 in September, most of them on war orders. Willkie saw these signs, and warned as strongly as he could against an industrial recovery based on armaments. As early as March of 1940, in an article called "The Court Is Now His" which he had written for the *Saturday Evening Post,* Willkie had named his central position on this issue. "If we cannot correct the present situation," he wrote, "recovery—based on peace rather than war— is not going to come. And if recovery does not come, the American may harbor a justifiable alarm for those principles of freedom, opportunity and enterprise that he holds most dear."

His challenge to the nation to find a peaceful incentive which could release its full productive power remains as valid as when he gave it. But it was a challenge and not an answer to the problem. And even the challenge lost political force when he kept on phrasing it negatively. "Nowadays," he told a crowd in Rainier Baseball Park in Seattle on September 23, "it is about as hard to start a new business as it is to rob a bank—and the risks of going to jail are about as great in both cases." The line was good for a laugh, but not as a rallying cry for the production-minded Americans Willkie was sure must rise in their power, cast off the shackles of Washington bureaucracy, and create the new goods and services and jobs the country needed. In the end, the war itself and the cold war which followed it accomplished the expansion that Willkie wanted, with other consequences that he deeply feared.

Willkie realized early in the campaign that his electoral chances depended partly on a serious break in the Democratic control of the farm vote. Even a new mobilization of the traditionally Republican business votes throughout the country, with such accessions of strength as he could win from industrial labor on his liberalism and the third-term issue, could not win alone. He was to prove more successful on the farms than in the cities. When the returns were all in, it was clear that Roosevelt's farmer-labor coalition had just begun to crack on the farmer side, with nine of the ten states he lost predominantly agricultural states. Yet during the campaign, Willkie was closer to a "me-too" position on agricultural policy than he was on any other issue.

He tried hard, in conferences with farmers' groups at Des Moines in August, at Rushville in September, and on all his long campaign trips through the West, to work out some smashing attack on the New Deal farm program. But most farmers were sold in 1940 on what Washington was doing for them, and Willkie was forced to concentrate his attack chiefly on the evils of remote and bureaucratic control. He repeated specific promises that he would make no change in farm benefits if elected. In Omaha on September 26 he said: "This, then, is my farm program. Let us take over—and improve—those elements of the present program which are helping the farmer in his battle against the contracting economy that the New Deal has brought about." This was a good deal less than all-out attack.

It was not for want of trying. The Republican platform had promised a soil conservation program "free from government-dominated production control." But Republican farmers knew that some kind of production control was an essential condition of commodity loans, which were in turn essential to farm relief and prosperity. So even production controls were given a silent blessing by the candidate before the election was over; he promised only to make them more efficient. From time to time he tried out more radical suggestions: he told a group of Indiana farmers on September 2, for instance, that high tariffs, Hitler's destruction of foreign markets, a tax structure based on acreage rather than on income, and the stagnation of American industry were the basic threats to agricultural prosperity. At Des Moines, in August, he tried out tentatively the idea of a great decentralization of industry to bring markets closer to the farms. But to have developed any of these themes at length would have meant stepping on too many Republican toes.

At Rushville, the day after his acceptance speech, he had said: "I am purely a conversational farmer. I have never done a stroke of work on a Rush County farm in my life, and I hope I never have to. Louis Berkemier and Joe Kramer and the other fellows [tenants on his farms] do the work. I merely do the talking." Then during the long campaign trips he was constantly being greeted at whistle stops by men who claimed to have known him during the summers when he worked on farms in the West. By September, he was opening a speech in Omaha with a reference to having worked as a farmhand in that section of the country, and adding: "I have never lost touch with the farm." The Republican National Committee released a movie short called "Willkie and McNary Know Their Farming." Few citizens knew that McNary's farming background consisted chiefly of having commercialized filbert growing in Oregon and later helping to develop a market for the imperial prune. The machine and the campaign were swallowing the candidates.

In his own position on labor, Willkie was as far from the traditional Republican position as he was on any single issue in the campaign. "Now let me tell you straight from the shoulder," he said in Seattle on September 23, "I stand for every single one of the social gains that labor has made. I stand for the National Labor Relations Act and the right of free collective bargaining. I stand for minimum wages and maximum hours, and for legislation to enforce them. I stand for social security benefits, and believe that they should be extended to other groups who do not yet enjoy them. I believe that we should be insured against unemployment, and that our old age should be protected by adequate pensions."

This was a big order for a Republican, but Willkie kept right on spelling it out, running the very real risk of an open split with his party. He promised that no person would be taken off relief until he had a job, and proposed a long-range program to improve the WPA by substitution of the merit system for political control. He denounced, it is true, crooked union racketeers and he called the New Deal administration of the NLRA "one of the most shocking tragedies in the history of American industrial relations." He hammered away steadily at "more jobs," in line with his central plea for more production, and his campaign estimate of more than 9,000,000 unemployed was not much in excess of the figures admitted by the Administration.

It did him no good at all. His reception in the grimy industrial districts of big cities was sometimes rough, always a little hostile. There were frequent boos, and sullen, unresponsive faces, in Homestead, Duquesne, and East Pittsburgh, along the winding Monongahela Valley, in contrast to showers of confetti and cheering crowds in Pittsburgh's "Golden Triangle." It was the same in Providence, Akron, Milwaukee, Chicago, and Seattle.

He made some mistakes. In his biggest speech on labor, made in Pittsburgh to a labor audience, he repeated his promises and added that he would appoint a Secretary of Labor directly from the ranks of organized labor. When the applause died down, he added: "And it will not be a woman, either."

Frances Perkins has remembered that Roosevelt, who listened to this speech on the radio, told her: "That was a boner Willkie pulled. He was right. He was going good when he said his ap-

Why Did Willkie Lose?

pointment of a Secretary of Labor would come from labor's ranks. That was legitimate political talk, but why didn't he have sense enough to leave well enough alone? Why did he have to insult every woman in the United States? It will make them mad, it will lose him votes."

Miss Perkins told the President that she had received some five hundred letters and telegrams expressing irritation at the remark, more than half of them from Republican women. "He's sure to make other boners as time goes on," Roosevelt told her. "If we don't do anything to break the spell, I'm pretty sure he will talk himself out of enough votes to carry me without much effort."

The trouble lay deeper than any slips the candidate made. There was no single labor union official who was known to be close to him. The Democrats were ringing every change on phrases like "economic royalists," "princes of privilege," and "minions of the House of Morgan." It did Willkie little good to go on explaining that he had never actually had an office on Wall Street, and that he had never fought a union in his business career. He found himself, in this regard, in the same dilemma as much of American business: organized labor was too new for him to know much about it, and while he was finding out he became ticketed in many minds with the views of the articulate minority of businessmen who knew about labor unions only that they were against them.

This failure of understanding had dramatic expression in the last-minute deal which brought John L. Lewis into Willkie's camp, without the C.I.O. of which he was then president. The circumstances of the deal were all tawdry, but Willkie had known nothing about them. Lewis indorsed Willkie in a radio broadcast on October 25, over 362 stations of the three major networks. The time was paid for—it cost approximately $45,000—by the Committee of Democrats-for-Willkie, of which Dr. Alan Valentine was executive director. Only after the election did it become known that the money, through an elaborate and lawyer-supervised round-robin of exchanged checks, had come in reality from William Rhodes Davis, a friend of Lewis and an oil man who had been involved with Germany in both oil business and peace feelers. Willkie had never heard of Davis before Pryor told him that he was willing to pay for the broadcast, and he said later that he would have rejected the offer if he had understood it. The only lucky break for the Republicans in the entire incident was the fact that their opponents did not learn about the sponsorship of the broadcast until after the election.

The Lewis speech was in his most characteristic style, and it convinced almost no one. He praised Willkie's "integrity and honor" in phrases certainly never used before or since about him. The Republican candidate was not an aristocrat, he said. "He has the common touch. He was born in the briar and not to the purple. He has worked with his hands, and has known pangs of hunger." It was a little late in the day to start this legend, but Lewis' real interest was not so much to elect Willkie as to oppose war and to defeat Roosevelt. He had plenty of scores to settle with the man he had helped to elect four years before. "You," he told prospective draftees, "who may be about to die in a foreign war, created at the whim of an international meddler, should you salute your Caesar? In cold, common sense, I think you should vote for Willkie." Even the strongholds of the C.I.O. and the U.M.W., both of which were Lewis' creations, voted overwhelmingly against his advice.

On balance, this question of the war cost Willkie an unknown but undoubtedly large number of votes. In their platforms both parties were firmly opposed to American involvement, and the personal convictions of the two candidates—as they were revealed to the public much later—were almost identical. It was the party system, again, which made the war an issue in the election. It gave Roosevelt the extremists in the interventionist camp, and they were quietly confident that in the long run he would prove to be their man. It gave Willkie the extremists in the isolationist camp, and they were quietly sure that in the long run he would abandon them. The great bulk of the voters, without extremist views, were given no chance to vote on the war, since both candidates promised not to send an American soldier unless we were attacked, but in such an emergency Roosevelt's

Why Did Willkie Lose?

experience counted heavily in many voters' minds to offset the argument against the third term.

The isolationists had good reason to suspect Willkie long before they voted for him. As early as 1939, he had taken part in the formation of William Allen White's Non-Partisan Committee for Peace through Revision of the Neutrality Law, the organization which was later to become the Committee to Defend America by Aiding the Allies. On October 20, 1939, Frederic R. Coudert gave a luncheon in New York at which White explained what his group was trying to do. Both Landon and Martin, then titular leaders of the Republicans, refused to join, but Willkie, who had been invited simply as a prominent businessman, spoke up after White had finished: "Well, if money is all that Mr. White needs, let's get it for him." When the Administration bill revising the 1935 Neutrality Law came before the House on November 3, 1939, 20 Republicans voted for it, 140 against.

During the summer honeymoon of Willkie and the Republican party, while still friendly forays were being made to Colorado Springs and Rushville to see how far the candidate would be reasonable, the isolationists did their best. Colonel McCormick went to see him. Senator Wheeler, Montana Democrat who was ready to bolt his own party on the war issue, tried to draw Willkie into a commitment against conscription. Father Coughlin's *Social Justice* and Joseph McWilliams of a Nazi Bund racket called the American Destiny party both praised his Elwood acceptance speech, with less sincerity than hope. Willkie repudiated them all by the time his campaign got under way, but there was no other place for many of these men to go and they did not repudiate him until after the election was over.

The Republican party's record on foreign policy was close to what the most extreme isolationists were working for. And many American businessmen approved of it. As late as October, 1940, in *Fortune's* forum of executive opinion, 30.7 per cent of a panel of powerful business leaders voted that Colonel Charles A. Lindbergh "has unselfishly and patriotically been making a useful effort to straighten out the nation's thinking on the war." In the preceding March, when Willkie had come out publicly for reciprocal tariffs and aid to nations attacked by an aggressor, Arthur Krock had written in the *New York Times* that this position alone showed why "he probably cannot be nominated by the Republicans." By the time he made his big campaign speech on foreign policy, in San Francisco on September 22, the gap between him and the party was as wide as the two-ocean foreign policy Willkie was advocating.

Willkie could not bring himself to leave the issue out of the campaign altogether, but once he attacked Roosevelt's foreign policy he was inviting examination of his own party's record and position. With Senator Hiram Johnson the ranking Republican member of the Senate Foreign Affairs Committee and Representative Hamilton Fish his counterpart in the House, with McNary and Martin the party's leaders in Congress, and with an unbroken record of heavy Republican votes on the isolationist side of all recent legislation, Willkie was in a tough spot. Somewhere in Iowa, in a session in his private car, a few of the reporters asked him what he would do with such men if he were in the White House. "Willkie brushed this aside impatiently," according to Marquis Childs, "saying that once he was elected, with the power of the Presidency behind him, such details could easily be taken care of. And I am sure he believed that. We from Washington looked skeptical."

The war news was crowding the campaign for headlines through the late summer and autumn. On September 19, London had its thirteenth consecutive night raid; on September 22, Germany, Italy, and Japan signed a ten-year mutual assistance pact; on October 4, Hitler met Mussolini at the Brenner Pass; and on October 27, eight days before the election, Mussolini's armies invaded Greece. If Willkie's problem was to show that he was no isolationist, Roosevelt was forced to prove that he would not declare war on Hitler the day after the election, and he was pushed, especially in the last weeks of the campaign, into statements he was later to regret. But his dilemma was simpler than Willkie's, he was enormously helped by the silent treatment he had given his opponent, and he was a far more skillful politician. "When I heard the President," Willkie later said, "hang the isolationist votes of Martin, Barton, and Fish on me, and get away with it, I knew I was licked." (Robert E. Sherwood, who heard him say it, commented: "I must say I doubt that statement; it was a virtue of Wendell Willkie's that he never knew when he was licked.")

The war was one issue on which the split in his party forced Willkie to change his tactics in mid-campaign. He started out by calling Roosevelt an appeaser, comparing him with Léon Blum. He charged that Roosevelt had intervened by telephone to speed the ultimate sell-out of Czechoslovakia at Munich. He quickly withdrew this charge, which had been written into his speech by Raymond L. Buell, a foreign affairs specialist, when Secretary of State Cordell Hull denied it. Hull's memoirs later made it clear that Roosevelt had indeed sent messages to both Hitler and Mussolini, although not by telephone and urging plain peace rather than peace necessarily on Axis terms. King George VI had written Roosevelt gratefully that "I have little doubt that your efforts contributed largely to the result." The campaign was no time to work out the niceties of responsibility involved.

Willkie attacked the President for his failure to support his own World Economic Conference in 1933, and he tried to enlist Winston Churchill on his side by quoting his words in 1937: "The Washington administration has waged so ruthless a war on private enterprise that the United States, with none of the perils and burdens of Europe upon it, is actually at the present moment leading the world back into the trough of depression." In 1940, Churchill was politically wise enough not to say anything, but he later wrote with what profound anxiety he had awaited the result. When it became known, he telegraphed Roosevelt: "Now I feel you will not mind my saying that I prayed for your success and that I am truly thankful for it."

Towards the end of October, the professionals had elbowed most of the amateurs away from Willkie, and they sold him on the reverse technique of calling Roosevelt a warmonger. In this their tactical judgment was strongly backed by their isolationist sympathies. The continuing gloomy reports from opinion polls and Willkie's gambling instinct led him to try it. By this time, he was pulling no punches in anything he said, and he struck out so violently, even if inconsistently, that he forced the President onto the defensive for the first and only time in the campaign. He asked whether there were secret agreements to take the United States into the war. "If his promise to keep our boys out of foreign wars is no better than his promise to balance the budget," he declared, "they're already almost on the transports." He worked up to the crescendo of predicting that "on the basis of his past performance with pledges to the people, you may expect war by April, 1941, if he is elected."

Whatever this new tactic did to ordinary people, it excited the professional politicians of both parties more than anything else in the campaign. On the Democratic side, they reacted with heavy pressure on Roosevelt which led him, in speeches in New York and Boston, to make serious concessions to the popular fear of war. These included the unqualified statement: "I have said this before, but I shall say it again and again and again: your boys are not going to be sent into any foreign wars." It was not a statement he was later glad to have on the record. On the Republican side, this first sign of panic in the enemy's camp led to moves which Willkie had no chance to control. Republican party advertisements were bought and paid for in the *Daily Worker*, since the Communist party was then chanting "The Yanks Are *Not* Coming," and in German-language newspapers which were anything but anti-Hitler. Hamilton Fish, whose Washington office was mailing out frankly pro-Nazi literature, wrote to the *New York Times* an exultant correction: "I do most emphatically endorse all of Mr. Willkie's recent statements on foreign policies."

One personal factor played a decisive part in pushing Willkie into this all-out charge of warmongering against Roosevelt. He had not been bothered by the first Democratic efforts to link him with appeasers, isolationists, and Fascists. Wallace had set their tone when he said: "The Republican candidate is not an appeaser and not a friend of Hitler. I'll say, too, that every Republican is not an appeaser. But you can be sure that every Nazi, every Hitlerite, and every appeaser is a Republican." This was no more than the usual campaign slugging, and it came while Willkie was himself trying to pin the same label on Roosevelt.

Why Did Willkie Lose?

As the campaign grew rougher, there were a good many whispers around the country about Willkie's German ancestry. Then in October the Colored Division of the Democratic National Committee released a truly scurrilous document linking his parents and his wife's parents with Hitler's statement that "Negroes are lower than apes." It called his nomination a *Blitzkrieg* triumph on the Hitler formula, and linked him with the wildest kind of isolationist and neo-Nazi fanatics. Unsigned leaflets were sent around the country, attacking his sister for marrying a German naval officer (she was married to Commander Paul E. Pihl, who was U. S. Naval Attaché in Berlin) and including such slander as the statement that Elwood, his home town, boasted public signs reading: "Nigger, don't let the sun go down on you."

Willkie answered this temperately in public. "Let me say this to you, also," he said in New York on October 8, "and I say this with the utmost sincerity: when anybody comes to you in a whispering campaign in an attempt to prejudice you, remember that you can teach a dog to fetch and you can teach a dog to carry. The very person who will attempt to stir up prejudice about another will stir up prejudice about you and about other people in America. All men should stop that, not only because it is their duty as American citizens but because if we once start that in American life then we are torn to pieces." But it was clear to those around him that the attack distressed him, and also threw him off balance. It explains the virulence of the last-minute warmongering charges against Roosevelt better than the "campaign oratory" statement for which Willkie was so often attacked later.

The statement that the Axis desired the defeat of Roosevelt was certainly believed by many Democrats. On October 9, Dorothy Thompson had come out for Roosevelt, and some of the Republican editors and readers of the *New York Herald Tribune,* as well as many of the other papers in which her column appeared, were seething with indignation. Undaunted, she wrote in her column prepared for October 14 that this was the deepest reason for her apostasy. "From Berlin there has been a systematic campaign against Franklin D. Roosevelt," she wrote, "in which the Nazis have seized upon every argument in opposition to him. Furthermore, the entire Fascist setup in this country, including a large section of the Italian and German press through all the many little sheets that they distribute, have conducted a base and virulent campaign against Mr. Roosevelt. They have instructed their followers to vote against him. Just now they are playing it all down a bit, in order not to have their open support injure Mr. Willkie. But they have done their work already and their followers are in the know.

"Wendell Willkie, as a character and a patriot, has nothing to do with the case. The Axis policy would have been the same whether the opponent had been Taft, Dewey, or Bob La Follette."

The article never saw print in the paper for which it was written. "Taken by itself it seemed to the Editor of the *Herald Tribune*," it was officially announced, "to be misleading, tending to inject into the campaign an un-American issue. The article was therefore withheld from publication pending the full development of Miss Thompson's views on this subject." That was the end of Miss Thompson on the *New York Herald Tribune*, and her column moved to another syndicate.

It is hard to estimate how many votes Willkie lost on the war issue. He was never sure himself. He had been even more sensitive than a professional politician to the problem of divided loyalties raised in America by the war. He spoke for Puerto Rican statehood, for the Y.M.C.A. on Founder's Day, for Christopher Columbus, for Leif Ericson, for Rosh Hashanah— all on dates which fell conveniently within the campaign. He was far more articulate and vociferous than any Republican candidate had been for a generation about Federal legislation against lynching, and about the elimination of Jim Crow practices in government work and contracts. Much of what he said on human rights and civil liberties made unpleasant reading for some Republicans. It was these speeches which gave rise to the anecdote of the fur-collared banker on a Westchester commuting train, reading his newspaper and commenting aloud: "I am afraid our candidate is talking too much."

In some regions, it can be shown that he actually won votes

because of the war. A clear shift of German or Italian votes in traditionally Democratic counties can be shown in South Dakota, in Texas, and in Staten Island. Samuel Lubell has calculated that Roosevelt's proportion of the major party vote dropped 7 per cent in 1940 against 1936; that in twenty counties his loss exceeded 35 per cent; and that nineteen of those twenty were predominantly German-speaking in background. But there is no way of measuring the reverse shift of voters whose "old country" feelings made them suspicious of Willkie and the Republican party.

Much *post mortem* analysis of the 1940 campaign has laid heavy emphasis on Willkie's personal independence of the party he was leading, and this has been attributed chiefly to his amateurism in politics and to his excessive personal self-confidence. Republicans have given this explanation the status of party doctrine by completely forgetting Willkie after, in the long run, they had repudiated him. This was a risk he ran during the 1940 campaign, with his ineradicable habit of calling them "You Republicans." Yet it would be a mistake to think that he did not know the risk. It is too simple to say, as some have said of Willkie, that he remained all his life a Wilsonian and an Indiana Democrat. This was not true. For four years of his life he tried hard to rebuild the Republican party on its old foundations in the American business and industrial world, by bringing into it the independent voters whose political function had been atrophied by the same pressures of modern American life which had made him an independent himself.

Willkie once told John Gunther that the first thing to find out about a state was the size and temper of its middle vote, its independents. He went into politics in 1940 as an independent, and his personal campaign strategy can be understood only if it is seen as an effort to appeal to men and women who were as independent as he was. Amateurism played its part, as did the personality factors which led him constantly to double his bets out of his deep need of winning. But the overriding consideration in his own mind was his plan to organize and lead an independent block of voters into the Republican party. Before he died, it could be said fairly that he had had more success in finding these voters than in squeezing them into the party he had chosen.

Granted the plan, the time was not badly chosen. In the 1936 election, a disturbingly small fraction of the qualified voters had bothered to go to the polls. There was clear evidence that both party machines, in the cities as well as in rural areas, were structural hangovers from an earlier and simpler period in American life. Millions of Americans had come to treat politics like baseball, with only occasional thumping of their sons' gloves to break a purely spectator relationship. The New Deal, in the preceding eight years, had brought a new block of independent voters into the Democratic party, which had creaked and groaned in the process of absorbing them, but had still survived. In 1940, Willkie was offering to do the same thing for the Republicans, and it was the decisive factor in all his campaign strategy.

By August there were 661 active Willkie Clubs, and more were being added at the rate of thirty or forty a day. Willkie made it transparently clear that he did not see them in any rivalry with the party apparatus; he was careful not to force their leaders onto party committees or even to give them any strong central headquarters. He saw them rather as incubators for independent citizens who might be drawn into the Republican party, much as some labor unions had served to recruit strength for the Democratic party over the preceding decade. When he talked to a meeting of their leaders in Des Moines on August 6, he addressed them as "Fellow Amateurs," to great applause. There is no reason to think that he ever saw these clubs as a potential machine to rival the regular Republican setup or that he would not have urged them to disband even if he had won the election.

The nucleus of most of these groups was in business. They also attracted many professional men, a few intellectuals, and very few workers. Their membership was heavily weighted in the younger age groups, and they included more women, relatively, than older political organizations. Few of them were concerned with local issues on the community level, which was

*"Hey, did you send my pajamas to the laundry
with my Willkie button on?"*

a central weakness. They produced almost no clear or incisive
political thinking—"The businessman dealing with a large political question is really a painful sight," the elder Senator Henry
Cabot Lodge once commented—and the Willkie Clubs gave
most of their members their first initiation into political thinking
as well as political activity. "Machinery's not important; ideas
are," Willkie once told Crum on the campaign train. This attitude was in large part to blame for his failure to keep the independent voters he enlisted in 1940 after he had disbanded the
Willkie Clubs because he did not think it right in a democracy

for any man to have a private political organization. Like the groups which had pushed through repeal of prohibition, the Willkie movement in 1940 seemed to be committed to a single political act, and then liquidation.

In addition to these young Republican voters Willkie looked to the business community at large for a big block of independent votes. He was, after all, the first businessman ever to run for President on a businessman's record. He was sure this would arouse enough new votes to upset the samplings on which the consistently discouraging political polls were based. In August, *Fortune's* forum of executive opinion showed business leaders to be five to one for Willkie against Roosevelt. Many of the 6,000,000 new votes he brought the Republican party, over the 1936 figure, may well have come from this source, but Willkie himself seriously overestimated it. One important reason was that he did not see the quiet but heavy drift of businessmen into passive and quiet support of the Democratic party. This had begun a few years earlier, when the New Deal had first begun to lose its New Deal spirit, and it was to grow for at least another dozen years after 1940. The business community as a whole was repeating what the utility industry had done in the 1930's. Its cohesion as an opposition was strong enough for slogans and public speeches, and for a good deal of private bitterness against Roosevelt and the Roosevelt family, but not strong enough for self-denial when Washington was in a mood to co-operate. Just as utility systems had quietly abandoned Willkie's fight against the holding company act when they were given acceptable reorganization plans, so many businessmen passed up his crusade for liberty and free enterprise when the smell of armament orders and government loans was heavy in the autumn, 1940, air.

The newspaper press gave Willkie all the opportunity he could have wanted to appeal to independent voters, but support by newspaper publishers proved to be no guaranty of support by newspaper readers. The percentage of the newspapers supporting Roosevelt, according to figures compiled by *Editor and Publisher,* the industry's trade journal, fell from 40 in 1932 to 36 in 1936 and to 23 in 1940. Willkie had an almost mesmeric influence over publishers, and as individuals they supported him with much more than normal Republican fervor. When the *New York Times* came out for him, it was the third time in fifty-six years (McKinley in 1900 and Taft in 1908 had been the first two) that the paper had backed a Republican for President. Besides the publishers, Willkie had much more personal support than most recent Republican candidates from working editors, columnists, and political reporters.

Among fashion-makers in the entertainment world, Willkie also had more support than Hoover or Landon had had. Hollywood gave Roosevelt a highly effective radio campaign just before the election. Although the list of motion picture celebrities supporting Willkie included names like those of Harold Lloyd, Joan Blondell, Bing Crosby, Walt Disney, Hedda Hopper, Robert Montgomery, Lionel Barrymore, Adolphe Menjou, Mary Pickford, Ann Sheridan, and Gary Cooper, they were never organized as shrewdly as the stars who backed the third term for Roosevelt. An organization called American Writers for Wendell L. Willkie enlisted an impressive array of writing talent to sign full-page advertisements in his behalf, but their campaign lacked much popular appeal beyond the glamour of the names. Don Herold wrote the copy for one of these, and among the reasons "Why I Want Willkie," he included: "He can add and subtract." It sounded too much like a banker's wisecrack to be anything but a boomerang to the candidate.

Once Willkie was the Republican candidate, the liberal press turned against him with virtual unanimity. It is doubtful that he lost many independent votes because of this, but it played a part in his failure to hold, during the next four years, any effective organized relationship with liberal groups in the United States, even when their members were individually for him. During the campaign, spokesmen for these groups attacked him with the fury peculiar to minority opinion groups. Bruce Bliven, writing in *Life* of October 14, 1940, and introduced as "perhaps the most distinguished radical journalist in the U. S.," literally tore Willkie apart. He found no good word to say for him except that he liked him personally. He called him a "front man and fixer" for the private utilities, "bull-headed," overeager, prone to talk too much. "Mr. Willkie's total," he concluded, "is that he is a victim of nostalgia who wants an impossible return to a dead and buried past."

On September 2, 1940, the *New Republic* devoted a special supplement to one man for the first time in its history, and "This Man Willkie" was strictly a campaign document rather than either scholarship or journalism. It called him a *condottiere,* a mouthpiece, a Wall Street insider as slick as they come, a super-salesman with his tongue in his cheek, hiring himself out to the highest bidder. This set the tone for nearly all liberal comment on him. By October 9, the newspaper *PM* was writing about the collapse of the Willkie boom. "The Republicans dreamed him up because they hated Roosevelt," its editor, Ralph Ingersoll, wrote. "The common people dreamed him up for a week or two because they are easygoing and good-natured and it's their habit to dream up heroes out of any handy material—like a baseball player who bats .400 or a movie actress who looks pretty with her hair mussed, or what have you? Mr. Willkie in this campaign, of course, was never either any better or worse than what he was before it began: a public utility front man and bond salesman who had charm for some people and a knack with the figures in a utility corporation balance sheet."

Professional politicians habitually shrug off this kind of comment, but it undoubtedly hurt Willkie's effort to mobilize new and independent voters behind his campaign. It was not confined to political liberals. Henry L. Mencken, who was an ardent anti-New Dealer, turned on Willkie savagely as soon as he saw that the candidate was no isolationist. "When he swallowed the Roosevelt foreign policy," Mencken wrote on September 15, "all the rest of the New Deal rumble-bumble went down with it, and he has since presented the spectacle of a man choking on his own false teeth." The editorials personally written by publishers themselves to point out, in the kind of prose publishers use, the parallel between Willkie and Lincoln were small help in mobilizing independent voters compared to this kind of attack.

Finally, Willkie expected to win more disgruntled Democrats on the third-term issue than he did. Especially at the beginning of the campaign, he gave a great deal of time to personal efforts to win over key figures in the Roosevelt camp; one estimate was that he made three hundred long-distance telephone calls himself from Colorado Springs in this effort. He got a few, but many of them were like John L. Lewis: their personal feuds with Roosevelt were too well known to give much conviction to their stand on principle against a third term. Al Smith, Raymond Moley, and General Johnson, although they had all been Democrats, would have made more news if they had come out for Roosevelt. During this time he was dragging his heels on seeing important Republican leaders. He wasted almost an entire month, for no gain. This helps to explain both his holding the Republicans at arm's length, figuring that they had no other place to go, and his subsequent return to their embrace.

Willkie directed his attack less against the third term itself than against the idea of the indispensable man. In *Look*, before he was nominated, he had himself written down the third-term issue. "The Fathers knew," he had said, "as we know, that the actual number of years was of no importance. Had they made the President's term two, six, or twelve years, it would have made little difference. They knew that the democracy that they built would stand or fall primarily on the attitude of the men who held office for whatever number of years."

This still left him plenty of room for attack, and the circumstances of the rigged and unspontaneous draft of Roosevelt by the Democratic convention seemed made to order for a real revolt. The word "leadership" had some ugly overtones in 1940 for many thoughtful Americans, and some of Roosevelt's idolaters used careless speech on this issue. Ickes, for example, gave Willkie ammunition he was to fire again and again in the campaign when he said: "Anything you do at this time to shake the confidence of the great mass of the American people in either the President or the national government is a sin against free enterprise, individual liberty, political democracy, and your own self-interest. No matter on what you may disagree with him, he is now a symbol of confidence whose loss of symbolic value would now make all agreements and disagreements utterly unimportant." This was more than a year before Pearl

Harbor, and its suggestion of leader-worship was asking for trouble.

Roosevelt, it is now clear, was as uncertain as Willkie about the probable political response to the third-term issue. On July 7, when Farley told him that Willkie might prove to be a formidable candidate, the President answered: "You are absolutely right. You know, if the war should be over before the election and I am running against Willkie, he would be elected." "I doubt very much," Samuel I. Rosenman has reported, "that [Roosevelt] would have made the campaign he did in 1940 if Willkie had not been making such great headway." Eleanor Roosevelt has said that this was the election her husband was least certain of winning, "not only because Mr. Willkie was a strong candidate but also because he thought the third-term issue would be a greater hurdle than it proved to be."

"Franklin had intended to make no speeches in this campaign except over the radio, but he was finally persuaded to make a few," according to Mrs. Roosevelt. "He liked Wendell Willkie very much: he never felt the bitterness toward him that he felt toward some of his other opponents, and I do not remember his ever saying anything derogatory to him in private conversation. This does not mean, however, that he did not feel the Democratic party should remain in power. I myself thought Mr. Willkie courageous and sincere, and I liked the way he stood for certain principles."

The fact that Roosevelt's popular vote declined, even if only from 27,475,673 to 27,243,466, suggested that some Democratic voters in 1940 were either disturbed by the third-term issue or alarmed by the threat of excessive personal leadership on which Willkie had hammered. But the war in Europe put a heavy premium in many voters' minds on Roosevelt's experience in handling foreign affairs. And the New Deal coalition of political forces was still growing larger as its reforming spirit declined. If Willkie had been able to communicate his own central positions on economic recovery and freedom in such a way as to mobilize some tangible nucleus for a new coalition, many more Democrats might well have deserted Roosevelt. But the independent voters he did enlist lay on the edges rather than at the core of such a coalition, and the Republican party was incapable of providing a nucleus which could accept them or hold them even for a few months.

The unhappy fact is that in 1940 Willkie had to find this out for himself. No one, especially after Philadelphia, could have been sure that it would work out in this way. The record of the Republican party was discouraging enough, and Willkie knew that it was the millstone around his neck. It is true that until July, 1940, he was thinking what he would do as President, and that after July he was thinking what to do to become President. Also, while the campaign was on, everyone was trying to make the candidate over in his own image. Immediately after the campaign, some of the amateurs and independents among his voters blamed him for even the lip service he had paid to party regularity. Since then it has become easy to say that he would have lost little and might have gained a great deal if he had broken with the party in the 1940 campaign with the same crash of chinaware that was heard in the land in 1944. It still took courage for him to break with the Old Guard as completely as he did, and literally no one knew for certain that he could not thus repeat on a national scale the miracle that had been worked in Philadelphia.

When Willkie finally conceded defeat in a radio broadcast on November 11, he turned his new independent voters over to the party for what it could do with them. The professionals knew they had won a minor victory in defeat by recapturing control of their party. "The outstanding note sounded by Mr. Willkie," said Senator John A. Danaher of Connecticut, "turns upon his recognition of the fact that intelligent scrutiny of Administration proposals must be supplied by the Republican party. His willingness to renounce in favor of the Republican party a large measure of support that was personal to him is not only gracious but is statesmanship of a high order."

The amateurs said little, and most of them went back to the great American game of watching politics. Two years later, one of them, the late and great reporter, Ray Clapper, who had guessed the end of the story even before the miracle in Philadelphia, summed it up: "Once, by accident and not because the leaders of the party wished it, a real leader appeared—Wendell Willkie. He was forced on the party. But as soon as the election was over, the party leaders tossed him out. The Republican party was even unable to recognize a real leader when it had the luck to find one on its doorstep."

CHAPTER FOURTEEN

London Under the Bombs

—————

A N AVALANCHE of mail—thirty thousand letters and telegrams in the five days following the election—was the first clear sign that the Willkie legend, far from having been killed, was only starting to grow. Electoral defeat is hardly martyrdom, but there was a new note of something close to dedication in the pledges of support which poured in on the defeated candidate. They were still filled with the crusading spirit, and it grew tougher, more resolute, in defeat. For many people there is a highly special pleasure, almost a feeling of nobility, in belonging to a minority, especially a minority which is twenty-two million strong. Throughout the four years of Willkie's political life, his following showed many strong points of resemblance to earlier movements for woman suffrage and for repeal of prohibition, and both of these had prospered on temporary defeat. By Armistice Day, when Willkie spoke "to the people of America" in an unprecedented postelection address over the three major radio networks, it was clear to everyone that this man was not going to disappear quietly back into the workaday business world from which he had emerged barely a year before.

The speech itself was a sober appeal for "a vigorous, loyal, and public-spirited opposition." Willkie repeated his major criticisms of the New Deal and his own deep belief in the need for a release of new energies, an expansion of production. He pledged full help in the national defense effort and reminded President Roosevelt of his promise to keep the country out of the war unless attacked. He did not mention the Republican party by name and that, as Mark Sullivan reported, "disturbed some Republicans." Then he went off with Mrs. Willkie for a vacation in Florida. They leased the house of Mr. and Mrs. Joseph Verner Reed on Jupiter Island, just off the coast at Hobe Sound, near the home of their friends the Pryors.

He broke the vacation twice. The first time was to make a long-promised radio broadcast for the National Inter-Fraternity Conference and to attend one of the newspapermen's banquets which no politician can afford to turn down unless he is already President. The second time, in the middle of December, he went north for another similar dinner, of the Gridiron Club in Washington, and to discuss the Willkie Clubs with Root and the Republican party with Martin. Except for these two trips and a speech on New Year's Day in the Rose Bowl, he sat on the beach for most of six weeks. The Davenports and some other friends came for short visits; he was especially fond of the Pryor children; he had an interesting day with Marjorie Kinnan Rawlings, author of *The Yearling*, at her orange grove in Florida. For most of the time he was bored, uncertain about his future, itching from inactivity. In the North, both politicians and newspapermen could only speculate on what new surprise he was likely to pull on them.

There was a good deal of speculation. Stanford alumni were looking for a new president and some of them were plugging Willkie; the same was true of the University of Vermont. There were rumors that three newspaper columns, two magazine editorships, a high industrial position, and a big public utilities post were among the more than a hundred jobs which were offered him. It was a safe bet that he could have a partnership in almost any law firm he chose. In his November 11 speech he had made it plain that he would not even consider an Administration job offer, but just what he was going to do and how he was going to lead his "loyal opposition" was uncertain.

Some time during these six weeks, he made up his mind that the first big job of his loyal opposition was to press for "all aid short of war" to Britain against the Axis powers. It was a major decision, perhaps more important than any other decision of his life. For it led logically to a series of other decisions and together

Harper in the Birmingham *Age-Herald*

"Defeat has its victories."

they determined the climax of his career. The initial decision
meant, during the months that were running out before Pearl
Harbor, a bitter and dirty fight against the isolationists and one
that was to leave more serious scars within the Republican party
than the campaign. Its high point was the debate over lend-
lease legislation. This effort led him to a more and more interventionist position, first expressed in the motion picture hearings
before the Senate, and, once the war had engulfed America, to
all-out support of bipartisan prosecution of the war. Finally, his
1942 trip around the world and the book he wrote about it made
him the champion of intelligent planning for a postwar world.

These three positions were each proved to have been histori-
cally correct, in the sense that fast-moving events and the

opinions of most Americans eventually caught up with him. But one can only guess at what the lag might have been, or how costly to the United States, if he had not moved out in front with the independent citizens who still looked to him for leadership. It seems clear now that at any one of these three points he could have materially strengthened his political position by waiting, like other Republican leaders, not getting too far out in front, consolidating his position, listening to the grass grow. Aloofness and reserve were obvious political responses to the war for ambitious Republicans, and nearly all except Willkie worked them into some patriotic but quiet formula. If Willkie failed to take the Republican party with him during these years, at least he stymied anyone else from taking it into a position which would have seriously hampered the American war effort. The verdict that Willkie was an opportunist, to whom power was more important than conviction, leaves out of account these four years in which he deliberately and repeatedly rejected a politically wise course in favor of one in which he deeply believed.

The fateful decision was announced on January 12, 1941, when Willkie called the reporters to his Commodore Hotel headquarters and told them he was supporting, with modifications, the President's aid-to-Britain bill and that he was shortly going to England to see for himself the danger he now rated greatest of all to the United States. He said later that working on a magazine article on foreign policy had crystallized the idea in his mind that he needed more information about the war; a friend, Harold Guinzburg, the book publisher, asked him why, then, he did not go to England to see it for himself. He discussed the press statement with no one except a few close friends, and with them only in reference to its style and phrasing. He had called Hull by telephone, to ask if he might have a passport, and the answer a few hours later had included an invitation from Roosevelt to visit the White House, if he wished, before leaving for London. Two friends, John Cowles and Landon K. Thorne, public utility banker and philanthropist, were going with him. None of the titular leaders of the Republican party knew about it before they read it in the newspapers.

London Under the Bombs

There were reasons for this. A good many top Republicans had already broken ranks after the election, abandoning the precarious formula on which the campaign had been fought in favor of the America First Committee and Colonel Lindbergh. They included some of the publishers, like Roy Howard, who had been close to Willkie in the campaign and who were now organizing Hoover, Dewey, Taft, and Landon into a strong opposition to lend-lease. During his Florida vacation Willkie had been visited by a series of emissaries who tried to convince him of the political capital still to be made out of denouncing Roosevelt as a warmonger. Two of these were William Rhodes Davis, the oil operator who had financed the John L. Lewis broadcast, and Verne Marshall, a Cedar Rapids, Iowa, newspaper editor who claimed that Davis had reasonable peace terms from Hitler in his pocket. They stayed for two days, but all they achieved was the special bitterness with which Willkie, in his formal statement, denounced the "appeasers, isolationists, or lip-service friends of Britain [who] will seek to sabotage the program for aid to Britain and her allies behind the screen of opposition to the bill."

It was clear that defeat had not changed Willkie. He talked to the reporters, when he announced his trip, with a mixture of deadly earnestness and boyish enthusiasm, munched a ham sandwich in each hand, kidded those he knew, and joked about the election. Whom did he expect to see in England? "I'll see everybody that will see me," he answered. This was the pre-Philadelphia Willkie.

The Republican reaction was swift. Willkie's friend Kenneth Simpson introduced a substitute bill in the House the next day to embody the modifications Willkie had asked in the lend-lease bill—chiefly a time limit on the emergency powers to be given the President and a Congressional right to debate which countries other than Britain could receive the aid. But Landon spoke for the party when he said: "If Mr. Willkie had revealed his position before the Republican convention he would never have been nominated." The overwhelming majority of Republicans in Congress used uglier language in the cloakrooms and on the floor. In New York, the *Daily News* called for a new Declaration of Independence from Britain, and the bill, officially HR 1776, was from that day on always referred to as "the dictatorship bill." The *Chicago Tribune* denounced Willkie's "treachery" and called him the "Republican Quisling."

To Willkie this was no surprise and he refused to be baited into making the issue, any more than he could help, a public fight within the Republican party. He knew that time was on his side. He stood up as a member of the audience at a Town Hall debate on January 16 to urge Americans to back President Roosevelt's program for aid to Britain to save America "so that we can debate with him again in another free election." Two days later, in an extemporaneous speech before the Women's National Republican Club, he urged Republicans not to become an isolationist party through blind opposition to the lend-lease bill.

"Let me say to you," he declared, and he was speaking without notes, "that if the Republican party in this year of 1941 makes a blind opposition to this bill and allows itself to be presented to the people as the isolationist party, it will never again gain control of the American government. I beg of you, I plead with you, you people who believe as I do in our great system of government, please do not in blind opposition, do not because of hate of an individual—and of all persons in the United States I have least cause to hold a brief for him—forget the critical world situation which confronts us and in which America is a part."

The setting of this luncheon and the other speakers, who were thirsting for Roosevelt's blood on this or any other issue, make it impossible to explain Willkie's outburst on any basis of personal ambition or opportunism. Another passage from the same speech explains it better, and in terms which were to stay fresh and meaningful for him until his death. "Whether we like it or not, America cannot remove itself from the world. Every development in the art of transportation, every development in the art of communication, has reduced the size of the world so that the world today actually is no larger than the thirteen original colonies were when we established our system of liberty in the United States. And much as we would like to withdraw within ourselves and much as we would like to disregard the rest of the world—we cannot. We cannot be indifferent to what happens in

Europe. We cannot forget the fighting men of Europe. They are defending our liberty as well as theirs.

"If they are permitted to fail, I say to you quite deliberately that I do not believe liberty can survive here. I take issue with all who say that we can survive with freedom in a totalitarian world."

Two days later Willkie saw Roosevelt in the White House, to pick up what he told reporters was "a very kindly letter" to Churchill. The President called him "Wendell"; he answered "Mr. Roosevelt." It was the day before the first third-term inaugural in United States history, and the President told him laughingly that he wished "Wendell" were going to be taking the oath in the cold instead of himself. "When I'm over there where the excitement is," Willkie told him, "you'll wish you were me, too." Sherwood has told how the President stopped his wheel-chair on his way to see Willkie, who came to the White House with Hull. The President asked Rosenman and Sherwood for some papers. "Which particular papers do you want, Mr. President?"

"Oh, it doesn't matter," said Roosevelt, "just give me a handful to strew around on my desk so that I will look very busy when Willkie comes in."

Willkie was relatively relaxed at this meeting with Roosevelt; he knew he had the ball and was running with it. He was bigger news than the inaugural the next day. "The household was so anxious to get a glimpse of him while he sat waiting in Franklin's study on the second floor of the White House," Eleanor Roosevelt wrote later, "that suddenly many people had errands that took them down the hall. I would have gone myself, but I didn't hear of his visit until Franklin told me of it later."

The letter Roosevelt gave him was addressed to "a certain naval person" and marked on the envelope: "Kindness of Honorable Wendell Willkie." This was a jest of which Roosevelt and Churchill never tired, referring to the First World War when Churchill had been First Lord of the Admiralty and Roosevelt Assistant Secretary of the Navy. The letter was unimportant except for the President's inclusion in it, in his own handwriting, of Longfellow's words:

245

Willkie

Sail on, O Ship of State!
Sail on, O Union, strong and great!
Humanity with all its fears,
With all the hopes of future years,
Is hanging breathless on thy fate!

Carl Sandburg wrote a poem about this incident, called "Mr. Longfellow and His Boy" and it has become part of the legend of the war. Less than three months later, Churchill referred to the Longfellow stanza, and answered it with another quotation which he might not have been able to use if Willkie had not come to England and swung his support behind the lend-lease bill:

For while the tired waves, vainly breaking,
Seem here no painful inch to gain,
Far back, through creeks and inlets making,
Comes silent, flooding in, the main.

And not by eastern windows only,
When daylight comes, comes in the light;
In front the sun climbs slow, how slowly,
But westward, look, the land is bright!

The Roosevelt letter also said that Willkie "is truly helping to keep politics out over here." Willkie saw Churchill at Checquers, and in the course of the conversation identified Longfellow for him as the author of the poem sent by Roosevelt; no one in the Prime Minister's office had been able to recognize or find it. Churchill recalled the meeting in his memoirs as "a long talk with this most able and forceful man, whose life was cut short so unexpectedly by illness two years later." Willkie lived nearly twice as long as Churchill remembered, and what he did to speed American help for Britain was in a simpler spirit than Churchill's comment in his memoirs that "every arrangement was made by us, with the assistance of the enemy, to let him see all he desired of London at bay." By the time Churchill wrote his memoirs he was not the only person to be having second thoughts about this strange American who had come to see beleaguered Britain

Hungerford in the Pittsburgh *Post-Gazette*

and was already wondering how it could survive even a victorious war without its empire and with the ideals it professed to be fighting for.

Willkie flew from New York in a Yankee Clipper on January 22 as a private citizen, paying his own way, "to see, hear, and learn." He came back on February 9, having covered thirteen thousand miles in eighteen days. Like the Philadelphia convention and the last weeks of the campaign, and like the trip around the world which was still to come, it was a short, explosive, foreshortened, and highly concentrated taste of his real power over the imaginations of men and women. He saw Salazar in Portugal, Churchill, King George VI and Queen Elizabeth in London, de Valera in Ireland, and an African celebrity named Thunderbolt McCoy

247

with an Oxford accent, a loincloth, and a stovepipe hat in Bolama on his way home. He had one long conference with Churchill, Foreign Secretary Anthony Eden, Clement Attlee, who was then Lord Privy Seal, and Lord Beaverbrook, Minister of Aircraft Production. Harry Hopkins called on him at the Dorchester. He talked with Professor Harold J. Laski, all the top Labor leaders, General Wladislaw Sikorski, and the Chinese Ambassador, Quo Tai-chi. He saw Coventry and Birmingham, the "Hell's Corner" at Dover, the shelters where British workers slept, a Communist party demonstration outside the Savoy Hotel, and the private estates of the Earl of Derby. He took time out to indulge in his own tastes, chiefly for a dinner party arranged by Rebecca West at the suggestion of their mutual friend, Irita Van Doren, so that he might meet some of Britain's top writers.

He caught the imagination of the British people, and they responded to him. He talked to policemen, soldiers, cab drivers, Cabinet ministers, and air-raid wardens, in the street, in shelters, in hotels, in trains, in homes and offices. He threw darts in pubs, and autographed everything from a package of tea to a ukulele. The *London Times* printed his picture on its main news page—an honor considerably more rare than knighthood. His bluff cheerfulness went over big; his stamina stuck out all over him. The Nazi air attack on Britain was in a period of lull and he was never in any great personal danger. But he was deeply impressed by the human courage he saw all around him. "I'm a tough old egg, I think," he said in a shelter during a raid, "but this moves me very deeply. I am almost spilling over." Another man from Indiana, Ernie Pyle, was in England at the same time; the Nazi *Blitz* had the same effect on them both.

The war and what Americans could do to help were inevitably on the top of his mind. "Last night I saw Wendell Willkie," Hopkins cabled to Roosevelt from London. "He told me that he believes the opposition to lend-lease is going to be vehemently expressed and it should not be underrated under any circumstances. It is his belief that the main campaign against the bill will be directed from Chicago and heavily financed. As perhaps he told you it's his opinion that Herbert Hoover is the real brains behind this opposition. Willkie said he hoped that you would make a radio speech, preferably from Chicago, and thereby take your case right to the people. He said that he himself might make some speeches after he returns home in about two weeks. He said that he approved the bill with some amendments but did not specify what they were. He is receiving all the attentions which the British know so well how to provide for distinguished guests. I shall have further observations to make on Willkie's visit here when I see you."

As often happens in such periods of concentrated frenzy, Willkie stored up impressions and ideas which colored his thinking as long as he lived. The trip had been a kind of emotional binge; he always had the capacity to let himself go in a parade, a demonstration, any outpouring of popular emotion, and then think about it afterwards. And he learned a great deal in England. The *Pictorial* wrote: "Mr. Willkie's great fact-finding trip has earned more newspaper, radio, and newsreel space than almost anything in the war. Mr. Willkie is not a visiting cowboy or film star. He is an important, powerful man. Let's treat him as such. Let's see that he gets a look at everything in his own way and in his own time." He did. He gave England what the *London Times* called "the impression of sincerity, friendship, boundless energy, and radiant high spirits which has been immensely heartening." He learned for himself that the British people could still win, and that Tory businessmen had a lot to do with their courage and determination. Neville Chamberlain in Great Britain had represented a segment of provincial business which had chosen appeasement because it feared what the war might do to strengthen the labor movement at home and revolution in Europe. Churchill represented an equally Tory slice of British thinking, one which was old-fashioned enough and ambitious enough to run the risk. These Englishmen had memories of a whole series of social revolutions, all of which their kind of people had survived, and they knew that more were sure to come. Willkie liked them, and he talked about them with respect and affection.

Willkie's trip to London achieved strictly intangible results. His pleading with de Valera for the use of Irish bases had been completely in vain, and with Hopkins in London at the same

Illingworth in *Punch*. Reproduced by permission of the Proprietors of *Punch*

"I guess that ought to fix it, Wendell."

time the Administration had not asked Willkie to play any part in negotiations over American aid to Britain. Yet his effect both on Europe and on the United States was clearly enormous. "Historians will say, I believe," Walter Lippmann wrote later, "that second only to the Battle of Britain, the sudden rise and nomination of Willkie was the decisive event, perhaps providential, which made it possible to rally the free world when it was almost conquered. Under any other leadership but his, the Republican party would have turned its back upon Great Britain, causing all who still resisted Hitler to feel that they were abandoned."

At home the debate over lend-lease was approaching a climax, and Willkie had to cut short his trip if he was to help with Congress. The isolationists saw correctly that lend-lease was a round they could not well afford to lose. Colonel Lindbergh, Father Coughlin, Norman Thomas, and General Robert E. Wood of Sears, Roebuck and Company and the America First Committee were by no means alone in opposing it. There were equally articulate Congressmen, including Senators Wheeler, Nye, and La Follette, and Representatives whose opposition was as deep as that of Fish and George H. Tinkham of Massachusetts. The Communist party was literally screaming against the measure as "the war bill." Landon, Hoover, and Taft had come out flat-footed against it; Dewey opposed it up to the last moment, when he changed his position just before the votes were taken. The great middle in American politics, both Democratic and Republican, was full of anxiety and suspicion; like the public it represented, it wished it could stay on the fence, with this bill as with the war itself.

It would be hard to exaggerate the bitterness of the issue at the time. This was the rock on which the *New York Daily News* tolerance of Roosevelt completely and finally foundered, and other large sections of the press, including the Scripps-Howard papers and the Hearst press and many more respectable papers, fulminated against aid to Britain. On March 8, the day after the Senate finally passed the bill, Senator Vandenberg wrote in his diary: "If America 'cracks up,' you can put your finger on this precise moment as the time when the crime was committed. I had the feeling, as the result of the ballot was announced, that I was witnessing the suicide of the Republic. . . . I do not believe we are rich enough to underwrite all of the wars of all the world. I fear it means the ultimate end of our democracy."

Willkie arrived on Sunday, February 9, the same day the

Nazi planes raided Iceland for the first time, and Churchill said, in a radio speech: "Give us the tools and we'll finish the job." By Tuesday, February 11, when Willkie testified before the Senate Committee holding public hearings on the bill, Merwin K. Hart, Joseph Curran, and the last of the bitter-end isolationists had finished their testimony. One of them, Miss Cathrine Curtis, chairman of the Women's National Committee to Keep the U. S. Out of War, had referred to Willkie as "Indiana's wandering—and wondering—son," who had "just returned from his circus tour of British pubs and London slums." Once again the stage had been set for him, and his appearance drew the largest crowd in history to the Senate Office Building.

The moment was historic as well as dramatic. Included in the twelve hundred persons who jammed into the ornate caucus room designed for five hundred were Senators and Representatives, members of the Cabinet, and many of the big names of Washington. They included, as Joseph Alsop and Robert Kintner reported, "the *vivandières* of isolationism, Mrs. Nicholas Longworth, Mrs. Bennett Champ Clark, and Mrs. Robert A. Taft, who sat like the sirens disappointed of Ulysses, in a special row of chairs, joking among themselves." Willkie, dressed in a blue suit and with his hair neatly brushed until the questions started, played his role quietly and confidently. He read a statement approving the bill with the modifications he had already suggested, and asking that from five to ten destroyers be turned over monthly to the British, with all patrol bombers not needed for training purposes, and more shipping. Republican Senators on the committee left him gingerly alone, for the most part, in the questioning, and even Senator Clark, a bitter-end isolationist from Missouri, failed to shake Willkie's patience or his good humor.

It was a true climax in more ways than one. There was no longer any serious question about the passage of lend-lease. And it can be understood why Willkie felt again that he could capture his party when he needed to. Walter Lippmann wrote the next day that Willkie would now "become not merely the titular leader but the effective leader of those who have in their keeping the future of the Republican party." Again, as in Philadelphia, Willkie had moved into a situation where there was a vacuum of leadership and had appealed directly to the people. Again his enemies could charge that it looked as if the stage management had been almost too skillful. Again he had played his role honestly, simply, without political guile, and again he had won hands down.

The next day he made the same appeal in a Lincoln Day address to the National Republican Club at the Waldorf in New York and to a national radio audience. He attacked the New Deal party as "without faith in people because its idea of winning elections and controlling votes is by the method of government pressures and expenditures." But most of the speech, delivered without notes, was an impassioned plea to the Republicans to abandon compromise and isolationism and to fight for the cause of freedom. Whatever the party notables on the dais thought, the 2,200-strong audience gave him a tumultuous ovation. By next morning there were 900 telegrams at his apartment and his Commodore Hotel office. His Senate testimony had catapulted him back onto the center of the national stage. The *New York Herald Tribune* said: "We can think of no precedent for a service by a private citizen as important as that which he has performed." Senator Nye, speaking to the Lincoln Day dinner in Philadelphia, said: "His explanations were arrogant and an insult to the American electorate and particularly to those millions who listened to him in all seriousness last fall." Both were Republican reactions, and if they showed how deeply split was the party, they also explained why it was so hard to drop Willkie into the discard.

The Senate committee reported out the bill favorably on February 12. Secretary Knox was against Willkie's proposal to give more destroyers to Britain, and the die-hard Republican Senators were fighting mad. Vandenberg called Willkie "the Clipper ambassador"; Nye referred with heavy sarcasm to him as "the great expert on European affairs"; Hiram W. Johnson of California said the hearings had been terminated abruptly by "a one-man circus intended to influence the citizens." Senator Prentiss M. Brown, Michigan Democrat, commented after listening to days of vituperative abuse of Willkie from the Republican side of the Senate: "I wish to say that evidently the gentleman from Indiana who ran on the Republican ticket is the most unpopular Republican in the country in the United States Senate, and probably the most popular Republican in the country outside the United States Senate."

It was not until March 7 that the Senate finally passed the bill. The Democrats split 49 to 13 in favor of it; the Republicans 17 to 10 against it. On March 11, the revised bill passed the House. It was immediately signed by Roosevelt, who five minutes later approved the first transfers of war material to Great Britain and Greece. Later in the day he asked for seven billions of additional funds with which to expand defense production.

One footnote to the Senate hearings was to plague Willkie for the rest of his life. Nye had read to him a quotation from a speech made by Willkie in Baltimore in the last week of the campaign. He had been discussing the President's record of broken promises, and the quotation was: "On the basis of his past performances with pledges to the people, you may expect we will be at war by April, 1941, if he is elected."

Willkie said: "You ask me whether or not I said that?"

Nye went on: "Do you still agree that that might be the case?"

"It might be," Willkie answered. Then, grinning, he added: "It was a bit of campaign oratory."

The phrase was innocent enough, and the record of the hearings pins it precisely to the prediction about Roosevelt. It had the effect of a fresh breeze, and the audience and the American public were both delighted. But the isolationists picked it up with shouts of glee and quoted it over and over again as if it applied to Willkie's own pledges during the campaign. Willkie denied it time and time again, patiently explaining just what he had said and that it had nothing to do with any pledge, but his enemies kept on blithely repeating it. It ended up, like George Washington's cherry tree, one of those legends that grow steadily stronger with every proof of their untruth.

Even his friends came ultimately to defend him for the meaning that he insisted the phrase did not originally have. "I'm 100 per cent sold for life on Wendell Willkie," William Allen White wrote to Justice William A. Smith of the Kansas Supreme Court, "and if I'm the only man in Kansas who is following him . . . I'm going to do it. I have made my living by being a pretty good judge of men, and never since Teddy Roosevelt have I known a man on whom I have pinned my faith as I pinned it on Wendell Willkie. I think one of the most courageous things any man ever said in public life was Willkie's 'campaign oratory' statement. It was not discreet, but it was deeply honest. Only three times in public life have I seen such honesty. The pretension that a candidate's utterances are omniscient when everyone knows he is talking damned nonsense is one of the large reasons why the American people lose faith in democracy."

Willkie had advance warning of the smear attacks which were to be made on him by the extreme isolationists throughout the rest of 1941. At Trinidad, he later wrote, on his return from England, "I received a cable message from a man who became one of the heads of America First that my reputation would be the subject of debasement in every town in America if I carried out my intention of testifying." In these last months of peace the isolationist camp was forced by the mounting pressure of events into a cohesion it had never had before. The Communists deserted after the Nazi attack on Russia in June, but not before one of their captive organizations, the American Peace Mobilization, had done its special kind of job on Willkie. The other fanatics in the isolationist coalition stayed bitter even after the great debate over intervention had been shatteringly interrupted by Pearl Harbor. One of their leaders, John T. Flynn, later wrote the formula with which they interpreted the crisis as it was developing. With its final sentence aimed directly at Willkie, it was a strictly propagandist formula which has never been repudiated by large and articulate sections of the Republican party although no honest historian has ever been able to defend or even document it.

"As America moved toward the war," ran Flynn's analysis, "there blossomed the most fantastic comradeship between flaming Red revolutionaries, foggy-eyed New Dealers, and deep purple conservatives. The war brought them together in an incongruous brotherhood. They were united in the drive for American entry into the war, but for a variety of different and contradictory reasons. But among these hostile elements the one group that was not foggy was the Communist group. Of them at least we can say that they knew what they wanted. The mere New Dealers, as that term came to be understood, comprised those wandering, vague dreamers who held to a shadowy conviction that somehow the safety of humankind depended upon the creation of some sort of ill-defined but benevolent state that would end poverty, give everybody a job and an easy old age, and who supposed that this could be done because they had discovered that money grew in government buildings. The others were largely devoted lovers of or worshipers at the ancient altars of Anglo-Saxon world hegemony. But they could all unite in a weird conventicle—Anglo-Saxon imperialists, groping New Dealers, and dogmatic Red bigots—under banners like those of the OWI, the OPA, and the BEW. And here and there was a fellow acutely conscious of the German blood in his veins and eager to purge himself of the stain."

The press was sharply divided on the issue. Roy Howard, William Randolph Hearst, and Colonel Robert R. McCormick were all prime movers in the attempt to rally the nation against Roosevelt's "war policy" and they fell on Willkie with the special savagery reserved for apostates. "Mr. Willkie," wrote the *Chicago Tribune* after he had endorsed the lend-lease bill, "entered the Republican party as a mysterious stranger, suddenly and to the astonishment of thousands of the party members who didn't recall the face or the name. He may now take his leave, quite as suddenly, still a stranger to the party's principles, although no longer mysterious. . . . The party will take leave of its late standard bearer with the hope that it will never again see him or he it."

Papers like the *New York Herald Tribune* and the *New York Times* supported Willkie's foreign policy on their editorial pages but some of their columnists were too close to leading Republican Senators to follow without careful hedging. Like many others, they wanted no part of appeasement, but nothing in the war in Europe seemed as important or as threatening as the growing power of Washington, and they made it clear in supporting Willkie that they believed he was sadly mixed up on priorities. "New Order's Architects Busy Behind Screen of Emergency" was a typical Mark Sullivan headline; Arthur Krock feared the lend-lease bill might entrench the New Deal for good. When Willkie made an appeal for national unity in his big speech of the summer on July 23 in the Hollywood Bowl, Heptisax summed up this reaction in the *New York Herald Tribune* by writing his regret that Willkie had not told the people and Washington "what the latter must do to deserve the confidence of the American people, without which all talk of unity is no more effective than the incantations of the rain makers." His erstwhile hero had learned nothing from what happened in November. "This splendid fellow has a job to do," he concluded, "and I believe I am voicing the opinion of many millions when I say that I wish he would come down out of the moral stratosphere and find out what it is."

Willkie took all the abuse as he had taken the eggs and the tomatoes during the campaign, with a broad grin. After a vacation in Rushville, he announced in New York that he was returning to law practice, as senior partner of the firm which had invited him through former Governor Miller more than a year before. It was renamed Willkie, Owen, Otis and Bailly (now Willkie, Owen, Farr, Gallagher and Walton), and Willkie moved in May into an office on the twenty-seventh floor at 15 Broad Street, looking out over the harbor of New York and the Statue of Liberty. The Commodore Hotel campaign office was closed at last, but with an incoming mail still running into thousands of letters daily his new law office looked and operated a little like a political headquarters. By June, he was still getting an average of two thousand letters a day.

He turned down offers of the Republican nomination for the seat in Congress of Representative Simpson, who had died suddenly in January. It would have given him the professional standing as a politician which he never had, but it was a forum he did not need and as a new member of the House he would have had small opportunity to influence legislation. He supported instead Joseph Clark Baldwin, a personal friend, who won a decisive victory in the special election on March 11 and credited it to his support "principally from Wendell Willkie, who is leading the fight in our party for national unity on foreign policy."

Willkie also went to Canada in March, making big speeches in Toronto and Montreal, touring Canadian war plants, and receiving noisy, friendly demonstrations everywhere. He had become a living symbol of hope to English-speaking peoples as a result of his trip to London and his support of aid to Britain. It was partly to counteract the charge of Anglo-Saxon exclusiveness which was being hurled at him by Communists and the extreme right that he threw himself at the same time into China relief work. He became a director of United China Relief and from March on he spoke with increasing frequency at meetings and rallies aimed at helping the Chinese people in their long war for freedom against Japan. Friends like Henry R. Luce, James G. Blaine, and Pearl Buck were also largely responsible for Willkie's interest in China. But basically it was a natural development of his unitary view of the world and of the war. During the 1940 campaign he had gone significantly further than Roosevelt in asking for a two-ocean defense policy and for help to China. By April 10, when the Nazis invaded Yugoslavia, he was supporting the bitter and desperate resistance which began in the mountains, and on April 16 he introduced General Sikorski to a mass meeting at Carnegie Hall for the support of underground Polish resistance to the Nazis. The phrase "One World" he did not use until two years later, but the idea had been central in Willkie's political thinking from the time of his support of Woodrow Wilson.

He was in enormous demand as a speaker and as a magazine writer. A list of his public appearances during 1941 shows that he had little time to practice law. It was during this period that he became an even more skilled extemporaneous speaker than he had always been. He was never in the same league with Roosevelt at delivering prepared speeches, from a platform or on the radio, but few men in America were his equal at public speaking without a manuscript.

The title of a piece he wrote for *Collier's* in May, 1941, was a fair summary of much of what he was saying at this time: "Americans, Stop Being Afraid." The article was an answer to one by Colonel Lindbergh, but the general feeling of anxiety and insecurity spread much further than the hard and bitter doctrines of the isolationists. February 17, 1941, was the date of the *Life* issue which carried Henry R. Luce's article called "The American Century." This had begun: "We Americans are unhappy. We are not happy about America. We are not happy about ourselves in relation to America. We are nervous—or gloomy—or apathetic." Against a background like this, what Willkie said sounded like a brass band playing in a funeral parlor.

Those who opposed Willkie, including many Republicans, saw something false and overeloquent in his constant appeals for unity and confidence. Others, who read differently the handwriting on the wall in Europe, became more fervent and emotional than ever in his support. The very disunity he was fighting widened the difference of opinion about him as a man. Nation after nation in 1941 was falling victim to this kind of disunity, and in each one the men who took strong positions against "the wave of the future" were guilty, as they were charged, of overstatement and oversimplification. But Willkie did his best to narrow the gap, and to check the growing bitterness with which Americans talked to each other in the summer of 1941.

Considering the violence of the 1940 campaign, impressive recognition of this was given by Roosevelt himself in his Jackson Day speech on March 29, 1941. "The leader of the Republican party himself—Mr. Wendell Willkie," the President said, "in word and in action is showing what patriotic Americans mean by rising above partisanship and rallying to the common cause." Such a statement only added fuel to the anger and indignation among isolationist Republicans, but Willkie played his case for unity both ways. When the audience booed and hissed Colonel Lindbergh's name at a labor "Beat Hitler" rally in New York in July, Willkie interrupted the proceedings. "Let's not boo any American citizen," he said. "We come here tonight, men and women of all faiths and parties, not to slander our fellow-citizens. We want all of them. Let's save all our boos for Hitler." When Lindbergh later wrote to the President demanding an apology from Ickes, who had attacked him sav-

259

agely, Willkie again moved in with a public statement: "I do hope the Administration will discontinue its constant, bitter attacks on individuals, companies, and others who may disagree with it."

This won him no protection for himself. It was during the summer of 1941 that personal slander against Willkie hit its all-time high. Both his private life and his public honesty were subjects of whispering smear campaigns. Some of it was not whispered. Senator Danaher's charge that he had won the nomination by pledging aid to Britain at a dinner party at the New York home of Mrs. Ogden Reid, with Taft and Thomas W. Lamont, Morgan financier, among the guests, was repeated again and again by leading Republicans, each time with a few new details added. The America First Committee charged publicly that Henry P. Davison, another Morgan partner, had paid Willkie for his speeches in support of Britain. Willkie denied each story as it became public. "I have never in my life," he said, "received a gift, loan, or consideration of any kind or character from anybody for making a speech either on the subject of aid to Britain or on any other subject. Nobody has ever paid me for any talk I have made on any subject nor has anyone influenced me or sought to influence me about what I was to say. I say what I want to say without any regard to what may be anyone else's opinion."

The attacks had greater currency in Republican circles than with the general public. "A lot of the boys are angry," the Republican national committeeman from Nebraska said in January; "he was a Democrat before he came into the party and I'm not so sure he still isn't a Democrat." To say that his relations with the regular party organization were strained was the euphemism used by reporters. Actually, they were all but broken. A national convention of the Young Republicans in Des Moines in January was barely prevented from coming out openly against Willkie, and in the following month, at an eleven-state conference of Republican leaders in Omaha, the problem was solved only by a curious ruling from the inevitable smoke-filled hotel room that the questions of lend-lease and Willkie's position were not to be mentioned, let alone discussed, on the floor of the conference.

The party machine could turn on the Willkie Clubs and it did so with a vengeance. They had been renamed in December as the Independent Clubs of America, in line with Willkie's expressed desire to turn them loose from his personal leadership. But his immediate re-emergence into national prominence and the quickening public interest in the war kept some of them active and growing. Root, who was still their chairman, was hopeful that they could form the nucleus for independent voters within, or in alliance with, the Republican party, and they did not actually suspend until after Pearl Harbor. But the Young Republican Federation passed a formal resolution inviting all independent political organizations "believing in the American form of government" to join the Republican party and urging the party in the future "to desist from fostering any independent organization."

Almost the only strong link Willkie maintained with the Republicans during 1941 was through his personal friendship with Martin and a few other leaders. Martin had wanted to resign as party chairman immediately after the election. Only Willkie's urging and the manifest impossibility of finding an acceptable successor kept him from doing so. He was still Republican leader in the House, and he was poles removed from Willkie's growing interventionist position on the war. But he tried hard to hold the party together by staying on as chairman, month after month, in spite of repeated stories that he would resign. "The Republican party is big enough and broad enough to have two opinions represented on any question which is being considered on a nonpartisan basis," he declared, and he kept on insisting to skeptical reporters that the heavy Republican vote in Congress against all legislation like the lend-lease bill was strictly nonpartisan.

Aside from his personal friendship for Willkie, the Republican chairman was in the same dilemma that had started with the miracle in Philadelphia. Whatever the party machine or the Republicans in Congress thought of Willkie or his views on the war, the man and his legend just would not go away. By March, after the lend-lease debate, a Gallup poll showed that only 14 per cent of Willkie voters in 1940 had come to like him better, with 24 per cent liking him less, but that among all voters, 22 per cent liked him better and only 14 per cent less. These were troubling figures for those Republicans who remembered that they were still a minority party. An official magazine, the *Republican,* polling Republicans in the same month, found that 61 per cent of them backed some parts of the domestic New Deal and that only 50 per cent were opposed to Roosevelt's foreign policy. By July the same trends were even more apparent. A Gallup poll in that month showed that only 9 per cent of the Republicans liked Willkie better, with 38 per cent liking him less. Of all voters, 20 per cent liked him better, 19 per cent less. It was also clear that he was gaining strength heavily in just those urban, middle-income groups where the Republicans most needed to win votes if they were ever to regain power. By September, he was far in front of all others, Democrat and Republican, in a Gallup poll which sought to measure popular rating of the Presidential timber available to succeed Roosevelt.

Willkie went away in August for a vacation, first to Rushville and then to Vermont and New Hampshire. The Nazi armies were pouring through Russia towards the outskirts of Moscow. German submarines were sinking tonnage in the Atlantic at a rate three times the combined British and American construction. American relations with Japan were slipping quietly but definitely out of the hands of the diplomats. William Allen White wrote Willkie on August 16 proposing an unadvertised and fairly discreet conference of Republicans who shared their views. "The time is short," he wrote, and "we just can't let Landon and Hoover and Taft and Lindbergh carry the Republican banner without a fight for it." But to Willkie the time ahead looked even shorter than it did to White. This was, of all times, not the moment for him to start worrying like a politician about his following; it was a time for leadership.

CHAPTER FIFTEEN

The Great Debate

B Y THE late summer of 1941, Willkie had been in the national
limelight for less than a year and a half. The forces which
were deeply changing both industry and politics in the United
States, and with them the place of America in the world, had carried him in a headlong rush from being a successful but relatively
unknown businessman to leadership on a national scale. He was
still a leader without office and without a party, and he had
hardly had time to catch his breath. Yet the evidence was overwhelming that he had understood the forces at work in the
world and in American thinking clearly enough to assert a kind
of public leadership when he wanted to, and get away with it.

Beginning with the autumn of that year, the war and America's increasing role in it cut the Willkie legend down to size.
American business and industry were moving jerkily along the
road to full mobilization, looking neither backward at still reluctant older leaders nor forward to men like Willkie who were
fumbling with blueprints of a future. The events of the next
twelve months followed each other with such speed and on
such a gigantic scale as to dwarf leadership of every kind. They
kept Willkie busy, and they kept him thinking. But civilians
quarreled in bars, beginning at the end of that summer, less
about political personalities than about global strategy, logis-
tics, and what their wife's young cousin wrote home. The headlines, like the thoughts with which people went to bed at night,
belonged first to the draftees, then to the soldiers.

Willkie sensed this quickly. His son, Philip, went into the
navy in 1941, and the war was never very far from Willkie's

mind. His own life had changed in important ways. He was more than ever a social lion, hunted by hostesses, women's clubs, universities, citizens' groups, all over the country. At long last he had been able to winnow out of these lion-hunters a small circle of close friends who had nothing to do with the electric power industry and not much to do with Republican party politics. Some of them were Republican moguls whom he liked personally even if he sometimes disagreed with them: Martin, Pryor, Marvin, Weeks, and Cake were among them. Some were newspaper editors: Geoffrey Parsons of the *New York Herald Tribune*, Charles Merz of the *New York Times*, White of the *Emporia Gazette*, Paul Smith of the *San Francisco Chronicle*. Many of the top Washington correspondents and newspaper columnists were now among his close personal friends. Irita Van Doren, one of the great professional editors of her generation, had become his leading adviser on the texts of speeches and articles, and through people like her, Willkie was thrown increasingly into contact with some of the most cosmopolitan-minded and civilized individuals of his time.

It was only late in 1941 that Willkie began to make a serious impression on the true fashion-setters in a democracy dominated by the mass media of communication—the editors of great newspapers rather than their publishers, the scholars in universities rather than their presidents, the production chiefs of corporations rather than the chairmen of their boards of directors. These men deepened and widened his outlook on the world. They also forced him to think through his positions more thoroughly. Some of these associations hurt him politically. There were strong traces of anti-intellectualism in the extreme nationalist and isolationist circles which had singled out Willkie as a chief target by 1941. Even less extreme critics charged that he was being seduced by the same kind of New York, long-haired, international-minded elements as had, in their opinion, dominated the New Deal for so many years—what the *Chicago Tribune* always calls "the champagne and caviar liberals of the East." In fact, Willkie's influence on these people was in most important ways far greater than theirs on him.

He had always been a restless man; it is significant that in no period of his active life did he carry over many close and intimate friendships from an earlier period. In the last phase, which was to last only three years, his circle of friends and associates changed again, but he dominated these as he had others before them. One of the compensations of having power without official responsibility in a democracy is that this makes it possible, although by no means easy, for a public figure to be both honest and frank. Willkie knew this and often talked about it. He felt a deep responsibility to the United States and to his times, and this drove him back to the ideas he had inherited and grown up with and to a constant effort to make contemporary sense out of his experience in American business.

He worked hard and lived hard. He was careless of his good health as only physically big men are. In 1941 he went back to earning money seriously, but he simply piled this on top of his speaking, his writing, seeing an endless stream of people on political business, traveling all over the country, going to interesting parties at the drop of an invitation. His library shows that after 1940 he bought and read a steadily increasing number of books, especially on contemporary social and political problems. He was trying to make sense the way a businessman tries to make money.

In political terms, there was little he could do. The Republicans in Congress were busy piling up an isolationist voting record so formidable as to suggest that they were determined to test Willkie's warning that this would lead to political suicide. They had voted 17 to 10 against lend-lease in the Senate, and 143 to 21 against it in the House. On the revision of the 1939 Neutrality Act, accomplished less than a month before Pearl Harbor, they voted 21 to 6 against it in the Senate, and 137 to 22 against it in the House. The Democrats failed to make good Willkie's 1940 campaign prediction that they would plunge America into war—one of Willkie's friends remembers his saying, in October, 1941, in reference to Roosevelt's promise to keep the nation out of war: "By God, I'm beginning to think he may have pulled it off!" The Republicans in Congress amply justified Roosevelt's warning that they were about as isolationist as Colonel Lindbergh.

Willkie

The Republican vote against the extension of selective service came as a serious shock to the country, since it caused the bill to be passed in the House by only one vote, 203 to 202. Conscription is never popular in any country, and least of all in the United States, but this seemed to many people a strange reaction in the face of imminent danger. The shock was dulled by the weight of bigger events. Leningrad was digging in for siege, building barricades in the streets. Odessa was still holding out but the Russians were forced to blow up the dam on the Dnieper River which was one of their greatest prides. The British and the Russians occupied Iran. Hitler and Mussolini met again for a conference which boded no good for anyone. Churchill and Roosevelt announced on August 14, two days after the selective service vote, that they had met at their secret Atlantic Conference, which produced the Atlantic Charter, and agreed on their mutual desire for "a better future for the world."

Willkie was never a military expert, and he never claimed to be one. Positions he later took on military questions, like his support of a second front and his opposition to a policy of expediency in North Africa, were primarily based on political considerations. But in the summer of 1941 he was far ahead of the Administration in recognizing the importance of naval warfare, and of the freedom of the seas as a major determinant of America's position on the war. On September 6, speaking with King Peter II of Yugoslavia to a national network audience, he called on President Roosevelt "to meet the challenge" in the North Atlantic posed by Nazi submarine warfare. "I hope and I know you hope," he said, "that the President of the United States serves notice upon Nazi Germany that the United States expects its ships to go unmolested in their passage across the North Atlantic and if they are interfered with those who interfere with them shall receive the results to which they are entitled. For there are certain things that no nation can concede without losing its strength and there are certain things that people cannot yield without losing their souls." A little later the same night, he was told that the Nazis had admitted an attack on the *U.S.S. Greer.*

A month later, he was still ahead of Roosevelt in believing

that the Neutrality Act of 1939, for which the President had claimed credit in the campaign, should be repealed. On October 6, in an important speech before the National Republican Club in honor of the British Ambassador, Viscount Halifax, he urged his party to take the leadership on this issue. "It is apparent to all thoughtful people," he said, "that this act should be repealed, and repealed promptly. The Administration is pursuing its usual course at critical moments—consulting the polls, putting up trial balloons, having some of its members make statements that others can deny—the same course that has led to so much of the people's confusion and misunderstanding." Three days later, on October 9, the President sent a message to Congress asking for amendment of the vital sections of the act.

The *New York Herald Tribune* and a few other Republican spokesmen backed Willkie up, but the Republicans in Congress never heard him. On October 17 the *U.S.S. Kearny* was hit by a Nazi torpedo, with eleven sailors killed, and on October 30 the *U.S.S. Reuben James* was sunk, with 115 lives lost. Willkie had gone right on talking as long as his voice lasted. On October 18, a cold had laid him up and Dorothy Thompson had to read to an N.B.C. audience a Willkie statement that the United States "must abandon the hope of peace." He had switched his personal allegiance from William Allen White's Committee to Defend America by Aiding the Allies to the Fight For Freedom group, which was much more frankly interventionist. "We can no more negotiate a peace with the war lords of Tokyo," he said, "than with the conquering dictator of Berlin." Willkie had persuaded three Republican Senators, Styles Bridges of New Hampshire, Warren R. Austin of Vermont, and Chan Gurney of South Dakota, to press a resolution for the lock, stock, and barrel repeal of the Neutrality Act, but this only increased the anger of the regular Republicans. "It is an action taken once more with chicane," said Senator Danaher, "once more with machinations, once more to deny to the American people the information they should have to make up their minds."

By October 22, Willkie had lined up more than one hundred prominent Republicans as signers of a public statement for outright repeal of the act. They came from forty states, including six governors, practically no members of Congress, and almost no names that were nationally identified with the Republican party rather than with their own jobs. Here he had got out in front of his own party and of Roosevelt, too. Landon came out with sharp criticism of "certain Republicans" for "running interference" for the President on foreign policy. But as Arthur Krock pointed out, "Mr. Willkie wasn't running interference this week. He grabbed the ball from a player on his own side and ran with it."

The outcry was loud. Hamilton Fish went on the air, over C.B.S., to challenge "Wendell Willkie, John W. Davis, Francis Biddle, the Attorney General of the United States, and the *New York Times* and *New York Herald Tribune*, all of whom believe in constitutional government, to issue a public statement repudiating an undeclared war as being un-American, undemocratic, and unconstitutional." Former Senator David A. Reed, Pennsylvania Republican, joined with John Cudahy, George N. Peek, Dr. Henry Noble MacCracken, president of Vassar, and the inevitable John T. Flynn, to denounce Willkie before the Senate committee holding hearings on the problem. Walter Lippmann answered them, calling them "Mr. Martin's Republicans." "They are not in opposition," he said, "they are an obstruction. . . . The country cannot stand much more of their obstruction and not find itself in dire peril. The country knows it, and Mr. Willkie and his fellow Republicans are sailing with a strong wind behind them."

It was a strong wind, but not among the Republicans. On November 7, exactly a month before Pearl Harbor, the Senate voted to repeal the sections of the Neutrality Act which prevented the arming of merchant ships and which barred U. S. ships from entering belligerent harbors and combat zones. The vote was 50 to 37, and the Republicans lined up 21 to 6 against it. Six days later, the House followed suit, 212 to 194, with 137 Republicans voting against the amendment and only 22 for it. On the same day, as if to prove the importance of the amendment, the Germans announced officially that they had sunk 14,500,000 tons of enemy shipping, just about the total for four years of the First World War. Willkie swallowed hard, breathed deeply, and issued a statement to show his party loyalty: "Undoubtedly, the vote was in part retaliation by Congress for the Administration's negligence and muddling in the solution of our industrial labor relations problem, and for its utter disregard of the needs and rights of large elements of our population in the handling of our domestic defense program." The Republicans, who should have been grateful for such forbearance on his part, set their teeth a little tighter.

Feeling was running much too high to be kept within the bounds of Congressional votes. In September, Leningrad was completely encircled by land and Kiev fell to the Nazis; on October 3, Hitler returned to Berlin from the Russian front to announce that "Russia is already broken and will never arise again." On October 19, Stalin declared Moscow itself in a state of siege. The thermometer was dropping fast. By December 5 it was to register 13 degrees below zero in Moscow, but General Winter had not yet been heard of on the Soviet General Staff as far as Americans were concerned, and Russian resistance was almost universally expected to collapse. Viscount Halifax had been given the eggs and tomatoes treatment by women on a Detroit street in November, shortly after Lindbergh and Wheeler had addressed twenty thousand wildly cheering Americans in a great America First Committee mass meeting in Madison Square Garden.

This was the setting in which Willkie agreed to speak up in public for the motion picture industry. Martin Dies, chairman of the House Un-American Activities Committee, had already spread wide and deep the charge that American films were being made a vehicle for Communist propaganda; it was one of the first tests of whether Hitler's theory of "the big lie" was applicable outside Germany. The production of a very few anti-Fascist pictures in 1941 led the isolationists to bring charges of "war propaganda disseminated by the motion picture industry." Willkie agreed on September 1 to defend the industry in hearings before the Senate.

Willkie's feelings about the war were only one factor in this decision. The attack on the movies was a tactic of the isolationists which showed them as more Fascist than they actually were.

Willkie

Colonel Lindbergh, speaking at Des Moines on September 11, had said: "The three most important groups which have been pressing this country toward war are the British, the Jewish, and the Roosevelt Administration." Going on to speak of the Jews, he had said: "their greatest danger to this country lies in their large ownership and influence in our motion pictures, our press, our radio, and our government." This kind of talk Willkie recognized as real dynamite, much more dangerous than opposition to the war, and it explains the alacrity with which he agreed to represent the industry at the Senate hearings.

His biggest job was to encourage Hollywood millionaires with Jewish names to stand up and be counted. They were by this time so intimidated that appeasement seemed the only way out. The Hays Office was also in favor of playing down any idea that any motion picture had ever contained any idea at all, and it urged the industry to lie low and wait for the storm to blow over. Willkie sat up night after night with Hollywood tycoons, before they were to testify, building up their morale, urging them to stand up and simply tell the story of their lives.

The hearings were a pushover for him from the start, although they brought a lot of sensational publicity. This was partly because the approach of Pearl Harbor made any talk of a Hollywood conspiracy seem like the plot of a Grade B movie, and partly because the sincere isolationists had been euchred out of control of their own movement by men like Colonel Lindbergh, Colonel McCormick, and the truly fanatic fringe.

The hearings were held before a subcommittee of the Senate Interstate Commerce Committee. They opened on September 9 with Senator D. Worth Clark, Idaho Democrat, in the chair. Senator Ernest MacFarland, Democrat of Arizona, was the only member of the subcommittee who was not an isolationist. Senator Nye had made a speech in St. Louis on the day he and Clark introduced the resolution calling for the hearings, and he had picked up the full Lindbergh line. He read a list of Hollywood executives with non-Anglo-Saxon names. "In each of these companies," according to Nye, "there are a number of production directors, many of whom come from Russia, Hungary, Germany, and the Balkan countries." Such men in times of world upset, he held, were susceptible to riotous and unreasonable national and racial emotions, and they were "trying to make America punch drunk with propaganda to push her into war."

Willkie was denied the right to cross-examine witnesses but it was hard to keep him quiet in the committee room and impossible to silence him in the newspapers. When Nye continued to denounce the Jews in Hollywood with frequent explanations that he was not himself anti-Semitic, Willkie commented: "I wish I could ask the Senator whether he believes the American public does not recognize the technique that he is using." When Clark suggested that one remedy for the situation they were investigating might be to require the film companies to present both sides of the international situation, Willkie said: "This, I presume, means that since Chaplin made a laughable caricature of Hitler, the industry should be forced to employ Charles Laughton to do the same on Winston Churchill."

Willkie had legal grounds for objection to the hearings—they had never been authorized by the Senate—but he soon realized that the sound strategy for Hollywood was to bury them with ridicule. He sat through long speeches by the Senators themselves, by John T. Flynn, and by a pair of Hollywood radio commentators, Jimmy Fidler and George Fisher, sure that at the end of each session the reporters would come to him. A few favorable witnesses were called, including Darryl F. Zanuck of Twentieth Century-Fox Film Corporation, to make a typically Hollywood defense with the argument that out of eleven hundred feature pictures produced since the war began, less than fifty had anything to do with the issues involved in the war or with the ideological beliefs of the warring nations. By the end of September, the hearings had wandered off into investigation of some Washington gossip that the British Purchasing Commission refused to employ Jews, Germans, or persons from the south of Ireland. They continued in suspended animation for another few weeks, and were completely forgotten after Pearl Harbor.

The episode was more important in the development of Willkie's ideas than in any political sense. He made a good many friends in the industry, including Spyros Skouras, who was about to take over control of the Twentieth Century-Fox Film Corporation after the conviction of Joseph M. Schenck on charges of income tax evasion. When Skouras, a one-time Greek shepherd boy, became president of the company in the following April, Willkie became chairman of the board and his law firm was retained as special counsel to the company. Besides defending the industry in the Washington hearings, he made the principal address at the annual awards dinner of the Academy of Motion Pictures, Arts and Sciences. Until his death he acted often as an unofficial spokesman for the entire industry. It was a situation which challenged his political beliefs, his interest in racial and other minorities, and his search for new media which could carry his ideas to greater and greater audiences.

These were months in which Willkie's public reputation was changing rapidly. He was becoming more widely known as a liberal and an internationalist; this cost him some old supporters and won him new ones. He was not changing convictions he had held all his life, but his urgent sense of the war speeded up their articulation, and his curious political position gave him freedom to state them with no strings attached. The New Deal itself played almost no part in this process; he remained bitter and sharp in his private criticism of Roosevelt and his Administration. His meetings with the President were infrequent and short, and if their old personal antagonism was less apparent it was not buried very deep.

They lunched together at the White House on July 9, 1941, chiefly for the President to make certain that Willkie would not publicly oppose the military occupation of Iceland. On August 25, Roosevelt wrote to him asking him to dedicate the Mount Rushmore Memorial, near Rapid City, in South Dakota, which had been carved by the late Gutzon Borglum. "I would be ingenuous," he wrote, "if I did not also mention that, geographically, this region is sadly in need of the kind of speeches you have been making." Willkie begged off on the ground of other commitments. Then in October, the President sent David Niles, one of his executive assistants specializing in politics and labor, to New York to sound Willkie out on the chances of his taking a major job with the Administration.

"I saw Wendell Willkie Friday afternoon at three o'clock in

his office," Niles reported back to the President on October 27. "I first told him that you would like to have him as part of your Administration, and also that you had said that this didn't mean that he was to give up any of his partisan ideology. He said that he was very much flattered and pleased, but thought that he would be much more useful to your foreign policy if he were not part of the Administration. I suggested that he ought not to say 'no' without further consideration and he replied that he would be glad to talk to you about it when you sent for him.

"I had told him that you would be glad to see him whenever you and he thought wise to discuss next year's political situation. You told me to suggest to you when that ought to be. I think the sooner the better, and I do not think it is necessary now to wait until these movie hearings are over. You will remember that you had thought it wise not to see him until the movie hearings were finished. I doubt if they will be resumed in the immediate future, if ever."

FDR wrote on the document a "memorandum for Pa" (General Edwin M. Watson): "Speak to me about seeing Wendell Willkie next week," but Willkie obviously had no interest in pursuing the matter, and the meeting hung fire. On December 5, Roosevelt wrote him enclosing a memorandum from Sumner Welles. The Australian Minister in Washington had delivered an invitation to Willkie from Sir Keith Murdock, a leading Australian newspaper publisher, and supported by the Prime Minister of Australia, to make an official visit to that country. Roosevelt offered to arrange his credentials in any way that Willkie might want.

"I leave this matter wholly in your hands," he wrote him, "as I think you should consult your own convenience—and I think both of us should be extremely careful, if you do go, lest it be said that I am 'sending you out of the country.'

"It would, of course, be of real value to cement our relations with New Zealand and Australia and would be useful not only now but in the future. There is always the Japanese matter to consider. The situation is definitely serious and there might be an armed clash any moment if the Japanese continue their forward progress against the Philippines, Dutch Indies, or Malaya or Burma. Perhaps the next four or five days will decide the matter.

"In any event I do wish you would let me know the next time you come to Washington as there are many things for us to talk over."

The letter was dated December 5, two days before Pearl Harbor, but postmarked December 8. There was a handwritten postcript: "This was dictated Friday morning—long before this vile attack started."

Willkie answered the letter:

My dear Mr. President:

I congratulate you very much on your Tuesday night talk.

I have your letter of December 5, which I appreciate. I am unable presently to appraise the potentialities or the wisdom of going to Australia since the Japanese attack. Perhaps it would now constitute a nuisance. I will think about it further.

I am coming to Washington on Monday, and, if your schedule presents a free moment, would you have one of your secretaries let me know before that date if it would be convenient for me to call on you in accordance with the suggestion in your letter? Please disregard this if you are at all pressed for time.

In case I do not see you Monday, there is something I would like to say to you. Of late a few people, friends of yours, have suggested to me various ways in which they thought you might make use of me in our national emergency. Since they have talked to me about this, I am afraid they may also have troubled you. You have incredibly anxious and burdensome days ahead and it should be plain to anyone that you can function with least strain and most effectiveness if you are free to choose your helpers and advisers for whom you must bear the responsibility, without any consideration other than your conception of the public welfare.

What I am trying to say—honestly, but awkwardly I am afraid, because it is not easy—is this: If any such well-meant suggestions about me are brought to you, I beg you to disregard them. There is on your shoulders the heaviest responsibility any man can carry and I would not add to it in the slightest way. Even to volunteer a willingness to serve seems to me now only an imposition on your attention. Every American is willing to serve.

In all sincerity, I am,

Respectfully yours,
Wendell Willkie

Willkie saw him as he had suggested, having lunch at the White House on December 15 immediately after Knox had given the President a long report on a flying trip to see the damage at Pearl Harbor. Willkie told the reporters afterwards that he had learned nothing to support the wild rumors of disaster which were then circulating. He insisted the President had not offered him a job, and when pressed as to whether he would take one, he replied: "I'm not running the government, although I tried very hard to get where I could. In times like these there is not any American who would not be willing to give everything he had in the service of his country."

The big job that was open was the direction of economic mobilization. Willkie would have liked this, and he had both powerful backing for it and strong arguments against it. Walter Lippmann wrote that Willkie "understands this war. He is trusted by business and by labor and by the country as a whole. He is a born leader of men. He has worked closely enough with industry to understand its problems, and yet not so near-sightedly as to be confused by its prejudices and shortcomings." White wrote Roy Roberts in January that he had seen Willkie in New York and "advised him, with all the earnestness of an ardent nature, not to get into the Administration under any circumstances, and he said he wouldn't." It would have been hard for Willkie to accept the job or to turn it down, but he had already told the President he would not ask for any post, and the offer was apparently never made to him.

Instead he was offered, together with Alfred E. Smith, Charles Evans Hughes, and James A. Farley, a post on the National War Labor Board which was being set up as a final court of appeal in labor disputes. The offer became known to reporters on January 13. The night before, Willkie had been called up by

Winston Churchill's secretary and told that the Prime Minister was at the White House and would like to see him. Frances Perkins reached Willkie at his Washington hotel by telephone, literally on his way to the White House, and asked him if he would accept the labor post. He asked for time to think it over. The White House reporters waited for him in the slushy driveway when he emerged, and they answered "Nuts" to his protests that he could not talk about what had happened. There was some stumbling talk about "a certain famous visitor" but Willkie gave no details. They pressed him on the labor board job, which Steve Early had told them about that morning; gossiping off the record, one of the reporters, Merriam Smith of the U.P., has written, Willkie "said he hadn't accepted such a post, knew little about it and that the situation was very indefinite."

Just what happened inside the White House that day it is impossible to state with precision; outside it there was vast confusion. According to James F. Byrnes, who was there, Willkie had called on Roosevelt, who "enjoyed talking with Mr. Willkie, and became so engrossed in the conversation that he was behind his schedule of engagements. Consequently, it was not until almost six o'clock that he told the Vice-President of his decision." The decision was that Wallace's job as chairman of the Economic Defense Board had been abolished, and that Donald Nelson had been named chairman of a new War Production Board.

As recently as the preceding weekend, according to Harry Hopkins' diary, the President had been talking at Hyde Park about naming Willkie, Nelson, and Supreme Court Justice William O. Douglas as a three-man committee to explore the matter for him and advise him about it. "I urged very strongly that this not be done," Hopkins wrote, "primarily because neither Willkie nor Douglas knew anything about production and because Willkie was apt to use it as a political football." Hopkins was certain that the final decision to appoint Nelson was known, until 5:30 on the afternoon of January 13, only to the President, himself, Justice Byrnes, and Harold Smith of the Bureau of the Budget.

"The amusing part of the whole business," Hopkins wrote in his diary the next day, "was that everybody was a candidate.

Wallace, I am sure, hoped the President would ask him. Bernie Baruch was in a hotel room in Washington spreading propaganda for himself. A great many of my friends were pushing Bill Douglas; Morgenthau wanted it worse than anything in the world. So did Jesse Jones and, of course, Knudsen."

Amusing as it was to Hopkins, it was confusion typical of the New Deal and typical of the early months of the war. Willkie had already released to the press the text of a major speech he was to make that night at the annual dinner of the United States Conference of Mayors in Washington. The heart of this speech was a blast at the Administration for failing to name one man to organize and co-ordinate the tremendous job of war production. The leading Republican exponent of unity in the war had spent a large part of the day in the White House and had not been told about a central decision in the planning of the national war effort. When the Nelson appointment was announced at 6 P.M., Willkie had literally a few minutes in which to revise a major public speech, making the necessary corrections and explanations to the wire services and the major newspapers. Evening editions of the Washington papers were carrying stories about his probable appointment to the National War Labor Board, a job he did not want and had not accepted. The explanations later made by Early about his premature announcement of this only served to confuse the whole affair. By the next day, columnists and correspondents were all writing about a major split between FDR and Willkie. Republicans were certain that their man had been tricked. There is no proof of malice or political trickery in the incident, but it followed a pattern Willkie had seen in his relations with the White House over nearly ten years. It is not hard to understand the feeling which was growing steadily stronger in him that the President's friendly manner toward him was full of guile.

The British Prime Minister has recorded his own contribution to the question of Roosevelt's political complexity at this time. He had been in Palm Beach for a week's holiday in the sun. "Mr. Willkie had asked to see me," Churchill's version runs. "At this time there was tension between him and the President. Roosevelt had not seemed at all keen about my meeting prominent members of the Opposition, and I had consequently so far not done so." But Churchill still felt cordially about Willkie's visit to London the year before, and Halifax advised him to see the Republican leader, so he telephoned Willkie from Florida.

When the call was put through there was an extremely awkward conversation about a prospective meeting until it became clear that the switchboard had made a mistake and Churchill was talking not to Willkie but to Roosevelt himself. When the confusion had been cleared up, Churchill asked: "I presume you do not mind my having wished to speak to Wendell Willkie?" To this Roosevelt said, "No." "And this was the end of our talk," according to Churchill's account of it.

It was not the end of Churchill's worrying about it, although he was not a man who bruised easily. When he got back to Washington he felt it necessary to write a formal inquiry to Hopkins to learn just how annoyed the President had been. "I rely on you to let me know if this action of mine in wishing to speak to the person named is in any way considered inappropriate, because I certainly thought I was acting in accordance with my duty to be civil to a public personage of importance, and unless you advise me to the contrary I still propose to do so." Hopkins reassured him that no harm had been done, but the incident is useful in any attempt to measure personal responsibility for whatever measure of political unity was eventually worked out during the war.

Willkie's support of much of Roosevelt's foreign policy at this time did not bring the two men any closer to each other and, in fact, served rather to sharpen the curious and old antagonism between them. Roosevelt's intimate associates agree without exception that he never expressed anything but friendly respect for Willkie, but the record is clear that in all his contacts with him, the President never for a moment forgot that he must act like a shrewd and sometimes over-cunning politician. On the other side, it is probable that this sharpened Willkie's dislike of complex personalities and complicated personal relationships. Willkie always had a capacity for highly diverse friendships, without any desire to bring ill-assorted friends together. Roosevelt seems to have loved doing this. Willkie always suspected the President of being over-tricky in their relationship as men, and he was as uncomfortable with him as he would have been in the presence of a group of highly different and contradictory friends.

They saw each other seldom. The President called him "Wendell"; he invariably answered "Mr. President" or "Mr. Roosevelt." There was a large and constantly growing number of prominent men who were close to both of them. When *Look* asked Willkie a series of questions, the answers to which were published on April 7, 1942, one of them concerned reports that he had "fallen out" with the President over the war effort. Using that phrase about two men, answered Willkie, "implies that there was once some sort of agreement or understanding between them. I don't have and never have had any personal relationship with President Roosevelt. There has never been any understanding between us that I should do or say certain things or that he should do or say certain things."

Another Churchill visit to the White House, in June, 1942, gave rise to another Roosevelt-Willkie legend. The President had taken Willkie upstairs to Churchill's room and after a little conversation prepared to leave the two men together. It was Churchill whom Willkie had come to see. The British Prime Minister waved Roosevelt's valet aside and insisted on pushing the wheel-chair out into the corridor, before beginning his talk with Willkie. The latter described the incident to friends, when he returned to New York, and at the same time he made clear, as he was consistently doing at this time, his growing fear that the Roosevelt-Churchill partnership threatened to involve the United States after the war in an unwise underwriting of the British Empire. The late Louis Adamic, in a book called *Dinner at the White House*, published what he called Willkie's version of the incident, including the wheel-chair, and quoted Willkie as saying he had been "shocked by the implication, haunted by the phrase 'taking him for a ride,' which came to my mind." This added a lurid, eastern European touch to the anecdote which was characteristic of Adamic but as unlike Willkie as anything could be. But Willkie was already genuinely concerned over the Anglo-Saxon monopoly of war and peace planning, and he believed that Roosevelt's personality was partly responsible for it.

Willkie had been earning a living during these months of heavy political activity, and he did this chiefly through the practice of law. He wrote a critic in 1944 that he had consistently earned more fees for his firm than he had drawn out. He was not an active trial lawyer, and much of what he did for the firm fell under the heading of new business, but this is a legitimate part of American legal practice. He said once in 1942 that he had convinced himself he could earn, if he wanted to, $500,000 a year, and that since he did not want to, he was going to go on working at the law only as hard as he needed to and not as if he wanted to become a millionaire.

During the months immediately after the 1940 election, he was widely touted for all sorts of industrial and banking jobs, including the management of the New York Stock Exchange. Actually, he moved slowly and carefully into the few directorships he took. In June, he became a director of the Federal Insurance Company, and in September of the Lehman Corporation, investment trust managed by the banking firm of Lehman Brothers, where he had several strong friends and supporters. In October, he was named as counsel by the National Coat and Suit Industry Recovery Board to defend it against charges of restraint of trade. This was a connection which gave him close and continuing relations both with clothing manufacturers and with the International Ladies Garment Workers Union, headed by David Dubinsky. In January, 1942, he returned to the board of the First National Bank of New York, at the request of its president, Leon Fraser, whom he counted among his close personal friends. By April, he had become chairman of the board of Twentieth Century-Fox Film Corporation; besides handling all its legal business, he negotiated in the summer of 1941 the settlement of a labor dispute for it and three other movie companies covering fifteen hundred clerical employees.

Willkie's bitter running fight with the isolationists in Congress deeply colored all his political activities in 1941 and 1942.

He continued to lead all Republicans in opinion polls, even those conducted officially by the Republican party. On the eve of Pearl Harbor, the *Republican* found in a poll of county and township Republican leaders that 42 per cent favored Willkie, 19 per cent Taft, and 15 per cent Dewey, with a scattering of votes for Hoover, Vandenberg, and Martin. By June, 1942, with the war six months old, a Gallup poll on a national sampling of Republicans, restricted to the two names, showed 52 per cent support for Willkie for the 1944 nomination against 48 per cent for Dewey. By this time Dewey was actively campaigning for the New York Governorship. The political experts were still agreed that if the Republicans were to find enough non-Republican votes to win a national election, Willkie was the only man who had a chance to deliver them.

Yet his unpopularity among the Republicans in Congress grew steadily, uninterrupted by the declaration of war. He had not caused much party trouble when he supported Mayor Fiorello H. LaGuardia in a Republican primary for the New York City mayoralty in September, 1941; LaGuardia himself, who had opposed him bitterly in 1940, said: "This is the most generous and sporting attitude taken in politics in a long time." But when in the same month he made a public statement that throughout 1942 he would work and speak for those Republican candidates who had backed President Roosevelt's foreign policy, he angered very nearly all the Republicans in the country who had a voice: the Congressmen, the newspaper publishers, and the conservative columnists.

"The complaint against Mr. Willkie uttered by many Republicans," wrote Mark Sullivan, "is that during the last six months he has made many speeches favoring the President's foreign policy—but has not, certainly not with conspicuousness, expressed that opposition to domestic policies of the New Deal which is part of the function of opposition leadership." The politicians went much further. It was unfortunate, Taft declared, that Mr. Willkie should attempt to read out of the party all who disagreed with him on foreign policy. Five Indiana Republicans, including Halleck, who had nominated him in 1940, and Senator Raymond E. Willis, issued a joint pledge of opposition to the Administration's effort "to involve this country in an undeclared war" which was clearly aimed at Willkie. Representative Dewey Short of Missouri, who had wanted to be candidate for Vice-President on the same ticket with Willkie, pleaded on the floor of the House: "May God forgive me for ever having supported such an impostor, this fifth columnist, this Trojan horse who is seeking to split the Republican party wide open."

Willkie stuck to his position. In the *American Magazine* for October he attacked leaders of both parties for their obstructionism in the face of national danger. He accused the Democrats of political manipulation of the defense effort, and he blamed the Republicans' isolationist record on their "psychopathic hatred of the President." The moral, he concluded, was obvious: "the party that pussyfoots, opposes, and obstructs during a national emergency writes its own death warrant; but the party that co-operates and encourages national unity survives with colors flying high. The choice stands clearly before the Republican party today."

Willkie carried his belief in unity as far as going to see Farley in January, 1942, to try to work out a general bipartisan agreement for the renomination and re-election of all Senators and Representatives who had supported the President's foreign policy. "I told him I was against any such agreement," according to Farley, "that the decision should be left to the voters concerned, and that neither he, the President, nor anyone else could successfully carry out such an agreement. As he left, I was convinced that he was still working for the Presidency." Willkie himself consistently parried reporters' questions about his 1944 ambitions. In Boston, on February 12, he answered a question on whether or not he would "like to meet the champ again" by saying that if his ideals prevailed he expected "to be a force in that election."

In April the isolationists in the party won a victory of uncertain value when Senator C. Wayland Brooks won an Illinois primary for renomination with the backing of the anti-Willkie *Chicago Tribune*. But when the Republican National Committee met in Chicago in the following week, Willkie scored a victory of considerable proportions. Four resolutions on national policy had been submitted to the committee: one by Willkie, a somewhat similar one by H. Alexander Smith, then Republican state chairman of New Jersey, and two by Taft and Brooks which went no further from the isolationist position than to state that the war must be won. On April 20, a resolution was unanimously adopted after seven hours of discussion in a small committee, which followed Willkie's wishes almost to the letter in committing the party to support international co-operation after the war. Willkie had had reservations on every plane for Chicago throughout the day in case he had needed to fly there to plead his views in person. He followed the meeting from New York with an open telephone circuit to his friends on the committee. He was openly jubilant. Taft did not hide his disappointment: "I think it is a great mistake for the national committee to have expressed any policy at all on postwar action."

Like all such victories, it had to be paid for. Martin was re-elected chairman of the party, and he announced that complete unity had been achieved inside the party. But if Willkie had won on the commitment to postwar internationalism, his opponents had won on the temporary glossing over of isolationism as an intra-party issue. They were seeking to keep their pre-Pearl Harbor records from the close examination Willkie had been threatening to give them. The measure of their victory was Martin's re-election. For, as the *New York Herald Tribune* pointed out on the day the meeting opened, "it is not merely that [Martin] was one of the last Republicans in the House to perceive the closeness of war to our shores and that he opposed measure after measure designed to secure for us allies and the sinews of war. The decisive point is that not by a word spoken since Pearl Harbor has he revealed the slightest awakening to the realities of the world today."

The truth was that the Republican Congressmen who voted for the compromise resolution were worried about the past, and Willkie was worried about the future. Both won their major objectives: there would be no party split in 1942 over isolationism and the party was on record, at long last, for an internationalist postwar policy. Only the party itself lost, in the sense that it continued to straddle on the central issue of the times.

For Pearl Harbor had interrupted but had not decided the great debate in which Americans were trying to come to terms with their new position of world leadership. The business community in which Willkie had grown up was uncertain about political slogans but not in the least uncertain about accepting the new challenge to it posed by the war. It was, in fact, so busy increasing the national product of the United States that the political wrangle over isolationism in 1941 and 1942 inside the Republican party reads today even more like double talk than when it was going on. Conservative Republican leaders, prodded by Willkie, were trying to look like anti-Fascist patriots without closing any doors behind them. But at the same time American business was becoming more and more permanently geared to a level of production which made the old Republican slogans of self-sufficiency, high tariffs, and no entangling alliances as obsolete as prohibition. When the Republican party failed to follow Willkie's lead, and went back at the end of the war through the doors it had so carefully left ajar, it found nobody there.

Willkie's running fight with his own party involved him in two local political situations during 1942. One of these was the attempt to unseat Representative Hamilton Fish in Orange, Putnam, and Dutchess Counties in New York. As early as February 21, the President wrote Willkie one of his genial notes, asking to see him, and adding: "By the way, it seems to me that the problem of Fish is just as much a problem as it was when we talked it over many months ago. I have various recommendations for candidates—some are inclined to think that if Warden Lawes could be persuaded to run, he would make the best showing. I think he calls himself an independent Republican. None of the other names are well known in all three counties." Willkie tried instead to rally support around Augustus W. Bennet, Newburgh lawyer.

Willkie did not live in the district, as Roosevelt did, and his interest in the fight stemmed from Fish's overt and extreme

position as an isolationist Republican. Dewey also opposed
Fish, although with considerably less gusto than Willkie. Fish
was a very small pawn in a bigger fight, but a symbolic one.
He could, and did, harp on the fact that "Wendell Willkie is
hardly dry behind the ears as a Republican" and he could,
and did, emphasize that the isolationist votes he had cast in
Congress, to which Willkie objected, had lined him up with
approximately 90 per cent of the Republicans in the House.
In the Republican primary, on August 12, Fish was renom- .
inated by almost a three to one margin.

A more important but less open struggle developed over
the nomination of a Repubican candidate for Governor of
New York in 1942. Coolness between Willkie and Dewey was
normal and expectable political weather considering the personalities of the two men; strong ambition was almost the only
trait they had in common. When Willkie's resolution was presented to the April meeting of the Republican National Committee, Dewey telegraphed J. Russel Sprague, his representative at the meeting: "I sincerely hope that skeletons of issues
buried in the bloodstained earth of Pearl Harbor and Bataan
will not be allowed to injure either our national or party
unity in the battle over words or resolutions to be adopted
at the Republican National Committee meeting." When the
vote had been taken, however, he said he thoroughly approved
of the resolution as it was adopted.

"Frankly, I'm puzzled," Willkie commented. "I'm not sure
whether he was recommending that the committee adopt a
doctrine of isolation or a position of world outlook and
co-operation by the United States after the war. I am glad
that he now commends the work of the committee."

Most of the rivalry which developed between the two men
over the next six months could be traced to Willkie's persistent
but vain attempt to commit Dewey to an internationalist
foreign policy, and to Dewey's quiet determination not to
close any doors behind him. Willkie himself never wanted to
run for Governor; in June and July a group of citizens calling
themselves Vote for Freedom, Inc., led by Richard B. Scan-
drett, Jr., and including some of the most widely known

internationalists in New York, tried to organize a "Draft Will-kie" movement. It won the strong support of Dubinsky and important fractions of the American Labor party, and many of Willkie's friends in New York City worked up a good deal of enthusiasm for the idea. Willkie discouraged it from the start, and never wavered in public from his flat statement that he had no intention of running for Governor. He had no state machine, as Dewey had, and no political need to run and win, as Dewey had, to stay in the running for the 1944 Presidential nomination. But he knew that Dewey, as Governor of New York, would be a more formidable candidate in 1944, and he also knew that Dewey was sure to continue as long as any man to straddle on the one issue on which Willkie was trying to reform and capture the Republican party.

So Willkie tried the extremely difficult political trick, for him, of staying on the fence about the nomination for Governor. At a legislative correspondents' dinner in Albany, in April, he described the man he felt the party should not nominate for Governor, and Dewey, who was present, could hardly have failed to resent the portrait. In the same month, he made public a list of twelve men he regarded as acceptable nominees: Dewey was not among them. Willkie had nothing to work with but his popular following and his fervent belief that any return to Harding isolationism would be fatal to the American system. In May, when he was made honorary chancellor of Union College at Schenectady, he made another reference to Dewey which could hardly have been plainer if he had mentioned his name. He urged his audience to choose leaders who had principles and the courage to state them plainly, "not men who examine each shift of sentiment and watch the polls to learn where they stand. I beg of you to vote for straight-out men—not wobblers. This is no time for ambiguity."

Willkie was shooting the works. On June 18, he paid tribute to Senator Robert F. Wagner at a dinner in his honor given by the Louis D. Brandeis Memorial Committee. "In my one attempt to occupy high political position, he opposed me mightily," Willkie said. "If I should aspire to public office again he would do the same. But I doubt if he ever gets the opportunity. I doubt if I shall ever aspire to public office again." His tribute to the author of the National Labor Relations Act was hardly calculated to endear him to the Old Guard Republicans. The next day, in a press interview, he went still further. "Our party should be the friend and advocate of the workingman," he said. "Ours is the party of production, the party of plenty, whether in war or in peace. It has always been our aim to produce, for the American workingman, the highest standard of living in the world, not alone in dollars of wage but in expansion and opportunity.

"Thus in so far as we have lost the workingman's confidence, we have lost our grip on our most basic purpose. We must regain it."

Hardly six months before, the emphasis in what he said about labor had been different. When an American Labor party rally had stood up and cheered him in Madison Square Garden in September, 1941, as he announced his support of LaGuardia for Mayor, he warned unions to avoid abuse of their new power if they wanted to keep it. "Any excesses in the policies of labor," he had said then, "are menacing primarily to the ultimate freedom and vitality of trade unionism itself. I want to ask that all of us in this period of emergency follow the course of moderation and keep this nation united in the cause of security and freedom." There was no doubt now that Willkie was changing, although men might and did quarrel over whether he was changing to something new or back to the basic pattern of beliefs which had shaped his whole life. In either case, much of American business was changing with him. It had been less than a year since the Ford Motor Company had given up its long and bitter fight with organized labor and signed a contract with a C.I.O. union granting everything the union asked for and throwing in the union shop and check-off for good measure.

Change was in the air in the summer of 1942. The war news continued black, yet no one living in America could help feeling the enormous military build-up which was under way. Willkie was determined to play his political cards in such a way as to profit from the stretching of men's minds and to stretch them still more. On June 19, he sat through what was described as a "harmonious" luncheon at the Capitol with about twenty Republican Senators. McNary was his host, and Willkie sat between Norris, against whom he had fought the TVA battle, and Nye, with whom he had fought over isolationism. By the next week he was campaigning for his friend Baldwin, in Connecticut, and telling Republicans "not to go about bemoaning your fate and talking about Franklin Roosevelt destroying the two-party system" but instead to "bring the leadership in this party to those men who will make the Republican party deserving of life and have it adopt principles that will make it live." On July 13 he announced flatly that he would take an active part in the autumn political campaign to help candidates committed to American participation in a new world order after the war.

"I'm a Republican," he declared, "and I expect to remain a Republican. Everything I do now has but one end: to bring the party to a realization of problems to be faced after the war. I want to help elect men to office who will see these problems. I'm dedicated to this one thing."

CHAPTER SIXTEEN

One World

THREE reporters languishing in the dreary Grand Hotel in Kuibishev, Russia's wartime capital on the Volga, helped Willkie to achieve the true climax of his public career. They were the first to suggest the trip which gave him, at least for a short time, leadership of men and women all over the world who wanted a victory with real meaning and promise for the future. They were Maurice Hindus, special correspondent of the *New York Herald Tribune*, Eddy Gilmore of the Associated Press, and the late Ben Robertson, representing *PM*. They all knew and liked Willkie, and in a friendly cablegram to him in July, 1942, they included strong advice that the moment was ripe for a good-will trip to Russia. "Nothing I would like to do so much," Willkie cabled back; "my personal regards to each of you." Within a month, after a White House luncheon on August 7 in honor of Queen Wilhelmina of the Netherlands, he stayed to talk about the idea with the President and some of the men at the head of the armed services. On August 26 he set off in a U. S. Army C-87 converted bomber, the *Gulliver*, on a trip around the world.

For all those who were committed emotionally and morally in the war, victory had become the overpowering consideration by the summer of 1942, and it was by no means a foregone conclusion. Ten years later, it is easy to forget that even the simple problem of a military verdict did not look at all simple at that time. Rommel's Afrika Korps had pounded deep into Egypt, and there was real fear that Cairo might fall in the days just before the *Gulliver's* arrival. The Russian armies were clinging to their toehold at Stalingrad, where eventual victory was still months away, Leningrad was besieged and Moscow evacuated by most of the Soviet government. The Chinese armies were deep in the western provinces and it was touch and go whether they could maintain even their symbolic resistance to Japan. With German armies in the Caucasus and Egypt and Japanese on the borders of India, the two strongest Axis powers were perilously close to establishing the land link between themselves which would have completely shattered the great strategic advantage of the Allies. In the South Pacific the Japanese still had supremacy in the air, and on the sea the decisive fifth battle of the Solomons was not to be fought until the middle of November.

For Willkie, victory meant much more than a military verdict. He had no doubt that in the long run American industrial production would prove to be the decisive factor, but he was afraid of what too long a run might do to the fighting spirit of the Allies. He had already worked out clearly in his own mind the thesis that nothing can be won in a war except what is fought for in that war. He knew that the great churning in human events which had brought on the war would require new patterns of world order after it ended, and he knew also that Pearl Harbor had broken off too sharply the slow, angry, American process of defining war aims which could help to set these new patterns. To start Americans thinking about them was a challenge to Willkie of truly passionate urgency. This belief in the importance of conscious, articulate war aims was no more original with Willkie than his older belief in the organic relation between productivity, national strength, and freedom. But both were central to all his political thinking, and the rights he established to them by persistent and passionate advocacy are the basis of his claim to a place in American history.

Willkie's desire to see the war at first hand had not been satisfied by his trip to England; it had grown steadily stronger. For a few weeks in February, 1941, he had thought of going to China. At the end of that year, the invitation from Australia had tempted him strongly until the Japanese attack filled all planes in the Pacific with more urgent cargo. By the summer of 1942, he had committed himself so deeply in public on the question of war aims that he badly needed some position or gesture dramatic enough to let him make his point without his voice sounding too shrill and passionate—his old danger. To work for the Administration in a civilian job was politically out of the question without a formal coalition. At the same time, he had pushed his position so far that he also had no chance, even had there been a desire, to hedge his bets by courting the regular Republicans or sharing their still-private dreams of a blessed return to normalcy. His old habit took over of going on to the offensive when he found himself in a tough spot.

He was also glad at the prospect of being out of the country for some of the weeks during which Dewey's campaign for Governor of New York was gaining momentum. The Republican columnists were wrong who wrote, as soon as the trip was announced, that Willkie was running out on the problem. He came back, as he promised he would, in time to face the difficult issue which Dewey's candidacy presented to him. But since he did not want to run against Dewey, his hope was to smoke him out, to force him to declare himself on international policy, and at the same time to keep the Willkie legend in the public eye if not in the hearts of Republicans.

Willkie left Mitchel Field, New York, on August 26, and returned to Washington fifty days later, on October 15. He had covered 31,000 miles in 160 hours of flying time, giving him about thirty days on the ground. He had flown over vast areas in Africa, Central Asia, Outer Mongolia, and Arctic Siberia which were unknown to the American public and just beginning to be mapped by American fliers. During this time he had met and had long talks with many of the world's leading statesmen and generals. He had seen at fairly close range three fighting fronts. He had talked to hundreds of soldiers and plain people. He came back fifteen pounds lighter, shorter on sleep than he had been since the end of the campaign, and committed as he had never been before to his crusade to persuade America to accept in a generous, creative spirit the world leadership which the war was thrusting on it.

There were six men in the army crew, led by Major (now Colonel) Richard T. Kight. Willkie had invited Gardner (Mike)

Cowles and this writer to go with him as his friends. Both of us were given leave of absence from the Office of War Information to make the trip. Its propaganda value was obvious, and it gave us a chance to see a good many of the foreign outposts of the government's wartime information service, as well as what was being done by our allies and by the enemy. Captain Paul Pihl of the U. S. Navy, Willkie's brother-in-law, and Major Grant Mason of the U. S. Army also went with him as representatives of those services, and the plane carried other officers for portions of the long trip.

The flight went by way of West Palm Beach to Puerto Rico,

One World

where Willkie had a chance to see his son, Philip, then stationed there at a navy post. After a short stop at Belém the plane flew to Natal for the take-off across the South Atlantic, via Ascension Island, to Accra. Ascension Island was then a secret U. S. air base, and was therefore not mentioned by Willkie in his book about the flight. There was a day's delay at Kano, the fantastic walled city of mud huts in the middle of Nigeria, a night in the Governor's Palace at Khartoum, and then a longer stay in Cairo to make possible a trip to the British Eighth Army, then building up for the battle of El Alamein. A smaller, nonmilitary plane was used to fly into neutral Turkey from the great British air base at Lydda. Jerusalem, Bagdad, and Teheran were all important stops on the trip. Then the *Gulliver* picked up Soviet fliers assigned to it for the long flights to Kuibishev, on to Moscow, and back via Tashkent and Urumchi (Tihwa), in Chinese Eastern Turkestan, to Lanchow and Chengtu in China. The airfield at Chungking was too small for the *Gulliver*, but Willkie picked up the big plane again at Chengtu, after his Chungking stay, for the final laps across North China and Mongolia to Chita, Yakutsk, and a frozen little village named Seimchan where a take-off could be made for the first eastward American flight during the war over the Bering Strait to Fairbanks in Alaska. The final flight was through Edmonton, in Alberta, and Minneapolis to the first really dangerous landing of the entire trip, in a heavy rainstorm, at the National Airport in Washington.

The plane had settled on runways in five continents, and had crossed the Equator twice. This was one of the obvious functions of the trip in terms of psychological warfare: it was a vivid demonstration to neutrals and the enemy that the great alliance fighting against Hitler had control of the strategic air routes which tied the world together. The South Atlantic route had been flown by Willkie the year before, at a very early stage in its development, and by 1942 was nothing new. The air link to Moscow through Teheran was also beginning to be well traveled by that time, at least by military planes. When the *Gulliver* dropped into the green valley around Tashkent, and then flew over the Altai Mountains into Urumchi and from there to Lanchow, it was being seen by men who had never seen an Ameri-

293

can plane before. The last laps, cutting north across China and Outer Mongolia (we circled Ulan Bator but did not land) and then flying over the Siberian Arctic and the Bering Strait to Alaska, were flights no American plane had ever undertaken before. They made real and believable for millions of Americans our new closeness to Asia. They dredged up from half-remembered legends in American minds words like Tamerlane and Samarkand and Genghis Khan. Just one war before, the commander-in-chief of the British Army, Lord Kitchener, had lost his life trying to visit his Russian ally. Willkie's trip was a dramatic illustration that war had changed, and that the Allies actually did control the air around the world.

A second goal of the trip was to pound home to people everywhere the story of American industrial production, and this was duck soup for Willkie. In the first place, he knew a good deal about the vast changes then taking place in American industry although he held no active industrial post. In one branch, the generation of power, he was as well informed as almost any man, and as a director of a big bank and through his business friends he had detailed knowledge of the production build-up which was then the American substitute for a second front. He talked it everywhere, to anyone who would listen, and he was a superb salesman for the kind of bigness that had attracted him so strongly all his life. In 1942 a C-87 looked as big as a B-36 looks today, and when Willkie stepped out of it, a towering man even without the flying clothes which were necessary on parts of the trip, and started to talk, on almost every airfield where we landed, the scene looked truly like an illustration for Dean Swift's story of Gulliver.

Finally, the propaganda importance of his being leader of the opposition party in the United States had not been lost on either Roosevelt or Willkie when the plan was made. It was a proof of national unity which was useful against the tales of internal dissension in America which the Nazis were spreading around the world. The fact that he was actively supporting the man who had defeated him for President two short years before was the theme for jokes which made Stalin laugh, made many politicians in the Middle East shake their heads confusedly, and

Seibel in the Richmond *Times-Dispatch*

drew from Generalissimo Chiang Kai-shek his warm, quiet, friendly smile, and Willkie never missed a chance to improvise some kind of wisecrack about it. There were stops on the trip at U. S. Army posts where Willkie's hosts were much more violently partisan on politics than he was. Everywhere he made it clear that he was still in opposition and that he would do his best to defeat the President in another two years, but his big theme was the unity of all Americans in backing the war to victory.

In the minds of those who planned the trip, including Willkie himself, these were his three basic assignments in what was then called by the fancy name of political warfare: to show the Allied control of strategic airways; to impress on people's minds what American industrial production was about to deliver; and to make vivid the degree of political unity behind the war in the United States. Willkie carried them out with considerable gusto and with measurable success. But he carved out for himself a fourth assignment during the trip, one which grew out of his earliest convictions about the war and which was reinforced by everything he saw and learned around the world. This was to argue for a working alliance of the nations fighting the Axis powers while they fought, an alliance based on open discussion of the problems of the war and on those of the peace.

His understanding with President Roosevelt before he left had made it perfectly clear that he remained free to state his own opinions in addition to carrying out the President's assignments. His critics jumped him for this, on the flimsy assumption that what he said on this score might be mistaken for official American policy. There was actually little danger of this. The Atlantic Charter had been the only approach to a statement of war aims; it had been framed by Roosevelt and Churchill alone; when the latter reported it to the House of Commons on September 9, 1941, he had pointed out that he was against any formulation of peace aims or war aims. "I deprecate it at this time," he had added, "when the end of the war is not in sight, when the conflict sways to and fro with alternating fortunes and when conditions and associations at the end of the war are unforeseeable." There could be no flatter statement of what Willkie was against, and he spoke against it without official sanction because of his belief that he had a free-wheeling mandate as an American citizen to speak his mind.

Everywhere Willkie went, men in positions of great power and ordinary citizens spoke to him briefly, hurriedly, with a sense that he would be gone the next morning and that this might be their last chance to say something outside official channels. So he inevitably picked up a remarkably detailed story of the creaking, timid, and negative working arrangements which had resulted from the Churchill-Roosevelt technique of keeping the planning of the war so closely in their own hands. Peoples who were not Anglo-Saxon were left in no uncertainty that they were junior partners in the enterprise. Military expediency formed the very structure of the arrangements. In every country Willkie visited, he discovered quickly that victory over the Nazis was only one of the goals for which men were fighting, and that on the other goals there was no agreement and no real effort to find it. Finally, there was a deep, human, irrational desire in the planning of the war in London and Washington to see it end with as little change as possible in the world as it had been in the summer of 1939. The chief thing Willkie learned on his trip around the world is that almost none of the people actually fighting the war liked this way of planning it.

The problem began to be clear in Egypt, when the *pashas* literally rolled out red carpet for Willkie to enter their palatial homes to be told, with great urbanity and cynicism, why Egypt, with Rommel's army deep inside its frontiers, was not in the war. The same story was set to music during a state dinner outside Beirut, at the Résidence des Pins then lived in by General Georges Catroux, the military ruler of Syria and the Lebanon. A house guest was the leader of the Free French, General Charles de Gaulle, whom Catroux recognized as his leader in terms of France but not in terms of the war. A dinner guest was Brigadier General E. L. Spears, then head of the British military mission there, a former supporter of de Gaulle but already his bitter political opponent. Willkie was taken by each of these men in turn along the paths of an elaborate formal garden under the Mediterranean stars. There, while the music played, he was told by each in blunt language what was wrong with the others, and in almost paranoiac terms what each planned to do about it. Willkie had passed the day before the dinner in the city listening to Lebanese tell him, some of them in a Brooklyn accent, what they planned to do about it, and it was, after all, their country.

It was not hard to smell trouble, and the smell grew steadily stronger. In Jerusalem, protocol required Willkie to be the guest of Sir Harold MacMichael, the British Resident High Commissioner for Palestine and Transjordan, a man who had stepped into real life out of the pages of Rudyard Kipling. In his massive and comfortable Government House, the problems of the Palestine mandate could be made to seem simple and old and eternal, and not much worth bothering about. But Lowell C. Pinkerton, U. S. Consul General at Jerusalem, loaned Willkie his house for one day. It had a double staircase which made it possible for Jewish and Arab leaders, desperately eager to tell their stories to Willkie, to follow each other alternately through a day-long debate that was filled with desperate and violent language. Willkie learned from them that the war against Hitler was only a part of a deeper process going on in Palestine, and that the problem of finding a peaceful end to this process was being smothered and not solved under a blanket of military expediency, diplomatic protocol, and Colonial Office formulas.

In Bagdad, members of the Iraq government told Willkie their suspicions of Great Britain behind a big screen which had been set up around a bar in order not to offend Moslem susceptibilities and yet give them all a chance to have a drink. In Teheran, the young Shah, Mohammed Riza Pahlevi, lunched alone with Willkie in an Arabian Nights garden and then took his first airplane flight with him, in the *Gulliver*, over his country neatly divided between the Russian and British armies. In Chungking, leaders of the factions in the uneasy coalition led by Chiang Kai-shek, members of the Generalissimo's immediate family, and United States officers like General Joseph W. Stilwell and General Claire L. Chennault all maneuvered Willkie into individual conferences where they could pour out their suspicions of each other and their fears of what was sure to happen when the discipline of war would be removed by victory, without any preliminary agreement on what the war had been fought for.

Everywhere he went, from Africa to Alaska, it was the same story. Everywhere he heard it in its clearest and fairest terms from Americans. Army officers, civilians on war missions, newspapermen, missionaries, and teachers were deeply worried about what was brewing, even when they disagreed over how Americans should use their great, new power. In its simplest version, what they told Willkie was that they had evidence that this war was much more than a military episode in an old balance of power struggle, and that they were afraid of what was sure to follow it if the war should end without a conscious and articulate effort at least to begin working on the deeper questions while a common enemy still held the peoples of the anti-Nazi world together.

It was this basic problem that led Willkie to make the two statements during the trip which caused major excitement all around the world. The first was in Moscow, on September 26, when he called for a second front in Europe "at the earliest possible moment our military leaders will approve," and added that "perhaps some of them will need some public prodding." The second was in Chungking, on October 7, when he said the war "must mean an end to the empire of nations over other nations" and called for firm timetables under which colonial peoples "can work out and train governments of their own choosing." Each statement was carefully tailored by him to its own situation, but both were deliberate and carefully planned efforts to start public discussion of problems which were vital to the future of the great alliance fighting Germany and Japan.

The Russian situation was full of dynamite for the simple reason that the Red Army was nearer defeat in the autumn of 1942 than Stalin was ever prepared to admit or Roosevelt and Churchill to recognize. From the very start of the Nazi-Soviet war, Western intelligence had been grievously wrong on Russian military strength; from a wrong underestimate in the summer of 1941 it had moved to an almost equally wrong overestimate in the following summer. Churchill had preceded Willkie to Moscow in August, 1942, primarily to cushion Soviet disappointment over the decision to establish a second front in North Africa instead of on the continent of Europe. Stalin had received the news badly; he was tough, obdurate, and deeply suspicious that even this watered-down promise would be repudiated. A considerable number of people outside Russia, including Stimson and Marshall, believed in 1942 that British military planners were trying to persuade their American colleagues to postpone a second front on the European continent. A noisy campaign for a second front, aimed at the people over the heads of their governments, was beginning in Hyde Park and Union Square, but the slavishly obedient Communist parties were not alone in thinking that the Russians needed help desperately. Willkie knew nothing of the North African plans—Roosevelt had let him go on this mission completely uninformed about them—and Stalin did not tell him of them. But he had plenty of reason to know that the Red Army, which was then battling against 5,000,-000 Germans, some 750,000 other Axis soldiers, and the entire industrial machine of western Europe, was in serious trouble and with it the whole anti-Hitler alliance.

First among his reasons for thinking this came his own evidence of the extent to which Stalin's ruthless defense strategy had strained the Soviet Union. He had had a chance to see a good deal for himself, in Kuibishev, then in Moscow, and at the front near Rzhev. He had seen a collective farm and several factories, all operated almost entirely by women. He had talked to the best-informed foreigners in Russia, who were nearly all less defeatist in 1941 and more worried in 1942 than officials in London and Washington. Everywhere Willkie went, he saw hard evidence of a nation strained almost to the breaking point. Ordinary Russians came up to him on the street to ask: "When will there be a second front?"

When Willkie said in his statement that "next summer might be too late" he had just had a long conference alone with Stalin. He kept no notes of what was said, but it was clear that he had heard a grim story. On October 5, the Soviet Ambassador in London, Ivan Maisky, gave Churchill a telegram from Stalin admitting that the situation at Stalingrad "had deteriorated since the beginning of September." He stressed German air superiority, and said: "Even the bravest troops are helpless if they lack air protection. We more particularly require Spitfires and Aircobras. I told all about that in great detail to Mr. Wendell Willkie."

At the dinner given for Willkie in the Kremlin, with most of the Politburo present to do him honor, both the strain and the suspicion it generated flared out for a few angry moments. Dive bombers operating from Norwegian bases had recently cut to pieces a convoy carrying lend-lease planes, and its British admiral had turned back. London was being blitzed again, and when Churchill heard about crated Lightnings (two-engined Lockheed P-38 pursuit planes) sitting on a dock in Scotland, he went to Averell Harriman and got them released for the defense of London. Unfortunately, no one except the ubiquitous Soviet intelligence service remembered to tell Stalin about it, or that other planes would be substituted for them. This was one of the main points Stalin had made to Willkie in their first conference, claiming that Churchill had been neither fair nor honest in taking the planes. Willkie had discussed the incident with both the United States Ambassador, Admiral William H. Standley, and the British Ambassador, Sir Archibald Clark Kerr (later Lord Inverchapel).

On the afternoon of the Kremlin banquet, a telephone inquiry had been received at the guest house where the Willkie party was staying, asking whether the British Ambassador might be included among the guests. Cowles answered in the affirmative, of course. Then in the endless succession of toasts which are an obligatory feature of Soviet banquets, Major Mason had proposed one to Russian and Allied pilots. Stalin remained on his feet when the toast had been drunk, and all but shouted a few bitter sentences about the failure of Russia's allies to supply the planes the Red Army needed. He specifically charged the British with having taken the 152 Lightnings. Stalin's voice was pitched low when he got to his point, but the words he used were rude and truculent. The British Ambassador stumbled back to his feet at once. He praised Stalin for his frankness, saying this was the reason he was so admired, but begged him to go on and explain the whole story.

At this point Willkie rose to his feet. In any great coalition, he said, there were always strains and misunderstandings, but we could not afford to lose sight of our common objectives. The British had held out alone for a long time before the Russians and the Americans were fighting by their side. If we stuck together now, he went on, we would beat the Nazis surely.

And if we could learn to stick together after the war, we would have a period of peace and prosperity such as the world had never seen. He put his arm down and turned Stalin around towards him, almost violently, and then proposed a new toast, to the Great Alliance. Stalin drank it.

There was nothing insulting in what Willkie said, but it was clear to everyone around the table that he was rebuking Stalin. "You are a plain-speaking man, I see," Stalin said to Willkie after the toast had been drunk. "I like plain-spokenness, but you wouldn't have stolen 152 planes from me."

The next day the British Ambassador called to thank Willkie for his intercession. The affair was never reported in the press, and gossip accounts of it were exaggerated out of all conscience. It remained Willkie's conviction that Stalin had spoken for the benefit of the other Russians in the room rather than for the British Ambassador. Stalin's position as dictator of an all-but-defeated nation, Marshal of a Red Army which was moving steadily backwards with seriously damaged morale, and leader of a desperately tired, suspicious, fanatic group of Communist commissars, may have forced him to use rough and dirty tactics. This was no excuse, but it was an explanation, and Willkie was trying to understand the Russians and what might keep them in the war.

Little of this was known or understood abroad, and when Willkie's statement about the second front was reported all over the world it provoked some angry answers. In Washington, the President told a press conference on October 6 that dispatches quoting Willkie were not worth reading because they were purely speculative. His old enemies, Senator Nye and Representative Rankin, denounced him roundly. Columnists were divided; some of them, like Mark Sullivan, wrote that it was a trick by Stalin and that the second front should be postponed as long as possible. The Hearst newspapers syndicated an article speculating on who was paying Willkie's expenses on the trip. (He paid his own personal expenses, and the U. S. Army provided the transportation.)

In England the reaction was equally adverse in official circles although a respectable section of the press welcomed what Willkie had said. Lord Croft, Parliamentary Secretary to the War Office, commented that Britain was already fighting on thirteen fronts. Clement R. Attlee, then Dominions Secretary, spoke of "demands made by irresponsible people." Churchill himself told the House of Commons about "the undesirability of public statements or speculation as to the time or place of future Allied offensive operations." There was laughter in the House when a member asked: "Will this be conveyed to Mr. Wendell Willkie?"

Stalin at least made it clear that Willkie had not dreamed up his fear of Russian resentment over the absence of a second front. Three days after Willkie had left Moscow, Stalin said in a letter to Henry Cassidy, A.P. correspondent in Russia:

"As compared with the aid which the Soviet Union is giving to the Allies by drawing upon itself the main force of the German Fascists, the aid of the Allies to the Soviet Union has so far been little effective. In order to amplify and improve this aid, only one thing is required: that the Allies fulfill their obligations fully and on time." A few days later, the Soviet press angrily demanded a public trial of Rudolph Hess, implying that the British might be dickering with him for a separate peace. The autumn of 1942 was not the beginning of the cold war between Russia and the West. Its true origins were much older, and the hot war against the Nazis was to keep the cold war awkwardly concealed for another three years. But this was the time, Willkie believed, when at least an effort might have been made to nail the Russians down to some postwar agreement. The effort was made later, but it was too little and too late.

Both on this trip to Moscow and on his later trip through Siberia on his way home, Willkie was enormously impressed by the Russian people and depressed by the nature of Communist control over them. The Russians had little chance, at that low point in their war, to conceal from him the enormous cost of the revolution, the shabbiness of the life they had wrested from it, or the increasing dangers of their authoritarian system and their growing isolation from the rest of the world. Willkie wrote in *One World* of his constant awareness of "the entire generation of men and women who had been destroyed, the families that had been scattered, the loyalties that had been broken, the thousands who had died from war and assassination and starvation, in the name of the revolution." A group of Soviet writers and newspapermen gave him an evening of wild talk, off the record, in which he heard the rude, intransigent, unfriendly kind of conversation which was to become the Communist "party line" when the war was over. Yet he liked much in the Russian national character as he saw it, especially in Siberia and especially in its lusty hunger for a higher standard of living. It was the contrast between these two reactions which drove Willkie to urge that some way be found to commit the Russians to a common set of war objectives and of terms of peace before the war was won.

Willkie's attack in Chungking on the colonial system was aimed at the same general target as his plea in Moscow for a second front: the forging of a real alliance to replace the complicated system of first-class, second-class, and third-class allies with which the war was being fought. Again he had been convinced of the merits of his case by first-hand observation. He had been treated well in the Soviet Union, but what happened in China was a kind of national ovation and it gave him a wonderful chance to learn what was going on in Asia.

"Since President Ulysses S. Grant, who came to China in 1879," the *Ta Kung Pao*, China's most influential independent newspaper, wrote on October 3, "Mr. Willkie is the first leading American statesman to visit China." He was helped by the fact that he entered the country through its Asiatic back door instead of through one of the ports which were symbols of foreign exploitation to the Chinese people. Again, he liked the Chinese people at once and genuinely. The result was that he had an unprecedented opportunity to learn for himself what Chinese were thinking and hoping, and this led him to speak up as loudly as he could for an American policy which would tie China into a free postwar world.

His language was even less tempered by discretion than it had been in Moscow. The war was not simply a technical problem for task forces, he said in his major statement on October 7, but a war for men's minds. He pleaded for an all-out offensive by the United Nations, for more help to China, and above all for an end to the entire system of colonial rule. "We believe," he said, "this war must mean an end to the empire of nations over other nations. No foot of Chinese soil, for example, should be or can be ruled from now on except by the people who live on it."

The statement was released after the fourth and longest of his conversations with Generalissimo Chiang Kai-shek. The latter had recently returned from long discussions in India with Nehru, and his mind was full of speculation about the new role of Asia in the world. Willkie also had long talks with

Mme. Chiang, with her two sisters, Mme. Sun Yat-sen and Mme. H. H. Kung, and with the latter's husband, who was then Finance Minister. Just before he left America, Willkie had talked for a long evening with the brother of these three remarkable sisters, T. V. Soong, then China's Foreign Minister. He saw General Ho Yin-ching, chief of staff of the Chinese Army, and General Chou En-lai, Communist leader who was later to become Prime Minister of the People's Republic of China. He talked to hundreds of others, Chinese and foreigners. Hollington Tong, then Vice-Minister of Information in Chiang's government, made a strong impression on him. So did Rewi Alley, New Zealander who had founded the Chinese industrial co-operative movement and whom he met in Lanchow. Most of all he liked the university professors, teachers, translators, doctors, engineers, the men of China's new generation who were determined to lift their country out of backwardness when the war was over.

These were the people who documented what Willkie said about the future of China and of all Asia. Even more than in Russia, the contrast between their hopes and the reality of China's position in the world was striking and profoundly discouraging. Willkie wrote frankly in *One World* about the impatience he found in all circles with the centralized control of Chinese life which was exercised by the Kuomintang in Chungking, and about the failure to adopt a sound fiscal policy to check the galloping inflation. At one luncheon given him by General Ho, China's top general, Willkie was asked by Stilwell about his plans to visit the front. When Willkie answered that his host had invited him to see the front near Sian in the great bend in the Yellow River, Stilwell told him that he would see there one of the great trading operations of modern China, with Chinese Nationalist troops engaged in heavy commerce with the Japanese. General Ho listened with bland imperturbability and did not deny it.

The courtesies and the attentions of the Chinese secret police were as ubiquitous as, and a little more apparent than, those of the Soviet secret police had been. Willkie was fairly well informed, by persons high in the Kuomintang, about the corruption in large sections of the government and about the central weaknesses of Chiang's regime. He could see for himself the grinding poverty of the Chinese people, and he was privately skeptical of the economic plans as well as the political plans with which the Generalissimo was hoping to implement his party's tutelary control of postwar China. Yet all this led him to believe more strongly than ever in the miraculous fighting which General Chennault was carrying on against incredible odds, and in the still greater gains to the Allied cause which might have come from greater help to China and from full Western recognition of China's new claim to sovereignty and independence.

Willkie's Chungking statement brought one immediate result. Two days after it had been issued, Sumner Welles announced to Dr. Wei Tao-ming, Chinese Ambassador in Washington, the readiness of the United States and Great Britain to begin final negotiations for the relinquishment of extraterritorial rights in China. These extraterritorial rights, which freed American and British citizens and companies in China from responsibility to Chinese courts, were the most galling symbol to Chinese of their subordinate status among the nations. Negotiations had been promised in 1934 and begun in 1937, but they had bogged down repeatedly in the absence of any public opinion behind them outside of China. This Willkie had created, literally overnight. Those who accused Willkie of threatening Allied unity by his attacks on the colonial system were comfortably ignorant of the degree to which this unity was confined to empty eloquence as long as extraterritorial rights in China were maintained.

For the most part, Americans liked what he said about the end of colonies. This was not true in Great Britain, nor among the ruling groups in many colonial regions who had made their own terms with Western powers and were afraid of the rise of nationalism among their own peoples because of the dangerous ideas which often come with freedom. In Great Britain, Willkie's reference to "no foot of Chinese soil" being ruled by foreigners after the war was rightly considered to have been aimed at Hong Kong. It provoked Churchill's angry retort on

Thomas in the Detroit *News*

November 10: "That there may be no mistake in any quarter, we intend to hold what we have. I have not become the King's First Minister to preside at the liquidation of the British Empire."

Not all British people felt the same way. The *Times* of London welcomed what Willkie had to say about the colonial system. "To deprecate the 'liquidation' of the British Empire," it stated, "is surely a false approach. The pride and achievement of the modern British Empire are that it has become in a certain sense a self-liquidating concern, dissolving itself by an orderly process into a commonwealth of peoples united by a common ideal of partnership in freedom." This reaction was common in other parts of the British Commonwealth. Walter Nash, New Zealand Minister to the United States, had been pressing for a

One World

supreme war council of the United Nations for almost as long as
Willkie, and Herbert Evatt, Australian Foreign Minister, joined
him in applauding Willkie's initiative in trying to establish some
kind of parity among the nations fighting the war.

Curiously enough, some Chinese felt that he was rocking the
boat, as did many leaders in the Near and Middle East. When
Willkie said in Chungking that Americans were ready "to stand
up and be counted upon for the freedom of others after the war
is over," he had traveled through thirteen countries, and he
made it clear that he was speaking about them all. When Roosevelt had first broached the Willkie trip to Marshall he had written that he was asking Willkie "especially to put some pep into
the officials of Egypt, Palestine, Syria, Iraq, Iran, and China."
Many of these officials wanted nothing less than they wanted
pep, or anything which might disturb their precarious local
power by developing the hunger of their peoples for freedom
and progress. Nearly ten years later, an American scholar, Dr.
E. A. Speiser, writing about the Arab world, pointed out what
One World had done in that region.

"Their social structure is top-heavy," he wrote, "and such essential instruments of society as public health and education,
or press and public opinion, are backward even by minimum
Western standards. It is this unconcealable backwardness that
shocks the ordinary visitor to the Near East. Wendell Willkie
carried away with him a strong impression of this shock, and
when Arabs read about it later they found it extremely difficult
to forgive the author for telling the truth."

On October 14, Willkie returned to an America which was
just beginning to feel the pinch of the war. Coffee was not always easy to find in stores, or whiskey, or hairpins, or some cos-
metics. "Praise the Lord and Pass the Ammunition" was the
most popular song. His first job was to report to the President,
and this he did in a seventy-five-minute conference at the White
House. For once Willkie did nearly all the talking, and his report was neither gentle nor encouraging.

He had been smarting under reports of Roosevelt's reaction
to his trip. He had heard in Chungking the comment attributed
to the President on October 6 that his Moscow statement had

been "not worth reading." He had fired back to the reporters that he had acted as the President's representative in all the matters on which he had been commissioned to act. "But when I speak for myself," he added, "I'm Wendell Willkie and I say what I damn please." It became clear later that the President had actually been referring to the controversy growing out of Willkie's statement as not worth reading, and not to the statement itself, but Willkie noted that the President had made no effort to correct the wrong impression, and it galled him. At a press conference on October 9, the President had been more careful and more precise. He said that Willkie was carrying out extraordinarily well just what he had asked him to do, and he refused to be drawn into any political discussion of what Willkie had said in China. But Willkie was almost pathologically suspicious by now, and his mood after his first report to the President on the trip was that of a man who had got a lot off his chest.

After a few hours in New York, Willkie went to Rushville to catch up on sleep and prepare a report to the American people on what he had seen. He inspected his pigs; standing among them he said to a reporter: "Now you might reckon this pig lot smells, which might be true. But you ought to smell Cairo." He worked hard on his report, for which the networks had offered time, and on October 26 he read it to a nation-wide audience. There was genuine curiosity about what he would say. No one else had yet come back to the United States from such a close view of the world at war. The Hooper rating of the speech was 48.0, which meant that an estimated 36,320,000 persons heard it. This was twice as large an audience as the top commercial program could get in 1942; the all-time high was then President Roosevelt's war message after Pearl Harbor, which had had an estimated audience of 62,100,000 persons.

The report was an extension of his Moscow and Chungking statements. He told the American people frankly that their reservoir of good will around the world was leaking dangerously. He blamed this partly on American failure to demand their own full mobilization for war, but much more on American failure to understand that even a military victory would not be

enough. "We must fight our way through not alone to the destruction of our enemies, but to a new world idea," he said. He
named three vital elements of this: "First, we must plan now for
peace on a global basis; second, the world must be free economically and politically, for nations and for men, that peace
may exist in it; third, America must play an active, constructive
part in freeing it and keeping its peace."

The broadcast brought him a heavier response, by mail and
telegram, than any speech Willkie ever made in his life, and 98
per cent of the messages were favorable. "Stay in there and
pitch," read one from Oregon. Another, from New Orleans,
signed "Two Able Seamen," said simply, "You got it." President
Roosevelt, at his press conference the next day, refused to pick
up the challenge to his policies which Willkie had thrown down.
Reporters thought he was having some unmalicious fun with
Willkie's pronunciation of the word "reservoir." (Roosevelt
later denied this to Willkie.) But the President kept on repeating that there was no controversy to be made out of the speech.
"I will sing it," he said, "if you want."

Actually, the speech had been full of controversy with Administration policies, and it could not be denied for long. Within a few weeks, at the *New York Herald Tribune's* Forum on
Current Problems on November 16, Willkie was scheduled to
speak on "The Economic Freedom of the World." The invasion
of North Africa had taken place on November 8, and three days
later had produced what came to be known as the "Darlan
deal." This was one of the high points of expediency in the
whole war; even important members of the Administration
were so deeply troubled by the apparent cynicism of dealing
with a notorious Vichy leader that Secretary of War Stimson
assembled a group of them at his home on November 16 to try
to convince them.

"That same evening," according to his memoirs, "hearing
that Wendell Willkie was about to attack the Agreement," Stimson telephoned to Willkie and did what he could to dissuade
him; that a man of Willkie's stature should attack Eisenhower's
stand seemed to Stimson very dangerous. " 'I told him flatly that,
if he criticized the Darlan Agreement at this juncture, he would

run the risk of jeopardizing the success of the United States Army in North Africa and would be rendering its task very much more difficult.' Willkie reluctantly withheld his attack for the time being, expressing himself forcefully, however, a little later when the immediate crisis had passed."

Stimson had told Willkie that his speech might cost sixty thousand American lives. Willkie answered that he could not believe this, but also could not risk it. So he was forced to change his speech forty-five minutes before he delivered it, and its transmission abroad was censored for twelve hours. By that time, the President released his own careful explanation of the Darlan deal, including his approval of the feelings which had caused so many Americans to be suspicious of it, and Willkie had good cause to wonder whether censorship had been applied to him for military or for political reasons. The next day, also speaking to the *New York Herald Tribune* Forum, the President spoke again about his troubles with the second-front clamor of "ignorant outsiders," and denounced especially "criticism from those who, as we know in our hearts, are actuated by political motives."

On December 14, in Berlin, Dr. Goebbels noted in his private diary the censorship of Willkie's attack on Darlan. His judgment of Willkie's motives differed from Roosevelt's. "Willkie is being spotlighted by certain circles," Goebbels wrote, "because they want him to be the next Presidential candidate for the Republicans. Willkie as President would possibly be even more dangerous to us than Roosevelt, for he is an opportunist, a politician without character and firm convictions, with whom nothing can be done. He would certainly be the man to intensify the United States war effort."

Willkie's decision to write a book grew directly out of the reception given to his broadcast speech. He had never written a book, but friends were pressing him to nail down his position on many points where he was vulnerable to misquotation. After another big speech, in Toronto on November 25, he set to work on a book which was to state his central beliefs about the world he had just seen at close range in the middle of the war.

He cared deeply about writing and he was unorthodox,

among contemporary political men, in his writing methods. In a document requested from him in 1943 to be auctioned for war relief funds, Willkie wrote: "As to writing, I write entirely with a purpose. I pretend to no literary skill; I write what I think and then rewrite." Somewhere in that statement is the secret of his success in communicating ideas at the end of his life. He had learned relatively early—internal evidence in his speeches would put the date in 1938—the lesson some public figures never learn: to use help from others only on outlines and initial drafts, and to do nearly all of his rewriting himself.

This had backfired on him in the 1940 campaign. One of his advisers, Raymond Leslie Buell, had offered the *Nation* a Willkie piece and had actually supplied it. After it had been set up in type and announced in the magazine, the piece had to be withdrawn because Willkie, on his campaign train, did not have time to rewrite what Buell had drafted. It offered a momentary triumph to the anti-Willkie liberal groups. Freda Kirchwey, editor of the *Nation*, was quite right in denouncing the miserable liaison work in Willkie's headquarters revealed by the incident. But when she added that "it also exposes the hollow void under the protestations of simple, hearty honesty that Mr. Willkie so sententiously lays before the public," she was wider of the mark. If anything, the incident showed that Willkie had a higher than average sense of responsibility for whatever appeared under his name.

In writing *One World*, Willkie used notes and outlines prepared by this writer and by "Mike" Cowles, as well as technical details on the flight prepared by Major Kight and background material on the countries he visited which had been prepared by the information services of a dozen nations. For six weeks he worked every morning from 9 until 12 at the apartment of his friend, Irita Van Doren, who had been his adviser on speeches and articles for many years. She helped him in assembling and organizing the material. But nobody ghostwrote *One World*. He would sit, sucking the end of his pencil, or walk up and down the room as he developed his ideas, talking them out, rewording them until he had just the effect he wanted. Even after the book was in galley proofs, and he had gone out to Rushville, he called back several times a day to have a phrase changed or an adjective removed in order that the emphasis might be just right. Willkie liked to work on typewritten copy which had been triple-spaced. He worked with a heavy black pencil, and he had a typical businessman's extravagance with the time of his typists. He deeply believed in rewriting. The last few manuscript versions of *One World,* which were deposited after his death in the Library of Congress, look as marked up as a college freshman's draft of an English composition theme.

In spite of the success of *One World,* Willkie was never a great writer in the traditional sense, or a phrase-maker, or a literary man. He had something to say, and he said it with enormous vigor and some hard-earned discipline and often genuine eloquence. He never thought of posterity when he was writing, or of literary fame, but he was quite literally transfixed with the need to communicate an idea. He was pre-eminently what is called a rewriteman in newspaper language, and he rewrote himself for three years between 1941 and 1944. No Roman orator ever worked so hard at polishing sentences. There are many in *One World,* and some whole paragraphs, which can be traced back through successive versions to speeches he had made in 1941 but which he had gone on working over, trying endlessly to give them more bite and conviction by slight changes in phrasing. The original title of his book was suggested by editors of Simon and Schuster, Inc. He had signed a contract with this publishing house before he knew any of its executives except one friend, Tom Torre Bevans, who was in charge of its manufacturing and for whom he had long before promised to write a book. Their suggestion was *One War, One Peace, One World.* Willkie's final title, which was to become part of the English language, was suggested by Bevans; he said: "Why not just *One World?*" Willkie accepted this with growing satisfaction after his characteristic tongue-rolling, gesturing, timing, rephrasing experimentation with the act of communicating an idea to a reader.

The book's success made publishing history. It appeared on April 8, 1943, with what looked like good but not sensational advance sales of 40,000 in a one-dollar paper-bound edition and 13,000 in a two-dollar cloth-bound edition. It had no initial book-

"Make room—you've got company."

club sponsorship. But spring was in the air. The war news was a little better. The baseball season was about to open. Most of the country was humming or whistling "Oh, What a Beautiful Morning" from *Oklahoma*. Something hopeful and challenging in the book set fire to the public imagination and it raced across the country.

Production was put quickly in the hands of two printing firms, each using two sets of plates and operating around the clock, but the supply of books still could not catch up with the demand. *One World* was the third nonfiction book since 1900 to sell more than 1,000,000 copies—H. G. Wells' *Outline of History* and Dale Carnegie's *How to Win Friends and Influence People* were the other two—but *One World* was unique in reaching the figure within seven weeks.

There is no way of computing the final sales of what was easily the most influential book published in America during the war. The original publishers sold 909,647 copies in paper

315

and 246,113 in cloth. In *Prefaces to Peace,* a Book-of-the-Month Club product, it sold 350,000 copies. Pocket Books sold 570,755 copies in a twenty-five-cent edition. A 50,000-copy edition was printed for soldiers overseas. Other editions were reprinted by the Readers' League of America and the Limited Editions Club. Several magazines published it in digest form; a condensed version of the book was syndicated in 107 daily newspapers.

Its appeal was not limited to America. It had almost equal popularity in nearly every modern language. It was printed on underground presses in Denmark and in Czechoslovakia. Copies were smuggled through all of occupied Europe. Three years later, when the war had ended, it jumped into the best-seller list in Germany.

Willkie sold the motion picture rights to Darryl Zanuck of the Twentieth Century-Fox Film Corporation, his own company, partly to ensure his own control of the way in which the book was to be filmed. Lamar Trotti completed a scenario, but the picture has never been produced. Revenue from the book was assigned by Willkie to a trust fund, with his friend "Mike" Cowles as sole trustee, to be distributed among various war-relief societies and public institutions. By 1952, the fund had received a total of $190,473.64.

The success of *One World* gave Willkie greater personal satisfaction than anything in his life, including his 1940 nomination. To a supreme degree, he had the satisfaction which came to him from every intellectual or literary job he ever did —articles, "Information Please" appearances, or personal friendships with scholars or writers. They all gave him the feeling that he was being successful in a field he had always revered and in which he always felt inferior. His personal elation over *One World* was on a scale with its spectacular success.

He also saw it as a vindication of his belief in the capacity of Americans to go on with the restless process of growth in which he was caught himself. And he saw it as a challenge which would continue to work in men's minds as long as the great process the book described, which "no man—certainly not Hitler—can stop. Men and women all over the world are on the march, physically, intellectually and spiritually. After centuries of ignorant and dull compliance, hundreds of millions of people in eastern Europe and Asia have opened the books. Old fears no longer frighten them. They are beginning to know that men's welfare throughout the world is interdependent. They are resolved, as we must be, that there is no more place for imperialism within their own society than in the society of nations. The big house on the hill surrounded by mud huts has lost its awesome charm."

CHAPTER SEVENTEEN

Our Domestic Imperialisms

W HEN Willkie appeared before the Supreme Court of the United States in November, 1942, to plead the case of an admitted Communist, his enemies were sure that it marked his final capture by the sinister forces of internationalism, liberalism, Jewry, and the Kremlin. "SAYS WILLKIE FAVORS REDS OVER G.O.P." ran a Hearst headline over a speech by Representative Paul Shafer, Michigan Republican. The 1940 Republican candidate had moved a long way, it is true, from the campaign which had been nicknamed "the commuters' counter-revolution," but the impelling forces behind his thinking were old, deeply rooted in his childhood and his life, and eminently respectable. On no single issue throughout both his business and his political career was Willkie so consistent or so articulate as on civil liberties.

Three separate issues on which he held strong beliefs came together in the struggle for civil liberties. His somewhat frustrated passion for study and writing, which had been developing slowly from his boyhood on, committed him to defense of freedom of speech. As a second-generation American, he was directly aware of the problems faced by minority groups in a conformist-minded society; German-Americans, Jews, and Negroes were alike in struggling for a kind of freedom which was more than an abstract human right. Finally, his political ideas were even more solidly based than were his economic ideas on a belief in competition; he was more prepared to accept some degree of rate regulation for the electric power industry than any control over the free market-place of ideas.

Our Domestic Imperialisms

His fight against the Klan in Akron had started when he was a delegate to the 1924 Democratic National Convention, where it was a major issue, and had continued the next year in the struggle to keep the Klan out of the city's school system. A large part of his opposition to the New Deal, especially in connection with its campaign to control utility holding companies, grew out of his conviction that techniques were being used against business which genuinely threatened all civil liberties. But he never restricted his protest to the field of free enterprise, even when he was engaged exclusively in business.

He attacked the Dies Committee, in public, before he ever thought of running for office. At a Columbia alumni luncheon at the Bankers Club in New York on November 1, 1939, he defined American liberties as "built upon a tripod—the democratic process, our civil liberties, and free enterprise. If any one of the parts of that tripod falls, all three will fall." He went on to attack the technique of Congressional investigation under which "men can be put upon the witness stand without the protection of counsel and without any adequate opportunity to answer. There is no more cruel way of destroying the reputation of a man than by publicity through inference and innuendo. It has been done to hundreds of businessmen and public figures heretofore, and I can speak of it now because it is not my kind that is being investigated, and for the moment—once in six years—I have no investigator in my office."

He knew the technique. "There is no quicker method to destroy the rights of an individual," he said, "because my property is worth nothing to me, it is obvious, without my reputation; and reputation is so rapidly destroyed by the process of putting a man on the witness stand and examining him very pleasantly until the eleven o'clock newspaper deadline for the afternoon newspapers, and then making a speech to him, and when he starts to answer, saying, 'Well, I will take the rest of that up with you later.' Screaming across the headlines of the country, his reputation is gone."

Even earlier, in February, 1939, he wrote to his close personal friend Gerard Swope, who was president of the General Electric Company, that "our men throughout our operating territory" were reporting to him a barrage of threatening attacks against the violently anti-Nazi commentator, Miss Dorothy Thompson, then being sponsored as a broadcaster by Swope's company. "If this is to become a parade of those who take business away because they are opposed to the truly magnificent stand Miss Thompson has taken on the Nazi and Jewish question, then I want to join the parade of those who take business away if there is any prospect of her being removed from the air for that reason. I think it is a perfectly outrageous situation when it can even be suggested that a noted journalist like Miss Thompson can be subjected to this kind of sabotage and both as a corporate official and an individual, I want to do all I can to prevent it."

Restrictions on civil liberties had been growing long before the war began. Congressional hearings had started in 1935 on the first Federal sedition law to be passed in time of peace since 1798, and the bill went through the House in July, 1939. Fears of foreign attack were not even mentioned in the debate. In Professor Zechariah Chafee, Jr.'s, words, "a nation which had successfully passed through six wars unprotected by teachers' oaths and the compulsory flag salutes of school children found them sweeping state after state like an epidemic, at least two years before anybody ever heard of a 'fifth column.'"

Willkie understood what was going on, and fought it. At that time the names of men like Elihu Root and Charles Evans Hughes, who had fought for civil liberties, were still mentioned proudly by Republican orators. William Allen White stood in their shadow when he reminded his fellow-Republicans that they could not invoke the Bill of Rights against Roosevelt without meaning it. Commenting on the late General Theodore Roosevelt, Jr., he wrote to Allan Nevins: "The danger of so many of these fellows who are howling for the Bill of Rights is that they want to use it for reactionary purposes to stop many of the necessary changes and reforms which must come eventually when we recover, if they cannot come along with recovery. The Bill of Rights, I fear, in the bright lexicon of young Teddy is to be the bulwark of privilege rather than a defense of democracy. There again I may not sense it right." Willkie had been throwing the Bill of Rights at the New Deal for ten years, but one difference between him and many of the Republicans who cheered him every time he mentioned it was that he had read it.

During his pre-convention campaign in 1940 he had spelled out exactly where he stood on civil liberties in an article called "Fair Trial," published in the *New Republic* on March 18, 1940. "Equal treatment under the law," he wrote, "means exactly what it says, whether the man before the tribunal is a crook, a Democrat, a Republican, a Communist, or a businessman; whether he is rich or poor, white or black, good or bad. You cannot have a democracy on any other basis. You cannot preserve human liberties on any other theory."

This article alone refutes the *Chicago Tribune* charge that Willkie changed course on civil liberties after his defeat in the 1940 election. "If for no other reason than self-interest," he wrote in the same piece, "we should all of us be vigilant to establish the principle of due process of law so firmly that neither a revolution of the right nor a revolution of the left can overthrow it. But I would not appeal to self-interest alone, because I believe that Americans have a genuine passion for liberty and a genuine passion for justice. Sometimes hatred obscures this instinct for fair play. It is well to remember that any man who denies justice to someone he hates prepares the way for a denial of justice to someone he loves."

As early as November, 1941, he had been named as a member, with Basil O'Connor, President Roosevelt's law partner, of the Committee on the Bill of Rights of the American Bar Association. A month later, speaking under the auspices of the National Conference of Christians and Jews, he said: "Under the stress and strain of combat the spirit of intolerance always rises. Suspicion begins to grow and fingers are pointed. I pledge myself to fight to the fullest extent against such intolerance. In the courtroom and from the public rostrum, I will fight for the preservation of civil liberties, no matter how unpopular the cause may be in any given instance."

The late Carol King persuaded him, alone and unaided and against the advice of his close friends, to plead the Schneiderman case before the Supreme Court. She was a specialist in deportation cases, and had defended many avowed Communists.

She sent him the brief through the mail, without a personal introduction to him of any kind, together with the writ of *certiorari* in which the Supreme Court had agreed to review the case. Later he told her, she remembered: "Your original letter came with the brief attached. I put it on the side of my desk as one of the things I wanted to read. It was about a week before I got around to reading the brief. I read it on a Saturday morning. I reread it. After that I could not, with my beliefs, have remained satisfied with myself if I refused to accept the case, if two conditions were true—(1) that Schneiderman was a decent fellow personally, and (2) that the record sustained the brief. That was the reason for my making inquiries about Schneiderman and asking you to send me the record."

He made his decision to accept the case before the United States was in the war. "I am sure I am right in representing Schneiderman," he wrote to his friend Crum on December 3, 1941; "of all the times when civil liberties should be defended, it is now." He pleaded the case twice before the Supreme Court, on November 9, 1942, just after his return from his trip around the world, and again on March 12, 1943, at a rehearing asked by the court. He served without compensation and paid his own expenses, Mrs. King remaining as associate counsel at his request.

The case involved the government's effort to revoke the citizenship of William Schneiderman, granted in 1927, on the grounds that his membership in the Young Communist League and the Communist party indicated belief in the overthrow of the government by force and violence, that he had concealed this in applying for citizenship, and that his citizenship had therefore been granted illegally. The American Civil Liberties Union and a few non-Communist newspapers backed Willkie's position that the decisions of the lower courts placed in jeopardy the constitutional rights of all naturalized citizens, whether Communist or not. The war had already softened some of the more bitter popular feeling against the Soviet Union—Willkie could score a point before the court by saying that Schneiderman had been born "in a town near Stalingrad"—but to defend an acknowledged Communist was no quick road to political popularity.

"Willkie had an informal and not too neat manner of working," Mrs. King observed. "He generally leaned back in his desk chair with his feet on the desk. Only at our very first conference had he managed to keep his feet on the floor. I would probably never have noticed that his shoes were rarely shined except for the fact that they were always in the immediate foreground. When he was busy, he would go right on talking as he ate a ham sandwich and swallowed coffee out of a container from the corner drugstore. He liked to mark the things on which he was working, himself. He would say, 'I can follow my own tracks.' He came to the argument in the Supreme Court with a much tracked-up record, a sheaf of quotations, and a page of notes scrawled in pencil. There wasn't much on the sheet either."

On June 21, 1943, the Supreme Court ruled in Schneiderman's favor. Justice Frank Murphy read the majority opinion, concurred in by Justices William O. Douglas, Wiley B. Rutledge, Hugo L. Black, and Stanley F. Reed. A minority opinion was filed by Chief Justice Harlan F. Stone, concurred in by Justices Felix Frankfurter and Owen J. Roberts. Justice Robert H. Jackson did not participate, having been Attorney General while the original case against Schneiderman was being prepared.

The basis of the majority decision was that there was no "clear, unequivocal, and convincing" proof that the Communist party as a whole was committed to the use of force or violence, or that Schneiderman personally followed those Communists who did believe in violence. Willkie had handled this latter problem by asking the court: "Am I to be held responsible for everything Ham Fish says?" He conceded that the founders of the Democratic, the Republican, and the Communist parties had all believed in the use of violence against their enemies where other methods were not available, and after quoting Jefferson, Lincoln, and Marx, he concluded that "the mildest of the three by far was Karl Marx."

It was an important decision. Willkie's plea for Schneiderman became the basis for the later defense of Harry Bridges against deportation charges, and his victory did much to delay the outlawry of the Communist party in the United States by judicial interpretation. Willkie pointed out to the court that Congress three times had refused to pass a bill outlawing Communism, and then added, after a little pause: "I suggest you leave it to Congress." Nine years later, Congress had still failed to make the Communist party illegal, but the Supreme Court had changed its position. Schneiderman himself was to be indicted in 1951 under the provisions of the Smith Act, which the Supreme Court ruled to be constitutional on almost the same concrete charges of belief in the overthrow of the government by force and violence which a majority of the court had ruled out in 1943.

Willkie was never fooled by Communists, nor was he frightened by them. "The best answer to Communism," ran his basic statement on the question, "is a living, vibrant, fearless democracy—economic, social, and political. All we need to do is stand up and perform according to our professed ideals. Then those ideals will be safe." He believed that freedom of expression gave the only guaranty that Americans could learn for themselves what is wrong with all authoritarian forms of government, and only a very clear and very present danger warranted, in his mind, any restriction on the right to think and talk and write freely. His own favorite criticism of Communism he had given to the production superintendent of an aviation factory in Kuibishev, in the Soviet Union, when he asked him: "How can you ever have political freedom and economic freedom when the state owns everything?" The Russian had no answers except for his Marxist theories, and Willkie wrote in *One World:* "to that basic question, Marxism gives no answer."

On his January, 1941, trip to England, Willkie was sitting in the Visitors' Gallery of the House of Commons with the sound of bombs and anti-aircraft fire in the distance. "As I sat there," he related later, "a member from Wales rose to attack the government for suppressing *The Daily Worker*. England was facing the greatest crisis of her history with the momentary expectation that the Germans would invade the country. Yet no man sought to suppress that speaker." At that moment, he believed, the British government had been right both in suppressing the Communist paper—the Hitler-Stalin pact was still in force—and in not silencing the member of the House of Commons who spoke in its defense.

"Our way of living together in America," he had written in *One World*, "is a strong but delicate fabric. It is made up of many threads. It has been woven over many centuries by the patience and sacrifices of countless liberty-loving men and women. It serves as a cloak for the protection of poor and rich, of black and white, of Jew and Gentile, of foreign- and native-born.

"Let us not tear it asunder. For no man knows, once it is destroyed, where or when man will find its protective warmth again."

Willkie was much more active and vociferous, all his life, in defending the rights of other, nonpolitical minorities. Although he had never joined any German-American society, he wrote the chapter on Carl Schurz for a book on famous Americans, *There Were Giants in the Land,* and in January, 1942, he ghosted an appeal to Americans of German blood for Miss Maud von Steuben, great-great-grandniece of Baron Wilhelm von Steuben, Revolutionary War hero. "Some of the most devoted Americans are those who come from across the sea," he told a Louis D. Brandeis Memorial Committee dinner in the same year. "They know what liberty is because they have tasted something else." He appeared frequently on "Voice of America" radio programs for broadcast to Europe, speaking with pride of the fact that his father had been born in Germany, and that he had grown up in the German revolutionary tradition.

Nazi doctrines on "race" and "blood" gave both the Jews and the Negroes a chance during the war to bring into the open the contrast between ideals and practices in the United States. Both were growing increasingly restless under what Willkie called "the counsels of patience and the assurances of kindly men," and Willkie welcomed their growing restlessness. It was good politics for a man aiming at the independent vote; more important, his own deepest convictions led him to champion both groups and to urge them to use the processes of democracy to better their position.

As early as February, 1941, he was given the annual award of the Jewish War Veterans of the United States for his "outstanding example of leadership in the promotion of Americanism and democracy." The National Conference of Christians and Jews gave him a similar honor in 1942. In the same year, he accepted "The American Hebrew" medal for 1942, but objected to the use of the word "tolerance" both in the official citation and in the comments, approving the award to him, made by President Roosevelt and by Eleanor Roosevelt. "It is not tolerance that one is entitled to in America," he said. "It is the right of every citizen in America to be treated by other citizens as an equal. No man has the right in America to treat any other man 'tolerantly,' for 'tolerance' is the assumption of superiority. Our liberties are the equal rights of every citizen."

The Jews had an unanswerable claim to the support of all Americans in their struggle against the Nazis in Germany. Willkie was an early supporter of the Emergency Committee to save the Jewish People of Europe, and on July 22, 1944, he made one of the first public proposals of a United Nations agency to work on this problem. But Willkie wanted to speed up the struggle against discrimination at home, too. In June, 1942, he wrote for the *Saturday Evening Post* an article called "The Case for the Minorities." This was an answer to what he called a "recent flagellation of the Jews" published in the same magazine by Milton Mayer.

"We are living once more in a period that is psychologically susceptible to witch-hanging and mob-baiting," he wrote here. He denounced "the excessive wartime activity of the investigating bureaus of Congress and the Administration, with their impertinent and indecent searching out of the private lives and the past political beliefs of individuals." In words that have not lost their relevance in the decade since they were written, he continued: "And each of us, if not alert, may find himself the unconscious carrier of the germ that will destroy our freedom. For each of us has within himself the inheritance of age-long hatreds, of racial and religious difference, and everyone has a tendency to find the cause for his own failures in some conspiracy of evil. . . .

"Within the tolerance of a democracy, minorities are the constant spring of new ideas, stimulating new thought and action, the constant source of new vigor. To suppress minority thinking and minority expression would tend to freeze society and prevent progress. For the majority itself is stimulated by the existence of minority groups. The human mind requires contrary expressions against which to test itself."

Even more than with the Jews, Willkie identified himself with the Negro struggle against discrimination. He was a trustee of Hampton Institute, one of the largest Negro colleges in the United States, and a supporter of the National Urban League in its efforts to improve the economic status of Negroes. But Willkie pushed his own position well beyond the point at which most political figures hesitate. In the spring of 1942, he played a large part in the campaign which led the Navy, Marine Corps, and Coast Guard to open their ranks for the first time in history to Negro volunteers. In July, he addressed the annual conference of the National Association for the Advancement of Colored People, at Los Angeles. This was before his trip around the world. The N.A.A.C.P. was an organization committed to direct political and legal action; its executive secretary, Walter White, was a personal friend of Willkie's.

"Today, it is becoming increasingly apparent to thoughtful Americans," he told the conference, "that we cannot fight the forces and ideas of imperialism abroad and maintain a form of imperialism at home. The war has done this to our thinking. . . . So we are finding under the pressures of this present conflict that long-standing barriers and prejudices are breaking down. The defense of our democracy against the forces that threaten it from without has made some of its failures to function at home glaringly apparent. Our very proclamations of what we are fighting for have rendered our own inequities self-evident. When we talk of freedom and opportunity for all nations the increasing paradoxes in our own society become so clear they can no longer be ignored."

Willkie

Joe Louis was his friend. When Louis defended his world heavyweight title against Buddy Baer, for the Navy Relief Society on January 9, 1942, Willkie thanked the crowd, before the fight started, for turning out for the benefit, and then turned to Baer and said: "About a year ago I took on a champion, too." The house went wild. A few months later, on March 11 at another navy relief show, it was from Mr. and Mrs. Willkie's box that Private Joe Louis climbed onto the Madison Square Garden stage to make his famous comment: "We're going to do our part and we're going to win, because we are on God's side."

The worst race riot of the war took place in Detroit in June, 1943. The Columbia Broadcasting System produced a special broadcast, written by William N. Robson, called "An Open Letter to the American People," and Willkie was asked to write and read the final message of the broadcast driving home the danger of such tragic outbreaks of mob madness. He took Walter White with him to Hollywood three times in the last two years of his life, wining and dining him with producers, directors, and movie executives. He was by then a power in Hollywood, and White was a skilled and patient propagandist for his cause. They pleaded together for a new treatment of Negroes in motion pictures, a break with the accepted Hollywood stereotypes of the Negro as a buffoon, a servant, or a minstrel. They were given eloquent promises that the situation would be changed.

"A few of the pledges were kept," White wrote in 1946. "But Willkie's tragic death damped and almost extinguished the reforms he stimulated. A highly vocal and belligerent minority which insisted that there be no change in film treatment of the Negro soon re-established the goblin of box-office returns in the thinking of Hollywood producers."

Underneath Willkie's support of both political and nonpolitical minority groups was the belief in freedom which his German ancestors had brought with them to this country and which he had absorbed as a boy in Indiana. In its simplest terms, this was always freedom of the mind to him. What he liked best about the Soviet Union was its schools and libraries; what he disliked most was its regimentation of thinking and expression, which meant the exact reverse of freedom to him. Deep in his distrust of the New Deal was his suspicion that too much power in Washington would multiply censorship, subsidize official propaganda, and penalize the unorthodox. His personal rejection of many of the social standards and ideas of modern American business was due to his feeling that they were against freedom.

The only time in his life he ever saw the late Samuel Insull, he told a Book and Author luncheon in New York on January 12, 1943, he had been called in as a consultant and found Insull grumbling about a growing spirit of radicalism in the country. "He said it was the fault of the publications and the newspapers," Willkie recalled. "He also blamed public leaders who stirred the people up. He said that if the people were told only what was best for them to know there would not be any of this growing radicalism.

"I dissented, I recall, very vigorously, and Mr. Insull said to me: 'Young man, when you get older you will know more.' So you can see that the doctrine of telling us what we should think did not originate with government in wartime. At least it was known by one of the greatest buccaneers of business of all time."

Championship of intellectual freedom, apart from minority rights, neither promised nor delivered any substantial political advantages in the middle of a great war, yet he gave it time and energy beyond any calculation of the votes it might win. Willkie always spoke deprecatingly of himself in the presence of scholars or writers; it was a habit not unrelated to the hard and almost arrogant conviction with which he spoke on matters he knew about. A large part of his humility was real. He was deeply aware of the intimate, subtle, and organic ties between freedom and the liberal arts. To be invited to speak before a group of writers, to make an award to Walter Lippmann, to succeed Archibald MacLeish as honorary chancellor of Union College —these were events that stirred him, and awakened his memories of his mother and father and of the old, unending struggle for human freedom through freedom of the mind. In an address he

Willkie

was invited to give on January 14, 1943, at Duke University, later reprinted by the *American Scholar*, he summed up what this meant to him:

"We must establish beyond any doubt the equality of men. And we shall find this equality, not in the different talents which we severally possess, nor in the different incomes which we severally earn, but in the great franchise of the mind, the universal franchise, which is bounded neither by color, nor by creed, nor by social status. Open the books, if you wish to be free."

CHAPTER EIGHTEEN

The Road to Wisconsin

B ARELY two weeks after his return in October, 1942, from his
trip around the world, Willkie renewed his standing offer
to the professional Republican politicians: party regularity in return for a liberal domestic program and an international-minded
foreign policy. For the next year and a half he was to keep this
offer standing, frequently restated. The professionals never
wavered in their desire to turn the offer down. But the war, the
success of *One World*, Willkie's growing appeal to the minority
groups which had given the New Deal so much of its political
strength, and his unvarying capacity to draw a bigger crowd
than any other Republican leader were all factors behind their
painful reluctance to turn it down in public. Between October,
1942, and April, 1944, Willkie was trying to repeat in slow motion the whirlwind courtship of 1940. The process often made
both him and the professionals look as awkward as adolescents
at their first dance. Neither party to the romance had any talent
for slow and patient courtship.

There was one major change in the relationship between 1940
and 1943. Willkie's independence of the professionals in his
first try had been based largely on a gambler's belief in himself. His political convictions were real and sincere, but the
crusading note in the 1940 campaign had been based on a negative purpose: throw the rascals out. By 1943, Willkie was a man
with a mission in positive terms. This mission had to do with the
war, and with the revolution in men's minds he had seen taking
place all over the world. This, even more than the drawn-out
time factor, caused him to change many of his political tech-

niques in 1943, and sometimes to look still more awkward. But it explains why the Republican party professionals, to their infinite dismay, found him so much harder to discard than Hoover or Landon had been. They were in no way stuck with him, but they were stuck with people who believed in him. After his One World trip, Willkie was a man without a party, but by no means a man without a country. This problem profoundly affected Willkie's attempt to win the 1944 Republican nomination. Its influence on the destiny of the Republican party will not have worked itself out until the party either splits or mends the deep fissure within it which made Willkie such an embarrassment to it at the end of his life.

On November 1, 1942, Willkie made a substantial down payment on his standing offer of party regularity by coming out for Dewey for Governor, confounding the critics who had said his trip around the world had been planned to let him duck the uncomfortable issue. He expected to vote the Republican state ticket, he announced, "anticipating from the state platform and from their statements that Mr. Dewey and his fellow-candidates will give New York a liberal government." He attacked the Roosevelt Administration for its lack of courageous leadership, "nowhere more plainly illustrated than by its continued recognition of the vicious and subversive Vichy government." He went as far as any member of a loyal opposition could then go when he continued: "Anyone who has made any study of conditions at home and abroad must know that the administration of our war effort is confused and, in many respects, inefficient."

With nearly two years to go before a Presidential election, the fissure within the Republican party cut much deeper than the personal ambitions of any leader. The old question of isolationism, renamed American nationalism for the duration of the war, still separated the *Chicago Tribune* from the *New York Herald Tribune,* the Midwest from the two coasts, tariff-protected businessmen from industrialists who looked forward to postwar foreign markets, the die-hard anti-New Dealers from those whom they called the "me-tooers." Martin had stayed on for two years as party chairman to keep this crack in party unity from becoming too apparent, but even his skill and his personal popularity could not mend it. When the Republican National Committee met in St. Louis in December to choose his successor, the fight flared up again into newspaper headlines.

The *Chicago Tribune* group was backing Werner W. Schroeder, a fifty-year-old lawyer with an expensive practice, close ties with Colonel McCormick's camp, and a clear-cut isolationist record. Senator Taft, who used the occasion to withdraw his own name as a 1944 candidate in favor of Governor John W. Bricker of Ohio, was the open leader at St. Louis of the Schroeder forces, with those known as Hoover's men solidly behind him. Dewey, publicly committed to serving four years as Governor of New York, was neutral. Willkie did not go to St. Louis, but members of the committee known to be close to him backed Frederick E. Baker, a thirty-five-year-old public relations counsel from Seattle.

The first ballot showed Schroeder and Baker tied at 40 votes each, with a scattering of votes for others. On the second ballot, the count was Baker 43, Schroeder 38, and Harrison E. Spangler, Iowa lawyer, 15. The Schroeder forces called for a recess, and Martin was given a chance to plead for another of the compromises with which the party had patched itself together on this issue since the 1940 election. This time it worked again, after some hours of private conference among the leaders, and both Schroeder and Baker withdrew in favor of Spangler. Taft gilded the lily of party harmony by offering a resolution specifically recommitting the party to the resolution on America's role in world affairs which Willkie had backed at the committee's meeting in Chicago the preceding April and which Taft had then called a mistake. Reporters covering the meeting called it a defeat for Colonel McCormick's side, which had first thrown in the sponge, and Willkie in New York made only the comment: "A man should never boast after victory." But the final choice had been made in one of those small rooms where Willkie's cause was never at its best, and the Republican National Committee, once Martin had stepped down, was never again to be even a referee in the continuing struggle for control of the party. From St. Louis on, it was enlisted in the struggle, and against Willkie.

Under these circumstances, Willkie was forced to improvise his own political machine between December, 1942, and the Wisconsin primary in April, 1944. Its core was the small group of party leaders who remained loyal to him, including Pryor, Weeks, and Cake. They helped to raise funds, together with a somewhat larger group of businessmen led by Hanes, and men like the Zellerbach brothers on the West Coast and the Cowles brothers in Minnesota and Iowa. No important effort was made to revive the Willkie Clubs. This was partly because the war itself was now absorbing some of the free-floating citizens' energy which had sparked them, and most of Willkie's ardent younger supporters were actually in the war. It was partly because Willkie had grown sensitive to the charge that manipulation and skilled public relations had alone worked the 1940 miracle in Philadelphia. Most of all, it was because the Republican party had stated clearly its implacable hostility to any personal effort to organize independents who might again threaten the tightly held control of the party machine.

Willkie's law office was the central headquarters for his political activity. During 1943 and 1944 he acquired a few assistants who were paid out of privately raised funds; they never numbered more than three and they inevitably represented the disparate groups backing Willkie more than they did Willkie himself. Willkie tried to manage them without amalgamating them. This was his way with people and sometimes with ideas: he saw himself as the co-ordinator of highly diverse elements, and he never felt under any pressure to get different groups of his friends to like each other. Willkie never had the pleasure in watching them dislike each other that Roosevelt had, but essentially the two men operated alliances of diverse supporters in much the same way.

In January, 1943, Willkie met the new party chairman, Spangler, in Washington for breakfast. It was their first meeting since the defeat of Schroeder in St. Louis, but it brought Willkie no good news. Spangler had just outlined the party's position, as he saw it, in the *American Magazine*. His demand for a return to "enterprise, opportunity, and thrift" was good Republican doctrine to which Willkie subscribed. But his further demand that the peace must be "without impairment of our national identity as an independent nation, without surrendering our individuality as an independent state," was impossible to square with Willkie's growing belief in the necessity for a strong postwar organization of the United Nations to keep the peace. Senator McNary had been re-elected minority leader of the Senate and Senator James J. Davis of Pennsylvania to the Senate's Foreign Relations Committee—choices which both the American nationalists and the Willkieites could still approve. But Willkie had good reason to think that it might be easier to capture the convention than the Republican National Committee.

In his own speeches he never stopped trying. He was turning back more and more, with the help of his friend Russell Davenport, to the past of the Republican party in an effort to give its traditions some contemporary meaning for those Republicans whose politics began and ended with the desire to "get rid of that man in the White House." He quoted James G. Blaine, William Howard Taft, President McKinley, John Hay, Charles Evans Hughes, and Elihu Root to show that a global viewpoint on trade and an internationalist foreign policy had been practically copyrighted by Republicans. "The startling fact abroad today," he told a Lincoln Day meeting in Indianapolis, "is that of the more than two billion people on the earth, the overwhelming majority have awakened. They fervently desire education, political emancipation, and the opportunity to raise their standards of living. . . . This should be a challenge to Republicans. For the Republican party is the party of production. It should be the party of expansion as well, and of dynamic industrial evolution."

Willkie returned to New York in March, 1943, from a trip which had taken him through Indiana, Illinois, Missouri, and Arkansas for nearly a month. Everywhere he had seen small groups of Republicans ranging from state committeemen to precinct captains. He was always a good listener, and now he was listening hard. In Rushville, he had bought for his mother-in-law, Mrs. Cora Wilk, in June, 1942, the ten-room house he had used during the 1940 campaign. Here he saw his tenant farmers, his neighbors, farm leaders, Indianans who always drifted in from all over the state when he was there. Grace Reynolds, national committee member from Indiana, and a few other state leaders had never abandoned him, and even the state Republican machine was beginning to have second thoughts about him as they appraised the dreary prospect of finding someone else to back. It was clear that large sections of the rank and file were still for him, and the inevitable political question: "Well, whom else can we win with?" was month by month becoming a more valuable ace in the hole.

On February 10, celebrating his seventy-fifth birthday, William Allen White told the country: "If the Republican convention were held today, Wendell Willkie is the only man whom the Republicans could nominate who could be elected. I say this realizing he could not be nominated if the Republican National Committee set up the convention as it too often has been set up in other years, notably in 1912, 1920, and 1924. That crowd never will take Willkie, and anyone that crowd names will be defeated." This was not said simply for public consumption. Two months later, he wrote Thomas W. Lamont, in a personal letter: "Of course, I am for Willkie. I still have faith that he will be able to breast the tide and buck the isolationist reaction against him. . . . This is a hunch and a guess. I have no facts to support it and have been wrong before; I may be wrong this time."

By the spring of 1943, Willkie's political strength was hard to estimate because he had no competition. Stassen finished the Naval Training School at Fort Schuyler, the Bronx, on July 23, 1943, and was immediately assigned to overseas duty. His last civilian statement on politics had been a plea for a nonisolationist candidate in 1944. When pressed on Willkie by the reporters, he had said: "As you know, I have a high regard for Mr. Willkie. He and I have seen most issues in the same light." Dewey was still insisting that he was not a candidate; he kept on calling isolationism a dead issue, unbothered by the refusal of the isolationist press, Congressmen, and business leaders to roll over and play dead. The Bricker candidacy, for which Taft had stepped aside, never succeeded in becoming air-borne. White had written a bitter attack on Bricker in the *Emporia Gazette*, saying the party "cannot be so craven that it would conspire to steal into victory with no issue but Bricker and a bellyache." He sent it to Willkie with the comment that he had received "a stack of letters as thick as a hired girl's leg. I just had to take a sock at that bird, and I hope this will find you the same."

Even without a strong candidate, Willkie's opponents knew what and whom they were against. On April 27, Thomas J. Curran, who had just been re-elected president of the National Republican Club, launched an entirely open "Stop Willkie" drive. When Willkie spoke in Detroit on May 30, the meeting was picketed by Gerald L. K. Smith's neo-Fascist America First party. The *Chicago Tribune*, the *New York Daily News*, and the Hearst press kept up a steady barrage of violent personal denunciation of Willkie. In June, Spangler set up a Republican council of forty-nine leaders to draft a postwar policy; it was clearly rigged against Willkie since it included neither him nor the internationalists in the party like Senators Joseph H. Ball, of Michigan, and Harold H. Burton, of Ohio. Deneen A. Watson, a Chicago lawyer, started an unofficial Republican Post-war Policy Association to counter this move. Leo Casey, who had been close to the Willkie camp since 1940, was its publicity director and it mustered substantial support for a conference in New York in July, but Willkie left it alone almost too ostentatiously in his desire not to confuse the issue of internationalism with his personal candidacy. *One World* was a sensational best seller across the country but, like nearly everything he did, it was making more friends for him outside the Republican organization than inside it.

Willkie saw this dilemma more clearly than some of his friends thought he did, but he was not prepared for appeasement. When Spangler's Council of Forty-Nine was announced, Willkie was receiving an honorary Doctor of Laws degree from Oberlin College. His prepared comment for the press was short: "I, of course, intend to fight for those things in which I believe, irrespective of the action of any pre-convention committee." Then he relaxed, and told the reporters that he was not yet sure that he would even be a candidate. "Ham Fish is against me," he went on. "Gerald L. K. Smith is against me, and I understand Landon is against me. If this keeps up, I may be nominated in spite of myself." After the reporters had filed out, he opened the door and called after them: "Say, add Colonel McCormick of the *Chicago Tribune* to that list."

None of the individuals who were close to Willkie on a day-to-day basis seem to have had any influence in building this truculence. For the most part, they were suggesting to him various devices by which he could strengthen his Republican orthodoxy without expensive appeasement of the die-hards. The intransigence with which Willkie lashed out at his opponents inside the party was largely self-generated. It was fed, naturally, by the emotional and sometimes almost hysterical reaction of many readers of *One World*. In 1943, the mood of great numbers of Americans was still tense, anxious, and expectant. The Administration's policy of military expediency in North Africa, Italy, France, and the colonial world literally pushed Willkie into becoming the outstanding champion of moral principles in the war. And the people who increasingly turned to him for forthright and challenging leadership were by no means confined to the country club circles who had first given emotional fervor to the 1940 crusade. From Kansas, White wrote him on June 26: "Either Hitler and the storm troopers, the boys in the pool hall under the leadership of Ham Fish, Martin Dies, Gerald Nye, and Colonel McCormick will come out and take leadership and bash the heads of liberals everywhere, or you will take leadership, and the time is short. . . . I earnestly beg of you to call your friends together, take counsel with them, and step out boldly into the position you must fill, and which if you do not fill will be filled by someone who will lead this country into revolution and bloody revolt. I feel this deeply and seriously or I should not be writing it."

Willkie replied in a self-joshing mood, and White came back at him on July 20: "Roosevelt has lost the ball; I doubt if he can ever get it again. Bricker will only fumble it. Dewey doesn't dare try to grab it at this time. Stassen is handicapped by his job; so is MacArthur. You are the only American of either party who can step out and take the moral, intellectual, and political

Ray in the Kansas City *Star*

leadership of this country. It must be done with dignity, but at the same time without a mealymouthed humility. You are quite right in saying 'Don't take yourself too seriously.' But after all, you are what you are, and the situation is what it is and not something else. . . ."

Willkie took the advice. August was nominally his vacation at Rushville, but there was little vacation in it for him. Most of the month was spent in a protracted huddle with those top Republicans who were still backing him: Weeks, Cake, Baker, Mrs. Reynolds, Wilson Williams of Atlanta, J. Kenneth Bradley of Connecticut, Harvey Jewett of South Dakota, and Robert

Burroughs of New Hampshire. Willkie laid it on the line to them that he would run, and he believed the Republicans could win, only on "a constructive, liberal domestic program of expanding economy" and a foreign policy of "enlightened self-interest." They represented a minority on the national committee; there was growing friction between them and Spangler. Most of them wanted to move the convention from Chicago, headquarters of the American nationalist movement, to Cleveland. They were apprehensive of what the Council of Forty-Nine might do at a meeting called for September on Mackinac Island in Michigan. Willkie returned to New York on August 29 and went almost at once to New Hampshire, as Weeks' guest, and then to Maine, talking steadily and hoping for a showdown with the politicians which would let him relax and be himself.

The Mackinac Island conference, which opened on September 6 without Willkie, Hoover, Landon, or Stassen present or invited, did not help him much. Partly because his absence made it doubly hard to repudiate him, partly because of a revolt by the Republican Governors against the Republican Congressmen, partly because it was becoming a party habit, the conference took a position on postwar policy which sounded liberal and committed nobody to anything. Willkie called it "a very distinct move in the right direction," but he was beginning to realize that each of these successive compromises for party harmony, whatever they might do to the future of the Republican party, was strengthening its control by the professionals who were determined to drop their 1940 candidate.

Essentially, Willkie was little more unpopular with the Republican party politicians at this time than Roosevelt was with the Democratic party politicians. Each was saying in effect to his party: "Win with me, on my terms, or lose. Take your choice." Willkie never could say it with the personal skill or experience Roosevelt had, nor did he have any power to back it up except what he could generate as a free-wheeling individual. At the end of September, he tried his hand at this kind of power again, in an article called "How the Republican Party Can Win in 1944" published by *Look*. "If the Republican party intends to drive heart and soul for liberal objectives . . ." he wrote, "I shall give

it my complete and undeviating service, whether as the convention's nominee or as a worker in the ranks." He then outlined,
in answers to five questions, what he felt those liberal objectives
should be. He based his answers on what he had learned in
one hundred private meetings with party leaders and workers
in twenty-two states, a far bigger sampling of opinion than any
other candidate had made. The magazine promoted the article
with a flamboyant advertising campaign based on the risky
suggestion that Willkie might be "another Lincoln," but most
political observers were quietly impressed by what Willkie
wrote. "The politicians here," Arthur Krock reported from Washington, "were more than ever disposed to concede, after reading
the *Look* article, that Mr. Willkie will be a formidable con-
tender for the 1944 Republican nomination, knows where his
fences are weak, and is setting out to repair them."

The repair job proved to be difficult from the very start. In
September, while Willkie was just getting started on this new
campaign to convince the party of his orthodoxy, a group of
Missouri Republicans sent him a list of nine questions carefully
phrased to make it hard for him to keep his temper. "Do you
believe," one of them ran, "in the free and unrestricted movement of people? If so, how do you propose to prevent peoples
from Asia . . . overrunning the United States?" Another asked:
"Do you believe that it is desirable for America to permit flooding our country with alien individuals and alien ideas?" The
questions had been prepared by a small group led by Edgar
M. Queeny, head of the Monsanto Chemical Corporation and
a large contributor to his 1940 campaign fund, privately checked
with Herbert Hoover, and signed by the thirty-five Missouri
delegates to the 1940 Republican convention. Willkie could
neither parry nor stall for long, although he tried, because Mark
Sullivan and a few other Republican commentators picked up
the questions with undisguised glee. So he agreed to speak in
St. Louis on October 12.

The incident could hardly have been more unhappy, more
rancorous, or more revealing of the power within the party of
the formerly isolationist, now American nationalist, die-hards.
When Willkie learned that fifty-dollar box seats were being sold

for the meeting, he offered personally to pay the cost of the hall, and they let him. There was a good deal of unfriendly preliminary comment back and forth, in which Queeny made what political use he could of Willkie's association with known internationalists like Henry R. Luce, Thomas W. Lamont, and his fellow-directors of Freedom House.

"Ed, let me give you a tip," Willkie wrote sarcastically to Queeny. "If you want to pursue this Administration policy of strong condemnation by frail association, I also belong to the board of directors of another public forum besides Freedom House. I am a member of the board of trustees of Town Hall. One of my fellow-directors is Mr. Norman Thomas, Socialist and pre-Pearl Harbor arch-isolationist. You can do wonders with that."

He made his speech a blistering attack on the Administration for its failure to encourage co-operation abroad and the revival of free enterprise at home. He made no attempt to answer one by one the "Have you stopped beating your wife?" type of questions which had been sent him, explaining that he did not believe anyone wanted him to answer them "in the manner of a schoolboy." The speech produced a tempestuous ovation in the hall, and extremely favorable editorials the next day in many of the country's leading newspapers. It utterly failed to satisfy the Missouri Republican leaders. They saw that Willkie was deliberately offering a savage criticism of the Administration in place of the abandonment of internationalism which they were trying to force from him, and they refused to make the deal. At a private luncheon given him the next day by Queeny and sixty St. Louis businessmen, Willkie learned what they really wanted from him. "I don't know whether you're going to support me or not," he answered at the luncheon, "and I don't give a damn. You're a bunch of political liabilities who don't know what's going on, anyway."

By now Willkie was angry, and in a fighting mood. He was covering the country in great swoops, from California to New York to St. Louis, back to New York, to Washington for a meeting with the Republican Congressmen, to Syracuse to speak

The Road to Wisconsin

for the Republican candidate for Lieutenant-Governor, to Wisconsin for a whirlwind speaking tour through the state where the first important primary was sure to come, to New Orleans and Dallas, Texas. He told Turner Catledge of the *New York Times* in October that he knew more of the down-to-the-precinct Republican workers throughout the nation than any other man in the party and that by the time of the convention he would know twice as many as anyone else.

The war in Europe was clearly approaching a great climax; the unconditional surrender of Italy was followed by massive but vague victories reported from the Russian front. Time would not wait for laggards; Willkie was desperate to see his idea of a grand alliance debated and accepted while the iron was still hot in men's minds and hearts. His sister, Julia, of whom he had always been especially fond, died on October 7 in Bridgeport, where she—an accomplished linguist and bacteriologist—had been working as priority director of an aircraft plant. The precise figuring of political angles and the appeasement of Republican leaders who were afraid of what victory might bring to the United States were not now, if they ever were, alluring jobs to this man in a hurry.

Willkie had now known for quite a while that he could neither capture nor appease the top levels of the Republican party machine, and his crack about "political liabilities" was less an angry indiscretion than it was a deliberate attempt to go over their heads to the rank and file of Republican voters. He had done this before; it seemed worth another try. The opinion polls had shown for more than a year that this was his only chance. Dewey, who was not a candidate, maintained a consistent but not heavy lead, with Willkie second, in all polls taken among Republican voters. In polls taken among politicians and Congressmen, his lead was much heavier, and Willkie was seldom higher than fourth, with Bricker and MacArthur ahead of him, too. By August, 1943, Dewey showed up in a Gallup poll for the first time as a stronger candidate against Roosevelt (45 to 55) than Willkie (41 to 59). But efforts to poll the independent vote or to predict how the "don't know" category would finally decide nearly always showed Willkie to be the only available Republican candidate with any kind of gambling chance against Roosevelt as long as the war continued.

This was still a long way from pledged delegate strength at the convention, and Willkie knew it. On December 11, 1943, the *St. Louis Post-Dispatch* published details of a thorough exploration which had been made by Willkie of the technical difficulties involved in getting a third party on to the ballot in each of the forty-eight states. "So many stories are circulated about me by both my friends and my enemies that I do not bother either to confirm or to deny them," Willkie said publicly. "I do not think I care to comment further at this time." Yet the story was true and the results of the exploration had been extremely discouraging to him. He was not married to the Republican party, he used to say, but still courting it. At other times he compared political parties to automobiles—machines to take you somewhere you wanted to go. In November, 1942, he had told an interviewer from *PM:* "Since I've already got a franchise, a license, to operate in the Republican party, why should I jump that? No, the thing to do is to take that instrumentality and make it better, then use it as the means to hasten the world's inevitable progress. Play along with it; be flexible; improve it; but never compromise your principles. And for God's sake don't make me sound stuffy." A year later, by the end of 1943, he was less sanguine about his franchise but his basic position had not changed, and there were still the primaries and the convention, in both of which a man could try to take control away from the professional party politicians.

To do this he needed the independent vote—those mugwumps of whom Willkie loved to quote the old definition: men sitting on the fence with their mugs on one side and their wumps on the other. They form a group in American political life whose voting behavior has fascinated and baffled politicians and political scientists since long before Willkie. They tend to wait out a labor dispute until the final phase of negotiation, an election campaign until all the speeches have been made, an argument in a bar until the early morning, before they make up their minds. Their final decisions are often influenced by

The Road to Wisconsin

desire to jump on a bandwagon, and they often vote for personalities rather than issues. In national elections there are nearly always a great many of them. Willkie knew at the beginning of 1944, more clearly than he did in 1940, that the bulk of these voters were to be found among industrial workers in the North, dissatisfied or progressive farmers, Negroes, and liberal-minded citizens in the lower- or middle-income brackets. They failed to tip the balance in his favor in 1944, as in 1940, despite his efforts to enlist them on his side. There were two basic reasons: most of them, although restless, were not yet ready to abandon Roosevelt and the New Deal; and the liberals who were their spokesmen and to some extent their guides were not at all ready to abandon their old picture of Willkie as a reactionary utility tycoon.

Samuel Grafton, columnist for the *New York Post*, went to Rushville in August, 1943, to check up on the new legend of Willkie as a liberal. He spent several days talking to Willkie and his neighbors, looking at his pigs, sitting on the front porch of the Harrison Street house. He came away "with the feeling that there are two fixed poles in Mr. Willkie's political life today, an interest in civil liberties and an interest in international collaboration. It seems to me highly unlikely that he can ever be shaken from his adherence to both. Would he accept political oblivion, if he had to, as the price for sticking to these concepts? I am certain, as of this moment, that he would." The report caused a minor sensation in New York at the time, because of the columnist's reputation as a liberal. It was almost the only favorable profile Willkie was to get during this preconvention period from any source even slightly to the left of center in American politics.

The liberal weeklies applauded *One World* and many of Willkie's individual statements during 1943, but not his campaign for the Republican nomination. The *New Republic*, which had devoted a special issue to proving him a reactionary in the 1940 campaign, published a new estimate of him by George Soule in August, 1943, which was less bitter but still far from friendly. By now he seemed not a tight-lipped, hide-bound conservative, but "a rumple-haired, simple-hearted boy from

345

Indiana" who was "perfectly capable of exploiting his sincere beliefs to gain public favor." In March, 1944, John Chamberlain wrote a major profile of Willkie in *Life*, critical but friendly in tone, in which he pointed out that to many of Willkie's new partisans among "the Negroes, the Jews, the liberal intellectuals, the Thurman Arnold anti-monopoly New Dealers, the foreign correspondents, the labor movement and the civil libertarians," he was still in the position of second-best friend, following Roosevelt. In the same month, *Harper's Magazine* published an article called "Wendell Willkie: Man of Words" by Professor Fred Rodell of the Yale Law School which was a virtuoso hatchet job in the pre-1940 New Deal style. It denied him any sincerity at all, repeated all the old stories of Commonwealth and Southern skullduggery, called him "Utility Magnate Willkie," and predicted that he would go down in history as "Wall Street's William Jennings Bryan."

Willkie was doing better with labor and the farmers than with professional liberals. Public opinion polls in 1943 showed that Roosevelt's 54 to 46 per cent lead over Willkie among farmers in 1940 had dropped to 50-50, and his 65 to 35 per cent lead among workers to 64 to 36 per cent. The changes were small but the direction was encouraging. In his November fence-building tour of Wisconsin, Willkie warned the Republican party that if it "were to adopt an anti-labor attitude it would take the road leading to certain defeat and deserved defeat." Both A. F. of L. and C.I.O. papers had begun to report him seriously, and with interest. For the first time in his career he included labor leaders among his personal friends. Columnists like Westbrook Pegler, attacking him for this shift, were more convinced of its sincerity than the liberal journalists who still tried to explain Willkie in formulas which dated from the 1930's.

More vicious personal attacks came from the extreme right. The McCormick press kept up a steady barrage of editorials throughout 1943 and the first half of 1944 attacking Willkie exclusively on the issue of internationalism. The language used in the *New York Daily News* was hardly distinguishable from that used by Mrs. Elizabeth Dilling, author of *The Red Network*, who wrote in her *Patriotic Research Bureau Newsletter*

Duffy in the Baltimore *Sun*

on August 7, 1943: "Will we have another phoney Willkie-FDR 'election' in 1944? Will we be given another 'choice' between the stooges of International Socialist-Communist-Collectivist-Judaistic world government? This query now haunts Americans who permit themselves to think."

This campaign reached a climax at the end of November, 1943, when a former mayor of Akron named C. Nelson Sparks published a scurrilous pamphlet written by himself and called "One Man—Wendell Willkie." It was designed to look as much as possible like the paper-bound edition of *One World*, and substantial funds were forthcoming from the most reactionary fringe of the Republican party to give it wide circulation. The pamphlet was an early and amateur example of the kind of personal smear technique which was to be applied to many other men in the years after Willkie's death. Its author, who had been campaign manager in 1940 for Frank E. Gannett, threw together a miscellaneous collection of easily disproved untruths about Willkie's career, wrapped them up in the fervid language of extreme nationalist isolationism, and topped the job with a forged letter, purporting to be from Harry Hopkins to Dr. Umphrey Lee, president of Southern Methodist University, and implying some sort of secret agreement between Willkie and the Administration. No responsible Republican dared to endorse the pamphlet publicly, but few of them were in any hurry to denounce it. It took more than a month to move the tawdry sensation it caused out of Congress and the front pages of the nation's press and into the courts. By then the smear had done much of what it had been designed to do. "It is a tragic thing," the Republican *New York Herald Tribune* commented, "that a situation should exist within the Republican party which should make such devices seem profitable to their authors, whoever they may be." It was an even more tragic thing that the device not only seemed profitable but was.

Willkie's personal relations with the Administration, in actual fact, had worsened steadily for two years. Marquis Childs listed the evidence of personal antipathy between Willkie and the President in an article in the *Saturday Evening Post*. It drew from the President this letter, written on March 6, 1943:

Dear Wendell:

Somebody called my attention to an article about you by an old friend of mine in the *Saturday Evening Post*.

In view of certain allegations made by Brother Childs, I want to tell you one or two things with the utmost simplicity.

First, I certainly did not give you any hint of the North African invasion plans. Nor, did I to anyone else except the top Army and Navy people who knew them anyway. Even the Vice-President and the Cabinet were given no hint.

Secondly, the records will show that I did not say I was too busy to read what you had had to say. What I did say was that I had been

The Road to Wisconsin

too busy to read the papers that morning and therefore did not know what you had said.

Third, I have in no way "seemed determined to belittle Willkie." The contrary is true. I have on many occasions done just the opposite.

Childs' article is a bit puerile. In regard to the press conference, I did not make a crack at your pronunciation of "reservahr." I used the word in my own way which happens to be very close to your own way. But it was the press and not me who treated the whole thing as a grand joke and made an episode out of nothing.

It is true, of course, that Stimson called you up about what you were going to say in the Darlan matter. That, however, is water over the dam and things in North Africa seem to be fairly quiet for the American Army forces behind the line.

I guess Childs was trying to make trouble between us because I honestly think you are doing your best to help all of us, from top to bottom, win the war.

Always sincerely,

FRANKLIN D. ROOSEVELT

Willkie told friends that he thought the letter had been written for history rather than for him, but he declined to make it public. He did not want to make public issues out of his relations with the White House, out of the personalities of the President and his family, or out of the increasing impatience, especially among businessmen, with wartime controls. "Some people," he wrote in a farming magazine in March, 1944, "have said to me: 'Mr. Willkie, get on this domestic thing. That's where you can make political hay.' But let me tell you this, I am not going to make an appeal to the gripes or lack of enthusiasm for the war in this country on any kind of a political basis.

"I am not going to make political capital of the reasonable or unreasonable objections by the people to the hardships and inconveniences of war. I will leave that for those who already tread so close to the subversive line it's hard to tell which side they are on."

From the first day of 1944, what little chance Willkie had to beat the isolationists and the professionals in his own party, before he could get a chance to test his strength among the independent voters, depended on the war. It was still the great unknown in every political equation. By this time, he had identified himself more than any other American with the twin ideas of a grand alliance of all the peoples fighting the Axis powers to win the war, and a strong, equal co-partnership after the war to win the peace. Every move in the war which seemed to strengthen either of these ideas was followed by a perceptible quickening of newspaper and public interest in Willkie; the reverse was equally true. For the first three months of 1944, with no second front in northern Europe, no resolution of the Vichy-de Gaulle impasse in France, no overt proof of the resistance strength in occupied countries, no break in the tight Anglo-American control of strategy through the Combined Chiefs of Staff, and no good political news from either Russia or China, the cards were running against him with fatal consistency.

Russian hostility over the absence of a second front had assumed Russian proportions. Willkie had made no secret in America of the fact that he and Stalin had at least been able to talk to each other; in those days it was good politics. His intercession in Moscow on behalf of Victor Alter and Henryk Ehrlich, Polish labor leaders, had been vain, and a later cablegram he sent in their behalf with Dr. Albert Einstein and others arrived after the two men had been executed. But another personal cablegram to Stalin had brought a friendly answer and permission for a foreign correspondent in Moscow, who was a friend of Willkie's, to marry his Russian fiancée. The Communist International had been officially dissolved; other American leaders were following Willkie's footsteps to receptions in the Kremlin; most important of all, it was now clear that reports from the Russian front were true and that enormous German armies were indeed being annihilated by the Red Army.

On January 2, 1944, the *New York Times* published an article by Willkie called "Don't Stir Distrust of Russia." It was an innocent and friendly piece in which he wrote that, "of course, one of the most pressing questions in everybody's mind is what Russia intends to do about the political integrity of small states around her borders—Finland, Poland, the Baltic and Balkan states." The article went on to plead that "our principal objective must now be to persuade Russia to accept and give the guarantees of a general organization, in which she and we are both members, rather than to seek her own protection by political and military control over adjoining territories."

Pravda, official Communist party newspaper in Moscow, replied on January 5 with a blistering article by its foreign commentator, David Zaslavski. He called Willkie "a political gambler," playing "strange tricks" on behalf of reactionary and secret adherents of the Fascists. He accused him of working with the British government and the Vatican. The question of the Baltic republics was an internal affair of the Soviet Union, Zaslavski insisted, and Willkie was "muddying the waters" with only sinister motives. Both the violence and the stupidity of the language were already typical of Soviet international manners. Willkie reaffirmed every word of what he had written and laughed off the incident. "I am at least in pretty good company," he said. "The British government, the Vatican, and Wendell Willkie—that's pretty good company for an Indiana boy." But the attack disturbed him, and it gave his enemies in the Hearst and McCormick newspapers a field day of poking fun at any idea of a grand alliance.

The incident had a curious sequel. Lord Inverchapel, who as Sir Archibald Clark Kerr had been British Ambassador in Moscow in 1942, was in New York on a short personal visit. He and Willkie had liked each other deeply from the day they met. Willkie asked him casually and half jokingly to tell Stalin, on his return, that a few more attacks like this would elect him to the White House. On February 29, 1944, the British Ambassador sent Willkie a personal letter from Moscow:

British Embassy,
Moscow
February 29th, 1944

PRIVATE AND PERSONAL

My dear Willkie:

A chance seems to offer itself to send you a word.

I got back here on the 30th of January, which was rather sooner than I expected. I saw Stalin on the 2nd of February and I gave him your message. It clearly shook him a bit. He said that no one here had liked your article and that it had been thought that it called for a reply. Here Molotov interjected: "Article for article." Stalin went on to say that probably it would have been better if no reply had been made, but he added, with a laugh, that Zaslavski lived by the articles he wrote and it would not do to deprive him of his daily bread. But he (Stalin) had no wish to hurt you. What about his sending you a message to the effect that he regretted what had happened and would see to it that it did not happen again? And should he add that he was not hoping that you would be the next president? I said that I thought some friendly message would go a long way to undo the harm Zaslavski's article had done to this country in the United States. Stalin then explained that he had been joking when he had suggested the inclusion of a phrase deprecating your candidature. What he really would say was that he was sorry about the whole business and that, if you wished it, he would prevent its happening again. That seemed all right to me.

When I saw him again yesterday I asked him if he had sent you the message he had had in mind. He said that he had not, because you had made some new statements about this country, both for and against it. He would keep his promise that the Soviet press would not attack you, but he did not propose to communicate with you direct. That was all that he would say.

I really enjoyed the glimpse I had of you in New York. All good luck to you.

Yours sincerely,

ARCHIBALD CLARK KERR

The news from China was no better for Willkie than the news from Russia. Mme. Chiang Kai-shek had come to the United States in 1943. Willkie had introduced her at her biggest meeting at Madison Square Garden and had seen her often, partly to return her hospitality in Chungking and partly as honorary national chairman of United China Relief. He continued to admire her, and to back China's claims to a full share in the peace. But it was already becoming clear that she, her husband, and her husband's party, the Kuomintang, saw the future in more personal terms than Willkie. Willkie died before the breakup of the wartime coalition between the Kuomintang and the Chinese Communists; the only Chinese Communist he ever saw had been a guest in the Chungking home of Chiang Kai-shek. But by 1944 the war in the Pacific had dwarfed the war in China, and the Kuomintang government was looking for friends with power.

Frances Perkins has told the story of Roosevelt's pressing Mme. Chiang on this trip for her candid opinion of Willkie. He rejected several courteous but bland answers until she told him: "Well, Mr. President, he is an adolescent, after all." The President pushed the question further by asking what, then, she thought of him. "Ah, Mr. President," she answered, "you are sophisticated."

"As Roosevelt told this story," Miss Perkins concluded her account, "there was a gleam of pleasure and, shall I say, simple human vanity in his eyes. His obvious pleasure belied its point." The story helps to explain why Willkie drew no political profit from his effort to back the Chinese people to a full share in the war and in the peace. His prediction that the Chiangs would lead, at the end of the war, a united, democratic, and strong China eager to take its rightful place in the world was already proving, at the beginning of 1944, a completely wrong guess.

During 1943 and 1944, Willkie's championship of Russia and China, as of Palestine and of the rights of colonial territories to some increase in self-government after the war, was based on his deep belief in the need for a United Nations Council to be set up while the war was still going on. He was not alone in this; Sumner Welles, former Under-Secretary of State, Walter Lippmann, and others were also demanding it. In the final speech of his campaign, in Omaha on April 5, Willkie asked: "What does a Frenchman in France, for example, or a Belgian in Belgium, or a Chinese in the conquered parts of China, or—for that matter— a Russian in the Soviet Union think of our failure to set up a United Nations Council? . . . The United States is the one country with enough strength and prestige and disinterestedness to take the leadership in setting up such a body." Neither Roosevelt nor Churchill was prepared to share their exclusive control over the strategy of war and peace except in the occasional big conferences like Teheran, Cairo, or Yalta. What would have happened if the war had ended with an already-existing United Nations Council, in which nations had worked out what they were fighting for while they were still fighting, as Willkie kept on urging, remains one of the central speculations of modern history.

If he felt a United Nations grand alliance was needed to shorten the war, he was even more convinced that it was needed to win the peace. In 1944 this became almost an obsession with him. He talked about it in almost every speech he made. He wanted to give the smaller nations a share in the planning of the peace, and he wanted to cushion by advance debate the shock to bigger nations which would come with knowledge that they would have to change their thinking on the nature of national sovereignty. In 1943 he played a leading part, through Stassen and Senator Ball, in the framing of the Ball-Hatch-Burton-Hill Resolution which first committed the United States to a postwar organization of the United Nations. For his friend Hamilton Fish Armstrong, editor of *Foreign Affairs*, he wrote an article in the April, 1944, issue of that magazine which went further in redefining the nature of sovereignty in the modern world than any American leader had yet gone.

The article was called "Our Sovereignty: Shall We Use It?" In its preparation he made more demands on his friends and advisers, including the editor of the magazine, than in any statement he wrote in the last year of his life, yet the final draft was his own. Its central purpose was to argue that membership in an international organization to keep the peace would increase our national sovereignty rather than limit it. He proposed to use our sovereignty and not to hoard it. This was an effort to head off a sterile repetition of the old debate about the League of Nations. He pointed out that a static isolationism no longer gives modern nations freedom of choice; the United States had not been free to choose peace or war in the twentieth century but only to decide that temporarily we would postpone going to war.

"In an international organization," he concluded, "which was backed by the machinery needed to enforce its decisions, the United States for the first time in history would be in a position to deal boldly and effectively with the problems which will confront it. In co-operation with our allies, we shall still be leaders by virtue of the strength and ingenuity of our people. To use this leadership, for our own enrichment and that of mankind, will not be to weaken the sovereign power of the American people; it will be to widen it and make it more real."

As late as January, 1944, Willkie was far more engrossed with this kind of long-range thinking than he was with thoughts of the primaries or of the convention. He still thought he had a gambling chance to win the nomination, if only by default since Dewey still insisted he would keep his promise to serve out his term as Governor and there were no other candidates with any appreciable popular support. Here he vastly underestimated the quiet determination of the professionals to be rid of him. Willkie knew that there were undercover moves, especially in the stimulation of "favorite-son" booms, to form a stop-Willkie movement, and his friend Governor William H. Wills of Vermont lashed out against these in a major speech at Montpelier on January 8. Wills heaped scorn on Landon, Hamilton, Nye, Joseph Pew, and Gerald L. K. Smith as the "four-year locusts" who agreed on nothing except their hatred of Willkie. "Up here in Vermont," he said, "where our Republicanism is unchallenged, we hail Wendell Willkie as a great Republican."

This time, unlike 1940, Willkie could not skip the primaries. He had hoped to use California in May as a test of his popularity, and he had gone to see Governor Earl Warren in Sacramento in October, 1943, to feel out his reception. He learned that Warren planned to run himself. Willkie's enemies later said he had alienated Republican politicians in that state by acting as if his Hollywood connections gave him a native-son franchise. Some of Willkie's friends said Warren was being used by the Old Guard to block a fair test for Willkie. All Warren said was that he was running in the California primary not as a true candidate but simply to hold together the state's fifty delegates to the convention. Crum, Willkie's 1940 campaign manager on the West Coast, urged Willkie to challenge Warren by entering the California primary anyway. When Warren assured him by telephone, at the end of January, that he would not become part of

Berryman in the Washington *Evening Star*

any stop-Willkie movement, and that one-half of his delegates
would be pro-Willkie men, Willkie announced that he would
not enter the California primary. It was the state he would have
preferred above all others for a test, but Warren left him no
alternative but to withdraw.

Since many states hold no popular Presidential primaries, this
left Willkie with very limited choice if he wanted a public demonstration of his political power. He had no choice in this. Pryor,
Weeks, Cake, Hanes, Helen Reid, and the Cowles brothers were
almost the only prominent Republicans left who were backing
him, and even they were running low on enthusiasm. If he was
determined to run again, they told him, he had to show some
strength against the party machine, and the primaries were his
only chance. His arrangement with them was that he would do
whatever they thought best politically, on the condition that
there would be no interference with his own expression of his

ideas and beliefs. So he formally filed to run in New Hampshire on March 14, in Wisconsin on April 4, in Nebraska on April 11, in Maryland on May 1, and in Oregon on May 19.

The mood in which he launched his last political campaign was clear in a major speech he made on February 2 at the New York Times Hall in New York on fiscal policy. He knew the odds were heavily against him, and he followed his old habit of doubling his bets. Many of his conservative business friends had been urging him to make a major speech on domestic problems, and especially on the fiscal policies of the New Deal, which would reassure sound-money circles on his orthodox financial views. He did it with a vengeance. Attacking the Administration for following "a fiscal primrose path," he lashed out at the public debt which was mortgaging the future of the free-enterprise system, demanded that the war be put on a pay-as-you-go basis, and suggested doubling the Treasury's proposal to raise $8,000,000,-000 by taxes. This was much too much of a good thing for many conservative Republicans, who liked talking about national solvency better than paying for it. It brought the *New York Times* and the *New York Herald Tribune*, both sound-money papers, to strong support of him as a candidate the next morning. But it literally stunned the politicians and those businessmen who, as Arthur Krock reported from Washington, "though Mr. Willkie was the first to fight their battle against the New Deal and spoke as one of them last night, have abandoned his cause."

Two days later, on February 4, he left New York on a speaking trip which took him across the continent and back. In Milwaukee he approved a full slate of delegates pledged to him in the primary. He covered Nebraska, Utah, Idaho, and Washington; and in Portland, on February 14, he formally announced his candidacy for the Republican nomination, naming his friend Cake as his pre-convention campaign manager. He came back through Montana, Wyoming, Minnesota, Iowa, and Illinois. He delivered set speeches every night, conferred all day with state Republican leaders, and shook hands with literally thousands of people. At the end of the trip, he figured that in the preceding twelve months he had visited all but four of the forty-eight states and had talked to virtually every Republican leader. Most of them had left him in no doubt that they resented his attempt to reform the Republican party while seeking to lead it and that they feared his liberal positions. Yet at the same time most of them were clearly measuring how and when they could jump on the bandwagon if it should start to roll.

The New Hampshire primary on March 14 gave Willkie six unpledged but favorable delegates out of a total of eleven, with two pledged delegates going to Dewey. Everyone conceded Willkie's strength in New England; the Middle West was another matter. On March 12, the Gallup poll showed that Dewey's November lead over him among Republicans of 55 to 35 per cent had climbed to 64 to 27 per cent. On March 17, he went to Wisconsin for the gamble which would make or break him.

Willkie's friends have debated for years what made him choose Wisconsin for the first major test in nearly four years of his popularity with voters. Wisconsin was the only state except Indiana in which he had run ahead of both the Republican candidates for Governor and Senator in 1940. He had the support of virtually every newspaper in the state except for McCormick and Hearst. He had spoken there repeatedly; the delegates pledged to him were outstanding citizens of excellent local repute.

On the other hand, every Wisconsin Republican in Congress had voted consistently against Willkie's policies in the pre-Pearl Harbor period. Their opposition had been unanimous to repeal of the arms embargo, to the arming of American merchant ships, to Secretary Hull's trade program, to selective service, to its extension on the very eve of Pearl Harbor, to lend-lease, and to the first lend-lease appropriation. The German origin of a considerable part of the state's population, which had helped him in 1940, was fertile ground for the isolationists. The young men were nearly all in uniform, not voting. Finally, the La Follette progressive traditions were no longer as strong as they had been or as they looked; two years later Joseph McCarthy was to defeat Senator Robert M. La Follette in another Republican primary.

But the real reason for Willkie's running was that he could do nothing else. With the California primary closed to him by

The Road to Wisconsin

Warren's candidacy, Willkie had to run in what he said frankly was the worst state for him except Illinois in the whole country, or admit that he was scared of it. He made forty speeches in thirteen days, traveling from one end of the state to the other, alternately denouncing the New Deal and the Old Guard of the Republican party, preaching his basic doctrines, hoping against hope that the problems of the war and the peace had bitten deeply enough into men's minds to give his ideas the kind of toehold he had been cutting for them ever since he started to practice politics.

None of the other candidates either went to Wisconsin or admitted that they were candidates. Stassen announced on March 21 that he would not actually seek the nomination but would take it if it were given to him. Dewey publicly asked his delegates to withdraw; after conferring with his close advisers, most of them continued in the race. General Douglas MacArthur was in the Pacific theater of war. The silent powers in the Republican party—Hoover, Landon, Sprague and Jaeckle of New York, Pew, Spangler, Lew Wentz of Oklahoma, Queeny —stayed in their respective bailiwicks, saying nothing.

The Stassen campaign in Wisconsin was originally in the hands of Dr. Frank L. Gullickson, a former Republican state chairman, but was later turned over to A. E. Smith, a political henchman of Fred R. Zimmerman, a former Governor who had been an outright isolationist and who was the leading Dewey delegate. The MacArthur campaign was managed by Lansing Hoyt, former Milwaukee chairman of the America First Committee. Jack Steele, reporting to the *New York Herald Tribune*, in a dispatch filed more than a month before the voting, described the technique used: "Delegates running in the names of Dewey and MacArthur are frankly using a double-barreled strategy. First, of course, they are trying to attract all the voters who are sincere admirers of either man. Then they are attempting to round up the votes of all the isolationist elements in the state, including those of the large population of Germanic descent. Their technique is to promise that, even if the candidates whose names they are using are not in the convention race, they will never switch their votes to Willkie."

Shadow and Substance.

Belfryman in the Washington *Evening Star*

Willkie's funds were completely inadequate for the job. His backers had no organization, and little spirit except what he could pump into them. There was no one to run interference for him, set up meetings, raise money, do advance publicity. Wisconsin utility leaders who had disliked him from the days when he refused to sacrifice his C. & S. stockholders in a political crusade against the TVA suddenly turned out to have long memories. At the end of the strange campaign in which all the candidates except Willkie pretended not to be running, large sums of money poured into the state for political meetings against him.

On March 29, Willkie finished his campaign, dog-tired, and after a one-day rest in Minneapolis began an eleven-day tour of Nebraska, where the next primary was scheduled. Willkie, like most of the reporters, thought his Wisconsin chances were 50-50. He spoke in York, Grand Island, and Norfolk, where in a hotel room at midnight on April 4 he learned the Wisconsin news. Dewey had won 17 delegates, Stassen 4, MacArthur 3, and Willkie 0.

Gardner Cowles was the only close friend who was with him. Willkie cheered up the disconsolate reporters who were traveling with him, read names in the Norfolk, Nebraska, telephone book for a while since he had no other reading matter handy, and then went to sleep. The next day he spoke in West Point and Freemont and then drove to a reception in Omaha and the inevitable hour of handshaking. He had been drafting statements all day, crumpling them up and throwing them away. After he had finished a prepared address on foreign policy that night, he announced in a five-paragraph statement that it was obvious he could not be nominated and that he was asking his friends to drop his campaign. He had cut it clean. It had taken two months short of four years to do the trick, but the professionals had had their revenge for 1940.

CHAPTER NINETEEN

The Long Summer

W ILLKIE canceled his speaking plans in Iowa and Michigan and took the train back to New York on the night he withdrew from the Presidential race. He played gin rummy, and reread *The Count of Monte Cristo*, one of his favorite novels. "I'm going back to New York to resume the practice of law," he told the reporters who boarded the train at every major stop, and when he was pressed for other plans he told them he was expecting to put about four hundred acres of his Indiana farms into corn. He was deeply tired, and discouraged, and uncertain about the future. Cake and Casey met him at the station, they arranged to close his improvised campaign headquarters in the Grand Central Building, and Willkie went home.

The legend that Willkie died of a broken heart seems a necessary climax in the dramatist's timing which arranged all the major events of the last four years of his life. Like all good climaxes, his death was preceded in the legend by a long summer of suspense, hope, and frustration. The legend of the broken heart was completely false, but the long summer was real and palpable. He was no more capable of retiring into the practice of law than he was of becoming a dirt farmer. He had lost a major round in a political fight which was manifestly still going on. Only fifty-two years old, he was too young to be an elder statesman—the only conventional role sometimes open to an unsuccessful candidate for President in the American party system. His convictions were brighter and sturdier than they had ever been. His personal following throughout the nation was larger and more devoted than that of any other man except the

President. He went to work, quiet, determined, a little grim, to carve out an unconventional role in which he could fight for the issues he believed in.

The first, and the last, major political problem of the summer was what to do about Governor Dewey's candidacy. There were two and a half months to go before the Republican convention, and Dewey had still not declared himself to be a candidate. But a "draft Dewey" bandwagon was already moving in high gear. Most political experts agreed that Willkie's stunning defeat in Wisconsin could be interpreted also as an overwhelming repudiation of the New Deal. The Republicans were listening again to Henry L. Mencken's quadrennial assurance that "any Chinaman" could beat Roosevelt this time. The "silent men" who had been the true victors in the Wisconsin primary—men like Hoover, Sprague, Jaeckle, Pew, Spangler, Wentz, and Queeny, the organization Republicans—were back in full control of their party, and after twelve long years in the wilderness, their hopes gave wings to their expectations.

D-Day had not yet come on the beaches of Normandy, and for those whose hearts were not wholly in the war there was none of that prickling sense of excitement which came with the long, slow build-up for the liberation of Europe. Gerald L. K. Smith called the Wisconsin primary a smashing victory for America First. On May 1, the Rev. Edward Lodge Curran told a packed and wildly cheering hall in Brooklyn that the Wisconsin vote had been the handwriting on the wall. "There the challenge was given," he said, "and there the people answered by consigning to political oblivion the man whose devotion to foreign alliance was greater than his devotion to the independence of his country." In Chicago, Colonel McCormick applied to the War Production Board for newsprint with which to start a new paper in Wisconsin because, he said, the primaries had amply shown that the people of that state had repudiated the Wisconsin newspapers which backed Willkie's candidacy. In the Illinois primary, a week after Wisconsin, all the Republican candidates recommended on the first page of the *Chicago Tribune* won by handsome majorities.

Willkie himself realized almost immediately after the Wisconsin vote that his power inside the Republican party in 1944 would be measured by the price he could exact for the support of his followers. He was also certain that the military news from Europe and from the Pacific would tend to raise that price in measure as it convinced more and more Americans, with the unanswerable logic of casualty figures, that the United States was already involved in world affairs. Now there could be neither profit nor morality in any effort to appease the organization Republicans, and Willkie began to state his program all over again, this time with a precision and a clarity which came more easily to a man who was no longer running for office.

On May 9, he wrote a personal letter to twenty editors and columnists who were his friends, enclosing a copy of a dispatch in the *New York Times* by Turner Catledge. The dispatch was an analysis of the political events in Wisconsin which began with Willkie's defeat and culminated, a month later, in the Republican and La Follette Progressive state conventions. The Progressives formally broke their twelve-year-old alliance with the New Deal and adopted, like the Republicans, a platform of extreme isolationist nationalism. Catledge reported that a nationalist movement of the first rank was taking shape in Wisconsin. Senator Robert M. La Follette, Jr., who was to be defeated two years later when Joseph McCarthy topped his bid for the nationalist voters, was trying to move back into the Republican party and, if the Republicans should win in November, the probable chairmanship of the Foreign Relations Committee of the Senate.

"Naturally, as a Republican," Willkie wrote in his letter, "I would prefer to work within the Republican party, but I will be damned if I am going to sit by while the peace of the world is wrecked again as it was in the 20's." It was a personal letter, and was never published until after his death, but it accomplished his purpose of letting key editors know what he was up to. He was going to try to force the Republican platform and the Republican candidate into an internationalist position. The only weapon he had was the unspoken threat of what Al Smith had called "taking a walk"; this could no longer hurt the professionals at the convention but the November election was a different matter.

The Long Summer

In June he wrote out his answers to what seemed to him the most important problems before the nation. In nothing he ever wrote did he pull fewer punches; there was no longer any personal reason for expediency, and he was determined to stimulate discussion and thinking among the large number of Americans with whom, according to opinion polls, his stature had actually risen after the Wisconsin defeat. Elmo Roper estimated in 1944 that the probable number of voters who strongly preferred Willkie above all other men for President was between five and six million. Even after Willkie withdrew from the race there were between a million and a half and two million people who, while firmly intending to vote against Roosevelt, still wanted to register themselves as believing that Willkie was the best man the Republicans offered. By September, 89.6 per cent of those who said they had voted for Willkie in 1940 said they intended to vote for Dewey in 1944. Eight per cent or about 1,800,000 of them said they intended to vote for Roosevelt.

Freed from the necessity of talking primarily to Republicans, Willkie turned directly to these more independent-minded voters in the seven newspaper articles in which he summed up his position. In the first, he dismissed states' rights as an issue, arguing that large Federal powers were necessary, and needed only to be more intelligently used. In the second, he spoke up for anti-poll tax and anti-lynching statutes. Social security should not be reduced, he claimed in the third, but extended, unified, and made simpler. A fourth article restated his old belief in an expansionist economic program to take up the slack of demobilization when the war was over. He demanded the repeal of the coercive Smith-Connally Act in the fifth article, a reassertion of labor's right to strike, and a greater sense of social responsibility among both employers and labor leaders. In the last two articles, he argued for progressive downward revision of tariffs and for a foreign policy based on the immediate creation of a functioning Council of the United Nations.

Compared to the pre-convention discussion of issues then going on in both parties, it was a breath of fresh air. Six newspapers had requested the series: the *New York Herald Tribune*, the *Boston Herald*, the *Minneapolis Star Journal and Tribune*, the *Des Moines Register and Tribune,* the *Portland Oregonian,* and the *San Francisco Chronicle,* but other papers all over the country reprinted the series because of popular interest in it. The articles formed the basis for a complete platform which Willkie drafted and submitted to the Republican convention.

Its reception by the professional Republicans was as cool as they could make it without running the risks of overt hostility. Mark Sullivan summed it up by reminding Willkie that an affirmative policy for the Republican party was not "what nature meant" and would be "a disservice to the country." "The real guide for the Republicans in their platform-making next week," he wrote, was in the rule that "the function of an opposition party is to be an opposition party." Willkie was never consulted in the drafting of the official party platform.

Willkie was offered a ticket to the convention by Spangler, "so I could get in the gate," but nothing else. Hoover had been asked to address the convention, and Landon attended as a delegate from Kansas, but Willkie had been running for the nomination when the New York delegates were chosen on March 23, and he was not included among the delegates-at-large who were named later. Some of his supporters in Oregon, Indiana, and Wisconsin were ostentatiously pushed into the background in pre-convention plans; a few others, like Crum and Davenport, made it clear that they would bolt the party if Dewey should be nominated on a weak and mealymouthed platform. But the nucleus of Willkie backers inside the party leadership, including Weeks, Cake, Pryor, Wilson Williams of Atlanta, the Cowles brothers, and Frank Baker of Seattle, came out for Dewey. The Dewey camp was so confident of winning the nomination that it could afford to make overtures to some of Willkie's friends. None was made to Willkie himself, and he stayed in New York throughout the convention. When Dewey and Bricker were nominated on June 28, Willkie wired the New York Governor at Albany: "Hearty congratulations to you on your nomination. You have one of the great opportunities of history."

To translate his bargaining power in independent-minded voters into effective influence on Dewey, his campaign, and his

"To tell you the truth, my voice has never been a hundred per cent right since that 'We Want Willkie' business."

administration if he should be elected, Willkie needed more than the threat of sulking in his tent. President Roosevelt was delighted to give him an extra threat. During the month between the two major party conventions, it took the form of speculation that Willkie might be tapped for the Vice-Presidential nomination on the Democratic ticket. During August and September, it shifted to the beginning of discussion of postelection plans which would have brought about revolutionary changes in the traditional American party system. As a step towards this, Roosevelt tried to persuade Willkie to go to Europe as his personal representative to set up civilian control over the victory which many, before the Battle of the Bulge, believed imminent. Willkie never used any of these offers publicly, but he did not need to. Leaks from the White House and the general public expectancy of some major political declaration by Willkie gave him the bargaining power he wanted, and he worked all summer to use it effectively for the policies he believed in.

Willkie never saw Roosevelt during this period. There is no record of their meeting after Willkie's report to the President when he returned from his One World trip on October 15, 1942. But by now there was a fairly considerable number of prominent men who had the confidence of both Roosevelt and Willkie, unlike 1940 when William Allen White was almost the only man in that position. The complete details of what transpired between the two men through intermediaries in the summer 1944 are not yet all available. Willkie had had enough experience by now with the President's extraordinary political cunning to move with extreme wariness. Roosevelt wanted the Willkie vote, but he did not want to pay any more for it than he had to and, as always, the element of sheer intrigue in the situation fascinated him almost as much as the tangible support he might gain. So the political maneuvering of the summer was carried on in almost storybook secrecy, with each of the two men eager to make a minimum of noise and to leave no footprints.

Yet there is a clear record that Roosevelt was in touch with Willkie before the Democratic convention and after it, by letter and through intermediaries. Whatever hopes the President may have had of splitting the Republicans before the election were clearly succeeded by hopes of a new political alignment, after the election, which would free each of the men from the reactionary Old Guard in his own party. This latter proposition, put forward by Roosevelt in the most concrete language, alone explodes the legend that Willkie died a defeated and brokenhearted man, with no future to live for. It shows his death to have been a major tragedy because of what lay ahead of him and not behind him.

The possibility that Willkie might be Roosevelt's choice for Democratic Vice-President was not as sensational, then or now, as the postelection plan for a new party. As early as July 14, 1943, a year before the conventions, Turner Catledge had written in the *New York Times* a "report . . . about a proffer of a one-to-twenty-five bet that the [Democratic] Vice-Presidential berth will be offered to Mr. Willkie if the Republicans turn him down, and therefore out, in 1944." Two days after the Wisconsin primary, on April 6, 1944, the *Boston Post* reported from Washington, on unnamed authority, that President Roosevelt would pick Willkie in order to form, in effect, a coalition government while the war was going on and to make more certain a stable and bipartisan peace.

Talk along these lines could hardly have been unusual in the White House. Robert E. Sherwood, who saw a good deal of the President in his more relaxed moments, has recorded that: "It was my belief in 1943 and early in 1944 that if Willkie were to win the Republican nomination Roosevelt would not run for a fourth term. I had no tangible basis for this belief, and it was a doubly hypothetical surmise because it was evident for a long time to Roosevelt that Willkie had no chance whatever of being nominated. Greatly as the Old Guard lords of the Republican machine hated Roosevelt, they had come to hate Willkie even more, and, be it said to his eternal credit, Willkie went out of his way to court their hatred by scorning their support."

Willkie kept his own counsel, even from his closest friends, on this problem. In May there were reports that he would be offered the Secretaryship of the Navy, as a device to make his name more acceptable to the Democrats at their convention. What he wrote about these rumors in a personal letter to Marquis Childs, on May 10, showed his basic position: "If I had a notion that I was the only one qualified to serve as Secretary of the Navy, or if I really thought that such action on my part would unify the people, I would, of course, accept.

Not believing either of these things, I would, of course, not accept. By the same token, the many suggestions that are made to me that I should in advance agree to accept some important position in government under the anticipated Republican administration as a condition of my support of Mr. Dewey, or support him in the hope of some position, leave me equally cold."

"I do not know whether I make my point clear," he concluded the letter. "If these were ordinary times, I might be moved by different motives. I happen to believe these are critical times, almost determinative times."

The exact terms of the pre-convention offer to Willkie are uncertain, as well as the intermediary who made it. The Constitution requires electors, in balloting for President and Vice-President, to vote for at least one from a state other than their own, and both Roosevelt and Willkie were legal residents of New York. Senator Wagner of New York was reported by one political columnist, Drew Pearson, to be the man at the center of the move for Willkie. Edward J. Flynn, Democratic National Committeeman from New York, commented on July 17 on his way to the convention in Chicago: "I feel we should nominate the man who will help the President most." Asked if this would cover Willkie, he hesitated briefly, and then said: "It includes anybody."

It seems extremely doubtful that the offer to Willkie ever went beyond an offer to submit his name to the convention, and by the time the convention opened on July 19 there was nothing secret about the fact that the Democratic party politicians, eager to be relieved of Wallace, had settled on Senator Harry S. Truman for the job. According to Rosenman, the decision was made at a meeting at the White House on July 11. Most important of all, Willkie was still far from having played out his hand as a Republican. For all he or anyone else knew in July, he might well hold the balance of power in the election in his hands. So he consistently shrugged off all inquiries about what kind of offer had been made to him. As late as July 15, he refused to confirm or to deny, to a reporter, Vice-Presidential overtures by the Democrats. In the course of his law business, he said, he saw many people, including representatives of all parties. Nor did he tell even his close friends any details of an offer, although it was clear from his general conversation that an offer had been made. He argued with Gardner Cowles, who tried to persuade him not even to consider it, that he distrusted Roosevelt too much, and liked his Republican friends who had supported him too much, to accept the offer. But he insisted he had every right to consider it.

President Roosevelt left almost as little record of any negotiations over the 1944 ticket. On July 5, three weeks before the Democratic convention, he had sent Judge Samuel I. Rosenman to see Willkie in New York, but the Judge's account of this discussion claims that it concerned postelection plans alone. On July 13, Roosevelt wrote Willkie a follow-up letter to this overture, asking for a meeting "but not on anything in relationship to the present campaign." There is only one proof in the Roosevelt records that Willkie's name played a part in the choice of a Vice-Presidential candidate. On his way to the Pacific Coast and Hawaii, the President received a blistering telegram from George Norris, who had heard that Willkie might get the Democratic nomination. From the very early days of the TVA, any mention of Willkie had always been enough to stir Norris into loud and violent denunciation. "Dear George," the President answered him on July 17, twelve days after he had himself written Willkie, "Your telegram reached me on the train while I was only one state away from McCook on my way to the Coast. I don't think there is any possible danger of Willkie, though feelers were put out about a week ago. . . ." The feelers were thus a fact. That they were almost certainly his own feelers cannot be proved against the master political operator of his generation.

The Rosenman meeting with Willkie, on July 5, was far more dramatic and it remained a closely kept secret for eight years. It took place at a luncheon, with only the two men present, in a private suite at the Hotel St. Regis in New York City. It lasted for two hours. Willkie was so apprehensive of the publicity which would surely have followed his recognition that he retired to the bedroom whenever a waiter appeared.

"Ever since the unsuccessful 'purge' of 1938," Rosenman

told Willkie according to his own version of the conversation, "the idea has been growing in the President's mind that the real future of progressivism in American politics lies in a realignment of the parties rather than intraparty conflict. The trouble is that all Democrats get together in a convention hall and the majority adopts a good liberal program; then, after election, the Southern conservatives, who do not depend on anyone outside their own conservative districts, just run out on the platform. The President learned in 1938, the hard way, that he cannot beat them in their own districts. He is now ready to form a new grouping, leaving them out of the new liberal party. You see, you both are thinking along the same lines. He wants to team up with you, for he is sure that the two of you can do it together; and he thinks the right time to start is immediately after the election."

Willkie answered that he was deeply interested in discussing the plan more fully, and in meeting the President for that purpose. But he insisted that the meeting should not take place until after the election. He did not want to look as if he were trading or being traded with, "and a meeting between the two before election—which could not possibly be kept secret—would give rise to many conjectures."

Eight days later, on July 13, and despite Judge Rosenman's report that it would be impossible to get Willkie to make a move before the Democratic convention and the election, President Roosevelt wrote him a letter. This may have been, as Judge Rosenman suggested, because he hated to let a good idea lie fallow, or there may have still been some indirect connection in his mind with the independently operated "feelers" about the Vice-Presidency. On July 11, two days before he wrote the letter, he had announced at a press conference that he would accept renomination for a fourth White House term. There was no public agreement yet on the man to run with him. The letter ran:

Dear Wendell:

I will not be able to sign this because I am dictating it just as I leave on a trip to the westward.

The Long Summer

What I want to tell you is that I want to see you when I come back, but not on anything in relation to the present campaign. I want to talk with you about the future, even the somewhat distant future, and in regard to the foreign-relations problems of the immediate future.

When you see in the papers that I am back, will you get in touch with General Watson? We can arrange a meeting either here in Washington, or, if you prefer, at Hyde Park—wholly off the record or otherwise, just as you think best.

Always sincerely yours,
FRANKLIN D. ROOSEVELT

Willkie answered this letter but never mailed the answer. The President's letter to him had leaked to a columnist in Washington, and Willkie was personally certain that Roosevelt had superb control over White House leaks. Willkie had not yet made up his mind on the election, and any report of negotiations with Roosevelt might be enough to ruin his last chances of a political future inside the Republican party. If he was determined not to be exploited, without his consent, by Dewey, he was even more determined not to let the President capture his support without paying any price for it in firm commitment to the issues Willkie believed in. This is what he had written but not mailed, found later in his files:

My dear Mr. President:

I have your gracious note of the thirteenth. The subjects concerning which you suggest we have a talk on your return from the West are, as you know, subjects in which I am intensely interested. I am fearful, however, that any talk between us before the campaign is over might well be the subject of misinterpretation and misunderstanding. And I do not believe, however much you and I might wish or plan otherwise, that we could possibly have such a talk without the fact becoming known.

Therefore, if it is agreeable with you, I would prefer postponement of any such talk until after the November election.

I hope you will understand that I make this suggestion solely because you in a great way, and I in a small one, have the trust and confidence of people who might see in the most innocent meeting

373

between us at this time some betrayal of the principles which each of us respectively hold so deeply.

Believe me, with great respect,

Sincerely yours,

(Unsigned)

There followed one of the most extraordinary of all the complicated incidents in which President Roosevelt's passion for personal politics involved him, especially towards the end of his life. The President had no reason to distrust Willkie, who was a model of discretion throughout a month—August—in which the President or his closest White House aides were leaking stories about the two men, denying them, and then withdrawing the denials. There is no clear proof that the President was trying to make political capital out of the confusion. If he was, he was turning down the much greater potential asset of Willkie's support, after the election if not before it. For Willkie, it was a month of deep and galling frustration; it did not break his heart but it confirmed some of his worst suspicions about Roosevelt and it wore his patience thin.

On August 1, Willkie gave a buffet dinner before the New York première of a motion picture on the life of Woodrow Wilson. Produced by his company, Twentieth Century-Fox, and written by Lamar Trotti, who had worked on the scenario for the never-produced picture of *One World* and had become a friend of Willkie's, it was a picture in which he had a deep personal stake. It was a serious subject, a major test of Hollywood's ability to handle important ideas. Its central character had been one of Willkie's political heroes for a quarter of a century. Finally, its central theme was the struggle for an international organization which had climaxed and ended Wilson's life. The end of another war could hardly be delayed long enough to keep the Wilson picture from being powerful ammunition in the cause which was more than ever at the center of Willkie's thinking.

He invited former Governor James M. Cox of Ohio to the dinner and the première, and arranged there to meet him the following morning for breakfast at the New York home of Albert

D. Lasker. They were together for three hours. The unanswered letter from the President was much on Willkie's mind. He talked with extreme frankness about his difficulties in deciding what to do in the election. He was convinced that Dewey could be forced, during the campaign, to continue and increase his public commitment to some kind of international co-operation, but he was afraid the Republican candidate's real convictions had been expressed in his earlier isolationist position. He had profound reservations about Roosevelt, but he felt that he was at least headed in the right direction on this issue. He wanted to be sure that Dewey's record was made clear to the people in the campaign, as he felt the Democrats were not making it clear, if only to leave Republicans like himself some freedom of choice. Finally, he asked Cox, as a man who had himself run for President and therefore knew the difficulties and dangers involved in Willkie's position, to make his state of mind known to the President and to serve as an intermediary between them on the various proposals which the President was making to him. He did not reveal to Cox the exact proposals which had been made to him.

By now Willkie was so cautious that he kept strictly separate all the channels the President was opening to him during the summer, and what he wanted from Cox was a channel of his own. Besides the proposals he had heard from Judge Rosenman, and the feelers about the Vice-Presidency, there were others. David Dubinsky, one of the leaders of the pro-New Deal Liberal party in New York, offered to back him for mayor of New York City if Willkie would endorse Roosevelt's campaign for a fourth term. Willkie never took this seriously. But still another subject was being broached to him through David K. Niles, one of Roosevelt's administrative assistants, and his close friend Crum. This was a proposal that Willkie be named the President's top representative in Europe in the event of a quick and sudden armistice. Like the Rosenman proposal, this was made independent of Willkie's decision on whom to back in the election. But it had to be talked about at once, after the Allied armies had broken out of Normandy on August 1. This was the day before Willkie asked Cox, in general terms, to set up some kind of secure communication channel between him and the President.

Governor Cox tried to do this, through the White House secretariat, before August 17, the day Roosevelt returned from his Pacific trip. Apparently, he did so with such discretion that there was some misunderstanding as to the man for whom he was speaking. Everywhere else there was an epidemic of indiscretion. Gossip column rumors of Roosevelt's July 13 letter to Willkie had been given page-one respectability a week before on August 10; Willkie answered all queries about it with "no comment." Willkie returned to New York on August 14 from a week-end at Moosehead Lake in Maine, intending to go to California two days later to plead a private case in court. But he found himself so deeply entangled in a web of gossip, leaks to the press, and misunderstanding that he postponed the trip.

What had happened was that Drew Pearson had published in his syndicated column an anecdote allegedly originating at Willkie's *Wilson* dinner and involving Governor Cox, Albert Lasker, and Bernard Baruch. There was some reason to think that the story had come via the White House. In any case, Presidential secretaries there jumped to the assumption that Baruch was the very well-known man to whom Cox had referred in his message to the President. Roosevelt returned from his trip to the West Coast and Hawaii on August 17; at his press conference the next day, speaking with a heavy cold in his voice and seeming irritated by the question, he denied any truth in published reports that he had been in touch with Willkie. Willkie immediately wrote Governor Cox to call off his earlier request that he serve as a friendly intermediary. The original leak of the President's letter to him, the leak of the garbled story about Cox and Baruch, and then the President's public denial that he had even been in touch with Willkie all combined to convince Willkie that either the President or men close to him were engaged in very complicated double-dealing.

It took a few days to unscramble the confusion. Roosevelt finally learned the true identity of the man for whom Cox had been speaking. On August 21, the President wrote Willkie directly:

The Long Summer

PERSONAL

Dear Wendell:—

A most unfortunate thing happened at my Press Conference on Friday. I had written you on July thirteenth, just as I was leaving for my trip to Hawaii and Alaska—a purely personal note telling you I hoped much to see you on a non-campaign subject sometime after I got back. Quite frankly when I was asked—in a series of questions about foreign affairs—whether I had written you to invite you to Washington, I said "no." That afternoon Steve Early said to me, "Are you sure you did not write to Wendell Willkie?" And it flashed into my mind then that I had written you before I left.

The interesting thing is how word of my note to you got out to the Press. I have been trying to find out where the leak was down here, as I regarded it as a purely personal note between you and me. As far as I can remember I said nothing about it to anybody, though it is possible that I told Leo Crowley that I was going to ask you if we could talk the subject over. I am awfully sorry that there was any leak on a silly thing like this—but I still hope that at your convenience—there is no immediate hurry—you will stop in and see me if you are in Washington or run up to Hyde Park if you prefer.

I hope you have had a good Summer. My trip in the Pacific was extraordinarily interesting. I hope to be able to tell you about it and about how I am trying to keep China going. Our friend, Madame Chiang, is in Brazil with her sister, Madame Kung, and I hope they will both come here before they return home.

Always sincerely,
FRANKLIN D. ROOSEVELT

Honorable Wendell L. Willkie,
15 Broad Street,
New York City,
New York

The entire incident had confirmed some of the worst things Willkie had ever said about the dangers of one-man administration on the Roosevelt model. On August 24, even this last letter found its devious way into print in Washington. "Once more, no comment," said Willkie in New York. Roosevelt finally con-

377

firmed the next day the fact that he had twice asked Willkie to come to see him. This enabled Willkie to release a one-paragraph statement repeating what he had consistently said: that he "would much prefer that no such conference occur until after the election. But if the President of the United States wishes to see me sooner, I shall of course comply."

Roosevelt kept on trying. Crum passed on to Willkie in late August an invitation, through Niles, to see the President at Hyde Park during the Labor Day weekend. Willkie had already made arrangements to go to Indiana, and he was still suspicious. But he arranged to have dinner with Crum the following Wednesday, to talk about it further. This proved to be the day he went into the hospital. Roosevelt asked for Willkie's Rushville telephone number—Rushville 2346—but if he talked to him from Hyde Park neither man left any record of it.

Willkie had good reason by now to suspect Roosevelt's motives; yet the President could hardly afford to wait. Paris had been liberated by August 25. By September 1, United States patrols were in Belgium and General Patton's Third Army had captured St. Mihiel, twenty miles southeast of Verdun, and was smashing on towards the German frontier. With Germans fighting on their own soil on both the western and eastern fronts, a surrender might take place at almost any moment. Roosevelt was to meet Churchill at Quebec on September 10, and he had behind him a badly divided Cabinet on nearly all the major problems on the agenda. The Morgenthau Plan was already the subject of bitter dispute. Admiral Leahy was expecting an imminent French revolution. No hard plans had been agreed on with the Russians. Roosevelt badly needed a civilian on the spot in Europe with enough stature and bipartisan support to make quick decisions, and Willkie was obviously the man.

It was Willkie's final illness which made this plan collapse, but the record of the summer shows how difficult it would have been in any case. Willkie had narrowly escaped losing what political leverage he still had, for no gain at all, through a long series of fumbled maneuvers on the White House side. Willkie was not sure who set the traps, if they had been traps and not

just personal politics and bumbling confusion around the White
House. In any case, he had failed to ease in any way the dilemma
in which he found himself over the election, and the fateful
discussion of the future which Roosevelt had originally had in
mind was never to take place.

Willkie's relations with the Dewey campaign during this
period were less complicated but equally sterile. There was
little the Republicans did that gave him heart or hope. Werner
Schroeder, whom Willkie had fought in 1940 and again in 1942
because he did not want the masthead of the *Chicago Tribune*
over the party, was Dewey's choice for vice-chairman of the
national committee. Dewey was now walking the tightrope
Willkie had walked in 1940, but the Republican Old Guard
could ask more from the candidate because they had given him
more than they ever gave Willkie. Herbert Brownell had become national committee chairman, with Spangler as general
counsel and James Scott Kemper, another McCormick supporter, as finance committee chairman. Weeks and Cake were
appointed to a new executive committee. Willkie believed that
the strongest single strategist in making campaign plans was
Herbert Hoover.

Willkie was careful to treat both parties with an even-handed
skepticism which confounded the political experts. On August
1, he wrote to Crum: "Don't be disturbed; there is not a chance
of my stating my position before I visit with you in California.
As a matter of fact, I don't know on what basis a man who is
uncontrolled, either by hates or partisanship, could make a decision at the present time." His intercession in local campaigns
was carefully controlled to reveal only the consistency of his
own basic position. When Representative Hamilton Fish, Jr.,
threatened to sue Maxwell Anderson, playwright, and some
others for a political advertisement attacking him in his campaign for re-election, Willkie offered cheerfully to serve as counsel without fee against the Congressman. Fish never sued. But
Willkie sent strong messages of support to two other Republican candidates for Congress, James Park of Kentucky and
William J. Otjen of Oklahoma, when they came out in public
for Senate ratification of treaties by a majority, instead of a

two-thirds vote. When his friend Russell Davenport came out openly against Dewey in a speech at Hartford, Willkie gently reminded reporters that no one was in a position to speak for him except himself.

In the middle of the mix-up over the Roosevelt letters, Dewey invited him to come to Albany for an exchange of views on foreign policy. The Governor's chief adviser on foreign matters, John Foster Dulles, was going to confer in Washington with Secretary of State Cordell Hull, and Dewey said that he wanted to bring into the discussion as many points of view as possible, especially on the role of small nations in a postwar world organization. Having failed to reach Willkie by telephone on Saturday night, August 19, Dewey telegraphed him the invitation on Sunday morning and followed it with another telephone call. By this time the reporters were camping downstairs in Willkie's apartment house. Even the newsreel companies wanted to get in the act. Willkie stalled while he tried to estimate the danger that this, like the White House overtures, might be designed to commit him in the campaign before he had made up his mind.

The way the meeting was being planned, Willkie later told the *New Yorker*, "we would solve all the world's problems and make the Atlantic Charter look like a piker. Did I say the Atlantic Charter? This was to be the Atlantic, Pacific, Indian, and Arabian Oceans Charter."

He telegraphed back to Dewey that he would be glad to see Dulles on his way to Washington. "I wish I had known of your desire for my views prior to your original statement," he could not help adding. "For several years I have been deeply concerned about the ill fate of the small nations inherent in military alliance between any or all of the great powers. But I have been equally concerned that there should not arise among our allies the notion that our party would in any way obstruct or endanger the success of an international conference. I, therefore, made inquiry about ten days ago of the Washington authorities to determine if our government intended to insist upon the protection of the position of the small nations in the forthcoming

Dumbarton Oaks conference. I was given strong affirmative assurances."

Switching the conference from Albany to New York gave Willkie a chance to control the statements and news photographs resulting from it which might otherwise have led to political assumptions he did not want. Late in the afternoon on Monday, August 21, he took a taxi to Dulles' New York City home—Dulles was laid up with a bad foot—and the two men had a ninety-minute conversation without reporters, cameramen, or the newsreel companies. Their joint statement after the conference said little, but included this sentence: "There was a full exchange of views not animated by partisan consideration nor having to do with any candidacy, but by the desire of both of us that the United States should play a constructive and responsible part in assuring world order."

Actually, the conference was important as part of the birth of postwar bipartisanship in foreign policy. "Our talk was somewhat strained," Mr. Dulles has since written of the conference, "for Mr. Willkie had not yet decided to support the Republican ticket. But he did respond to Governor Dewey's and my invitation to talk over the future of world organization, in which he was deeply interested." Dulles met Hull on August 23, and in three days of conference the groundwork was laid for the compromises on both sides which were to produce bipartisan support for the organization of the United Nations in the following year.

Since nearly all of Willkie's closest friends and associates had themselves chosen sides by this time, there were many who thought he was being excessively jittery in his determination not to be trapped into commitment on the election until he had made up his mind. Both his pro-Dewey friends and his pro-Roosevelt friends wanted him to relax, but each in a different direction. Inevitably the impression grew that his mood was one of disappointed personal ambition. In actual fact, he had not made up his own mind and he had some reason to believe that his refusal to choose sides was forcing both candidates to resist the growing pressures of American nationalism. He was watching this process literally on a day-to-day basis, turning on all the public heat he felt the situation could stand. As an exercise in political virtuosity, the last months of Willkie's life are hard to match in American history: the flat certainty with which men stated, after his death, how he would have voted and the complete contradiction between their statements were unconscious tributes to both his skill and his sincerity. His effect on the voting, as distinguished from his influence on the candidates, was clearly to reinforce the factors which led voters to stay at home. The total poll declined in 1944. Dewey increased the Republican electoral vote from 82 to 99, but his popular vote fell to 22,018,177 from Willkie's 1940 figure of 22,304,755.

Willkie saw newspapermen almost every day during this period, and wrote them letters much franker than any he had ever written before. A week before Willkie went into a hospital, Arthur Krock summed up from Washington the moves Willkie had made to avoid being committed to either Roosevelt or Dewey, and the success with which he had confounded the cynics on both sides who had been sure all summer of what Willkie would do. Willkie had demonstrated, according to Krock, writing on August 24, these things:

"He is absolutely earnest in his plan to know what kind of foreign policy, postwar and for the long span of years, will be pursued by the candidate he will support.

"He is not yet satisfied with his inquiry with respect either to the President or to Mr. Dewey.

"Meanwhile he will not be used for any political build-ups, be the instrument of any public misconception, or yield to blandishment from highly placed persons or any possible design on their part to improve their own chances at his expense, and, more important, that of the cause to which he is committed."

Willkie thanked him for the article in a letter dated August 28. "I happen to think," he wrote, "of both Mr. Roosevelt and Mr. Dewey as what I call pragmatic politicians. If one states it kindly, one says they seek to articulate the opinion of the masses. If one says it unkindly, one says that they follow the polls and engage in vote-catching.

"I am not interested in the characterization, but I am greatly interested in creating a body of public opinion which will force either or both of them to go in the direction in which I believe they should. In other words, I believe that either one of them can be classified under either of those general terms, internationalist or isolationist. When it became politically expedient, Franklin Roosevelt repudiated the League of Nations. When it became politically expedient, Thomas Dewey attacked the Lease-Lend Bill. Likewise, both of them have made strong statements in favor of international co-operation. In the foreign field, I want to do what I can to help force them in the latter direction. You helped to make this very clear in your article. I am very grateful to you because I appreciate in the process I have undertaken, I am violating both the clichés and the code which politicians seek to impose upon the rest of us."

It was during August that he wrote two pieces for *Collier's*, both published in September. The first, called "Cowardice at Chicago," was a blistering attack on both the major party platforms for their evasions on the issues of foreign policy and postwar security. The second carried the attack further by analyzing the positions of both parties on racial minorities. The struggle for freedom among colonial, subject, and minority peoples looked to Willkie like "the great quest of our times." He foresaw with more accuracy than can be found in other 1944 political statements the progressive worsening of America's position if we could not quickly frame a foreign policy and a domestic behavior pattern which would recognize this central fact. In his last book, *An American Program*, which was published the day before he died, he put together the seven newspaper articles he had published in June with his own draft platform for the Republican convention and these two articles on foreign policy and the problems of Negro citizens. The last two were to him the questions which really mattered, far more than the candidates in the election. "For our attitude on our racial minorities and on our international obligations," he wrote on September

25 in a foreword to the book, "will constitute a test of our sincerity at home and abroad and of our ability to bring about, with other nations, a world of peace and security."

A total of 67,812 copies of the book were sold, almost all immediately on its appearance, in spite of the fact that it was a reprint of already-published material. Its original purpose had been simply to increase Willkie's leverage on Roosevelt and Dewey before the election, but it summed up his own last convictions more neatly than is the luck of most men who die suddenly. "Wendell Willkie," Bernard De Voto wrote in his review of the book, "was a man who actually believed in republican government by democratic means, in the health of American institutions, in mankind and in the future. He actually believed that an informed people could make wise decisions, that it was not only safe but best to debate issues openly, that governor must be responsible to the governed. In 1944 he was the only public leader willing to commit himself to the iron and awful complicities on which our way of life is based. But another one will appear the sooner because of his example."

On September 6, Willkie returned to New York from a visit to Rushville. He had been planning to go on to California, on his long-postponed legal business, but a severe heart attack changed all plans. He first realized he was in trouble when he had difficulty and pain trying to open the door of the diner on the train to Indiana; the night after he arrived in Rushville, the trouble became serious. He had never taken good care of himself; too much work, too little exercise, heavy eating and little relaxation or diversion had cost him heavily in resistance. Yet his first reaction was a desperate hope that he could keep the heart attack a secret and fight his way out of this difficulty as he had fought his way out of others before. "I've got too many things still to do and say," he told Mary Sleeth, who took care of him in Rushville, "to be written off as an old man with a bum heart."

At first, he was so desperately eager to keep the attack a secret that he refused even to see a doctor. He saw one, finally, in Indianapolis, but he refused to follow his advice to go into a hospital at once, and insisted on returning to New York. He went directly to his apartment from the train, and after his pain had been relieved by sedatives was taken in an ambulance to the Lenox Hill Hospital.

He lived there for a month and two days. The public explanation of his illness was that a stomach disorder and a run-down condition from overwork required a checkup and a rest. He was cheered by his success in keeping the true nature of his illness a secret. He was alternately grave and cheerful while he tried to give up smoking, to rest, and to wait for the specialists to report on just how bad the situation was. Helen and Loretta Tucker, his secretaries, kept things going at his office, while he worked in his hospital room on the final editing of *An American Program,* wrote a number of personal letters, and saw a few close friends.

Up to the very end, the record is clear that no break came in his continuing indecision on exactly how to treat the final phase of his long pre-election summer. On September 27, he wrote to Governor Leverett Saltonstall of Massachusetts that he did not think Dewey's most recent speech, at Louisville, had clarified the situation. "On the contrary," he wrote, "it further muddied the problem. And because I am so desperately anxious to see the Republican party survive, at least as a party with ideals and a nucleus of influence around which we can rebuild, I hope you do not get yourself so closely tied up with the recent nonsense Dewey has been talking that you sink with him if he sinks. Of course, as a Republican Governor, you will want to support him formally, but for God's sake don't sacrifice your principles. Much more is at stake even than your own political future. And the only way that fellows like you and me can really contribute to our party's welfare at this time is by a certain aloofness which may force the candidate to take the right course, if anything can do so."

On Saturday morning, September 30, he saw a friend, Roscoe Drummond of the *Christian Science Monitor,* who has recorded that he looked rested, robust, and buoyant, filling the small, newspaper-cluttered hospital room with his energy. The next Monday, Drummond received a personal note from Willkie which said: "I enjoyed our talk this morning very much.

Frankly, I cannot answer your ultimate question [whom he would support] yet because I have not finally decided."

While he was in the hospital, he had fourteen separate heart attacks. On Wednesday, October 4, he contracted a streptococcic throat and a lung congestion. His temperature rose to 104 on Thursday, but penicillin brought a rally, and the first news that he was seriously ill, released to the press on Friday, carried the reassuring report that he was out of danger. On Saturday night, his cardiac condition became acute. At 2:20 on Sunday morning, October 8, after the last three heart attacks, he died of a coronary thrombosis.

The news of his death came too late for all except the late editions of the Sunday papers. The U. S. First Army had broken through the Siegfried Line north of Aachen, and the Cards had beaten the Browns to tie the World Series. Through the day the news spread that Willkie had died. The quick, hard shock was accentuated for many people by sudden surprise, since few had known how ill he was, and by an almost guilty sense of waste that came with the flat statement in the obituaries that he was only fifty-two.

This was followed by a flood of tributes from all over the world. They came from President Roosevelt and Governor Dewey, from Herbert Hoover and Harry Bridges, from the Old Guard of the Republican party and from its liberals, from old opponents like Lilienthal and Senator Nye, from London and Moscow and Chungking, from the Association of Red Caps at Pennsylvania Terminal and from Prime Ministers and Foreign Ministers of countries encircling the globe. They all paid tribute to the man, and most of them to his ideas, since now that he was dead the ideas could be safely praised.

Sixty thousand New Yorkers filed through the aisles of the Fifth Avenue Presbyterian Church before the funeral services on October 10. Thirty-five thousand packed the streets outside when friends, national officials, and notables jammed the church to hear the service conducted by its pastor, the Rev. Dr. John Sutherland Bonnell. In the silent crowds were many Negroes, soldiers and sailors, and men in working clothes. A week later, he was buried in Rushville's East Hill Cemetery. The grave was

Ding in the New York *Herald Tribune*

afterwards marked by a twelve-foot granite cross, its carving
designed by Willkie's friend Malvina Hoffman, the sculptor,
and by an open granite book containing quotations from his
speeches and from *One World*.

When he died, there was only a month to go before the election. Inevitably the politicians, including many of his friends,

387

and the gossip columnists issued strong and sure statements about how he would have voted had he lived. The fact that these statements flatly contradicted each other only increased their news value. They stopped only when Mrs. Willkie, in Rushville after the burial service, issued a short and dignified statement to the press: "I am distressed because many people are saying that they knew how Wendell Willkie intended to vote in the coming election. I am sure he had not made his decision. No one could speak for him while he was living; and I ask, out of respect for his memory, that no one should attempt to speak for him now."

After the formal tributes by the great had been published, there was a period during which newspapermen, columnists, and writers who had known Willkie personally could wrestle with the job of trying to sum up what Archibald MacLeish, then Librarian of Congress, called "the stopped voice—the uncompleted sentence." Even the first obituary accounts of his life had been written with an undertone of affection and of personal sincerity which are usually barred from professional newspaper copy. No American in his generation except President Roosevelt confronted men who write or preach or teach with a harder or more challenging task of trying to reduce, in words, the complexity and power of a living man to the hard core of what he left behind him. At least for a few weeks of mourning, Willkie's deepest convictions—the issues for which he had fought—were restated by men and women of literally every political camp with something of the confidence and the sincerity he gave them.

Then began the great silence. The war was still to be won, and the peace—as Willkie had feared and warned—to be fumbled and lost. The American people were still grappling with the forces within themselves which had shaped Willkie's past and were to shape their own future. But the time had passed, and had not yet come again, when large numbers of men and women could find themselves, through the alchemy of leadership in a democracy, in his image. Less than four years later, when the Republicans met to pick a Presidential candidate again, Willkie's name was never once mentioned in the long, florid speeches of the convention. Yet the same forces which made Willkie were still working deeply in America. They were opening the books, and churning men's minds, in Indiana, in Akron, in the Tennessee Valley, in New York, in every whistle-stop where he had ever spoken. Whatever else he had done, Willkie had made his own life one of these forces, in memories for living men and in the record for persons not yet born.

ACKNOWLEDGMENTS

THE documentation on which this book is based, especially the texts of Willkie's speeches and writings and the newspaper reports of his activities, is too lengthy to warrant printing but is, of course, available to anyone interested in checking the accuracy of the factual statements made in the book or in pursuing them further.

My greatest debt is to the reporters, some with by-lines and some without, who covered Willkie. Only someone who writes a book about a period in the immediate past knows the degree to which he is inevitably a rewriteman, dependent on the leg-work and the reporting skill of the men who work for American newspapers.

To name in a long list the individuals who have given me help and information and advice does not mean that any of them agrees with my interpretation of the facts of Willkie's life. Nor does it begin to express my gratitude to them. They include: Bert Andrews, Frederic Attwood, Margaret Bevans, Tom Torre Bevans, Lillie L. Brown, Lillian Conrad, Gardner Cowles, Bartley C. Crum, Roscoe Drummond, Morris L. Ernst, Felix Frankfurter, Lewis Galantiere, Harold Gallagher, Jack A. Goodman, Harold Guinzburg, Clarence B. Hanson, Jr., Maurice Hindus, Arthur Krock, Albert D. Lasker, David Lawrence, Albert R. Leventhal, David E. Lilienthal, Bert Loewenberg, Kingsley Martin, Thomas W. Martin, George Fort Milton, David K. Niles, Geoffrey Parsons, Frances Perkins, Mrs. Gifford Pinchot, Samuel I. Rosenman, Oswald Ryan, M. Lincoln Schuster, Robert E. Sherwood, Leon Shimkin, Richard L. Simon, Mary Sleeth, Mrs. Howland S. Stedman, W. L. Sturdevant, Gerard Swope, Helen Tucker, Irita Van Doren, James P. Warburg, M. R. Werner, Aubrey Williams, Edith Willkie, Edward Willkie, Philip Willkie.

INDEX

393

Index

Index

395

Index

Index

Index

Index

Index

Index

Index

Index

Index

Index

A NOTE
ABOUT THE AUTHOR

In 1942, Willkie asked Joseph Barnes and Gardner Cowles Jr. to go around the world with him as his friends, with Barnes also serving as combined secretary and interpreter. The friendship, which grew steadily stronger until Willkie's death in 1944, had begun when Barnes was a newspaperman, working as Foreign Editor of the New York Herald Tribune *after some years of being a foreign correspondent for that newspaper. Since then he has been an official of the Office of War Information, a war correspondent, editor of the* New York Star, *and currently an editor of Simon and Schuster and a member of the faculty at Sarah Lawrence College. He has translated novels from the French and Russian, but this is his first book of his own.*

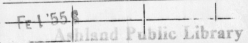